Studies in Colloquial Chinese and Its History

Studies in Colloquial Chinese and Its History

Dialect and Text

Edited by Richard VanNess Simmons

Hong Kong University Press
The University of Hong Kong
Pokfulam Road
Hong Kong
https://hkupress.hku.hk

© 2022 Hong Kong University Press

ISBN 978-988-8754-09-0 (*Hardback*)

All rights reserved. No portion of this publication may be reproduced or transmitted in any form or by any means, electronic or mechanical, including photocopying, recording, or any information storage or retrieval system, without prior permission in writing from the publisher.

British Library Cataloguing-in-Publication Data
A catalogue record for this book is available from the British Library.

Digitally printed

Contents

List of Figures and Map   vii

List of Tables   viii

Acknowledgments   x

Introduction: Facets of the History of Colloquial Chinese as Reflected in the Dialects and in Texts   1
Richard VanNess Simmons

I. Chinese Dialects in Texts

1. Does Taiwanese Cantillation Reflect the Sound of the Táng?   15
   David Prager Branner

2. Vernacular Written Cantonese in the Twentieth Century: The Role of Cantonese Opera in Its Growth and Spread   36
   Marjorie K. M. Chan

3. The Mix of Dialect and Guānhuà Elements in the Wú Folk Songs Collected in Féng Mènglóng's *Shāngē*   59
   SHÍ Rǔjié

4. Changes in Language Use as Reflected in *Shuǐhǔ zhuàn* Passages Embedded in the *Jīn Píng Méi cíhuà*   88
   HUÁNG Lín

5. Wordplay in *Jīn Píng Méi*   104
   ZHĀNG Huìyīng

6. Division of Old and New Shànghǎi Dialects: A Comparative Study of *Tǔhuà zhǐnán* and *Hùyǔ zhǐnán*   121
   ZHĀNG Měilán

7. The Origin and Evolution of the Dialect Word *yá* 伢 'Child'   137
   NÍ Zhìjiā

II. Chinese Dialects and Their History

8. The Demarcation of Western Mandarin and the Designation of the Chéngdū Dialect as Its Standard Form in Modern China   153
   Kengo CHIBA

9. A Question in the Final Systems of Míng-Time Guānhuà   173
   W. South Coblin

10. The Hénán Xìnyáng Dialect of 150 Years Ago: Evidence from Dialect Islands in Jiāngsū, Zhèjiāng, and Ānhuī   179
    HUÁNG Xiǎodōng

11. An Exploration of the Nature of Nánjīng Mandarin in the Míng Dynasty   194
    ZĒNG Xiǎoyú

12. Language Use in the Chinese Community of Manila in the Seventeenth Century: A Case of Occasional Diglossia?   206
    Henning Klöter

13. Frontier Mandarins and Lán Mào's *Yùnlüè yìtōng* in the Míng   220
    Richard VanNess Simmons

14. On the Variation of the *Rù* Tone in the Shānyīn Dialect of Shānxī   248
    GUŌ Lìxiá

15. Tonal Features Based on Acoustic Analysis and Historical Development in Mùlěi Mandarin in Xīnjiāng   266
    LIÚ Xīnzhōng

List of Contributors   275

Index   279

Figures and Map

Figures

Figure 1.1:   A couplet displaying all of the prosodic features discussed here — 25

Figure 2.1:   Lines of colloquial Cantonese in the *Maai⁶ faa¹ dak¹ mei⁵* opera text — 47

Figure 2.2:   Opening lines of 2005 hip hop *Ou³-wan⁶-wui⁶* — 53

Figure 12.1: Excerpt from the *Dictionario*, f. 87v, with permission of Archivo de la Universidad de Santo Tomás, Manila — 213

Figure 12.2: Excerpt from the *Dictionario*, f. 213v, with permission of Archivo de la Universidad de Santo Tomás, Manila — 214

Figure 15.1: Contour of Mùlán Mandarin tones — 268

Figure 15.2: CDC tone correspondence to the three tone contours of Mùlán Mandarin — 271

Map

Map 7.1:   Distribution of words with the morpheme *yá* 伢 in modern dialects — 143

Tables

1.1:	Inconsistent Taiwanese reflection of some medieval initials	19
1.2:	Accommodated rhyming (*xiéyùn* 叶韻)	20
1.3:	Raising of /a/ without effect on rhyming	20
1.4:	Taiwanese tones *yīnqù* and *yángqù* rhyme	21
1.5:	Táng tones *shǎng* (with voiced obstruent initials) and *qù* rhyme	22
1.6:	Average duration of each syllable by tone category	23
1.7:	Average duration of each syllable by both syllable-position and *píng-zè*	23
1.8:	Average duration of each syllable by both place and tone category	24
1.9:	Percentage of each tone category displaying melisma	24
2.1:	Twelve words across three periods of orthographic changes of the *Huājiān jì* (花箋記)	52
8.1:	Phonological features of regional variants of Mandarin	157
10.1:	Alveopalatals in the Hénán dialect islands of Jiāngsū, Zhèjiāng, and Ānhuī	183
10.2:	Pronunciation of the initial *rì* in Hénán, Jiāngsū, Zhèjiāng, and Ānhuī dialect islands (with *róng* 榮 and *yòng* 用 included for comparison)	184
10.3:	The distinction between velar fricatives and labiodental fricatives in the Hénán dialect islands of Jiāngsū, Zhèjiāng, and Ānhuī	186
10.4:	Presence or absence of rounded main vowels and medials in the Hénán dialect islands of Jiāngsū, Zhèjiāng, and Ānhuī	187
10.5:	Comparison of tone contours in the Hénán dialect islands of Jiāngsū, Zhèjiāng, and Ānhuī	190
11.1:	Phonological features found in the texts	198
11.2:	Comparison of the transliterations with Mandarin dialect phonology	200
14.1:	The Shānyīn pronunciations of *rù* tone syllables	250
14.2:	List of informants by background	252
14.3:	List of the *rù* tone syllables surveyed	253

14.4: The correspondence of Shānyīn tones with Middle Chinese initial types 254
14.5: Variant pronunciations on *rù* tone syllables 255
14.6: The state of change in the *rù* tone syllables surveyed 259
15.1: The average value of Mùlán Mandarin tones (pitch_Hz, duration_ms, and number of syllables) 267
15.2: The value of Mùlán Mandarin tones (logarithm value) 267
15.3: The correspondence of tone categories with the tone pitch of modern Mùlěi 269

Acknowledgments

This volume evolved out of presentations and discussions that took place at a workshop held at Rutgers University on March 11–12, 2016, on the topic of "The History of Colloquial Chinese—written or spoken." The workshop was generously sponsored by the Chiang Ching-kuo Foundation for International Scholarly Exchange, USA, with additional support provided by the Rutgers Center for Chinese Studies and the Rutgers University Department of Asian Languages and Cultures. The editor and workshop participants are grateful for the support provided by these institutions. Following the workshop, the chapters and the form they take in this volume gradually came together through a process of translation and compilation in which the editor-translator was assisted by many hands at several different times. In the 2016–2017 academic year, Blair Donner, Kristina Poon, and Ruolan Zhang, three undergraduate research assistants provided by the Rutgers Aresty Undergraduate Research Program, helped with preparing selected preliminary translations and provided bibliographic checking and support. During that year we held an informal weekly seminar at which we discussed much of the translation work in great detail. These seminar discussions were greatly enhanced by the participation of several visiting scholars who were at Rutgers that year, LOU Yu, YANG Wei, BA Xiaojin, and a visiting graduate student, XU Yi. More recently, after the translations were finalized and the volume had come fully together, Julianna Johnson, a Rutgers Aresty Undergraduate Assistant in 2020–2021, and Man Shan HUI, an MPhil research graduate student at the University of Hong Kong, helped with getting the full manuscript into final shape. The editor is deeply grateful for the assistance and input from all of these students and colleagues during the compilation process. The editor also extends thanks to the two anonymous reviewers of the book proposal for their constructive and useful comments. Many thanks are also due to Clara Ho and Kenneth Yung at Hong Kong University Press for their generous editorial advice and assistance. Thanks as well to Corynn Smith, who assisted with designing the cover for the original workshop program, from which the cover for this volume is adapted. Lastly thanks also go to all the contributors, whose keen scholarship and hard work forms the core of this volume. Of course, all remaining errors and textual issues are entirely the editor's responsibility.

Introduction
Facets of the History of Colloquial Chinese as Reflected in the Dialects and in Texts

Richard VanNess Simmons

This volume aims to broaden perspectives on the history of colloquial Chinese in the millennium following the age of Middle Chinese, which is generally dated to the early Táng dynasty (618–907). The general focus of the studies collected here is on the history of spoken Chinese as it is reflected in the dialects, and its influences on the languages used and represented in texts. That history is usually framed within the post Táng rise and evolution of Mandarin and centers on what is usually simply characterized as Old and/or Early Mandarin. Old and Early Mandarin are roughly contiguous with what is characterized in Chinese as *Jìndài Hànyǔ* 近代漢語, which refers to the language underlying the vernacular texts written in *báihuàwén* 白話文.

Yet little attention has been paid to the actual spoken languages behind the *báihuà* texts, beyond a general sense that they are a form of Mandarin or in making note of some apparent, though often coincidental, connection between words used in a text and some modern Mandarin dialect. An example is the connection purported to be seen between the language of the *Jīn Píng Méi* and the dialects of Shāndōng and other places—a connection that has been a frequent subject of discussion in the past couple of decades.[1] At the same time, non-Mandarin influences on the development of *báihuà* and the texts that take it as a medium are also neglected. Suffering as it does as primarily a history of the words and vocabulary of *báihuà* texts, the study of the language of vernacular texts is often strictly on the words in the texts and the graphs with which they are written. This can lead to infelicities in our understanding of the texts themselves. For instance, David Roy's generally masterful translation of the *Jīn Píng Méi* consistently renders the frequent occurrences of negative epithets containing the morpheme *qiú* 囚 as 'jailbird', for he was unaware of coarser meanings conveyed by that graph thorough its homonymic connection to vulgar Wú dialect words (see Zhāng Huìyīng in this volume).

Beyond the vernacular literary texts, phonologies of the language of the Old and Early Mandarin periods generally revolve around rime books and rime tables

---

1. For examples, see Yīn Xiǎojié 殷曉傑 (2011) and Yáo Jígāng 姚吉剛 (2019). But also see Zhāng Huìyīng 張惠英 (2016).

that present standards of various ages, from *Zhōngyuán yīnyùn* 中原音韻 in the Yuán (1271–1368), to *Hóngwǔ zhèngyùn* 洪武正韻 in the early Míng (1368–1644), and encompassing various texts between, or following. However, attention to the connection between those standards and the living dialects of their time is limited to how contemporaneous dialects might have influenced sundry arcane and puzzling features of the various phonological texts themselves.[2] Such studies usually focus on the formal structures of the phonologies represented and how those phonologies correspond to, or differ from, the early authoritative model of the *Qièyùn* 切韻 of 601 CE. Rarely do scholars seek to understand the background of the authors or compilers and the dialects they might have actually spoken and how the history of those dialects might be reflected in the phonologies of texts. This volume is a preliminary effort to bring greater attention to some of these areas of neglect.

The studies collected in this volume grew out of a two-day workshop funded primarily by the Chiang Ching-Kuo Foundation and held at Rutgers University in March 2016. Its subject was "The History of Colloquial Chinese—Written and Spoken." The workshop's participants explored various issues related to colloquial languages in China in their spoken forms, the relationship between those spoken forms and written forms, colloquial literary language, and the Chinese phonological tradition. The chapters presented here are for the most part the result of the presentations made and discussions held at the workshop.

The dialect groups with the most substantial connections to written tradition include Mandarin, Wú, Mǐn, and Cantonese, in north, central, eastern coastal, and southern China, respectively. The studies in this collection focus on aspects of the histories of these dialects in their written and spoken forms, including regional variants, and their evolution and influence. These studies also bring new detail to our understanding of the underlying factors in the formation of supra-regional common languages in China, as well as the written forms to which they gave rise—specifically Guānhuà 官話 and *báihuà* 白話, respectively.

There are fifteen chapters in this collection. Eight of them were first written in Chinese, one first in Japanese. All were then translated expressly for this volume. Though a few of the authors offered their own translations, the editor (Richard V. N. Simmons) provided most of them, while also revising the other translations as necessary. Hence this collection presents authoritative representatives of the most current Chinese and Japanese scholarship on the history of Chinese to a broader English-speaking audience. Many of the ideas and issues touched on in the collection have not been widely considered outside China, such as the themes of the studies by Guō Lìxiá, Huáng Lín, Huáng Xiǎodōng, Liú Xīnzhōng, Ní Zhìjiā, Shí Rǔjié, Zēng Xiǎoyú, Zhāng Huìyīng, and Zhāng Měilán. It is hoped that this volume can thus provide scholars working outside China and those who may not know Chinese with

---

2. The most recent, up-to-date, and state-of-the-art example of this approach can be found in Shen (2020).

a more nuanced picture of the history of Chinese and the Chinese dialects than is generally available in English.

We have divided the studies into two broad categories. The section titled "Chinese Dialects in Texts" comprises chapters that treat textual reflections of the dialects as well as the nature of dialects and their influence in the texts. The chapters in the section titled "Chinese Dialects and Their History" focus more directly on questions of language itself and how it evolved over time. But these categories can overlap, and the division is arbitrary in some cases.

Indeed, the first chapter in the collection straddles the categories of texts, dialects, and the history pertaining to both: David Prager Branner's "Does Taiwanese Cantillation Reflect the Sound of the Táng?" This examination of a Taiwanese tradition of intoning received texts considers whether that traditional form of recitation reflects authentic features of the sounds of early literature and the prosodic tradition contained therein. The focus is on the rendering of received texts through reading and interpretation in a modern dialect that was not the language of the texts' long-ago authors. Branner's discussion reveals that while there is an oral reading tradition in the modern dialect, that tradition is constrained by both the dominant prosodic tradition in Chinese history and the inherent prosody of the original text, whose composition reflects resonances of its author's contemporary dialect. Those resonances are then refracted into the sounds of the performer's modern dialect following the conventions of the Taiwanese cantillation tradition. Branner concludes that the tradition allows "native speakers to take possession of premodern literature using their own phonology." The dialect of the texts' origin and that of the performance can be quite different. Branner's discussion reveals that something of the history of each can be discerned through careful analysis of the outcome.

The interplay between text and language is also the subject of the chapter by Marjorie Chan. Her study examines a relationship between dialect performance and text that differs from the one Branner discusses, one in which the transcribed content of performances in the Cantonese dialect informed and nurtured the development of the Cantonese written vernacular. Focusing particularly on written materials that were unabashedly intended to represent vernacular Cantonese, such as opera scripts for mass readership, songbooks, and printed lyrics, Chan shows how a non-Mandarin dialect was able to develop a flourishing written tradition that fed into, and reciprocally spun out of, popular culture from historical times (at least as early as the eighteenth century) into the present. While written Modern Standard Chinese, which is Mandarin, still serves as a higher, more formal register that is indispensable in overall literacy among Cantonese speakers, Chan presents to us a purely Cantonese realm of literate activity, literary composition, and textual interaction. Within this realm one is able to enjoy the delights of a form of Chinese literacy that is free to function in its own milieu and move beyond the confines of Mandarin traditions, standards, and usage.

In contrast, in the seventeenth-century literature of Wú dialect provenance, which often cheekily and sometimes liberally incorporated Wù vernacular, Mandarin remained ever-present. A purely Wú dialect presentation is not easily found on the written page. Thus Shí Rǔjié, in his contribution, finds that Féng Mènglóng's 馮夢龍 (1574–1646) *Shāngē* 山歌, which ostensibly is written purely in the Sūzhōu 蘇州 Wú dialect of its author, frequently mixes in Mandarin vocabulary and grammatical forms. Nevertheless, Shí Rǔjié finds that overall, Féng Mènglóng's book is written primarily in Wú dialect, albeit with many Mandarin elements folded in, often unconsciously. As such, the volume does not represent what would have been actual spoken dialect of Féng Mènglóng's time and place. Even so, it serves as a treasure trove of Wú dialect vocabulary and usage that allows Shí Rǔjié to glean and describe much detail about the dialect of seventeenth-century Sūzhōu.

The mixing of dialect type and register in vernacular Chinese texts is often a result of the transmission process: story elements from earlier texts and authors are adopted and developed by later authors in the production of new editions or new stories. In his chapter, Huáng Lín offers an example of the mixing process in his examination of the adoption of textual content from the *Shuǐhǔ zhuàn* 水滸傳 in the *Jīn Píng Méi*. It is generally known that the author of the *Jīn Píng Méi cíhuà* incorporated a popular story from the *Shuǐhǔ zhuàn* as a starting point for an entirely new and different novel. The story was folded into the *Jīn Píng Méi* through a process whereby the author embedded whole passages from the *Shuǐhǔ zhuàn* into the new novel but then augmented and embellished them with words and phrases in colloquial dialect (*súyǔ* 俗語) that contrast with the basically Mandarin plain vernacular (*báihuà* 白話) that the *Shuǐhǔ* was written in. The result is that the language in the *Jīn Píng Méi cíhuà* deviates so much from the Mandarin-based *báihuà* that, as Huáng Lín tells us, the novel is considered by some scholars to be close to a novel in dialect (*fāngyán xiǎoshuō* 方言小說). But which dialect? To answer that question, Huáng Lín reviews the arguments that the author was from Shāndōng and adopted elements from the Shāndōng dialect. In the end, though, he finds a stronger connection to the Wú dialects on the basis of vocabulary found in the dialect elements as well as some matters of homophony that are more clearly explained by Wú pronunciation. Nevertheless, Huáng Lín is hesitant to regard this judgment as conclusive; and he remains puzzled by an issue that seems to undermine his argument.

In her contribution, Zhāng Huìyīng argues that the issue troubling Huáng Lín can be easily attributed to the *Jīn Píng Méi* author's love of wordplay, which is found in abundant measure in the dialect-influenced language of the novel. Zhāng Huìyīng has no doubt that the author was a Wú dialect speaker and that the wordplay in the novel, including the author's frequent punning, earthy expressions, double-entendre, and clever use of homophony, is all overwhelmingly based on Wú dialect phonology and usage. Elsewhere she has definitively argued that "the language of the *Jīn Píng Méi* is composed of non-Mandarin dialect elements layered onto a Mandarin foundation, among which Wú dialect elements comprise the largest concentration, particularly Zhèjiāng 浙江 Wú elements."[3] In her chapter in this volume, Zhāng Huìyīng further bolsters her case with an examination of the Wú dialect coloring of vulgarisms and obscenities, both of which are liberally sprinkled throughout the *Jīn Píng Méi*. While the identity of the author of the *Jīn Píng Méi* remains obscure to this day, his linguistic background is clearly discernable in the liberal layering of his beloved colloquial Wú dialect vocabulary and wordplay across the surface of the northern *báihuà* vernacular foundation of the novel's language.

Missionaries' efforts to learn and teach dialects in the nineteenth century led them to compile textbooks for the purpose. Though these textbooks were expressly intended to teach natural spoken dialect, they were often modeled on textbooks that had been compiled to teach Mandarin. Thus, we are left with a conundrum similar to the one we face when teasing out colloquial dialect from Guānhuà and *báihuà* in the texts of vernacular literature. Zhāng Měilán tackles this issue in her chapter in this volume, which looks at two late nineteenth-century Shanghainese textbooks (*Tǔhuà zhǐnán* 土話指南 and *Hùyǔ zhǐnán* 滬語指南) that were modeled on a Mandarin textbook (*Guide to Kuan Hua* or *Guānhuà zhǐnán* 官話指南) that had been compiled a few years prior. The Shanghainese texts methodically translated all of the examples in the *Guide to Kuan Hua*. This allows Zhāng Měilán to carry out a systematic comparison. Her discussion provides an overview of the similarities and differences between the Shanghainese and the Mandarin versions with regard to vocabulary and grammar as well as a comparison of the Shanghainese of the texts in light of what is known about older and younger varieties of that language. She finds that the two dialect textbooks accurately reflect the Shanghainese of the late nineteenth century, both lexically and grammatically.

Ní Zhìjiā's chapter takes a different direction in the exploration of dialect in text. Instead of sorting through one or two texts for clues to the disparate dialect elements they may contain, he probes a wide variety of texts in search of the origin, etymological development, and dialect distribution of a single word of interest: *yá'ér* 牙兒, which started out meaning 'infant' but came to mean 'child'. Ní Zhìjiā finds that this word was probably the more common word for 'child' in the Mandarin koine of the Northern Sòng (960–1127) and was widely distributed from central China south into the middle and lower Yangtze River watershed region. Following the collapse of the Northern Sòng, *yá'ér* diffused as far south as Hángzhōu 杭州, the capital of the Southern Sòng (1127–1279) and faded in use in central China. The word eventually also fell out of use in the prestige varieties of Mandarin and is only preserved in dialects, primarily those in the Yangtze watershed. Ní Zhìjiā's examination of the geographic and historical distribution of this key colloquial word uncovers some of the history and layering that have affected Mandarin over the centuries, within both its prestige and non-prestige varieties.

---

3. Zhāng Huiyīng 張惠英 (2016, 703): "《金瓶梅》的語言是在北方話的基礎上，吸收了其他方言，其中，吳方言特別是浙江吳語顯得比較集中。"

The interplay between normative koines and prestige and non-prestige varieties of Mandarin is a frequent focus of the chapters in the section on Chinese dialects and their history. Kengo Chiba's chapter looks at one case of the development of a norm for a Mandarin koine that is remarkably easy to delineate historically. In the mid-nineteenth century, missionaries working in the Western Mandarin region chose the dialect of Chéngdū 成都 in Sìchuān 四川 as the base dialect for their transcriptions of the regional koine, both in Romanized form and in Chinese characters. Chiba argues that by "codifying" the dialect in a written form, building on nascent roots in local tradition and developing a large variety of written materials in the dialect, which were then widely disseminated, the missionaries provided the Chéngdū dialect with prestige and a foundation to serve as the regional Mandarin koine standard. The missionaries also used the Chéngdū standard in their teaching in West China Union University, which they had established, thus further burnishing the koine's prestige throughout China's southwestern territories. In contrast to what Chiba finds with regard to the influence of missionary preference and activity on the rise of the dialect of Chéngdū as the standard for the regional Mandarin koine, this volume's editor has argued elsewhere that the influence of Westerners on the choice of Běijīng as the underlying standard for the national language is far more diluted than is generally assumed.[4] However, Chiba's overview of the Western and Japanese switch of preference from the Southern Mandarin Nánjīng-based koine to a Běijīng-based standard in the course of the nineteenth century provides a useful overview of the situation.

The reference works and other materials developed by the earliest Western missionaries to China for use in their study of Chinese reveal much about the nature and details of the Míng Mandarin koine. Some of those details can be unexpected, such as in the situation discussed by W. South Coblin in his contribution to this volume. Coblin examines the formal pronunciation of the finals in a series of syllables recorded by the Korean sinologist Sin Sukchu 申叔舟 (1417–1475) in the mid-fifteenth century that is quite unusual and thus has been considered of suspect reliability by modern scholars. The unexpected pronunciation relates to the lack of a medial -u- in syllables where most Mandarin dialects have the medial, such as seen in the Běijīng pronunciation of *chuāng* 窗 'window' and *zhuàng* 壯 'strong, robust'. Exploring the record of the pronunciation of the forms in question as produced by missionaries in the sixteenth and seventeenth centuries, Coblin finds representations of the exact same apparently anomalous pronunciation. Although he does not identify a corresponding pronunciation in modern Mandarin dialects, Coblin demonstrates that the missionary sources coincide closely with Sin Sukchu in this feature, thus providing several independent witnesses to the pronunciation within a broad geographic range and time span. Hence the unusual pronunciation must surely have had a basis in living versions of the Míng Mandarin koine and cannot be easily dismissed.

---

4. See Simmons (2017, 2020).

Indeed, the feature Coblin discusses is found in the set of Mandarin dialects examined in Huáng Xiǎodōng's contribution. In this comparative and historical look at dialects originating in Hénán 河南, Huáng Xiǎodōng examines how dialect islands preserve historical features that may or may not have changed in their source dialects. He compares a set of dialect islands in Jiāngsū 江蘇, Zhèjiāng 浙江, and Ānhuī 安徽 that are descended from the language of migrants from Hénán in the area of modern Xìnyáng 信陽 and provides a detailed inventory of their similarities and differences. Features that the dialect islands share with the Hénán source would be preservations of features that were common to all when they first separated 150 years ago. Among all the various features that Huáng Xiǎodōng examines, he notes that both the dialect islands and the Xìnyáng source share a lack of the medial -u- in the set of syllables that include *chuāng* 'window' and *zhuàng* 'strong, robust'. So, the feature discussed by Coblin in this volume does indeed exist in some varieties of Mandarin, and Huáng Xiǎodōng has shown us that it also was found in living Hénán dialects a century and a half ago and likely even earlier.

Variation in the characteristics of the historical Mandarin koine, such as the divergent pronunciations for the same set of words that Coblin discusses, is in fact a predictable element in the basic nature of the koine itself. Many scholars seek a single identifiable dialect as the source or foundation for the Míng koine that came to be called Guānhuà 官話. Some find that the dialect of Nánjīng was that source; others argue that the source is to be found in Jiāng-Huái 江淮 variants with a connection to Central Plains dialects. After summarizing these competing views in her contribution, Zēng Xiǎoyú shows that the koine was in fact a dynamic, flexible language that allowed for variation and that accommodated a variety of features. She makes her case through comparison of a variety of Míng and Qīng period descriptions of the Mandarin koine compiled by Chinese, Korean, Japanese, and Western scholars. She finds that Guānhuà can best be characterized with a small set of distinguishing features that are generally shared by all the versions represented in the sources she examines. Moreover, a majority of the descriptions she looks at reflect an additional small set of features that are specifically characteristic of the Mandarin dialects of the Jiāng-Huái region. She concludes that the Míng Mandarin koine thus was a "flexible amalgam" of characteristics that came together in a "dynamic elastic system and without a rigidly fixed model" and that allowed for features not necessarily fully shared by both the northern Zhōngyuán 中原 and the southern Jiāng-Huái type Mandarins.

The chapter by Henning Klöter explores the reach of Míng Guānhuà beyond China's borders and the status and role that the koine might have played in an overseas Chinese community in Míng times. Klöter's approach is primarily a sociolinguistic one, through which he seeks to characterize how Mandarin might have been perceived and used in an overseas community where it was not the dominantly spoken Chinese language. Looking at the use of Mandarin in a Chinese Hokkien (southern Mǐn dialect) speech community, known as the Sangleys, in Manila in the seventeenth century, Klöter finds that Mandarin had a prestige "High" status that was underpinned by "social beliefs deeply anchored in the culture of" the Chinese community and bolstered by visits of government officials from China (mandarins). But the historical evidence he has uncovered to date does not shed much light on whether that status led to any significant use of Mandarin in local communication and interaction. At most all that can be discerned so far are minor traces of the use of Mandarin, traces that Klöter designates as "occasional diglossia." Nevertheless, the fact that the prestige of the Míng Guānhuà koine had purchase in the imagination of Chinese living so far from the homeland is strong evidence of the strength of that prestige and the importance of the koine within China proper.

The spread of Guānhuà inside Míng China is the subject of the chapter by Simmons. His study examines the Mandarin of dialect islands in southeastern China that formed in the Míng period and compares them to a Mandarin phonology recorded in a fifteenth-century Guānhuà rime book, the *Yùnlüè yìtōng* 韻畧易通. The Mandarin phonology of that rhyme book was conservative for its time as it does not include innovations in Mandarin that occurred in the north earlier in the Yuán and are also not seen in the modern dialects of the Yúnnán 雲南 homeland of its author, Lán Mào 蘭茂 (1397–1476). Yet several of the conservative features of the *Yùnlüè yìtōng* are shared by the Mandarin dialect islands in the southeast. As noted earlier, dialect islands preserve historical features that may or may not have changed in their modern source dialects. While Lán Mào's Yúnnán dialect, which likely had recently migrated from Luòyáng 洛陽 in Hénán 河南, was not the specific source of the various Mandarin dialect islands, it is highly likely that they had roughly contiguous source dialects. Thus, the dialect islands have preserved features shared by source dialects that were subsequently lost in the Yúnnán descendant of Lán Mào's language. Simmons argues that a set of those shared features also encompasses the most salient characteristics of the type of Guānhuà that had the widest geographical currency in early Míng times: the southern variety of the Mandarin koine that Zēng Xiǎoyú in her chapter refers to as the Jiāng-Huái type. Simmons's findings also resonate with those of Zēng Xiǎoyú in noting that the Guānhuà koine had a flexible, dynamic nature that allowed for a degree of variation. But Simmons emphasizes that there was a core set of features that were consistently shared across the koine and the dialects related to it. The aggregate of that core set of features also likely functioned as a kind of hallmark that identified the Guānhuà koine and outlined the parameters of the prestige language that its speakers embodied or aspired to emulate.

One of the most dramatic changes that happened in the set of Mandarin dialects that includes the Běijīng dialect was the loss of the *rù* tone, which broadly went missing in Northern Mandarin and the northern variety of the Guānhuà koine and, as a result, is also missing in Modern Standard Chinese. The loss of the *rù* tone has left the standard language critically bereft of an important actor in traditional prosody, which is consequently impossible to fully grasp when reading in the Běijīng-based pronunciation of Modern Standard Chinese. The changes that led to the loss of the *rù* tone happened according to regular patterns in most Mandarin dialects, but for social and historical reasons, the outcome in Běijīng was partly irregular. The changes caused by the loss were completed at least a couple of centuries ago in Northern Mandarin dialects. The resulting Běijīng version of the situation has now become fixed for the standard language and codified in modern dictionaries.

Guō Lìxiá's contribution presents a view of *rù* tone change in progress in the Shānyīn 山陰 dialect of Shānxī 山西 (belonging to the Jìn 晉 group of northern dialects that are closely related to Mandarin), providing a modern example of the kinds of sociolinguistic factors that come into play as well as the paths the changes can take among competing influences. These competing factors include pressure from the dominant prestige language—spoken Pǔtōnghuà 普通話 (Modern Standard Chinese)—as well as word frequency and sociolinguistic register. Similar factors must also have been in play when the *rù* tone was reshuffled into the other tones in the Běijīng dialect. But their effects arose at a time when the dominant prestige dialect was the Nánjīng-like variety of Guānhuà, the Southern Mandarin koine; and thus it was the colloquial language of Běijīng that was affected by the outside pressure.

The loss of the *rù* tone is also a central point of attention in Liú Xīnzhōng's contribution to this volume, which examines the evolution of the tones in the northwestern Mandarin dialect of Mùlěi 木壘. That dialect has only three contrastive tone categories, *píng*, *shǎng*, and *qù*, which differs from the usual situation in Mandarin dialects wherein the *píng* tone is split into two registers, *yīnpíng* and *yángpíng*. Liú Xīnzhong approaches the question through the lens of experimental phonetics and a detailed analysis of a large database of recordings of the syllables of that dialect. In the results of his analysis, Liú Xīnzhōng demonstrates what happened in Mùlěi in the wake of the loss of the *rù* tone category in that dialect. He finds that the changes followed regular patterns that merged most of the *rù* tone syllables with the *qù* tone, while a set of the *rù* syllables that corresponded to Middle Chinese ancestral forms that had voiced obstruent initials are merged instead with the *shǎng* tone. Liú Xīnzhōng also tells us that the set of syllables originally belonging to an earlier *yángpíng* tone also merged entirely with the *shǎng* tone. We can infer from this state of affairs that there was likely an intermediate stage in which that latter set of *rù* syllables had first merged with a premodern *yángpíng* tone and then moved together with the *yángpíng* syllables into the *shǎng* tone. This path of evolution corresponds fairly neatly with the general pattern of tonal evolution in Northern Mandarin dialects.

In broad perspective, the studies collected in this volume are connected by several shared historical developments and related trends and influences that affected the dialects both internally and in their relationship to texts and the language of literature. These studies have identified clues to those developments and trends in the history of colloquial Chinese and dialects in a variety of sources that serve as witnesses to the languages in earlier times. These witnesses include texts written in language that contains or mixes in colloquial forms, dialect islands that preserve features of historical stages of the languages, contemporary Chinese descriptions and materials such as rime tables and rime books from outside the orthodox phonological tradition that reveal features of their compilers' languages, and descriptions of Chinese languages by people from outside China who studied and made a record of the Chinese they heard. The missionaries held a particularly broad role in the latter case, not only by recording, and sometimes even codifying, varieties of Mandarin, but also in bringing written form to non-Mandarin dialects. Below is a collective summary of conclusions that can be culled from what the chapters in this volume drew from their sources:

- There was regular interaction between text and spoken Chinese that had a variety of effects and outcomes, in both the composition of texts and in their reading or performance. This holds true even though the nature of the Chinese written language and Chinese characters obscures the orality and phonology of the spoken Chinese language and dialects.
- The language of vernacular literature, *báihuàwén* 白話文, while based on a Mandarin foundation that was closely related to, and counterpart to, colloquial Guānhuà and its varieties, still often absorbed non-Mandarin dialect elements. But the power, prestige, and normative influence of Guānhuà was for the most part an insurmountable obstacle in efforts to break fully free of Mandarin in *báihuà* writing and literacy.
- Guānhuà was not a single, well-defined language like Modern Standard Chinese. The Guānhuà Mandarin koine was instead characterized by significant flexibility and diversity in historical times. Nevertheless, it had a powerful prestige and a broad geographic reach in the Míng and the Qīng. Within this state of affairs, the strongest Guānhuà variety was the Southern Mandarin variety, which had the widest geographic spread and held the greatest prestige in both dynasties.
- Of all the phonological features discussed, the *rù* tone played the most critical role in the history of colloquial Chinese. Its loss in Northern Mandarin dialects created a dramatic difference between the northern and southern varieties of the Guānhuà koine. The greater prestige of the southern variety of Guānhuà was in part due to the fact that it was the variety that maintained a *rù* tone, which held a prominent place in literature, in the koine, and in many dialects.

The chapters in this volume present much detail that illustrates and fleshes out these conclusions. These are not the only findings contained within these chapters, as can be seen in the above discussion. Yet this summary of conclusions should help guide interested readers in navigating the various arguments and discoveries of the contributors, as well as in identifying areas for further investigation, of which many remain.

References

Shen, Zhongwei. 2020. *A Phonological History of Chinese*. Cambridge: Cambridge University Press.

Simmons, Richard VanNess. 2017. "Whence Came Mandarin? Qīng Guānhuà, the Běijīng Dialect, and the National Language Standard in Early Republican China." *Journal of the American Oriental Society* 137 (1): 63–88.

Simmons, Richard VanNess. 2020. "What Was Standard Chinese in the 19th Century? Divergent Views in the Times of Transition." In *Language Diversity in the Sinophone World: Historical Trajectories, Language Planning, and Multilingual Practices*, edited by Henning Klöter and Mårten Söderblom Saarela, 13–38. New York and London: Routledge.

Yáo Jígāng 姚吉剛. 2019. "*Jīn Píng Méi* zhōng de Héféi fāngyán yánjiū" 《金瓶梅》中的合肥方言研究 [A study of the Héféi dialect in the *Jīn Píng Méi*]. Chóngqìng: Chóngqìng kējì xuéyuàn xuébào (shèhuì kēxué bǎn) 重慶科技學院學報 (社會科學版) 4: 75–79.

Yīn Xiǎojié 殷曉傑. 2011. *Míng-Qīng Shāndōng fāngyán cíhuì yánjiū: yǐ* Jīn Píng Méi cíhuà, Xǐngshì yīnyuán zhuàn, Liáozhāi lǐqǔ *wéi zhōngxīn* 明清山東方言詞彙研究：以《金瓶梅詞話》,《醒世姻緣傳》,《聊齋俚曲》為中心 [The lexicon of the Míng-Qīng Shāndōng dialect of the Míng: With a focus on *Jīn Píng Méi cíhuà, Xǐngshì yīnyuán zhuàn*, and *Liáozhāi lǐqǔ*]. Běijīng: Zhōngguó shèhuì kēxué chūbǎnshè 中國社會科學出版社.

Zhāng Huìyīng 張惠英. 2016. "*Jīn Píng Méi* fēi Shāndōng fāngyán bǔ zhèng" 《金瓶梅》非山東方言補證 [Supplemental evidence showing that the *Jīn Píng Méi* is not written in the Shāndōng dialect]. *Zhōngguó yǔwén* 中國語文 6: 703–6.

I. Chinese Dialects in Texts

1
Does Taiwanese Cantillation Reflect the Sound of the Táng?*

David Prager Branner

Introduction

Among the many questions we can ask when studying one given variety of Chinese language, an important one is this: how is this variety related to earlier and especially ancient forms? For the most part we consider the question in terms of linguistic features that are discrete and that can be rigorously compared, such as phonological units. Historicity tends to be part of the pride of identity in Chinese societies, and for that reason of some popular interest—though the technical aspects by which historicity could be validated are not part of popular awareness. Among people who speak major southern varieties of Chinese such as Cantonese and Hokkien, it is a commonplace that reading Táng literature in their accents is truest to the sound of history.

How does one actually verify that? Surely what most people mean when they say that is that 文讀 *wéndú* 'learnèd character-readings' in the southern dialects have oral stop-endings in the 入聲 *rùshēng* tone category: Taiwanese 急 *kip* [kɪp32], 不 *put* [puɒt32], 客 *khek* [khi̯ɛk32]. But the claim can be examined linguistically in greater detail—we have a fair amount of information about the phonological features that held a Táng-style poem together, and we can examine those features as expressed in modern renderings of Táng poetry.

Here I take as research data a long performance of an important Táng poem, rendered in Taiwanese reading pronunciation and elaborated into melody by a leading contemporary practitioner, who observes well-established artistic custom. This is a preliminary study, intended to explore the question itself and to establish workflow for future study.

---

* Initial research on this project was presented at the Annual Meeting of the T'ang Studies Society, March 24, 2001, Chicago. The workflow for collecting statistics on transcribed song, together with a script in the Python programming language, was presented on October 23, 2014, at Hacker School (now the Recurse Center), New York; the present chapter's conclusions were presented on 1 November, 2014, at the meeting of the American Oriental Society (Western Branch), at Stanford University, and, with revisions, on March 11, 2016, at the International Workshop on the History of Colloquial Chinese—Written and Spoken, at Rutgers University, as "Taiwanese Cantillation Prosody and the Standard Tradition of Regulated Verse." Research on this subject has been supported in part by a Small Research Grant from the T'ang Studies Society. Thanks to Garrett Fischbach for reviewing the musical notation.

This form of performance is called 吟誦 *yínsòng*, which I translate (for reasons justified below) as "cantillation" rather than "chanting." In comparing Taiwanese cantillation to Táng poetic internals, I consider two types of issues: faithfulness of individual phonological categories and expression of traditional tonal prosody. Phonological issues chiefly concern syllable finals (especially vocalism) and tone, as they affect rhyming; tonal prosody is chiefly the expression of the 平仄 *píng-zè* distinction.

Terminology and Technical Matters

Chinese *yínsòng*, the melodic expression of literature (including even literature that we would strictly consider prose), is usually rendered as "chanting" in English. That is a poor translation because "to chant" suggests monotony, especially that of plainsong. I use "cantillation" not because it is technically more correct, but because it is already current as the name for florid melodic ornamentation in another literary language, liturgical Hebrew, so that its associations are more expressive of musical artistry. Chinese traditional *yínsòng* is ornamented. All Chinese words bear intrinsic syllable-tones, and in cantillation those tones are elaborated into melody. As a form of artistic embellishment, the practice recalls in sound the way written characters are elaborated into calligraphy for the eye. This analogy is quite a productive one, but discussion here would be a departure from the topic at hand.

There are traditions of cantillation all over the Chinese-speaking world, and the practice is well-known in texts from the ancient period; 鄭玄 Zhèng Xuán (127–200) comments on the *Zhōu lǐ*: "倍文曰諷，以聲節之曰誦" [to recite literature from memory is called *fěng*; to add rhythm (or "measure") to it using sound is called *sòng*].[1] In much of continental China there was a steep, decades-long hiatus and decline in the practice of this tradition. During the twentieth century two major political movements militated against cantillation: the May Fourth Movement, which sought to promote vernacular language at the expense of the conservative prose style and associated literary learning; and the Movement to Smash the Four Old Things (破四舊 *pò sìjiù*), an expression of mid-century Communist ideology. But Taiwan experienced neither of the upheavals of these "Two Fours." Literati cantillation there has survived in a number of traditions, with recordings attested at least from the 1960s and 1970s. It was not a wholly intellectual or educational practice; during the period of Japanese rule, one of these traditions was associated in part with *geisha* entertainment—women cantillated traditional poetry at drinking establishments, as part of entertainment for male customers.

In historical-comparative linguistics we are accustomed to treating linguistic evidence as though it were a naturally occurring substance—but in fact, it must

---

1. Scholium on 周禮 *Zhōu lǐ* "春官 Chūnguān," "大司樂 Dà sīyuè": "以樂語教國子，興、道、諷、誦、言、語."

be put into written form through patient labor by native speakers, fieldworkers, and philologists. (The process by which it is collected is part of the data itself—the metadata, if you will—though many hands neglect to document that closely.) Here we are dealing not only with words and sentences but also with a through-composed work of performance art—a composition that has an author and a specific, recorded performance of the composition, used as the basis of the conclusions in the present chapter. I take as my data a performance of the 琵琶行 "Pípá xíng" of 白居易 Bái Jūyì (772–846; Hóng Zénán 2002). The composer, 洪澤南 Hóng Zénán, is a passed master of Chinese literati cantillation (文人調 wénrén diào) in the styles of Taiwan's "Sword-House Studio" (劍樓書房 Jiànlóu Shūfáng, founded by 趙益山 Zhào Yìshān) and "Pipes of Heaven Cantillation Society" (天籟吟社 Tiānlài Yínshè, founded by 林述三 Lín Shùsān, 1887–1957). Note that this is a living tradition, not an effort to recover the practice of any former era. For the purposes of this chapter, the performance has been transcribed inelegantly into traditional Western musical notation, found in the appendix to this chapter.

Features of the composition, such as repeating motifs that unify it melodically, are not discussed here, since the aim is to consider how the performance expresses the Táng-time prosodic order of the poem. There are some changes of apparent key in the recording, most notably following bar 165, but they are corrected in the transcription, and this is of no consequence to the analysis.

A number of romanization systems compete as to how to transcribe this language. The governments of both Taiwan and the People's Republic of China have issued official systems. Here I use so-called Church romanization (called 白話字 pe̍h-ōe-jī in Taiwanese), which was devised by Carstairs Douglas (1830–1877) and is used in many dictionaries and textbooks. Campbell (1913) is an important and comprehensive source for character readings —wéndú in particular—in Church romanization. The rules of the system are rather different from those of the more familiar Hànyǔ Pīnyīn for Mandarin. Very briefly, Taiwanese vowels o and ɔ are distinguished as [ə] (or [o]) vs. [ɔ];[2] raised ⁿ represents nasalization of the preceding vowels and is distinct from n; finals -eng and -ek are pronounced as though they have a preceding medial -i-: seng [ɕieŋ] and sek [ɕiek], respectively. There is a three-way distinction in stops and obstruents: p-, ph-, b-, and so on. Every syllable belongs to one of the seven tone categories, distinguished mainly by diacritics and syllable-codas:

The 平 píng categories:

    陰平 yīnpíng: vowels a e i o ɔ u without diacritics, and without codas -h, -p, -t, or -k

    陽平 yángpíng: â ê î ô ɔ̂ û

---

2. Vowel ɔ may also be seen as oo, o·, and ɔ. Note that vowel ɔ does not normally occur in rù tones.

The 仄 *zè* or non-*píng* categories:

陰上 *yīnshǎng*: *á é í ó ó̇ ú*
陰去 *yīnqù*: *à è ì ò ò̇ ù*
陽去 *yángqù*: *ā ē ī ō ō̇ ū*
陰入 *yīnrù*: *a e i o u* without diacritics but with coda -*h*, -*p*, -*t*, or -*k*;
陽入 *yángrù*: *ā ē ī ō ō̇ ū* (and always ending in -*h*, -*p*, -*t*, or -*k*)

All syllables within a given "word" are joined by hyphens, although what constitutes a "word"—either in modern Taiwanese or in the language of a Táng poem—is a vexed question that would take us beyond our present domain of discussion.

Wéndú Segmentals

There are two technical features of Táng poetic language to compare with modern Taiwanese performance: segmentals (consonants and vowels—sounds that can be transcribed in Roman letters) and prosody (suprasegmentals, i.e., tones, and their organization in literature).

Wéndú are not a consistent representation of the linguistic past. They represent a model of historical language in terms of contemporary phonology, something quite distinct from linguistic reconstruction proper, which attempts to recover historical sounds either literally or in the abstract. Exactly where *wéndú* come from in any given variety of southern Chinese is often uncertain. They usually appear to be accretions of different things, rather than having been derived from prescriptive records of some stage of language (spoken or literary) of some single point in time. In terms of their place in a language overall, however, they tend to dominate the high diglossic register—they are associated with the pronunciation of written or written-sounding Chinese rather than purely oral language. But we are subtly in error when we call them "character-readings," since they do not exist in isolation as the readings of characters and nothing else. In Taiwanese they are plentiful in living speech, in diverse vocabulary of educated origin, while some characters are conversely read using words of popular rather than learnèd origin. Normally, a contemporary performer uses a dictionary to learn all the readings necessary to cantillate a piece of pre-modern literature—some, such as Hóng Zénán, the composer of the piece examined here, also consult traditional Taiwanese rimebooks (韻書 *yùnshū*), along with the 廣韻 *Guǎngyùn* and other formal sources of medieval phonology.

Some sixteen initials are heard in common Taiwanese *wéndú*, whereas medieval phonology requires between thirty-five and forty-one. Naturally, Taiwanese cannot distinguish all thirty-five medieval initials with its sixteen. There are also various places where medieval categories are simply mixed up in Taiwanese—one medieval initial corresponding to different initials in Taiwanese—mostly among the voiced initials. That means that correspondence sets, the bread and butter of historical phonology, are confused in relating Taiwanese *wéndú* and Táng phonology. A few examples will suffice and are shown in Table 1.1.[3] All come from the "Pípá xíng" transcription.

Table 1.1: Inconsistent Taiwanese reflection of some medieval initials

Initial	字	Medieval phonology	Taiwanese
定母一、四等	彈	dan-1	*tân*
	弟	deiQ-4	*tē*
	停	deing-4	*thêng*
	頭	dou-1	*thiû*
定母二、三等 (澄母)	茶	dra-2	*chhâ*
	宅	dreik-2a	*thėk*
	纏	dran-3b	*tiân*
	沉	drem-3	*tîm*
來母	羅	le-1	*lô*
	老	lauQ-1	*nóⁿ*
日母	人	nyen-3b	*lîn*
	耳	nyiQ-3d	*níⁿ*

Note in passing that the inconsistencies in *wéndú* initials have no relevance in the case of the present poem, which is not "regulated verse" (律詩 *lùshī*). Furthermore, comparing lists of initials affords us only a static view of both phonologies. Since we are really talking about the historicity of current performance tradition, let us turn now to more dynamic evidence.

First, consider rhyming. Because *wéndú* reflects standard categories imperfectly, people make small adjustments to how characters are read in order to improve prosodic effects. The most salient such adjustments are those applied to rhyming, called 叶韻 (or 協韻) *xiéyùn* 'accommodated rhyming'. This term originated in early medieval times, when it had become evident that the rhyming behavior of the ancient 詩經 *Shījīng* required a system of pronunciation distinct from then-current phonology—an interesting parallel to modern performance of Táng literature. In the examples in Table 1.2, the rhymewords are in a mixture of finals -*u* and -*o*, but cases of the latter are coerced to -*u* for the sake of assonance; an arrow shows the coercion.

---

3. Medieval phonology is transcribed as in Branner (2006: 271–302).

Table 1.2: Accommodated rhyming (*xiéyùn* 叶韻)

	Non-rhyming foot	Rhyming foot		Non-rhyming foot	Rhyming foot
自言本是京城女	*lú*		今年歡笑復明年	*liân*	
家在蝦蟆陵下住		*chū*	秋月春風等閒度		*tō̄ → tū*
十三學得琵琶成	*sêng*		弟走從軍阿姨死	*sú*	
名屬教坊第一部		*pū*	暮去朝來顏色故		*kò̍ → kù*
曲罷曾教善才服	*ho̍k*		門前冷落車馬稀	*hi*	
妝成每被秋娘妒		*tù*	老大嫁作商人婦		*hū*
五陵年少爭纏頭	*thiû*		商人重利輕別離	*lî*	
一曲紅綃不知數		*sò̍ → sù*	前月浮梁買茶去		*khù*
鈿頭雲篦擊節碎	*suì*				
血色羅裙翻酒污		*ù*			

The practice of accommodated rhyming is faithful to Táng-time reading of much older poetry. But the need for it confesses a discrepancy between Táng phonology and modern Taiwanese *wéndú*.

And not all discrepancies are resolved in the Taiwanese data. One such case is imperfect rhyming of words in the medieval 山攝 *shānshè* category—words ending in *-an* and *-at* in Taiwanese. In these rimes, the presence of medial /i/ has the effect of raising and fronting the vowel /a/, just as it does in Mandarin. As shown in Table 1.3, Taiwanese rimes *-an* and *-oan* are phonetically [an] and [u̯an] but *-ian* is phonetically [-ɛn] or [-i̯ɛn], and similarly *-at/-oat* and *-iat* are [at]/[u̯an] and [-ɛt] or [-i̯ɛt]. The vowels [a] and [ɛ] do not sound alike. But there is no effort to normalize either vowel by accommodated rhyming.

Table 1.3: Raising of /a/ without effect on rhyming

	Non-rhyming foot	Rhyming foot	Phonetically
主人下馬客在船		*sôan*	[su̯an]
舉酒欲飲無管弦		*hiân*	[χɛn] ~ [χi̯ɛn]
醉不成歡慘將別		*pia̍t*	[pɛt] ~ [pi̯ɛt]
別時茫茫江浸月		*goa̍t*	[gu̯at]
忽聞水上琵琶聲	*seng*		
主人忘歸客不發		*hoat*	[χu̯at]
水泉冷澀弦凝絕		*choa̍t*	[tshu̯at]
凝絕不通聲暫歇		*hiat*	[χɛt] ~ [χi̯ɛt]

And there is a second point here. Raising of *a* after medial *i* or *j* and before an alveolar coda is very widespread in diverse forms of Chinese, so it is reasonable to hazard that it was a feature of Táng pronunciation. But if so, it seems to have left no trace on Táng rhyming practice. We are supposed to recognize that the two endings are considered to rhyme, even though the assonance is imperfect.

The raising of *a* after medial *i* or *j* is not the only case of imperfect assonance. Look again at the rhyme-words in Table 1.2. They are in two different Taiwanese tones: *yīnqù* (Taiwanese final *-ù*) rhymes with *yángqù* tone (Taiwanese final *-ū*).[4] This point is shown more clearly in Table 1.4.

Table 1.4: Taiwanese tones *yīnqù* and *yángqù* rhyme

Tone	住	部	妒	數	污	度	故	婦	去
yīnqù			*tù*	*sù*	*ù*		*kù*		*khù*
yángqù	*chū*	*pū*				*tū*		*hū*	

In the early Táng, these words were all in the same single tone: *qùshēng*. But at some point each early Táng tone divided into two in much of Chinese, producing the pairs of *yīn*- and *yáng*-tone categories we now find in Taiwan.

Yet hearers have continued to accept them as a single category for poetic purposes, as have poets, even though objectively they sound different. We know that there was already a *yin*- and *yáng*-tone split some time during the Táng and that *yáng* was already behaving differently from *yīn*, at least for the *shǎng* tone—because of doublets in Táng redactions of the 切韻 *Qièyùn* and the comments of 李涪 Lǐ Fú in the late ninth century. Standard poetic practice was still to rhyme in a conservative fashion, where there were only four tone categories, even though at least one of those tone categories and possibly all of them had by then split into two and did not actually sound the same in ordinary language. But poetic language is not necessarily ordinary language; at a minimum it often differs in register.

Bái himself, writing around Lǐ Fú's time, tends to rhyme 全濁上聲 *quánzhuó shǎngshēng* words the standard way—with other *shǎngshēng* words—in much of his poetry. For example, in "初入峽有感 Chū rùxiá yǒugǎn" he rhymes 峙 *zhì* {driQ-3d} and 恃 *zhì* {dzyiQ-3d} in a block encompassing 水、葦、起、齒、里、趾、此、矣、子、死. But in the present, more ballad-like work, intended to be comprehensible to the uneducated ear, he rhymes two *shǎngshēng* words into a *qùshēng* rhyming block, as shown in Table 1.5.

---

4. The foot-word 女 *lǔ* in the first line of Table 2 does not "enter the rhyming" (不入韻 *bú rùyùn*) in Táng phonology.

Table 1.5: Táng tones *shǎng* (with voiced obstruent initials) and *qù* rhyme

Tone	住	部	妒	數	污	度	故	婦	去
shǎng 上聲		bouQ-1						bouQ-3b	
qù 去聲	druoH-3c		tuoH-1	sruoH-3c	weH-1	duoH-1	kuoH-1		khuoH-3b

That is an intrusion of living phonetics into literature—the *shǎngshēng* words would not rhyme with *qùshēng* words in stricter poetry, but Bái's ear has permitted him to rhyme them.

It bears repeating that the phonology of cantillated literature is not natural language of the kind we usually assume speech to be. It is through-composed, and at times altered consciously for literary effect. Since Taiwanese distinguishes *yīnqù* and *yángqù* tone categories, even when they are treated as a single category in Táng rhyming, the composer has felt no need to harmonize them here. But close examination of cantillation performances shows that composers commonly adjust their readings in various ways. In bar 83, for example, the composer has chosen to read 事 as Taiwanese *sī* (a reading unattested in standard sources for *wéndú*) so that it rhymes properly. Its regular *wéndú* pronunciation, however, is *sū* as in bar 259 (the "popular," most historically conservative reflex of the morpheme is *tāi*, as in *tāi-chì*, 'matter').

There is a high-level lesson here. In reconstructing forms of Chinese earlier than the present day, we typically draw on written materials of many sorts, including rhyming practice in fine literature and the character readings prescribed in rime books. Yet at least since middle antiquity—the Táng—the phonology of natural language and that prescribed for the performance of literature have diverged. The implications of this matter reach far past the scope of this chapter, however.

Tonal Prosody

So far, all the examples have been segmental. But how is Táng tonal prosody expressed in Taiwanese cantillation? By syllable length and by ornamentation. Syllables of different tones are not of the same average duration; Table 1.6 shows a distinct tendency to prolong *píng* syllables overall, and particularly the *yángpíng*.

Table 1.6: Average duration of each syllable by tone category

Tone category	Average duration ($\quarternote = 1.0$)
○ (*píng* 平) average	1.3
yīnpíng	1.2
yángpíng	1.3
● (*zè* 仄) average	1.0
yīnshǎng	1.0
yīnqù	1.0
yángqù	1.0
yángrù	1.0
yīnrù	1.0

The prolongation of *píng* tones does not occur in every case, but when we look at averages we see it to a greater degree in certain of the seven different positions. Data are summarized in Table 1.7.

Table 1.7: Average duration of each syllable by both syllable-position and *píng-zè*

Syllable position	1	2	3	4	5	6	7
píng tones	1.0	1.7	1.0	1.4	1.0	1.0	1.8
zè tones	1.0	0.9	0.9	0.8	0.9	0.8	1.6

Final syllables, regardless of tone, tend strongly to be prolonged—that is presumably an effect of the musical organization of the poetry into more-or-less discrete couplets, drawn out on the last foot. But line-caesura positions—positions 2 and 4 in a seven-syllable line—are also prolonged in *píng* tones, while inner (positions 2 to 6) *zè* tones are all slightly shorter on average. The overall effect is to make *píng* tones prominent at the caesuras. This prolongation is a tradition attested widely in modern practice all over the Chinese cantillating world, and summarized in the maxim "平聲長，仄聲短 *píngshēng cháng, zèshēng duǎn* [*Píng* tones are longer and *zè* tones are shorter]," although whether the practice is of Táng date is unknown. But the practice is interesting because the *píngzè* contrast is an organizing feature of prosody only in regulated verse, while "Pípá xíng" is an example of "new Music Bureau poetry" (新樂府詩 *xīn yuèfǔ shī*), which does not observe regulated rules. Such caesura-prolongation of *píng* tones is common among cantillators from diverse dialect traditions. So, ancient or not, it is not an expression of known Táng prosody; it may well be the modern expression of regulated prosody being extended onto non-regulated poetry.

The details of the data are presented in Table 1.8. Interestingly, there is some prolongation in position-2 *yīnshǎng*, too. I can suggest no explanation for that without further data.

Table 1.8: Average duration of each syllable by both place and tone category

Position	1	2	3	4	5	6	7
yīnpíng	1.0	1.6	1.0	1.2	1.0	1.1	1.9
yángpíng	1.1	1.7	1.0	1.6	1.0	0.9	1.8
yīnshǎng	1.0	1.3	1.0	0.8	1.0	0.9	1.5
yīnqù	1.0	0.6	0.9	0.6	0.9	0.9	1.6
yángqù	1.0	0.8	0.8	0.8	1.1	0.8	1.8
yīnrù	1.0	0.6	0.8	0.8	0.8	0.8	1.7
yángrù	1.2	0.8	0.9	0.8	0.8	0.7	1.5

There is another special tonal feature in this performance: ornamentation of *yángpíng*-tone syllables. This ornamentation is melisma (more than one note to a vowel), and to varying extents it occurs in all tones. But it occurs with highest frequency in *yángpíng* tones, and *yángpíng* tones alone are mainly melismatized so as to contain rising contours—melisma in all the other tone categories produces falling contours. The data appears in Table 1.9.

Table 1.9: Percentage of each tone category displaying melisma

Tone	Melismatic		Non-melismatic
	Fall	Rise	
yīnpíng	27.7%	1.5%	67.9%
yángpíng	4.6%	54.3%	41.1%
yīnshǎng	44.2%	6.5%	49.4%
yīnqù	31.9%	0.0%	68.1%
yángqù	25.4%	0.0%	73.1%
yīnrù	44.4%	1.4%	52.8%
yángrù	26.8%	0.0%	65.9%

Yángpíng is the only tone category whose basic form has a rising contour in ordinary Taiwanese, so it is a natural way of marking the *yángpíng* in cantillation.[5] That

---

5. All Taiwanese tones have a "basic" form (本調 *běndiào*) and a "sandhi" form (變調 *biàndiào*). These total fourteen, of which only one (the *yángpíng*'s basic form) is a rising contour in most forms of Taiwanese. A rare exception is retriplicated morphology, which Traditional Church romanization lacks any regular system to notate. This morphology appears with adjectives of intensive degree, introducing a rising contour in the *yīnpíng*, *yángpíng*, *yángqù*, and *yángrù* tones (only):
   hiam 'spicy' → [hiam$_{25}$ hiam$_{33}$ hiam$_{44}$] 'extremely spicy';
   kôan 'tall, high' → [kuan$_{25}$ kuan$_{33}$ kuan$_{24}$] 'extremely tall or high';
   kāu 'thick' → [kau$_{25}$ kau$_{22}$ kau$_{33}$] 'extremely thick';
   kut 'slippery' → [kuot$_{25}$ kuot$_{22}$ kuot$_{33}$] 'extremely slippery'.
   The other tone categories use contour [44] in the antepenultimate syllable in this morphological pattern:
   thiám 'sleepy' → [thiam$_{44}$ thiam$_{44}$ thiam$_{53}$] 'extremely sleepy';
   tshàu 'foul-smelling' → [tshau$_{44}$ tshau$_{53}$ tshau$_{21}$] 'extremely foul-smelling';
   siap 'astringent' → [siap$_{4}$ siap$_{53}$ siap$_{32}$] 'extremely astringent'.
   (Examples from the 台灣宜蘭壯圍 Zhuàngwéi region of Taiwan's Yílán County.)

means that rising melisma is being used to draw special attention to the *yángpíng* category, and that is something unattested in the Táng prosodic tradition.

Conclusion

To summarize: Segmentally, Taiwanese *wéndú* is a poor match for medieval phonology: much of the older tradition is lost or confused in the modern praxis. Taiwanese cantillators today employ strategies used in earlier times to improve the sound of poetry: accommodated rhyming and overlooking palatalization of *-an/-at* and the tone-split. As for prosody, there are ornamental developments beyond what is known in Táng tradition. Even in a non-regulated poem, the *píng-zè* distinction is expressed as a length-distinction—especially at the caesura but also in general. The *yángpíng* has the strongest tendency to be melismatic and at those times has a distinctive rising contour, unlike the other tones, which tend to fall in melisma. These features may not be innovations, but their historicity is uncertain.

Figure 1.1 shows one couplet (bars 157–164) exhibiting the various prosodic features discussed above. The base syllable length is a quarter note: ♩. Line feet are longer than the base. *Píng* tones at the caesuras are longer than the base (*gîm, siông*); *zè* tones at the caesuras are base-length or shorter (*poat, tùn*). There are four *yángpíng* syllables whose melisma involves a rising contour (*gîm, hiân, siông, iông*); there are another four non-*yángpíng* syllables whose melisma involves a falling contour (*hòng, poat, chhap, liām*).

Figure 1.1: **A couplet displaying all of the prosodic features discussed here**

Broadly speaking, the Taiwanese cantillation tradition pays attention to traditional large tonal categories and their ornamentation, and to the integrity of traditional rhyming groups, without being true to the medieval phonology on which finer-grained prosodic rules rested. Tonal ornamentation is the primary expression of non-musical linguistic prosody in musical performance and is imposed even on compositions entirely outside of the regulated praxis—even on Classical prose.

In the end, we have no way to settle the question posed at the beginning of this chapter—to tell whether that tonal ornamentation is true to the historical sound of Táng times. It is, however, beautiful to hear, and even if it is only a modern tradition, it has historical roots and allows native speakers to take possession of pre-modern literature using their own phonology.

Note on the Transcription

Transcription was done using the open-source MuseScore application (musescore.com). The finished transcription was exported to "extensible markup language for music" format (MusicXML), and analyzed statistically with an original script in the Python programming language. Although the melody is lovely, musically the transcription itself is unattractive. My goal was to produce MusicXML output in an equal-tempered tuning system, so in the interest of speed the only accidentals I used were sharps, even when flats would have made more structural sense (e.g., d♯ always appears, rather than e♭).

The vowel bears essentially the whole of the pitch or pitches to which any given syllable is set. The voiceless stops -p, -t, and -k cannot be prolonged, so where they occur, they close the syllable at the very end of the note to which it is set.

There are frequent changes of time signature in places, because I have started a new bar with each apparent downbeat.

References

Branner, David Prager. 2006. "Comparative Transcriptions of Rime Table Phonology." In *The Chinese Rime Tables*, edited by David Prager Branner, 265–302. Amsterdam: John Benjamins.

Campbell, William [Gān Wéilín 甘為霖]. (1913) 1955. *A Dictionary of the Amoy Vernacular Spoken Throughout the Prefectures of Chin-chiu, Chiang-chiu, and Formosa*. Tainan: Presbyterian Church. Reprint, Tainan 臺南: Táiwān Jiàohuì Gōngbàoshè 臺灣教會公報社.

Hóng Zénán 洪澤南. 2002. "Bái Jūyì, Pípá xíng" 白居易，琵琶行 [The 'Pípá xíng' of Bái Jūyì]. Performed by Xǔ Yītíng 許樟娗 in a setting composed by Hóng Zénán 洪澤南. Audio supplement to [No author], *Gāojí zhíyè xuéxiào guówén* 高級職業學校國文 [Literary Chinese for Vocational Schools]. Taipei: Sanmin Book Co., Ltd. 三民書局 (Dōngdà shūjú 東大書局), 民國91年. The copyright holder of the composition and the recording, Mr. Hóng Zénán, has graciously given permission to publish the transcription.

白居易『琵琶行』
[Bái Jūyì, "Pípá xíng" in Taiwanese]

Composition by Hóng Zénán 洪澤南　作曲
Performed by Xǔ Yīting 許樟姃　　唱
Transcribed by David Prager Branner 林德威　譜

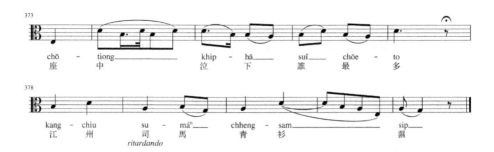

This transcription is dated 8 November, 2021, and represents a significant change from the version originally presented. The original recording contains a slight increase in speed and a rise in pitch, beginning at bar 165 and continuing for most of the composition thereafter. I interpret them now as the result of mechanical issues relating to tape-playback. That means this transcription represents the composer's presumed intention more closely than it does the literal performance in the published recording.

I am most grateful to the violinist Garrett Fischbach for criticism and suggestions about the improvement of this transcription. The final result, however, is my own responsibility.

2
Vernacular Written Cantonese in the Twentieth Century

The Role of Cantonese Opera in Its Growth and Spread

Marjorie K. M. Chan

Introduction

During the past three or so decades, vernacular written Cantonese ('written Cantonese,' for short)—that is, the written form of Cantonese that reflects the vernacular language used in the informal register—has become very widespread in popular print media in Hong Kong and overseas Cantonese-speaking communities. Written Cantonese, with respect to vernacular Cantonese characters and Cantonese lexicon and syntax, is often found in advertisements, comic strips, newspaper headlines and columns, entertainment magazine articles, personal correspondence, and written transcripts of spoken discourse, as well as in written forms of social media.

Since Bauer's (1988) pioneering study on written Cantonese, a fair amount has been written about linguistic matters such as code-mixing, dialect literature, and diglossia.[1] An important starting point is the definition of 'written Cantonese'. For heuristic purposes, this chapter follows Bauer (1988) in defining it as "any text which contains at least one Cantonese lexical item *and* is intended by its writer to be read by a Cantonese-speaking reader" (emphasis MC's). Truly vernacular written Cantonese text should, however, contain a larger inventory, or a larger proportion, of written Cantonese than a single token of what is clearly identifiable as Cantonese that is not part of standard written Chinese taught in school. That is a starting point, and leaves for future discussion the proportion to be deemed sufficient (see, for example, Bauer 2018).

An illustration of text with written Cantonese is found in a weekly magazine in a lively article on Andy Lau (劉德華), a well-known Hong Kong Canto-pop singer and movie star. The weekly is *Star Magazine* (星周刊), the Vancouver (Canada) edition of the *Sing Tao Daily* (星島) for local Cantonese readers, many of whom have immigrated from Hong Kong. Published on October 9, 2005, the text of the main article (on page 52) is printed in traditional format, with vertical columns going from

---

1. Examples of some linguistic literature concerning vernacular written Cantonese include Bauer (1984), Chiu (2005), Lau (1995), Li (1997), Li (1998, 2000), Lo and Wong (1990), Lock (2003), Snow (1993, 2004, 2008, 2010), Starr and Li (2015), Wu (2003), Yan (2005, 2008), and sources cited therein.

right to left, and written in simple language that requires only limited education and literacy level. It is also in standard Chinese. The caption under the inserted photos differs both in layout—horizontal text from left to right—and in dialect; it is written with the intention that it be read silently or aloud in Cantonese and as direct speech, precisely to capture the full flavor of the megastar's own words. In his monologue given in (1), with Jyutping romanization and English translation added, Andy Lau recounts an incident from his China trip.

(1) a. 呢朝八點幾，去機場途中見到隻蟹，
 我即刻叫司機駛入去！
 嘩！一世人都未曾見過咁大隻蟹呀！
 真係令我好激動！
 於是我哋架車直劏草原，
 我立刻落車衝埋去，
 唔使九秒九就爬咗上去！

b. *Ni¹-ziu¹ baat³-dim²-gei², heoi³ gei¹-coeng⁴ tou⁴-zung¹ gin³-dou³ zek³-haai⁵, ngo⁵ zik¹-hak¹ giu³ si¹-gei¹ sai²-jap⁶-heoi³!*
 Waa⁴! Jat¹-sai³-jan⁴ dou¹ mei⁶-cang⁴ gin³-gwo³ gam³ daai⁶ zek³-haai⁵ aa³!
 Zan¹ hai⁶ ling⁶ ngo⁵ hou² gik¹ dung⁶!
 Jyu¹-si⁶ ngo⁵-dei⁶ gaa³ ce¹ zik⁶ caan² cou²-jyun⁴,
 ngo⁵ lap⁶-hak¹ lok⁶ ce¹ cung¹ maai⁴-heoi³,
 m⁴-sai² gau²-miu⁵-gau² zau⁶ paa⁴-zo²-soeng⁵-heoi³!

c. 'That morning at a bit after eight, en route to the airport, (I) encountered a crab.
 I immediately told the chauffeur to drive in!
 Wow! In my entire life I've never seen such a huge crab!
 It got me really excited!
 As a result, our car mowed straight through,
 I dashed out of the car and rushed over,
 and in less than 9.9 seconds I had already climbed on!'

Written text such as this short example—containing marked Cantonese mixed with standard written Chinese (and potentially more literary language)—abounds in Hong Kong, where the vast majority of the population can speak Cantonese.[2] Extensive use of written Cantonese is similarly evident in Chinese communities with a large population of former Hong Kong residents. While this phenomenon is far less observed in cities in Guangdong province in China, as a result of tighter government

---

2. Some census and language survey data from late twentieth century for Hong Kong are available. For example, the results of a 1993 survey in Hong Kong (Bacon-Shone and Bolton 1998) show that 81.6% of the Hong Kong residents speak Cantonese as their 'mother tongue.' Some Hong Kong residents learn Cantonese after starting school. Thus, the total figure for Hong Kong residents who can speak Cantonese is higher still, namely, 91.9%. These statistics do not appear to have changed drastically two decades later, based on 2012 data provided from the Hong Kong government's Census and Statistics Department website.

controls on dialect use,[3] the growth and development of vernacular written Cantonese forms a vital part of Cantonese dialect history.

This study is on written Cantonese that is found in Cantonese operas, focusing on its peak of popularity in the early decades of the twentieth century through to the post–World War II decades. The aim is to show that Cantonese opera played a vital role during that period in the spread of vernacular written Cantonese. Thus, its use in Hong Kong popular culture today—from the lyrics of Canto-pop in the 1970s onwards, to advertisements and printed media, and to handwritten and digitally based written communication—did not develop in a vacuum. To the contrary, written Cantonese forms part of a long and rich legacy of rendering into a written medium the vernacular language of a region for a reading public with varying degrees of literacy and education.

The remainder of this chapter is organized into three broad historical periods concerning the contribution of Cantonese operas to the growth in use of written Cantonese in recent decades. Section 1 discusses some historical background and sources on written Cantonese, which as a literary genre is an integral part of Cantonese opera. Section 2 presents the period of relative peace between 1920 and 1937, years that can be called the 'golden age' of Cantonese opera. This very creative and very productive period was cut short by the outbreak of the war of resistance against the Japanese (kàng-Rì zhànzhēng 抗日戰爭, 1937–1945), the end of which also marked the end of World War II. Section 3 discusses the post–WWII decades with respect to the impact of the different political systems in Hong Kong and China on Cantonese opera and on the fate of written Cantonese during that period, leading up to the present. Section 4 presents some concluding remarks.

Written Cantonese Prior to the Twentieth Century

The origins of written Cantonese will probably never be known, although speculations link its emergence and development to the influence of Buddhism (Snow 2004, based on Mair's 1994 study). While written Cantonese texts very likely extend back to at least the late Ming dynasty (1368–1644), extant texts containing written Cantonese only date back to the early Qing dynasty (1644–1911). Written Cantonese, with an extensive repertoire of vernacular characters, has a continuous recorded history of just over three centuries, from the earliest extant source in 1713 (or 1714) to the present. It has never been subjected to standardization or government-imposed script reform. As a result, over the centuries, users have been relatively free to make their own choices of orthographic forms, and many of these have become conventionalized

---

3. See, for example, China's Language Law of 2001 (Zhōnghuá Rénmín Gònghéguó guójiā tōngyòng yǔyán wénzì fǎ 中華人民共和國國家通用語言文字法) and recent efforts by the State Administration of Radio Film and Television (Guójiā guǎngbō diànyǐng diànshì zǒngjú 國家廣播電影電視總局) to suppress the use of local, non-standard speech on television. Exempt for cultural reasons are regional dramas, such as local operas that are performed using regional dialects. http://www.gov.cn/gzdt/2005-10/14/content_77613.htm.

and instantly recognizable. Thus, very familiar to Cantonese speakers are such vernacular graphs as *mou*[5] 冇 'not have' (with a formally established, standard Chinese pronunciation of *mǎo*). Users also resort to phonetic loans, such as *zung*[6] 重 'heavy' (literary reading) for the meaning of 'still, yet' in the dialect. At times, an obsolete—and long-forgotten—choice, such as *tai*[2] 體 for 'to see,' is replaced by a semantically more transparent *xíngshēng* 形聲 graph, *tai*[3] 睇, containing the 'eye' (*mù* 目) radical.[4] Other strategies include taking an existing Chinese character and giving it a vernacular, *xùndú* (訓讀) reading, such as treating *zī* 孖 'twins' as its local equivalent, *maa*[1].

The earliest extant text containing written Cantonese is an anonymous, book-length literary work, a love ballad titled *Huājiān jì* (花箋記, "Romance of the Fancy Note-Paper").[5] While the extant edition is a Qing dynasty product, with the preface date of the 52nd year of the reign of the Kangxi Emperor (thus, 1713 or 1714), the work is generally accepted as having been written during the preceding Ming dynasty. It was explicitly identified as a Ming text by Peter Perring Thoms (1824) in his English translation of the ballad. Moreover, words sensitive to the Manchu conquerors appear to have been removed from the woodblocks, leaving conspicuous blanks on the pages where those words would have appeared. Words such as *hú* 胡 'foreign' and *fān* 番 'foreign' (*húbīng* 胡兵 and *fānbīng* 番兵 'foreign troops'), were in fact added to later editions, precisely where those blanks appeared in the 1713 edition, thus essentially "reconstructing" the missing words.

The *Huājiān jì* contains about 1,700 lines of poetry. It was written in a colloquial style that reflects the Cantonese dialect. In the three centuries since the 1713 edition, it has been reprinted and, in the process, transformed: from printed editions with commentaries to stanza-formatted performance texts that contain poetry only. In the late twentieth century, the text migrated to the internet, undergoing orthographic changes along the way. It is now available digitally in both running text and stanza format.

The *Huājiān jì* and other such works belong to the genre of *mùyúgē* 木魚歌 'wooden-fish songs'. These vary both in length and in literary refinement, from very colloquial to highly classical. These songs are sung in Cantonese without musical accompaniment[6] and are published in 'wooden-fish books' (*mùyúshū* 木魚書).[7] Transmission in printed form of such orally performed folk literature is probably our

---

4. In fact, K. C. Leung (1999) criticized Thoms (1824) for careless "misprints," such as "體 occasionally used for 睇" in his Chinese text of the *Huājiān jì*. In all likelihood, Thoms had based his text on a nineteenth-century edition that had used both 體 and 睇 in the same text. We witness the transition from use of 體 only in the earliest extant edition to the sole use of 睇 in twentieth-century editions.
5. For further studies on various topics concerning this love ballad, see Leung (1999), Liáng (1998), and Chan (2010b, 2013, 2014).
6. *Mùyú* performances may be sung without any instrumental accompaniment or with some simple percussion instrument, such as a pair of bamboo strips, musical clappers, or a *mùyú* (木魚), 'wooden fish.' *Mùyú* is a percussion instrument consisting of a hollow wooden block shaped like a skull that was originally used by Buddhist priests to beat out the rhythm when chanting scriptures.
7. Liáng (1978, xiii) notes that "*Mu-yü-shu* had once a great influence on persons of limited education, especially on women." Yue-Hashimoto's (2005, 411–12) field recording provides an example from the Dancun (Taishan) dialect of Cantonese, on 'Learning *Muyu* Songs' 學木魚歌.

richest source for early records of a regional variety of a language. This is certainly true for Cantonese. Singing *mùyú* (木魚) 'wooden-fish' poetry in Cantonese in the Pearl River Delta dates back to at least the late seventeenth century, based on historical and textual sources that mention such poetry (Ching 1996, 55).

Given that songbooks printed prior to the eighteenth century are unavailable, the 1713 edition of the *Huājiān jì* (花箋記) is an especially precious resource, being the earliest extant text that offers a glimpse of an early stage in the history of the Cantonese dialect. From a literature perspective, the *Huājiān jì* is also significant in having been translated into various European languages in the nineteenth century, after others had read Thoms's (1824) English translation, which influenced writers such as Goethe. Equally importantly, the *Huājiān jì* predates some of our earliest sources on the Cantonese dialect, namely, Zhāo Zǐyōng's (招子庸) 1828 collection of *Yuè'ōu* (粵謳), Morrison's three-volume compilation of Cantonese vocabulary that same year, subsequent poets' *yuè'ōu* collections, and a trove of pedagogical materials on Cantonese produced by missionaries in the decades that followed.

By the early twentieth century, *mùyú* song style had made its way into Cantonese opera as an aria type. These songs are performed without any instrumental accompaniment and the lyrics tend to be quite literary in flavor. Nevertheless, as noted earlier, wooden-fish songs *per se* may also reflect a more informal style of spoken Cantonese. *Huājiān jì*, for example, is written in a fairly literary style, yet one can still find scattered through it quite vernacular Cantonese, both in descriptive narrations and in discourse contexts. In fact, in his English translation of this narrative song, Thoms (1824, v) describes it as having been written "in a colloquial style, peculiar to the province of Kwang-tung, and is much read by persons of both sexes."[8]

To illustrate, consider the four lines of ballad in (2), from Thoms's (1824, 19) translation of the *Huājiān jì*, where a number of colloquial Cantonese words can be sighted. Provided in (2) is Thoms's Chinese–English bilingual text, along with Jyutping romanization for modern Cantonese. Three of these lines (2a–2c) are from the point in the verse where the young ladies are playing chess when Master Liang (Young Leang) espies the young mistress of the house and is smitten by her beauty. In the fourth line (2d), the maid, Biyue, is returning to the pavilion to retrieve the chess board.

(2) a. 的息金蓮二寸長
Dik¹-sik¹ gam¹-lin⁴ ji⁶-cyun³ coeng⁴
He beheld the golden lilies (her small feet), which exceeded not three inches

---

8. Thoms (1824, v) notes its unknown authorship, but states that it is "supposed to be the production of two persons of Canton, who had acquired high literary honors" and that it has been ranked next to "Se-seang" (*Xīxiāng jì* 西廂記).

b. 佢 重 回 頭 開 一 個 笑 臉
   Keoi⁵ zung⁶ wui⁴-tau⁴ hoi¹ jat¹-go³ siu³-lim⁵
   On her looking round, with a smiling countenance
c. 我 咕 哩 條 殘 命 死 花 旁
   Ngo⁵ gu² li¹ tiu⁴ caan⁴-ming⁶ sei² faa¹-pong⁴
   He was one death-smitten by the side of the flowers
d. 做 乜 俾 佢 直 入 到 欄 杆
   Zou⁶ mat¹ bei² keoi⁵ zik⁶-jap⁶ dou³ laan⁴-gon¹
   Why permit that youth to approach without announcing him?

In (2a), the adjective *dik¹-sik¹* 的息 (or 的式 in some modern sources) means 'small, exquisite'; it is still used colloquially today in Cantonese. Similarly, in (2b) and (2d), the pronoun *keoi⁵* 佢 's/he' is in current usage; it is a dialect word generally associated with Cantonese, although historically it had a much wider geographical distribution.[9] The strategy of using standard Chinese as phonetic loans for colloquial vocabulary is not limited to the use of *dik¹* 的 for its sound value. Other examples are *zung⁶* 重 'still' in (2b), *gu³* 咕 'to guess' and *li¹* 哩 'this' in (2c), and for *mat¹* 乜 'what' (in *zou⁶ mat¹* 做乜 'why') and *bei²* 俾 'to allow' in (2d).[10]

Another early genre relevant to written Cantonese in Cantonese opera is *nányīn* 南音 'southern songs', which are sung in Cantonese with string accompaniment. Similar to *mùyú* songs, *nányīn* were incorporated as an aria type into Cantonese opera during the early twentieth century. Both genres and their sub-varieties have remained integral to the stock of tunes in Cantonese opera, and both are identified as such in stage performances, karaoke, and published opera librettos.

Note that these and other ballads that were chanted or sung in the Cantonese dialect appealed especially to women. And for some who were semi-literate, the songbooks containing these ballads might very well have been their initial, or even main, source of reading materials. Instructive here is a description by Kulp (1925, cited in Hayes 1985) of life in Phenix (Phoenix?) village in northeastern Guangdong province: "the women like to gather in a reading circle and listen to one of their number 'sing' ballads. These ballads are in simple and rhythmic popular language, especially designed for women to read or sing."

In a similar vein, regarding the eighteenth- and nineteenth-century Cantonese ballads in the Munich State Library Collection, Eberhard (1972, 2) notes that they

---

9. *Keoi⁵* 佢 's/he' *keoi⁵* [kʰøy²³] is also used in other dialect groups, such as Wú (Wēnzhōu), Gàn (Nánchāng), Kèjiā (Méixiàn), and Northeastern Mǐn (Jiàn'ōu), as shown in the *Hànyǔ Fāngyán Cíhuì* (Beijing Daxue 1995, 549). Wáng (1958, 270) notes the importance of the third-person pronouns *yī* 伊 *and qú* 渠 during the Six Dynasties (222–589) and the following Tang dynasty (618–907). Unlike modern standard Cantonese, where the third person pronoun is pronounced in the *yángshǎng* 陽上 tone, some subvarieties of Yuè (粵 'Cantonese')—such as Zhōngshān 中山, Yángjiāng 陽江, Nánhǎi 南海, and Shùndé 順德— still pronounce 's/he' with the *yángpíng* 陽平 tone of *keoi⁴* 渠 'canal, ditch' (Chan 1980; Běijīng dàxué 1995; Zhan and Cheung 1988).

10. Graphic variants from these four lines can be found in other editions, as shown by Liáng (1998) and Chan (2013, 2014).

"are written *by* simple writers, not by scholars, and *for* simple folk to be read by them or to be listened to." In fact, it is possible that songbooks served as textbooks or primers for teaching women to read. An illustrative example is a touching story recounted by a ninety-five-year-old Dongguan man to a journalist in 2004.[11] He told that journalist about the popularity of *mùyú* songs among the populace when he was a young man in Dongguan (a district in the Pearl River Delta region of Guangdong province). He himself had used these ballads to teach his wife how to read. He transcribed the lyrics of his wife's beloved songs, then used the songbook he compiled in this manner to teach her, patiently, character by character, the written text of those songs, which she already could sing and knew by heart. Within a year, she had learned several thousand Chinese characters, and from there she learned to read the newspaper and even Liáng Yǔshēng's 梁羽生 knight-errant (*wǔxiá* 武俠) novels.

During the Ming and Qing dynasties, late Qing in particular, many ballads were published in printing centers in China, including Cantonese ballads published in the Pearl River Delta region (Magang, Foshan, Guangzhou) (Rawski 1970). The Cantonese ballads were printed in quantity on low-quality paper for local consumption, to be sold quickly and cheaply. The fact that there was a market for these publications, which ranged from two-page flyers to multi-volume sets, speaks to the extent of literacy, or semi-literacy, among the populace—the male population in particular. As Snow (2004, 79) notes, more than fifty publishers were producing *mùyú* books, hundreds of which are still extant today. Of particular significance here is that the mass printing of *mùyú* books and booklets would be extended to the mass printing of opera libretti (*jùběn* 劇本) in the early twentieth century. Clearly, there was a strong appetite for reading materials published in the vernacular for popular consumption—materials that did not require a formal education to read and enjoy.

Rawski's (1972, 1985) research findings on popular literacy suggest that during the Ming and Qing dynasties, the number of Chinese who were literate (i.e., able to read at least popular literature) was larger than scholars have long supposed. Literacy *per se* should not be measured against a level of mastery attained by the scholar-gentry class through classical education, a point made well by Twitchett (1962, 188):

> We often make the mistake of accepting at its face value the Chinese literati's view that literacy is to be equated with a thorough grounding in Confucian learning. By this standard, the literate class was very small indeed. But undoubtedly there was always a very large number of persons who, although uneducated by the yardstick of classical scholarship, were nevertheless literate. The evidence for this, from Tunhuang MSS, from early popular literature and even more from the vast quantities of practical handbooks designed for popular use . . . speak eloquently of a mass readership, and their authors constantly stress that they are designed for the members of all four classes.

---

11. The original article is no longer online but can be retrieved via the Wayback Machine at https://archive.org/web/.

With regard to female literacy, Rawski (1972, 6) notes that formal education was neither approved nor systematically provided to women prior to the twentieth century. She cites early nineteenth-century estimates of only 1 to 10 percent for female literacy, albeit probably with great regional variance. Against that backdrop, it is significant that she identifies Guangdong province as seemingly having had high levels of female literacy; for example, she provides statistics from the 1896 census for Hawai'i that record a 25 percent literacy rate for Chinese female immigrants.[12] In imperial China, household educational level might also have factored into this: female literacy was likely more common in literati homes, as literacy would have helped women attend to their household duties and aided them in the early education of their children.

As part of more recent scholarship on women in Chinese history, Mann (1997, 58) notes that the education of daughters appears to have become increasingly important in the High Qing period (c. 1683–1839): "In the marriage market, erudition marked a woman as a highly desirable marriage partner, one who could provide not only sons but also the very best in early childhood education for them. Moreover, she was seen by her kinfolk and by society at large as the heir to her family's tradition of 'house learning' or 'family learning' (*jiāxué* 家學)." Historical records (Mann 1997) also indicate that literacy education for girls began with family members, and that those who were gifted and who had no brothers may in fact have been doted on by fathers who recognized and appreciated their talents. The low estimates on female literacy cited in Rawski (1972) should probably be revised, taking into consideration the need to review what constitutes literacy as well as the need to re-evaluate female literacy in light of more recent scholarship on the education of females in Chinese history. The statistics on Hawai'i mentioned earlier may perhaps reflect higher overall literacy attainment by females in the Guangdong region and a broader, more universal, understanding of literacy—one that was not narrowly confined to the fruits of an elite Confucian education. The issue of literacy is important, for it has a direct bearing on the ability to read written Cantonese, be it ballads or opera libretti or dialogues in spoken Cantonese. All of this sets the stage for the next section of this chapter, which discusses the time when Cantonese opera libretti containing both verse and spoken colloquial dialogue became widely read.

Cantonese Opera and Written Cantonese in the Early Twentieth Century

Much has been published on Cantonese opera, its history, artists, plots, and so forth.[13] What is known today as Cantonese opera (*yuèjù* 粵劇, or *dàxì* 大戲 in street

---

12. In addition to 48 Hawaii-born Chinese women living in Hawai'i in 1896, the 1896 census statistics for Hawai'i give a total of 1,419 foreign-born Chinese women living there that year (Glick 1980, 119).
13. See, for example, Guō (1988), Lài (2001), Lí (1993), Liú and Xiǎn (1995), Mackerras (1975), Xiānggǎng shizhèngjú (2003), Zhōngguó xìqǔ zhì (1993), *inter alia*.

parlance) is usually traced back to an actor, Zhāng Wǔ 張五, who performed in the capital (Běijīng) during the Yōngzhèng 雍正 reign (1723–1735) in the Qing dynasty. The Manchu government considered his acting subversive and exiled him from the capital. He travelled south, eventually settling in the bustling commercial city of Foshan, a short distance from a second major commercial city, Guangzhou (Canton City). Zhāng Wǔ founded an opera company in Foshan, accepted pupils, and established a guild hall for actors that became extremely influential. The region around Foshan and Guangzhou would become the center of Cantonese opera over the following centuries. The development of Cantonese opera was temporarily interrupted by their banning, the result of the performers' participation in the Taiping Rebellion in the 1850s, led by Lǐ Wénmào 李文茂 (d. 1858).[14]

Over time, the Cantonese operatic tradition absorbed local characteristics, including the use of the vernacular language. We have no historical records documenting the use of Cantonese in opera performances of the eighteenth and early nineteenth centuries, but it is likely that those performances were using Cantonese dialect prior to their being banned in the aftermath of local performers' anti-Manchu activities (Luo 1993). Given the popularity among the locals of their beloved Cantonese ballads and songs, it is hardly plausible that the company would not have used the regional dialect for opera performances. At any rate, with the government authorities' prohibition of Cantonese opera performances—only performances of *kūnqǔ* 崑曲 and Beijing opera (*jīngjù* 京劇) were permitted—the Cantonese performers renounced (at least outwardly) their local operatic tradition and either outwardly adopted the northern-style operas or joined the 'non-local' theatrical companies that had not been similarly condemned and proscribed by the Qing government (Sū 2003; Mackerras 1975). Eventually, the ban on local Cantonese operas was relaxed, and by the late Qing and the early years of Republican era in the twentieth century, the Cantonese dialect had replaced Mandarin (Guānhuà 官話) for performances of Cantonese opera.

An important change during this time was the development of opera libretti (*jùběn* 劇本). In the late Qing dynasty, opera troupes did not use scripts; instead, they relied on brief outlines of stories from a small stock of seventeenth-century and later play scripts, as well as on notes that matched performer with role (rank of character). As Sū (2003, 89) notes, "Major dramatic highlights would have their lyrics and music written down, but the remainder would be improvised by the actors, who were allowed to sing away as long as they continued to make sense." The need to entertain the audience with new story lines led to the expansion of the story repertoire and the preparation of original scripts. By the 1920s, fully written scripts for spoken and sung lines were being produced (Liáng 1995).

The switch from Mandarin to Cantonese had additional consequences, one of which was the eventual replacement of the male falsetto voice with the natural voice

---

14. While Zhōngguó xìqǔ zhì (1993, 598) gives his year of death as 1858, Mackerras (1975, 148) gives 1861.

(*pínghóu* 平喉) for young male roles. Lài (2001) attributes this change to differences in the two phonological systems (the number of lexical tones in Cantonese, the preponderance of *píngshēng* 平聲 syllables, the heavier use of nasal sounds, etc.); that is, the change addressed the mismatch that arose when Cantonese was sung in falsetto. The audience's warm reception of the natural male voice as used by Zhū Cìbó 朱次伯 (d. 1922) and Jīn Shānbǐng 金山炳 (n.d.) led to its gradual adoption by other performers (Zhōngguó xìqǔ zhì 1993).

The replacement of Mandarin with Cantonese for performances of Cantonese opera precipitated other changes as well, such as the incorporation of colloquial vocabulary and expressions, which can be seen in scripts from as early as the 1920s and 1930s. The frequent use of vernacular written Cantonese characters is amply demonstrated in Huáng (1995), with English gloss added here: *keoi*[5] 佢 's/he', *ngaam*[1] 啱 'correct', *mou*[5] 冇 'not have', *mai*[5] 咪 'don't', *nau*[1] 嬲 'be mad at', *tam*[4] 氹 'puddle', *di*[1] 啲 'more, -er, some, a few' (e.g., *faai*[3]-*di*[1] 快啲 'faster'), *m*[4] 唔 'not' (e.g., *m*[4] *hou*[2] 唔好 'not good', *m*[4] *gau*[3] 唔夠 'not enough', *m*[4] *wui*[5] 唔噲 'will not', and *m*[4] *hai*[6] 唔係 'not be', and even opera titles such as in *M*[4] *Gaa*[3] 唔嫁 'Won't Get Married'), in addition to a host of Cantonese sentence-final particles that are still in use today. Some particles from these scripts appear in the utterances in (3) and (4). (SP = sentence-final particle, ASP = aspect marker, CL = classifier)

(3) a. 搵 到 嘞 噃
    Wan[2] *dou*[2] *laak*[3] *bo*[3].
    find-arrive SP SP
    'Found it.'

  b. 你 番(返) 咗 嚟 哩 咩
    Nei[5] *faan*[1] *zo*[2] *lai*[4] *le*[1] *me*[1].
    you return ASP come SP SP (咗: perfective aspect marker)
    '(So) you're back?'

(4) a. 將 你 來 蝦
    Zoeng[1] *nei*[5] *loi*[4] *haa*[1].
    ZOENG you come bully
    'pick on you'

  b. 我 係 一 個 初 歸 新 婦 (婦: 讀 "抱" 音)
    Ngo[5] *hai*[6] *jat*[1] *go*[3] *co*[1] *gwai*[1] *san*[1] *pou*[5].
    I be one CL first return new married.woman.
    'I am a first-time returning (home) daughter-in-law.'

  c. 呢 個 係 我 新 抱 嚟 㗎
    Nei[1] *go*[3] *hai*[6] *ngo*[5] *san*[1] *pou*[5] *lai*[4] *gaa*[3].
    this CL be my new married.woman ASP SP (嚟: similar to Mandarin 來著)
    'This is my new daughter-in-law.'

Other colloquial and slangy expressions from Huáng (1995) include *ham⁶-baang⁶-laang⁶* (or, *ham⁶-baa⁶-laang⁶*) 冚崩冷 'all', *zan¹ leon⁶-zeon⁶* 真論盡 'so clumsy', *daai⁶-paau¹-wo⁴* 大泡和 'dummy', and even curse words, such as *ham⁶-gaa¹-caan²* 冚家剷 'annihilation of the entire family'. Chinese characters may also be used strictly for their phonetic value—that is, as phonetic loans (*jièyòng* 借用)— harking back to an earlier 'read as' (*dúruò* 讀若) tradition in Chinese that preceded the use of *fǎnqiè* 反切 spelling. The reading based on phonetic loan may not be explicitly noted in the script, as in the case of (4a), where the character for the noun 'shrimp' (*haa¹* 蝦) is used simply for its sound value to spell out a homophonous word in Cantonese meaning 'to pick on, to bully'. Phonetic loans or changes in pronunciation may be indicated, as in the case of (4b). There, *san¹-pou⁵* 新婦 'bride, daughter-in-law', a word in standard Chinese, *fu⁵* 婦 [fu²⁴] is pronounced with a labiodental fricative onset in that syllable in Cantonese, as in Mandarin *fù* in *xīnfù*; in spoken Cantonese, however, the second syllable of the word is pronounced with a bilabial stop: *pou⁵* 抱 [pʰou²⁴]; for that reason, a note of instruction was inserted in the script on pronouncing the character *fu⁵* 婦 as one would the character *pou⁵* 抱.¹⁵ In (4c), the colloquial pronunciation is not similarly flagged; the phonetic-loan character 抱 is used in lieu of 婦.

The vernacular language is not limited to spoken dialogues. It even penetrates the sung lyrics, as illustrated in (5) from Huáng (1995), where the line is sung in the aria type known as *gwan²-faa¹* 滾花 (Mandarin *gǔnhuā*), which is the most frequently used aria type in Cantonese opera today (Yung 1989). In (5), evoking the devil (*gwai²* 鬼) is very much part of Cantonese vulgar (unrefined) language, and the derogatory expression, *laan⁴-sei²-gu¹-lou⁶* 躝死咕路 (although unfamiliar to this author), corresponds very closely to Mandarin *gǔndàn* 滾蛋 'beat it, scram'.

(5) [滾花] 快啲 躝 死 咕 路, 鬼 嫁 你 個 大 泡 和
   [*Gwan²-faa¹*] *faai³ di¹ laan¹-sei²-gu¹-lou⁶, gwai² gaa³ nei⁵ go³ daai⁶-paau¹-wo⁴.*
   quick-ly beat-it/scram, devil marry you CL dummy
   'Beat it! Scram! Who wants to marry (you), you big dummy!'

There are even English loanwords in these scripts from the 1920s and 1930s. Some examples are *kut³-baai²* 括擺 'good-bye', *o¹-lai⁵* 柯禮 'alright', and *mei⁵-li⁴* 尾厘 'minute'.¹⁶ As further illustration of the extent to which colloquial Cantonese shows up in these early scripts of the 1920s and 1930s, Huáng (1995) provides two

---

15. The colloquial pronunciation of *fu⁵* 婦 with a bilabial stop can actually be analyzed as a preservation of an earlier bilabial onset for the word in the Chinese language. What is not clear is if at that time, there was, already, labial assimilation in the sequence of *san¹* 新 plus *fu⁵* 婦, such that the first syllable has a bilabial nasal coda, *-m*, such that the word could be rendered orthographically as *sam¹-pou⁵* 心抱.
16. Some examples in Lín (2003) that are not mentioned in Huáng (1995) include *aa¹-lou⁶* 丫路 or *haa¹-lou⁴* 蝦勞 'hello', *je⁴-si⁶* 爺是 'yes', *si⁶-dik¹* 士的 'stick', *sin¹-si⁶* 仙士 'cents', and *jin³-so¹* 燕梳 'insurance.' Note that the production of the syllables may actually differ from the lexical tones, such that 爺是, for example, might have been pronounced *je¹-si⁴*.

Figure 2.1: Lines of colloquial Cantonese in *Maai⁶ faa¹ dak¹ mei⁵* opera text

「同下」、「滾花」、「朱氏上唱」乖女買線、都去幾咁耐・乜重唔見、佢闖來・

「六上作人門介白」錢奶奶、「珠白」六嫂、乜野呀、「六白」冇錯㗎、隔離街

個位史萬年、聞得你位千金、好想成過佢個仔亞生呀、所以叫我嚟做媒、

你點呢、佢個仔唔錯呀、「珠白」哦、就係賣花個個亞生呀、係幾好、而且

pages from one such opera, *Maai⁶ faa¹ dak¹ mei⁵* 賣花得美. The text of only four lines from page 12 is given here in Figure 2.1 (undated). The opera title that Huáng gives in his caption includes the name of the performer, Shézǎi Lì (*Se⁴-zai² Lei⁶* 蛇仔利, d. 1962). He also provides the following title for the opera: *Se⁴-zai² Lei⁶ maai⁶ faa¹ dak¹ mei⁵* 蛇仔利賣花得美 (Shézǎi Lì sells flowers and wins a beauty). Shézǎi Lì, well-known for playing the clown role, was at his height of fame in the 1920s and 1930s. This opera is one of his earlier operas (Zhōngguó xìqǔ zhì 1993). The 1920s also happens to have been the peak period for the opera troupe that produced the script, the Zhū Huá-nián Opera Troupe (祝華年劇團). So it is quite likely that this script was published some time during the 1920s. There is an astonishing amount of very colloquial, vernacular written Cantonese on those two pages, both for the arias and for the spoken lines. The fact that this is a comedy undoubtedly contributes to the high degree of colloquialism in the script. Such colloquialisms so early in Cantonese operas would not be obvious without a perusal of these early scripts.[17] What is significant is that such vernacular language continued to be produced in the scripts in China until the founding of the People's Republic of China in 1949. Furthermore, such language continued unimpeded in Hong Kong, spreading into opera films and other genres.

Starting in the 1920s, there was tremendous demand from both audiences and readers for Cantonese opera libretti, which were printed locally and in high volume. They sold well, and popular libretti were reprinted multiple times. Huang (1995) mentions a script connected with a well-known performer that had undergone a fifth reprinting by 1 March 1927. There was an avid readership, who regularly encountered vernacular written Cantonese through these libretti, which were an important source of inexpensive, popular reading materials for Cantonese. To meet the huge demand for both published scripts and live performances, old scripts were modified and new scripts were written that tapped multiple sources of inspiration: traditional plots from classical novels, adaptations of plots from Beijing opera and other regional Chinese operas, as well as Chinese folktales and local stories. Casting the net even more widely, plots from foreign literature and foreign films were also adapted, such

---

17. While Snow (2004, 229) states that his opera example, with 7% marked Cantonese characters, is "a fairly typical example of Cantonese opera," this is not necessarily so, since there is an overall elevated register used, despite colloquialisms in the spoken dialogue of even the emperor.

as Shakespeare's *Taming of the Shrew*, rewritten as *Diu¹-maan⁴ gung¹-zyu² ngong⁶ fu⁶-maa⁵* 刁蠻公主戇駙馬 (The unruly princess and the foolish prince consort), and so forth (Liáng 1995).

On the mainland after 1949, with the emphasis on standardization and the promotion of Putonghua, the use of written Cantonese to capture the flavor and authenticity of the local dialect came to a halt. As a quick illustration, a circa-1950 publication of the script for *Liǔ Yì chuán shū* 柳毅傳書, (Liu Yi delivers a letter), written by Tán Qīngshuāng 譚青霜 (1928–1993), was published as a thirty-three-page handwritten booklet reminiscent of the inexpensively produced scripts of the 1920s and 1930s; it contains the rich flavor of the Cantonese vernacular. In stark contrast, a much-modified version of the script in a 1993 collected volume (Guǎngzhōu zhènxīng Yuèjù jījīnhuì) virtually erased from the dialogues and lyrics the lively and colloquial flavor of Cantonese that had featured prominently in the earlier edition. (See Chan [2010a] for more detailed study of this opera.)

The focus here has been on developments pertaining to linguistic and orthographic issues. But other developments were taking place at this time in the world of Cantonese opera, such as the division of operas into scenes and the use of new props, costumes, scenery, tunes, and musical instruments. The 1920s and the pre-war years in the 1930s were a time of relative peace and stability that was conducive to much experimentation and innovation. Changes that were adopted during that period became established, forming a critical part of what we understand to be Cantonese opera today. Given the vitality, creativity, and productivity of that period, it is apt that the 1920s and 1930s were dubbed the 'golden age' of Cantonese opera. The tremendous innovations that took place during that period would not be repeated in the decades after World War II.

Written Cantonese and the Legacy of Cantonese Operas in Post–World War II

The founding of the People's Republic of China in 1949 brought a different political system to China, one that embraced a strong ideology concerning language standardization, both spoken and written. With the political changes, the colloquially written Cantonese scripts ceased production and earlier scripts were revised to serve the new regime. While spoken lines retained the language of the local dialect, the cruder, livelier, and more colorful vocabulary and expressions, which were frowned upon by the new government, were scrubbed. The speech now reflected a blander, more neutral form of Chinese, one that was sanitized and standardized, with more 'respectable' vocabulary and expressions, as revealed in video recordings of live, post–Cultural Revolution performances that were commercially available on videotapes and subsequently on VCDs and DVDs. In post-1949 China, the folksier humor and the coarser, more vulgar language found in Cantonese operas of the 1920s and 1930s had all been expunged;[18] at the same time, the lyrics in the arias had been placed on an elevated plane, so that there were almost no Cantonese colloquialisms in those arias—only literary language that cannot easily be identified as markedly Cantonese. Based on a viewing of video-recorded stage performances of Cantonese operas from China, there is only the occasional intrusion of vernacular Cantonese in the arias; and this may be because the performers ad-libbed them. For example, the standard Chinese third-person plural pronoun, ngo^5-mun^4 我們 'we', that is given in the subtitles on a VCD or DVD, may in fact be sung based on the corresponding colloquial Cantonese counterpart, ngo^5-dei^6 我哋, where the plural suffix is dei^6 哋 and not mun^4 們.

The suppression of non-standard Chinese writing can also be seen in the broader societal context. To illustrate, Snow (2004) charted the use of written Cantonese in newspapers in Guangzhou (Canton City) in the two years after the Communists gained control of the city in 1949, and noted that by August 1951, "there is very little evidence of Cantonese in Guangzhou newspapers after that time" (121). Clearly, written Cantonese in opera scripts and in local Cantonese newspapers shared the same fate.

The postwar scene was very different in the British colony of Hong Kong, where the colonial government took a laissez-faire approach to its ethnic Chinese citizens' language use. Written Cantonese was left to follow its own course without suppression or standardization, and there was no imposed standardization of graphic variants that existed alongside phonetic loans. The result was texts that looked superficially like standard Chinese but were incomprehensible to readers who lacked some knowledge of spoken Cantonese.

Cantonese opera played a vital role in the spread of vernacular written Cantonese in the twentieth century, initially through the publication of opera libretti. The booming film industry in postwar Hong Kong added a new dimension, for it brought Cantonese operas to the silver screen. Because movie tickets cost far less than tickets for live opera performances, many Cantonese opera fans of low or average income were able to see far more Cantonese operas. In fact, Cantonese opera films eventually supplanted opera theater. At its peak in the 1950s, the Cantonese opera film genre became so popular that it constituted one third of all Cantonese cinema production in Hong Kong; more than 500 Cantonese opera films were produced in that decade alone (Xiānggǎng Shìzhèngjú [Urban Council, Hong Kong] 2003, 9).

In these opera films, written Cantonese is customarily included onscreen for the lyrics when arias are sung. These onscreen lyrics provide visual reinforcement of Cantonese vocabulary and syntax, as well as vernacular Cantonese characters. In some films, even spoken lines are accompanied by written Cantonese text. In this way, Cantonese opera filmgoers encounter written Cantonese in regular doses at the cinema.

---

18. Moser's (2004) online article suggests some parallels in the fate of bawdier humor in comic dialogues (xiàngshēng 相声 'crosstalk') in post-1949 China.

As noted earlier, Cantonese operas of the 1920s and 1930s were influenced by the West (adaptation of scripts, English loanwords, etc.). These influences also extended to Cantonese opera films in Hong Kong, including theme songs. For example, *Fung⁶ gok³ jan¹-cau⁴ mei⁶-liu⁵-cing⁴* 鳳閣恩仇未了情 (Romance of the Phoenix Chamber), a 1962 opera film directed by Huáng Hèshēng 黃鶴聲 based on a stage version, was exceptional in having its theme song at the beginning rather than at the end of the opera. These theme songs and other Cantonese operatic songs (*Yuèqǔ* 粵曲), as well as excerpts from Cantonese operas that included spoken dialogue, have been collected into popular anthologies. One such publication from that era[19] is a 494-page collection titled *Jīnpái Yuèqǔ huáng* 金牌粵曲皇 (Cantonese operatic golden oldies). A splashy, entertainment-magazine type cover boldly advertises that "Every song is popular" (*Zi¹-zi¹ lau⁴-hang⁴* 支支流行, in which *zi¹* 支 is the Cantonese classifier for 'song') and that the book contains "Mostly famous songs" (*Ming⁴-kuk¹ zeoi³ do¹* 名曲最多). These Cantonese operatic songs and excerpts from Cantonese operas—and even full-length operas—were the "Canto-pop" of the pre-Canto-pop song era in 1950s and 1960s Hong Kong. And, in terms of the presence of written Cantonese, there is probably more written Cantonese in Cantonese operas, even in the arias, than in Canto-pop songs.

The difference between Cantonese operatic tunes and Canto-pop music in twentieth-century Hong Kong is rather fuzzy. One finds, in fact, a continuum rather than an abrupt, categorical shift between the two genres. At one end are the very traditional Cantonese opera arias; at the other are the heavy-beat rap songs of more recent decades. The main reason there is no sharp break is that, in addition to traditional opera tunes, early Cantonese operas absorbed local folk melodies, later incorporating other popular tunes, including Western tunes. At the same time, 1950s and 1960s Hong Kong cinema occasionally produced Cantonese operas with Western garb and modern themes. An example is the 1957 film *Syun⁴ gung¹ jim⁶ si²* 璇宮艷史 ('My kingdom for a husband'), directed by Zuǒ Jī 左几. Billed as a romantic musical comedy, it is based on an earlier Cantonese opera that itself is an adaptation of an early Paramount musical directed by Ernst Lubitsch, *The Love Parade* (1929). While the Cantonese film opens with modern Westernized songs, the film is essentially a Cantonese opera using modern dress and modern themes, and includes both romance and comedy. Predictably, given this combination, there was much room for the vernacular language, slang expressions, English loanwords, and so forth, to be embedded in the arias and for these lyrics to be displayed onscreen. In many ways, the creativity and experimentation in 1950s Hong Kong Cantonese opera films harkens back to the creative and innovative changes that took place in Cantonese opera during the 1920s and 1930s, but in cinematic mode this time.

With respect to written Cantonese, lyrics of Cantonese opera songs are available not just in songbooks and on-screen (in theaters and, later, in homes and on

---

19. Originally undated, the most recent reprint sports a simple cover and a publication year of 1998.

television); they were also printed on the backs of phonograph record sleeves or printed separately and slipped into record albums, and later into audiocassette cases and CD jewel cases.

Cantonese opera films were declining in popularity by the mid-1960s (Xiānggǎng shìzhèngjú 2003); even so, there remained strong sentiments toward Cantonese opera songs. As a result, traditional Cantonese opera songs have found a place amidst modern Canto-pop songs sung to karaoke. It is also notable that, unlike in the West, where opera singing style is very different from pop singing style, Canto-pop singers popular in the latter part of the twentieth century, such as Roman Tam, Anita Mui, Leslie Cheung, Jackie Chan, Andy Lau, Lisa Wang, and Adam Cheng, have all enjoyed singing opera songs, sometimes even donning opera costumes, especially for charity programs to help raise funds for worthy causes. And the proliferation of Cantonese opera songs and excerpts available in audio and video formats and subsequently placed on YouTube and elsewhere on the Web attest to their staying power.

Concluding Remarks

Cantonese opera played an important role in popular Cantonese culture throughout the twentieth century. Although that role has diminished in the early decades of the twenty-first century, it is worth noting that even in the new millennium, Cantonese opera still captures the heart, as reflected in a Cantonese opera musical version of the 2019 Hong Kong protesters' song, "Glory to Hong Kong" (*Jyun^6 wing^4-gwong^1 gwai^1 Hoeng^1 Gong^2* 願榮光歸香港), which is widely available online. Moreover, while that protest song consists of formally written lyrics in standard Chinese, and is thus understandable to all who can read Chinese, the Cantonese opera rendition adds a number of spoken lines in colloquial Cantonese. For example, addressing the police is the line "*M^4-hou^2 hoi^6 jan^4-dei^6 ge^3 zai^2-neoi^5 laa^1* (唔好害人哋嘅仔女啦 'Stop hurting our children'), transcribed in vernacular written Cantonese. Thus, Cantonese opera, a quintessential component of Cantonese culture, remains a deeply intimate part of today's Cantonese-speaking world.

Vernacular written Cantonese has been an indispensable part of Cantonese popular culture, whether in print media (libretti, songbooks, printed lyrics accompanying audio recordings) or in the multitude of video formats. The ubiquitous presence of written Cantonese in Hong Kong culture today is, thus, partly due to the important role that Cantonese opera played throughout the twentieth century: it provided the populace with access to written Cantonese. In the last decade of the twentieth century and into the new millennium, the vernacular written language has continued to thrive with the growing importance of the Web. New opportunities have arisen for creative innovations in the use of new orthographic forms, sometimes due to input and character selection, such that inputting *qú* might retrieve *qú* 拘 more quickly than *qú* 佢 and the variant *qú* 拘, for the third-person pronoun is born and used interchangeably with qú 佢. And in Hong Kong television programs today, one continues to find delightfully playful uses of written Cantonese. This can be seen in such program titles as *Ngo⁵ sik⁶ faan⁶ nei⁵ maai⁴ daan¹* 我食飯你埋單 "Treat Me A Meal," *Maa⁴-maa¹ m⁴ ji⁶ 'zou⁶'* 媽媽唔易'造' "Mom No Easy," and *Hau⁶-saang¹-zai² king¹ haa⁵ gai²* 後生仔傾吓偈 "Young and Restless."

Looking back at the earliest extant source written in the dialect, the *Huājiān Jì* (花箋記) provides a valuable illustration of changes over the past three centuries in the history of written Cantonese. Table 2.1 divides the different editions of the *Huājiān Jì* into three periods of orthographic changes. Twelve monosyllabic words are selected across a number of different editions, from the 1713 edition to twentieth-century online texts of the ballad. As the online texts of the *Huājiān Jì* have, on the whole, preserved the conventionally used characters in the text, an additional column is inserted into the table to include some orthographic forms that are not used in the various editions of the *Huājiān Jì* but that can be found on the Internet, in emails, texting, blogging, pop, rap lyrics, and so on. Most notable is the use of the lower-case letter 'o' for the 'mouth' (*kǒu* 口) radical, as a very creative and speedy means to input some of these vernacular Cantonese characters.

Table 2.1: Twelve words across three periods of orthographic changes of the *Huājiān jì* (花箋記)

| | | *Huājiān Jì* (花箋記 / 花笺记) | | | Internet age of email, texting, blogging, pop and rap lyrics, etc. |
		Period 1 18th c. 1713 post-1713	Period 2 19th c.	Period 3 20th–21st c.	
1. *tai2*	'to look'	體	體 睇	睇	睇
2. *keoi5*	'he/she'	渠	渠 佢	佢 (渠)	渠 偶 佢 距 拒
3. *dei6*	(plural suffix)		地		地 哋 o地
4. *hai6*	'to be'		係	系 (係)	係 系
5. *m4*	'not'		唔 無	唔 (無) 无	唔 无
6. *mou5*	'not have'		冇 無	冇 (無) 无	冇 无 o無 o无
7. *gam3*	'so, such'		泔	咁	咁
8. *bei2*	'to allow'		被 俾	俾	畀 (俾)	畀 俾
9. *go2*	'that'*		個	吤	嗰个 (個)	嗰 個 个 哥 果 o个
10. *zoi6*	'to be at'			〔在〕		喺 系 o系
11. *se1*	'some'			〔些〕		的 啲 D d 尐
12. *mat1*	'what'				乜	

* One more variant in Cantonese language materials that is not included in this row: 箇
 ( ) : A potential graphic form based on traditional Chinese script is absent due to PRC sources that use simplified Chinese script.
 〔 〕 : A different, or more literary, word is used in the text.

An illustration of a deliciously playful use vernacular Cantonese characters containing 'o' for the 'mouth' radical—mixed with other written Cantonese, English words, letters and numbers—is Fama's (*Nung⁴-fu¹* 農夫 'farmer') 2005 hip hop, *Ou³-wan⁶-wui⁶* 奧運會 "Olympic Games," which is readily available online. A representation of a screenshot of the opening lines is shown in Figure 2.2. The words are copied to (6), along with adding of Jyutping romanization and an English translation. Subscripted forms are the conventional graphs with the 'mouth' radical.

(6) a. "各位聽眾你o地哋好,
我o地哋係代表香港
電台Teenpower o既嘅
農夫C君同農夫6永呀."

b. "*Gok³-wai² ting³-zung³ nei⁵-dei⁶ hou²,
ngo⁵-dei⁶ hai⁶ doi⁶-biu² Hoeng¹-gong²
din⁶-toi⁴ Teenpower ge³
Nung⁴-fu¹ Si¹ Gwan¹ tung⁴ Nung⁴-fu¹ Luk⁶ Wing⁵ aa⁶.*"

c. "Our listening audience, greetings.
We represent Hong Kong
TV Station Teenpower's
Fama C-Kwan and Fama 6-Wing."

Figure 2.2: Opening lines of 2005 hip hop *Ou³-wan⁶-wui⁶*

The two members of the Fama group are 6-Wing (*Luk⁶ Wing⁵ Kyun⁴* 陸永權) and C-Kwan (C君 *gwan¹*: *Zeng⁶ Si¹ Gwan¹* 鄭詩君). The lyrics contain several layers of delightful wordplay. The group's name, Fama, itself comes from 'Farmer', the English translation of *Nung⁴-fu¹* 農夫. In the case of the name, 6-Wing, '6' comes from the hip hop artist's surname, *Luk⁴* 陸, where the number '6' and his surname are homophonous. 'Wing' comes from the romanization of the first syllable of his given name, *Wing⁵ Kyun¹* 永權. In the case of C-Kwan, it comes from his given name, *Si¹ Gwan¹* 詩君, where *Si¹* and the letter 'C' are homophonous. Devilishly clever! Example (6) offers a quick glimpse into a very creative and dynamic future for vernacular written Cantonese in the hands of our young!

This playful, subversive translanguaging is what Li and Zhu (2019, 151) have coined "tranßcripting," the linguistic process of "creating a script with elements from different writing systems, such as Chinese and English, or by mixing conventional language scripts with other symbols and signs, including emoji" that is seen in Hong Kong as well as on the mainland in the twenty-first century. Recent additional examples can be found in some 2019–2020 Hong Kong protest signs (Gomes and Chan 2021). As long as the Cantonese language and culture survive, vernacular written Cantonese will thrive as an integral part of the culture of the speakers of that community.

Acknowledgments

Friends, students, and colleagues have helped in different ways with this research, which was part of a larger project on written Cantonese supported in part by a 2005 Seed Grant in the Arts and Humanities, Office of Research, Ohio State University. My special thanks to the many friends, colleagues, and students for discussions and for making some Cantonese materials available to me over the years: K. K. Luke, Benjamin T'sou, Peggy Wong, Yan Jing, Carine Yiu, Samuel Cheung, Peggy Wong, Thomas Chan, Patricia Sieber, Roxana Fung, Andy Chin, Zheng Rongbin, Tan Yutian, Chen Litong, Tsui Tsz-Him, and our Ohio State University librarian, Li Guoqing. An earlier, shorter version of this chapter appears in Chan (2005). My sincere thanks to Richard VanNess Simmons for his assistance with manuscript preparation for this volume. My heartfelt thanks also go to the two anonymous reviewers for their assistance.

References

Bacon-Shone, John, and Kingsley Bolton. 1998. "Charting Multilingualism: Language Censuses and Language Surveys in Hong Kong." In *Language in Hong Kong at Century's End*, edited by Martha C. Pennington, 43–90. Hong Kong: Hong Kong University Press.

Bauer, Robert. 1984. "The Hong Kong Cantonese Speech Community." *Cahier de Linguistique Asie Orientale* 13 (1): 57–90.

Bauer, Robert. 1988. "Written Cantonese of Hong Kong." *Cahier de Linguistique Asie Orientale* 17 (2): 245–93.

Bauer, Robert. 2018. "Cantonese as Written Language in Hong Kong." *Global Chinese* 4 (1): 103–42.

Běijīng dàxué Zhōngguó yǔyán wénxué xì yǔyánxué jiàoyánshì 北京大學中國語言文學系語言學教研室. 1995. *Hànyǔ fāngyán cíhuì* 漢語方言詞匯 [Lexicon of Chinese dialects]. Second edition. Běijīng: Yǔwén chūbǎnshè.

Chan, Marjorie K. M. 1980. "Zhong-shan Phonology: A Synchronic and Diachronic Analysis of a Yue (Cantonese) Dialect." MA thesis, University of British Columbia.

Chan, Marjorie K. M. 2005. "Cantonese Opera and the Growth and Spread of Vernacular Written Cantonese in the Twentieth Century." In *Proceedings of the Seventeenth North American Conference on Chinese Linguistics (NACCL-17)*, edited by Qian Gao, 1–18. GSIL Publications, University of Southern California.

Chan, Marjorie K. M. 2010a. "Liu Yi and the Dragon Princess: Cantonese Opera Adaptations of a Yuan Dynasty Drama." In *Perspectives on Chinese Language and Culture*, edited by Ik-sang Eom, Shi-Chang Hsin, and Yea-Fen Chen, 55–84. Taipei: Crane Publisher.

Chan, Marjorie K. M. 2010b. "The *Huajian Ji* (花箋記): Glimpses into Early 18th Century Vernacular Written Cantonese." Presented at the 2010 Midwest Conference on Asian Affairs, October 1–3, 2010, Ohio State University, Columbus.

Chan, Marjorie K. M. 2013. "Three Centuries of Orthographic Changes in Written Cantonese: Glimpses from 18th to 21st Century Sources." (Invited keynote speaker.) Presented at the 25th North American Conference on Chinese Linguistics (NACCL-25), June 21–23, 2013, University of Michigan, Ann Arbor, Michigan.

Chan, Marjorie K. M. 2014. "Orthographic Variants in the Cantonese Love Ballad, *Romance of the Fancy Notepaper* (*Huajian Ji* 花箋記): 1713 to Present-Day Editions." (Invited keynote speaker.) Presented at the Second Workshop on Innovations in Cantonese Linguistics (WICL 2). March 7, 2014, University of Chicago.

Ching, Ching, May-bo. 1996. "Literary, Ethnic or Territorial? Definitions of Guangdong Culture in the Late Qing and the Early Republic." In *Unity and Diversity: Local Cultures and Identities in China*, edited by Tao Tao Liu and David Faure, 51–66. Hong Kong: Hong Kong University Press.

Chiu, Wai-nga. 2005. "Language Choice on the Internet: The Use of Written Cantonese on Web Sites." MA thesis, University of Hong Kong.

Eberhard, Wolfram. 1972. *Chinese Ballads and Songs* [Guǎngdōng chàngběn tíyào 廣東唱本提要]. (= Issue 30 of Asian Folklore and Social Life Monographs). Taipei: Dōngfāng wénhuà shūjǔ.

Glick, Clarence E. 1980. *Sojourners and Settlers: Chinese Migrants in Hawaii*. Honolulu: Hawaii Chinese History Center and University of Hawaiʻi Press.

Gomes, Skylor E., and Marjorie K. M. Chan. Forthcoming. "The 2019–2020 Hong Kong Protests: Dueling Messages of the Authorities and the Protesters." In *DEALL 50th Anniversary Celebration Volume: Current Issues in East Asian Languages and Literatures*, edited by Mineharu Nakayama, Richard Torrance, Zhiguo Xie, John Bundschuh, Jennifer Nunes and Lindsey Stirek. [= *Buckeye East Asian Linguistics 5.*] Columbus: OSU Knowledge Bank.

Guǎngzhōu zhènxīng Yuèjù jījīnhuì 廣州振興粵劇基金會. 1993. *Guǎngzhōu Yuèjù jùběn xuǎn* 廣州粵劇劇本選 [A selection of Guangzhou Cantonese opera scripts]. Volume 1. Guǎngzhōu: Guǎngzhōu chūbǎnshè.

Guō Bǐngzhēn 郭秉箴. 1988. *Yuèjù yìshù lùn* 粵劇藝術論 [On the art of Guangdong opera]. Běijīng: Zhōngguó xìjù chūbǎnshè.

Hayes, James. 1985. "Specialists and Written Materials in the Village World." In *Popular Culture in Late Imperial China*, edited by David Johnson, Andrew J. Nathan, and Evelyn S. Rawski, 75–111. Berkeley: University of California Press.

Huáng Zhàohàn 黃兆漢. 1995. Èr-sān-shí niándài de Yuèjù jùběn 二三十年代的粵劇劇本. In *Yuèjù yántǎohuì lùnwénjí* 粵劇研討會論文集 [Papers and Proceedings of the International Seminar on Cantonese Opera] (= Studies of Ethnomusicology, No. 4)], edited by Liú

Jìngzhī 劉靖之 and Xiǎn Yùyí 冼玉儀, 99–117. Hong Kong: Joint Publishing (H.K.) Co., Ltd.

Jīnpái Yuèqǔ huáng 金牌粵曲皇 [Cantonese operatic golden oldies]. (Originally undated, from the 1960s?) 1998. Hong Kong: Háojiāng liánhé chūbǎnshè 濠江聯合出版社.

Kulp, Daniel Harrison. 1925. *Country Life in South China: The Sociology of Familism.* Volume 1. Phenix village, Kwantung. New York: Bureau of Publications, Teachers College, Columbia University.

Lài Bójiāng 賴伯疆. 2001. *Guǎngdōng xìqǔ jiǎnshǐ* 廣東戲曲簡史 [A concise history of Guangdong operas]. Guǎngzhōu: Guǎngdōng rénmín chūbǎnshè.

Lau, Arthur Chunip. 1995. "Written Representation of Oral Features in Cantonese Chinese." EdD dissertation, Columbia University.

Leung, K. C. 1999. "*Chinese Courtship:* The *Huajian Ji* 花箋記 in English translation." *Chinoperl Papers* 20–22: 269–88.

Li, David C. S. 1998. "The Plight of the Purist." In *Language in Hong Kong at Century's End*, edited by Martha C. Pennington, 161–90. Hong Kong: Hong Kong University Press.

Li, David C. S. 2000. "Phonetic Borrowing: Key to the Vitality of Written Cantonese in Hong Kong." *Written Language and Literacy* 3 (2): 199–233.

Lí Jiàn 黎鍵, ed. 1993. *Xiānggǎng Yuèjù kǒushù shǐ* 香港粵劇口述史 Hong Kong: Joint Publishing (H.K.) Co., Ltd.

Li, Mi Fong. 1997. "Attitudes toward Written Cantonese and Mixed Codes in Written Language in Hong Kong." MEd thesis, University of Hong Kong.

Li, Wei, and Zhu Hua. 2019. "Tranßcripting: Playful Subversion with Chinese Characters." *International Journal of Multilingualism* 16 (2): 145–61.

Liáng Péichì (Leung Pui-chee) 梁培熾. 1978. *Xiānggǎng dàxué suǒ cáng mùyú shū xùlù yǔ yánjiū* 香港大學所藏木魚書叙錄與研究 [Wooden-fish books: Critical essays and an annotated catalogue based on the collections in the University of Hong Kong]. Hong Kong: Centre of Asian Studies, the University of Hong Kong.

Liáng Péichì (Leung Pui-chee) 梁培熾. 1998. *Huā jiān jì huìjiào huìpíng běn* 花箋記會校會評本 [An annotated volume of editions of the *Hua jian ji*]. Guǎngzhōu: Jì'nán dàxué chūbǎnshè.

Liáng Wēi 梁威. 1995. "Qiǎnxī Yuèjù jùběn yǔ chàngcí" 淺析粵劇劇本與唱詞. In *Yuèjù yántǎohuì lùnwénjí* 粵劇研討會論文集 [Papers and Proceedings of the International Seminar on Cantonese Opera] (= *Studies of Ethnomusicology*, No. 4)], edited by Liú Jìngzhī 劉靖之 and Xiǎn Yùyí 冼玉儀, 137–59. Hong Kong: Joint Publishing (H.K.) Co., Ltd.

Lín Fèngshān 林鳳珊. 2003. "Dú èr-sān-shí niándài (1920–1936) Yuèjù jùběn shíqù" 讀二、三十年代 (1920–1936) 粵劇劇本拾趣 [Interesting tidbits on reading 1920s and 1930s Cantonese opera scripts]. In *Xiānggǎng xìqǔ tōngxùn* 香港戲曲通訊 [Hong Kong Cantonese opera newsletter]. Volume 7: *Èrshí shìjì chū Yuèjù, Yuèqǔ wénxì* 二十世紀初粵劇、粵曲文獻 [Early twentieth-century Cantonese opera: Cantonese opera documents]. Part 1. Hong Kong: Chinese Opera Information Center, Chinese University of Hong Kong.

Liú Jìngzhī 劉靖之, and Xiǎn Yùyí 冼玉儀, eds. 1995. *Yuèjù yántǎohuì lùnwénjí* 粵劇研討會論文集 [English title: Papers and Proceedings of the International Seminar on Cantonese Opera] (= *Studies of Ethnomusicology*, No. 4). Hong Kong: Joint Publishing (H.K.) Co., Ltd.

Lo, Terence, and Colleen Wong. 1990. "Polyglossia in the 'Printed Cantonese' Mass Media in Hong Kong." *Journal of Asian Pacific Communication* 1 (1): 27–43.

Lock, Graham. 2003. "Being International, Local, and Chinese: Advertisements on the Hong Kong Mass Transit Railway." *Visual Communication* 2 (2): 195–214.

Luó Pǐnchāo 羅品超. 1993. "Yuèjù 'Nánpài' chuántǒng yìshù" 粵劇'南派'傳統藝術 [Art of the Guangdong opera 'southern school' tradition]. In *Xiānggǎng Yuèjù kǐushù shǐ* 香港粵劇口述史 [Hong Kong Cantonese opera oral history], edited by Lí Jiàn 黎鍵, 3–11. Hong Kong: Joint Publishing (H.K.) Co., Ltd.

Mackerras, Colin. 1975. *The Chinese Theatre in Modern Times: From 1840 to the Present Day*. London: Thames and Hudson.

Mair, Victor. 1994. "Buddhism and the Rise of the Written Vernacular in East Asia: The Making of National Languages." *Journal of Asian Studies* 53 (3): 707–51.

Mann, Susan. 1997. *Precious Records: Women in China's Long Eighteenth Century*. Stanford: Stanford University Press.

Morrison, Robert. 1828. *A Vocabulary of the Canton Dialect*. 3 volumes. Macao: The Honorable East India Company's Press.

Moser, David. 2004. "No Laughing Matter: A Hilarious Investigation into the Destruction of Modern Chinese Humor." Posted online elsewhere in 2004, and reposted at harvard.edu on January 29, 2009. https://blogs.harvard.edu/guorui/2009/01/29/no-laughing-matter-a-hilarious-investigation-into-the-destruction-of-modern-chinese-humor/.

Rawski, Evelyn Sakakida. 1972. *Education and Popular Literacy in Ch'ing China*. Ann Arbor: University of Michigan Press.

Rawski, Evelyn S. 1985. "Economic and social foundations of late imperial culture." In *Popular Culture in Late Imperial China*, edited by David Johnson, Andrew J. Nathan, and Evelyn S. Rawski, 3–33. Berkeley: University of California Press.

Snow, Don. 1993. "Chinese Dialect as Written Language: The Cases of Taiwanese and Cantonese." *Journal of Asian Pacific Communication* 4 (1): 15–30.

Snow, Don. 2004. *Cantonese as Written Language: The Growth of a Written Chinese Vernacular*. Hong Kong: Hong Kong University Press.

Snow, Don. 2008. "Cantonese as Written Standard?" *Journal of Asian Pacific Communication* 18 (2): 190–208.

Snow, Don. 2010. "Hong Kong and Modern Diglossia." *International Journal of the Sociology of Language* 206: 155–79.

Starr, Rebecca L., and Xingxing Li. 2015. "Predicting NP Forms in Vernacular Written Cantonese." *Journal of Chinese Linguistics* 43 (1A): 54–89.

Sū Wēng 蘇翁. 2003. "Yuèjù jùběn shǐhuà 粵劇劇本史話" [The development of Cantonese opera libretti]. In *Dì shíyī jiè Xiānggǎng guójì diànyǐngjié - Yuèyǔ xìqǔ piàn huígù* 第十一屆香港國際電影節 • 粵語戲曲片回顧 [Cantonese opera film retrospective, The 11th Hong Kong International Film Festival]. Rev. ed., edited by the Xiānggǎng shìzhèngjú 香港市政局 (Urban Council, Hong Kong), 87–88, 89–91. Hong Kong: Hong Kong Film Archive.

Tán Qīngshuāng 譚青霜. 1950. *Liǔ Yì chuán shū* 柳毅傳書. (Publication date is provided by WorldCat.)

Thoms, Peter Perring. 1824. *Huā jiān* 花箋 *Chinese Courtship. In Verse*. London: Parbury, Allen, and Kingsbury.

Twitchett, Denis. 1962. [Review] Joseph Needham, *Science and Civilization in China*. Volume 3 (Cambridge, 1959). *Bulletin of the School of Oriental and African Studies* 25 (1): 186–89.

Wáng, Lì 王力. 1958. *Hànyǔ shǐgǎo* 漢語史稿 [History of the Chinese language]. Volume 2. Běijīng: Kēxué chūbǎnshè.

Wu, Fung Hoi. 2003. "A Study of Written Cantonese in Hong Kong Culture: The Development of Cantonese Dialect Literature before and after the Change of Sovereignty." MA thesis, University of Hong Kong.

Xiānggǎng Shìzhèngjú 香港市政局 (Urban Council, Hong Kong), eds. 2003. *Dì shíyī jiè Xiānggǎng guójì diànyǐngjié—Yuèyǔ xìqǔ piàn huígù* 第十一屆香港國際電影節・粵語戲曲片回顧 [Cantonese opera film retrospective, The 11th Hong Kong International Film Festival]. Revised edition. Hong Kong: Hong Kong Film Archive.

Yan, Jing. 2005. "[Bin^1-di^1 hai^6 ngaam^1-ge^3] 邊D系啱嘅 vs. [Nǎxiē shì duìde] 哪些是對的 'What Things Are Correct'—Written Variables in a Cantonese Internet Community." In *Proceedings of the Seventeenth North American Conference on Chinese Linguistics (NACCL-17)*, edited by Qian Gao, 483–94. GSIL Publications, University of Southern California.

Yan, Jing. 2008. "Social Variation of Vernacular Written Cantonese in Guangzhou (Canton City), China." PhD dissertation, Ohio State University.

Yue-Hashimoto, Anne O. 2005. *The Dancun Dialect of Taishan* [Computational and Linguistic Analysis of Asian Languages, Monograph Series No. 1]. Hong Kong: Language Information Sciences Research Centre, City University of Hong Kong.

Yung, Bell. 1989. *Cantonese Opera: Performance as Creative Process*. Cambridge: Cambridge University Press.

Zhan, Bohui 詹伯慧, and Yat-Shing Cheung 張日昇, eds. 1988. *A Survey of Dialects in the Pearl River Delta*, vol. 2: *Comparative Lexicon*. [Chinese Title: 珠江三角洲方言調查報告之一. 珠江三角洲方言詞匯對照.] Hong Kong: New Century Publishing House.

Zhōngguó xìqǔ zhì – Guǎngdōng juàn biānjí wěiyuánhuì 中國戲曲志・廣東卷 編輯委員會 [China's traditional operas: Guangdong volume compilation committee]. 1993. *Zhōngguó xìqǔ zhì – Guǎngdōng juàn* 中國戲曲志・廣東卷 [China's traditional operas: Guangdong volume]. Běijīng: Zhōngguó ISBN zhōngxīn.

3
The Mix of Dialect and Guānhuà Elements in the Wú Folk Songs Collected in Féng Mènglóng's *Shāngē*

Shí Rǔjié

Introduction

This chapter examines the mix of Wú dialect and Mandarin colloquial elements in the *Shāngē* 山歌 [Mountain songs], transcribed and compiled by Féng Mènglóng 馮夢龍 (1574–1646). *Shāngē* is a ten-chapter collection of often ribald folk songs transcribed primarily in the Wú dialect in which they were undoubtedly performed in their time. As such, the book is an invaluable record of the Sūzhōu 蘇州 language of four centuries ago (Ōki and Santangelo 2011, 3). The language used in the *Shāngē* is essentially pure Wú dialect. However, this collection of songs actually contains a great deal of vocabulary and grammatical forms from Guānhuà 官話 (the Mandarin koinē, or *tōng yǔ* 通語 of the time), all generally mixed in with the Wú dialect forms. This underscores a realization we came to when compiling *A Dictionary of Wú Dialect in the Míng and Qīng Dynasties*: it is well-nigh impossible to find literature that was written entirely in dialect in the pre-modern period. Below we examine in detail identifiable Wú and Mandarin forms in the *Shāngē* and consider the causes and implications of the linguistic mélange within Féng Mènglóng's compilation.

Féng Mènglóng's Use of Language in the *Shāngē*

Féng Mènglóng is an author who really focused on language phenomena. He provided explicit descriptions or explanations of language forms in a wide variety of forums. For example, in the comedic work he compiled titled *Xiàofǔ* 笑府 [Treasury of laughs], there is the punning he explains in "Wāizuǐ qiú yào" 歪嘴求藥 [Crooked-mouth seeks a remedy] (*juàn* 4, 5b):

> A fellow suffering from crooked-mouth consulted a doctor in search of an herbal remedy. The doctor politely declined, saying "I specialize in internal medicine, and don't have that kind of drug." The crooked-mouthed fellow replied, "You mean you've gone to the trouble to be a doctor and yet don't have Bitter Orange Rhizome 'Mouth-straightening' Pills at your home-clinic?" (Féng Mènglóng's annotation: In

Wú dialect *zuǐ* 'mouth' [tsʮ⁵²] is homophonous with *zhǐ* 'bitter orange' [tsʮ⁵²] and *zhí* 'straight' [zəʔ²³] is homophonous with *zhú* 'rhizome' [zəʔ²³].)

有患嘴歪者，叩醫求藥，辭云："我是裡科，無此等藥。" 歪嘴曰："難道特地做一個郎中，枳 ₍嘴₎ 朮 ₍直₎ 丸也沒得在家裡？"（吳音"嘴"同"枳"，"直"同"朮"。）

And there is also that of "Chì bí" 赤鼻 [Red nose] (*Xiàofǔ, juàn* 10, 5b):

> There was a fellow who saw a man with an elongated chin. He said to him, "I would like to put up a scaffold on your face." Horrified, the man said, "What for?" "To knock down your chin," was the reply. The man retorted, "How can a chin be knocked down?" To which the response was, "If your chin cannot be knocked down, how come your nose is knocked-red?" (Féng Mènglóng's annotation: *chāi* "knock down" and *chì* "red" are homophonous in Wú dialect: [tsʻaʔ⁵].)
>
> 有見長下頦者，曰："我欲借你面上搭一鷹架。"其人駭曰："為何？"曰："要拆你的下頦。"其人曰："下頦如何拆得？"曰："下頦拆不得，鼻頭如何拆 ₍赤₎ 了？"（吳語"赤、拆"同音。）

These examples reveal that Féng Mènglóng's linguistic sensibility is sharpened by his delight in wordplay, a delight he explicitly articulates in the preface to *Xiàofǔ* (see Zhāng Huìyīng's contribution in this volume). *Shāngē* too has many similar examples in which Féng Mènglóng explains the dialect elements, as in "Xiézi" 鞋子 [Shoes] (*juàn* 9, no. 3):

> A bit of advice to you dear young lady: Don't say it is because you have a strong patron. Even wearing woven reed slippers, you would still have the advantage over a remarried widow. (Féng Mènglóng's annotation: Wú dialect refers to a widow who has remarried as *zuǒjiàrén* [tsi⁵⁵kaʻ⁵⁵ɲin¹] in which *zuǒ* has the dialect pronunciation [tsi⁵⁵].)
>
> 奉勸姐兒沒要自道是腳力大，就是拖腳蒲鞋還勝子左嫁人。（吳語再醮曰"左嫁人"。左，俗音"際"。）

In overall perspective, the distinction between dialect and Mandarin (Guānhuà) is rather obvious in the *Shāngē*. Yet while Féng Mènglóng could highlight the subtle differences in language in the ways illustrated above, we find in a careful reading of *Shāngē* that he could not avoid the influence of Mandarin even when expressly writing in dialect. The *Shāngē* is clearly written primarily in the Wú dialect. Only the "Tóngchéng shíxīng gē" 桐城時興歌 [Fashionable songs of Tóngchéng] in *juàn* 卷 10 completely use Mandarin. For example, in the book as a whole, the Mandarin conjunction *hé* 和 is used four times, and three of these instances are found in *juàn* 10. There are a total of twenty-one examples of the Mandarin preposition *bǎ* 把. Eight of these are found in *juàn* 10, while another six appear scattered among the Wú dialect verses, including the old-style poems and the songs. Yet there are also

Mandarin examples in the ballads, such as in "Mán niáng" 瞞娘 [Deceiving mother] (*juàn* 1, no. 20):[1]

> *Ā-niáng guǎn wǒ hǔ yī-bān, wǒ **bǎ** niáng lái gǔ lǐ mán.*
> 阿娘管我虎一般，我**把**娘來鼓裏瞞。
> 'My mother watches me like a tiger, and so I deceive her with my lies.' (Ō&S, 91)

And in "Hébāo" 荷包 [The pouch] (*juàn* 6, no. 13):

> *Nǐ yǒu zi tóng-qián yínzi dàn píng nǐ gé lái hē,*
> *Zhǐ mò yào wú qián kōng **bǎ** bù-qún xiāo.*
> 你有子銅錢銀子但憑你閣來呵，只沒要無錢空**把**布裙囂。
> 'Whatever coins you have, copper or silver, you can set it right down;
> But if you have no money, please do not roll up my skirt in vain.' (Ō&S, 234)

Yet we find that Mandarin appears frequently in Féng Mènglóng's *Shāngē* even if we exclude *juàn* 10 from examination (as we will do in the remainder of this study). Why is this? Obviously, one can conjecture that it is because in his day Guānhuà was already heavily influencing the written language. Even Féng Mènglóng had no way to completely distinguish the boundary between dialect and Guānhuà; and he could not fully resist or avoid inadvertently using Mandarin elements.[2] This is highlighted in the analysis of *Shāngē* language that we undertake below, as we investigate the mix of Wú and Guānhuà elements in the text with regard to pronunciation, vocabulary, and grammar. We also consider the influences behind the various elements in the mix and ponder their origins.

Issues of Wú and Guānhuà Rhyme

Rhyming in *Shāngē* follows definite prosodic structures. For example, the rhyming syllable is generally at the end of lines 1, 2 and 4. The rhymes reveal clear dialect influence. For instance, "Ménshén" 門神 [The Door God] (*juàn* 9, no. 2) includes the following syllables in rhyming position, alternating between two rhymes in this order: 神、情、經、神、庭、門、星、聲、承、塵、景、人、人、心、停、聲、真、情、情、聽、人、新. As illustrated below, this reveals that the rhyming did not distinguish between Common Dialectal Chinese (CDC) final nasal consonants

---

[1]. The *Shāngē* passages are numbered as ordered in Shí Rǔjié and Huáng Míngmíng (2007–8a, b). Here and following, translations for passages in *juàn* 1 through *juàn* 7 are based on Ōki and Santangelo 2011, but frequently modifications are made to allow the English to more clearly demonstrate the point being illustrated. For reference, page numbers for the original translations in Ōki and Santangelo 2011 are indicated using the format "(Ō&S: #)". Translations for passages in *juàn* 8 and *juàn* 9 are by the editor and translator of this article. For the convenience of readers, *pīnyīn* transcriptions are also provided for words under discussion and selected passages, which of course represent the pronunciation of Modern Standard Chinese and not the Sūzhōu pronunciation of the original.

[2]. For additional consideration of Féng Mènglóng's views on language, dialect, and humor also see Zhāng Huìyīng contribution to this volume in Chapter 5.

*-m, *-n, *-ng, a situation also seen in modern Sūzhōu dialect, as the following table illustrates:[3]

Pīnyīn	English	Common Wú	Sūzhōu	CDC
jǐng 景	'scene'	/jing³/	[tɕin⁵²]	*kiang³
jīng 經	(zhèngjīng 正經 'proper')	/jing¹/	[tɕin⁴⁴]	*kiang¹
qíng 情	'emotion'	/dzing²/	[zin²³]	*dziang²
rén 人	'person'	/gning²/	[ɲin²³]	*nhin²
tíng 停	'stop'	/dhing²/	[din²³]	*diang²
tīng 聽	'listen'	/ting¹/	[tʻin⁴⁴]	*thiang¹
tíng 庭	'hall'	/dhing²/	[din²³]	*diang²
xīn 心	'mind'	/sing¹/	[sin⁴⁴]	*sim¹
xīn 新	'new'	/sing¹/	[sin⁴⁴]	*sin¹
xīng 星	'star'	/sing¹/	[sin⁴⁴]	*siang¹
chén 塵	'dust'	/djeng²/	[zən²³]	*jin²
chéng 承	(fèngchéng 奉承 'flatter')	/djeng²/	[zən²³]	*jing²
mén 門	'door'	/meng²/	[mən²³]	*mun²
shén 神	'god'	/jheng²/	[zən²³]	*jin²
shēng 聲	'voice'	/sheng¹/	[sən⁴⁴]	*shiang¹
zhēn 真	'true'	/jeng¹/	[tsən⁴⁴]	*cin¹

The situation is rather more complicated in the following examples:

I. From "Gé/Yòu gé" 隔/又隔 [Variations on "Separation"] (juàn 2, no. 34; Ōki and Santangelo 2011, 147)

Pīnyīn	English	Common Wú	Sūzhōu	CDC
bāng 浜	'brook'	/báng¹/	[pã⁴⁴]	*bang¹
gēng 更	'night hour'	/gáng¹/	[kã⁴⁴]	*kang¹
cháng 長	'long'	/djáng²/	[zã²³]	*jiong²
...				
qiáng 牆	'wall'	/dziang²/	[ziã²³]	*dziong²
chuáng 床	'bed'	/dzuang²/	[zã²³]	*jong²
qiáng 牆	'wall'	/dziang²/	[ziã²³]	*dziong²

---

3. It is possible that the neighboring Southern Mandarin Jiāng-Huái 江淮 dialects also did not distinguish *-m, *-n, *-ng in the late Míng. Here and following, Common Wú (between slashes '/ /') is based on Chao 1956; Sūzhōu forms (between square brackets '[ ]') are based on Shí and Chén 1989, with corrections or emendations by the author; CDC forms (starred '*') are based on Norman 2006 and 2011.

II. From "Jià" 嫁 [Marrying] (*juàn* 3, no. 18; Ōki and Santangelo 2011, 166)

Pīnyīn	English	Common Wú	Sūzhōu	CDC
bāng 浜	'brook'	/báng¹/	[pã⁴⁴]	*bang¹
shēng 生	(*hòushēng* 後生 'lad')	/sáng¹/	[sã⁴⁴⁻¹]	*shang¹
shēng 甥	(*wàishēng* 外甥 'nephew')	/sáng¹/	[sã⁴⁴⁻⁴]	*shang¹

III. From "Bú yùn" 不孕 [Barrenness] (*juàn* 1, no. 33; Ōki and Santangelo 2011, 110)

Pīnyīn	English	Common Wú	Sūzhōu	CDC
tiān 天	'heavens'	/tien¹/	[tʻiɪ⁴⁴]	*thian¹
yān 煙	'smoke (of incense)'	/ien¹/	[iɪ⁴⁴]	*ian¹
nián 年	'year'	/gnien¹/	[ɲiɪ²³]	*nian²
...				
nián 年	'year'	/gnien¹/	[ɲiɪ²³]	*nian²
chuán 傳	'transmit'	/djón¹/	[zø²³]	*jion²
yān 煙	'smoke (of incense)'	/ien¹/	[iɪ⁴⁴]	*ian¹

IV. From "Zuànzi" 鑽子 [The drill] (*juàn* 8, no. 6)

Pīnyīn	English	Common Wú	Sūzhōu	CDC
bān 般	'same kind'	/bón¹/	[pø⁴⁴]	*pon¹
kuān 寬	'wide'	/kuon¹/	[kʻuø⁴⁴]	*khuon¹
zuān 鑽	'drill'	/tzon¹/	[tsø⁴⁴]	*tson¹
...				
zuān 鑽	'drill'	/tzon¹/	[tsø⁴⁴]	*tson¹
fān 番	'time(s)'	/fan¹/	[fɛ⁴⁴]	*phon¹
guān 関	'shut'	/guan¹/	[kuɛ⁴⁴]	*kuan¹
...				
yān 煙	'smoke'	/ien¹/	[iɪ⁴⁴]	*ian¹
tān 癱	'paralyzed'	/tan¹/	[tʻɛ⁴⁴]	*than¹

The first two sets of rhymes (I and II) basically conform with Wú phonology. But note that in modern Sūzhōu the main vowel of *chuáng* 'bed' is [ã], which is distinct from the main vowel [ã] of the other syllables. [Editor's notes: This is evidence that the Common Wú medial -u- may have not yet affected the main vowel in Féng Mènglóng's time.] The second two sets of rhymes (III and IV) mix Common Wú finals—main vowel and ending—/en/, /on/, and /an/ (Sūzhōu [ɪ], [ø], and [ɛ]). There are many examples of this type in *Shāngē*, too many to enumerate. We can only conjecture that while most of the rhyming in the *Shāngē* accords with dialect phonology, occasionally there is influence from Guānhuà rhyming conventions. For instance, the rhyming in sets III and IV matches the *hán-shān* 寒刪 type rimes in the *Cílín zhèngyùn* 詞林正韻 [Correct rimes of the forest of words] by Gē Zài 戈載 (1786–1856). [Editor's notes: This would represent a stage in Mandarin in which CDC *on had already merged with *an and the main vowel in CDC *ian had not yet raised to the [iɛn] of modern Mandarin. The *Cílín zhèngyùn* example is in "*Dì qī bù*" 第七部 [Part seven] (*juànzhōng* 卷中, p. 9a).]

Pronouns

In this section we discuss the various pronouns used in *Shāngē*, both personal pronouns and interrogative pronouns. While there is a rich and varied set of Wú dialect pronouns in the text, various Guānhuà forms are also dispersed throughout.

First-person pronouns

In the *Shāngē*, there are 492 examples of *wǒ* 我 'I, me' used alone (for both male and female). There are 2 cases of *wǒ-nóng* 我儂 'I, me'. The female pronoun *nú* 奴 'I, me' appears 48 times, while there are 6 instances of *ā-nú* 阿奴 'I, me', 55 instances of *ā-nú-nú* 阿奴奴 'I, me', and 8 appearances of *nú-nú* 奴奴. The following are examples:

我儂 *wǒ-nóng* /ngú⁴nong²/ [ŋəu²²noŋ⁴]

> "Mùshū" 木梳 [Wooden comb] (*juàn* 8, no. 4):
> 結識私情好像木梳能，**我儂**柱子聽你介相思結髮情。
> 'Getting involved in a secret love affair is like a wooden comb. **I** yearn in vain for you, begetting a knot of matrimonial desire.'
> [Editor's note: '*Jiéfà-qíng* 結髮情' combines *jiéfà* 結髮 'comb into a bun' (figure of speech meaning 'get married') with *qíng* 情 'feeling, desire'.]

奴 *nú* /nu²/ [nəu³¹]

> "Sīqíng sìjù" 私情四句 [On secret loves in four lines] (*juàn* 4, no. 2):
> 被蓋子郎來郎蓋子我，席襯子**奴**來**奴**襯子郎。
> 'The quilt is covering you and you are covering me, The bed mat lies under **me** and **I** lie under you.' (Ō&S, 172)

阿奴 *ā-nú* /aq⁷-nu²/ [aʔ⁵nəu³⁴]

> "Kuíhuā" 葵花 [The hollyhock] (*juàn* 6, no. 49):
> 我捉你當子天上日頭，一心只對子你，你沒要陰晴無准弗照**阿奴**心。
> 'All my heart is devoted to you, considering you are the sun in my heaven,
> So please do not change like the weather and do not stop the shining on **my** heart.'
> (Ō&S, 262)

奴奴 *nú-nú* /nu²-nu²/ [nəu³⁴nəu¹]

"Yòu (yùn)" 又 (孕) [Variation on "pregnancy"] (*juàn* 1, no. 32):
玉指尖尖抱在紅燈下看，半像奴奴半像郎。
'Held in slender jade fingers, and looked at under the red lantern, he looks half like **me** and half like my lover!' (Ō&S, 109)

Nú 奴 /nu²/ [nəu³⁴] in the vast majority of instances is used by women to refer to themselves, especially in the cases of *ā-nú-nú* 阿奴奴 and *nú-nú* 奴奴. These are nouns formed with *nú* 奴 that serve as pronouns used by young women or teenage girls. But *Tǔfēnglù* 土風錄 [Record of Local Customs] (by Gù Zhāngsī 顧張思 [n.d.] of the Qīng) notes that *nú* is a term of endearment for children. Only the dialects of Zhōuzhuāng 周莊 and Chénmù 陳墓 in Kūnshān 崑山 Municipality, as well as the suburbs of modern Sūzhōu, use *nú* as a common first-person (singular) pronoun, pronouncing it in the *qù* tone. (Zhū Wénxióng 朱文熊 [1883–1961], the author of *Jiāngsū xīn zìmǔ* 江蘇新字母 [A new spelling system for Jiāngsū] [preface 1906], was from Chénmù.) [Editor's notes: Chao (1928, 95) indicates a *qù* tone /nou⁶/ ("*now*") as a first-person pronoun in Sūzhōu; in his *Wúyīn dānzì biǎo* (1956, 186) he gives /nhu³/ as the Sūzhōu pronunciation for 奴, and /nu²/ as the pronunciation elsewhere.]

Shāngē has the following first-person plural pronoun forms: 34 instances of *wǒlǐ* 我裡, 3 of *wǒlī* 我哩, and 3 of *wǒlǐ* 我裏. These forms probably arose earlier and are seen in a variety of literature from the Míng to the twentieth century. They are also still found in many modern Wú dialects. Here is an example:

我哩 *wǒ-lī* /ngú⁴li⁴/ [ŋəu²⁴li¹]

"Shān rén" 山人 [Hill people] (*juàn* 9, no. 7):
我哩個些人，道假咦弗假，道真咦弗真。
'**We** folk, when we say it's fake it's not fake; when [we] say it's real, it's not real.'

Second-person pronouns

For the second-person singular pronoun, *Shāngē* utilizes *nǐ* 你 'you' 358 times, *ěr* 爾 'you' 13 times (only in the first 6 volumes), and *nǐ-nóng* 你儂 'you' 4 times. Sometimes *nǐ* 你 and *ěr* 爾 are found used in the same song.

你/爾 *nǐ/ěr* /gni⁴/ [ni⁴⁴]

"Zhēng" 爭 [Dispute] (*juàn* 4, no. 18):
我十六歲貪花養子你箇娘，娘十七歲上貪花養子爾。
'I enjoyed sexual pleasure and bore **your** mother when I was 16; Your mother enjoyed sexual pleasure and bore **you** when she was 17.' (Ō&S, 193)

"Yīyún (Jiùrén)" 一云(舊人) [Variation on "My Old Lover"] (*juàn* 3, no. 16):
姐兒說向我郎聽:"我聽**你**也是隔年桃核舊時仁,**爾**沒要做子桑葉交秋弗採子我,囉匡**爾**再是黃梅天日出弗長晴。"
'She says to her lover: "**You** and I are old lovers, just like the old kernel from the stone of last year's peach; don't **you** treat me like the mulberry leaves in Autumn and ignore me; and don't **you** be like 'the sun in the rainy season,' as love lasts no longer than fine weather then."' (Ō&S, 165)

你儂 *nǐ-nóng* /gni⁴nong²/ [ni⁵⁵noŋ¹]

"Pò zōng-mào gē" 破騣帽歌 [Song of the ragged bristle cap] (*juàn* 9, no. 6):
你儂弗要出言吐氣,我儂唱介一隻曲子你聽聽。
'Don't **you** say a word or make a sound; I will sing this song for you to have a listen.'

For the second-person pronoun plural form, *nǐ-dā* 你搭 is used, for which there are 18 occurrences.

你搭 *nǐ-dā* /gni¹dáq⁷/ [ni⁵⁵taʔ¹]

"Xiōng-dì" 兄弟 [Brothers] (*juàn* 4, no. 11):
結識子兄弟又結識子箇哥,**你搭**弟兄兩箇要調和。
'I commit adultery with the younger brother, and I also commit adultery with the older brother; **you** two brothers must maintain the harmony between you.' (Ō&S, 185)

"Mén shén" 門神 [Door god] (*juàn* 9, no. 2):
我只是聲色弗動,並弗容介個閒神野鬼,上**你搭**箇大門。
'I am simply unmoved by voice or looks; and I will not allow this idle spirit and wild lout to come through **your** gate.'

The suffix *dā* 搭 in this form is derived from its use in place words. For example, 'the place where you are' (Mandarin *nǐ-nàlǐ* 你那裏) in modern Suzhou is [nE²⁴taʔ¹] 倷搭 and is probably of related origin.

Third-person pronouns

Within *Shāngē*, the third-person singular pronoun *qú* 渠 'he/she/him/her' is used 53 times, but Mandarin *tā* 他 is also used. From a historical perspective, *qú* 渠 is probably an earlier form.

渠 *qú* /djiu²/ [dʑy²³]

"Fú huán quán" 弗還拳 [Do not react to beating] (*juàn* 2, no. 22):
喫**渠**罵子喫渠打,憶郎君好處只是弗還拳。
'I was insulted and beaten by **him**. But remembering his good points, I decided not to fight back.' (Ō&S, 139)

The third-person plural pronoun *qú-dā* 渠搭 only has one example.

渠搭 *qú-dā* /djiu²dáq⁷/ [dʑy²²taʔ⁴]

"Xiézi" 鞋子 [Shoes] (*juàn* 9, no. 3):
耍[喻]來頭現在**渠搭**四箇冤魂個眼睛？
'For what reason now do the four of **them** have eyes of the unjustly accused?'

他 *tā* /ta¹/ [tʻɑ⁴⁴] is used 21 times. But only two of those are as the third-person pronoun.

"Dìng guǐ mén" 釘鬼門 [Watch the gate of hell—stir up rumors] (*juàn* 7, no. 12):
私情起意未曾曾，咦有閒人搬來我裏箇聽，并無形跡，由**他**講論。
'When our affair had just started and nothing had yet happened, a troublesome man came and told me husband about it. As there is no evidence, I will let **him** talk as much as **he** likes.' (Ō&S, 280)

"Lǎo Ā-jiě" 老阿姐 [The old spinster] (*juàn* 7, no. 14):
千方百計，騙他動情，脫裙解褲，抱**他**上身。
'With a hundred tricks and a thousand stratagems, she succeeded in seducing and exciting him. Removing her skirt, she took off his trousers and hugged **him** tightly.' (Ō&S, 280)

All other examples are in literary words such as *tārì* 他日 'another day' and *tārén* 他人 'others'.

Interrogative pronouns

In *Shāngē* there are seven instances of the Mandarin word *shéi* 誰 'who' that are used in special sections of the song (such as in the *páigē* 排歌 'free verse ballads'). There are also two other dialect forms, *shuǎ-rén* 耍人 'what person, who' (usually *shà-rén* 啥人 in modern orthography) and *luó-gè* 囉个 (equivalent to Mandarin *nǎge* 哪个) literally 'which one'. Comparatively, the dialect forms are used much less frequently.

囉箇 *luó-gè* /lo²geq⁷/ [lo²⁴kəʔ¹]

"Yǒuxīn" 有心 [Love] (*juàn* 2, no. 5):
結識私情只要自即伶，閒人**囉箇**能當心？
'When you have a love affair, cleverness is paramount. For **who** among strangers would ever bother to notice?' (Ō&S, 119)

耍人 *shuǎ-rén* /sha⁵gning²/ [sɑ⁴¹ȵin³⁴]

"Yòu (yùn)" 又(孕) [Variation on "pregnancy"] (*juàn* 1, no. 32):
眼淚汪汪哭向郎，"我喫腹中有孕**耍人**當？"
'A girl asks her lover tearfully: "I have been knocked up, **who** will take the blame?"' (Ō&S, 108)

誰 *shéi* /jhé²/ [ZE³¹]

> "Zhòumà" 咒罵 [The curse] (*juàn* 7, no. 9):
> 當初來往，是誰請你？如今撇我，被人説是講非。
> 'When we began our romance, who asked you to come? Now I have been cast aside. People criticize me with their gossip.' (Ō&S, 277)

Difficulties in distinguishing Wú and Guānhuà pronouns in *Shāngē*

The *Shāngē* does not use Mandarin plural pronouns such as *wǒmén* 我們, *nǐmén* 你們, *tāmen* 他們. But the singular forms of *wǒ* 我 and *nǐ* 你 are used. It is hard to know whether or not these are Mandarin forms. Shěn Chǒngsuí's 沈寵綏 (d. ca. 1645) *Dùqǔ xūzhī* 度曲須知 [What you need to know to go through the Qǔ-type songs], notes (*juàn* A, p. 15a):

> Wú dialect colloquial has the words "*wǒ-nóng*" and "*nǐ-nóng*." In the latter the syllable "*nǐ*" is not pronounced like "*nǐ*" 'mud'. It has another colloquial pronunciation that is similar to a voiced alveolar (*shìshéyīn*, [ṇ]).
> 吳俗有「我儂、你儂」之稱，其「你」字不作「泥」音，另有土音，與舐舌音相似。

The colloquial voiced alveolar pronunciation that he is referring to here is a syllabic nasal [ṇ]. In light of Shěn's description, these forms should be understood to be dialect forms. But since they are written with the same character as their Guānhuà counterparts they can be considered to represent a kind of *xùndú* 訓讀 (*kunyomi*) 'popular or non-etymological dialect reading' of the character. However, the cases of the third-person pronoun *tā* and the interrogative pronoun *shéi* are clearly Guānhuà forms.

Substantives or Full Words

In this section we will cite only a few examples of types of substantives or full words (*shící* 實詞), primarily verbs for 'holding', 'carrying', 'putting', and 'placing'. Again, we observe that both Wú and Guānhuà forms are found. First are examples of verbs with the meaning 'hold, take, carry'.

擔 *dān* /dan¹/ [TE⁴⁴] has seven examples in the *Shāngē* (other than its use in such words as *tiāo-dàn* 挑擔 'shoulder a load' and *fù-dān* 負擔 'a burden'), such as in "Chī yīngtáo" 喫櫻桃 [Eating cherries] (*juàn* 7, no. 6):

> 日落西山影弗高，姐擔子竹榜打櫻桃。
> 'The sun is setting behind the western mountains, but our shadows are still not very long. **Holding** a bamboo plank, she knocks down the cherries.' (Ō&S, 274)

拿 *ná* /no²/ [no²³/⁴⁴] The text uses *ná* 拿 26 times, such as in "Shāo xiāng niáng-niáng" 燒香娘娘 [The Incense Lady] (*juàn* 9, no. 5):

收捉銅杓、注子兩件，同兩領補打個衣裳，替我**拿**來典當里去當當。
'Gather up the copper ladle and decanter, both things, together with two well-patched items of clothing, and **take** them to the pawn shop for me to pawn off.'

There are also cases where meanings of *dān* 擔 overlap, as in the following example, in which *dān* means 'bring to' or 'take to' in addition to 'carry on a shoulder pole', as in "Yī yún (gé)" 一云(隔) [Variation on "Separation"] (*juàn* 2, no. 34):

結識私情隔條街，又**擔**米了又**擔**柴，朝**擔**暮**擔**，**擔**弗了，一性搬來合子家。
'I have a secret lover who lives across the street. He **brings** me rice, and then **brings** firewood. He **carries** some in the morning and **carries** more in the evening, until he can no longer carry things. I would rather move out into his home and turn two houses into one.' (Ō&S, 148)

It can be observed here that both *dān* 擔 and *ná* 拿 were in general usage. *Ná* had probably originated in the Guānhuà *lingua franca* — *tōngyǔ* 通語—and had a powerful, prevailing influence.

Our second set of examples is verbs having the meaning 'put, place'. We find three different verbs with this meaning, though the examples are few:

放 **fàng** /fang⁵/ [fɑ̃⁴¹²]

"Suō" 睃 [A glance] (*juàn* 1, no. 2):
珊瑚樹兒玉瓶裡栽。呀，輕輕**放**，心肝愛。
'A coral tree is planted in a jade vase. Ah, **place** it gently, my love!' (Ō&S, 68–70)

(*juàn* 8, no. 8):
贈錢買我家去，**放**我來紅紗帳子裡安身。
'Add some money to purchase me and bring me home; **put** me in the red netting bed curtain to comfortably reside.'

安 **ān** /on¹/ [ø⁴⁴]

"Chī yīng-táo" 喫櫻桃 [Eating cherries] (*juàn* 7, no. 6):
打子四九三十六個櫻桃**安**來紅籃裏。
'Beating four times nine, thirty-six cherries are **put** into her red basket.' (Ō&S, 274)

(*juàn* 9, no. 4):
安我來糞箕裡，一丟丟子我來炉裡去。
'**Put** me in the dustpan, and toss me away in the stove.'

擺 **bǎi** /ba³/ [pɑ⁵²]

"Bǎi cí-táng" 擺祠堂 [Setting up an altar to her dead lover] (*juàn* 7, no. 4):
袖裏藏，袖裏藏，再來檢妝裏面**擺**祠堂。
'Hiding it in my sleeve, hiding it in my sleeve, I also **place** an altar to him on my dressing table.' (Ō&S, 272)

From the perspective of modern Chinese, *fàng* 放 is the most common of the words for 'put, place' in the Mandarin *tōngyǔ* (*Pǔtōnghuà*), while *ān* 安 is mainly a dialect word. Yet the word most commonly used in present-day Sūzhōu, *bǎi* 擺, has only a single example in the *Shāngē*, which however is not the most typical meaning of 'put, place'.

Function Words and Grammatical Forms

In this section we discuss various function words (*xūcí* 虛詞) and grammatical forms, including passive markers, conjunctions, prepositions used in the disposal construction, verbs indicating position or existence, and words for the negative imperative. In usage, these kinds of functional forms are highly characteristic of a given dialect type. Yet Féng Mènglóng still could not avoid mixing in Guānhuà forms, often in ways that borrowed the nuances of Wú counterparts.

Passive markers

The passive in *Shāngē* uses the preposition *chī* 喫 (吃) the most. We find it used 80 times, followed by 7 instances of *bō-lái* 撥來, while there are only 5 cases of *bèi* 被. The first 2 are original Wú dialect forms. During the period that the *Shāngē* were composed, the passive *bō-lái* 撥來 had just begun to be used. It would eventually replace *chī* 喫, while *bèi* 被 is clearly not original to the Wú dialect.

喫 *chī* /chieq[7]/ [tɕ'iə?[5]] **(1)** Preposition and passive marker indicating the actor or initiator of an action. For example, in "Chě bù-qún" 扯布裙 [Tearing the skirt] (*juàn* 1, no. 21):

> 喫情哥郎扯斷子布裙腰。
> 'Her skirt's waist was torn **by** her lover.' (Ō&S, 92)

"Yuè shàng" 月上 [When the moon rises] (*juàn* 1, no. 15):
> 約郎約到月上天，再喫箇借住夜箇閒人僭子大門前。
> 'I have a date with my lover when the moon rises; but I am obstructed **by** an idle evening wanderer at the doorway.' (Ō&S, 84)

"Fú huán quán" 弗還拳 [Do not react to beating] (*juàn* 2, no. 22):
> 喫渠罵子喫渠打，憶郎君好處只是弗還拳。
> 'I was insulted **by** him and beaten **by** him. But remembering his good points, I decided not to fight back.' (Ō&S, 139)

喫 *chī* sometimes is followed by an object, for instance in "Tān huā" 貪花 [Indulging in flowers (obsession for sexual pleasures)] (*juàn* 2, no. 14):

> 拿花弗着喫郎摸子妳(奶)。郎貪白妳(奶)．姐貪花。
> 'Before she can pick the flower, her breast was touched **by** him. He longingly desires to touch her breast, just as she longingly desires to pick the flower.' (Ō&S, 133)

"Shāi yóu" 篩油 [Pouring oil] (*juàn* 5, no. 5):
> 喫鄉下箇篩油蠻子討子小便宜。
> 'She was taken advantage of **by** a country oil-merchant.' (Ō&S, 203)

"Huòzi" 鑊子 [The pot] (*juàn* 9, no. 4):
你搭自弗小心，喫箇白日撞偷子物事。
'You are so careless to have had your stuff stolen **by** a daytime thief.'

(2) Verb, indicative of unsatisfactory cause and followed by a verb phrase. There are many examples of this kind such as in "Yòu (yùn)" 又(孕) [Variation on "Pregnancy"] (*juàn* 1, no. 32):

眼淚汪汪哭向郎，"我喫腹中有孕耍人當？"
'A girl asks her lover tearfully: "I **have been** knocked up, who will take the blame?"' (Ō&S, 108)

Yòu (yùn)" 又(孕) [Variation on "Pregnancy"] (*juàn* 1, no. 32):
姐兒囑咐小風流，只有喫箇羅帳裏無郎弗好留。
'She tells her tiny love child, "**Having been** left with no man [to rely on] inside the boudoir curtains, I cannot keep you."' (Ō&S, 110)

"Yīyún (xiǎo nān'er)" 一云(小囡兒) [Variation on "A Girl"] (*juàn* 7, no. 13):
我喫箇打生舡上人多，落弗得箇腳，眼看鮮魚忍肚饑。
'Eyed **by** so many hunters on the boats, I cannot come down to you. I have to resist my hunger, although my eyes see a fresh fish.' (Ō&S, 282)

"Zhú fūrén" 竹夫人 [The bamboo pillow] (*juàn* 8, no. 8):
我喫箇傷心了，唱介兩句曲子，自家嘆箇自身。
'I've **been left** grieving; I'll sing a few lines, and sigh my own sorrows.'

The aspect marker *zi* 子 can be added after 喫 *chī*, for example in "Zhuōjiān" 捉奸 [Catching the adulterer in the act] (*juàn* 1, no. 29):

歪嘴油瓶喫子箇口弗好，鱅臭泥出弗得好香菱。
'Despoiled **by** words from crooked mouths, as twisted as the spout of an oil jar. Fragrant water chestnuts cannot grow from foul-smelling mud.' (Ō&S, 101)

It sometimes means to suffer through unsatisfactory treatment, such as in "Pò zōngmào gē" 破騣帽歌 [Song of the ragged bristle cap] (*juàn* 9, no. 6):

捉箇豬膽去油，教我受子多少醃臢苦腦？捉箇百藥箭上色，教我喫子多少烏皂泥筋？
'Squeezing the oil from a pig's gallbladder, how much filthy vexation have I endured? Clutching a hundred poisoned arrows, how much dastardly indignation have I **suffered**?'

撥來 *bō-lái* /beq⁷leq⁸/ [pəʔ⁵ləʔ⁵] Originally composed of the verb *bō* 撥 (like the Mandarin verb *gěi* 給 'give') and the preposition *lái* 來 (like the Mandarin proposition *gěi* 給 [as passive marker]), it has the same meaning as *bō* 撥 'give' alone. However, the construction must be used with or followed by a person object, such as in "Yòu (Jiě-er sheng-dé)" 又(姐兒生得) [Variation on "Such a Beautiful Girl!"] (*juàn* 2, no. 1):

爾弗要**撥**箇粗枝硬梗屑**來我**，連起子羅裙憑你椏(=控)。
'Don't you **get me** soiled **by** giving me the leavings of that thick branch and hard stalk of yours. I would rather pull up my silk skirt and let you poke to your heart's desire.' (Ō&S, 112)

"Yòu (gé)" 又 (隔) [Variation on "Separation"] (*juàn* 2, no. 34):
郲(=哪)得針變子槍，**撥來**小阿奴奴半夜三更掘開子牆。
'How can a needle become a spear? **Give [it to] me** at midnight on the third watch to open up my wall.' (Ō&S, 147)

Such a combination is often more like a compound preposition that is used in the passive. It marks the subject of the action—the actor, as in "Pà lǎo-gōng" 怕老公 [Fearing my husband] (*juàn* 3, no. 19):

寧可**撥來老公**打子頓，郲(=哪)捨得從小私情一旦空。
'However, I would prefer to **be beaten by my husband**; how could I bear to give up my secret childhood lover in sudden emptiness.' (Ō&S, 167)

"Yī biān ài" 一邊愛 [Unrequited love] (*juàn* 3, no. 3):
放我在腳跟頭睏介夜，情願**撥來你**千憎萬厭到大天光。
'Allow me to sleep at your feet tonight; I would willingly be hated and detested **by you** through the night into bright day.' (Ō&S, 153)

Shāngē does not use the Mandarin passive *gěi* 給, but it does use Mandarin *bèi* 被.

被 *bèi* /bhé⁶/ [bɛ³¹]

"Mán-rén" 瞞人 [Deception] (*juàn* 1, no. 27):
結識私情要放乖，弗要眉來眼去**被**人猜。
'When you have an illicit affair, you must be skillful. You must not exchange glances with your lover and be guessed about **by** others.' (Ō&S, 98)

"Zhòu-mà" 咒罵 [The curse] (*juàn* 7, no. 9):
當初來往，是誰請你？如今撇我，**被**人説是講非。
'When we began our romance, who asked you to come? Now I have been cast aside, and am criticized and gossiped about **by** others.' (Ō&S, 277)

"Hòu tíng-xīn" 後庭心 [The back courtyard] (*juàn* 7, no. 11):
硬郎不過，只得順情。**被**人看見，壞奴好名。
'Resisting him in vain, all one can do is obey him. If seen **by** others, I will lose my reputation.' (Ō&S, 278)

"Zhú fū-rén" 竹夫人 [The bamboo pillow] (*juàn* 8, no. 11):
穿窗入戶，到奴枕旁，奴的東西**被你**長偷慣。
'Through the window into the house, arriving beside my pillow, my stuff is accustomed to being frequently stolen **by** you.'

In the recent history of Chinese, many examples of the passive *chī* 吃/喫 are found across a wide area (Liú and Jiāng 1992, 210). In the present day it survives only rarely in the Wú dialects. But it is still rather common in Mǐn dialects, where it is normally written as *qǐ* 乞 (Chén Zhāngtài 1991, 301). This is a rather interesting phenomenon.

Conjunctions indicating connections

Conjunctions that indicate connection primarily include *tīng* 聽, which is used most (40 times), *dā (zi)* 搭 (子), and *tì* 替. The Mandarin conjunction *hé* 和 appears only four times, of which three are in *juàn* 10.

聽 ***tīng*** /ting¹/ [t'in⁴⁴] (1) As a conjunction that connects two equal sentence components, usually nouns, meaning 'and', as in

"Yòu [Mánfū]" 又 (瞞夫) [Variation on "Being Unfaithful to My Husband"] (*juàn* 1, no. 25):
姐**聽**情哥拍面來，再喫我裏親夫看見子了兩分開。
'Although she **and** her lover passed each other face to face, she was seen by her husband, so each of them went their separate way.' (Ō&S, 97)

"Yòu (Zhuō jiān)" 又(捉姦) [Variation on "Catching the Adulterer in the Act"] (*juàn* 1, no. 29):
郎呀，我**聽**你并膽同心一箇人能介好。
'Darling, you **and** I are like one person who share a gall bladder and one heart.' (Ō&S, 103)

(2a) As a preposition meaning 'with', 'together with', as in "Zhēng" 爭 [Dispute] (*juàn* 4, no. 18):
爹爹也弗要來娘房裏去，哥哥也弗許**聽**箇嫂同床。
'But father must not go to mom's room, either; and my older brother must not go to bed **with** his wife, my sister-in-law.' (Ō&S, 193)

"Wāi-chán" 歪纏 [Disputation] (*juàn* 8, no. 13):
我也無介氣力**聽**渠叉嘴，自**聽**賣魚個開言。
'I have no energy to cut in the conversation **with** her. I'll talk **with** the fish seller.'

(2b) As a preposition indicating beneficiaries of an action meaning 'for', 'on behalf of', as in "Cǎi huā" 採花 [Picking flowers] (*juàn* 2, no. 15):
隔河看見野花開，寄聲情郎**聽我**採朵來。
Seeing wildflowers blooming across the river, I send word to my lover to pick one **for me**. (Ō&S, 134)

"Zhēnglóng" 蒸籠 [Bamboo steamer tray] (*juàn* 8, no. 5):
我為你受子幾呵頭頭腦腦，盡閣在肚裡；長長短短，儕**聽你**包容。
'For you I've put up with lots of bossy complaints, I keep it all in my belly; the long and the short of it, I put up with it all **for you**.'

(2c) As a preposition indicating the person being spoken to or of whom a request is made meaning 'from' or 'to', as in modern Mandarin *gēn* 跟, *xiàng* 向.

"Zuì-gōng chuáng" 醉公床 [A rocking chair] (*juàn* 2, no. 26):
使盡機謀湊子我裡箇郎，**聽箇外婆**借子醉公床。
'Having lured my lover to my room with many tricks, I have borrowed a reclining bed **from my grandmother**.' (Ō&S, 142)

"Shē-zhē" 奢遮 [Cleverness] (*juàn* 2, no. 31):
結識箇姐兒忒奢遮，**聽渠**咦討荷包咦討鞋。
'The girl with whom I have fallen in love is so clever; I once asked for both a small bag and a pair of shoes **from her**.' (Ō&S, 145)

Dāzi 搭(子) and *tì* 替 are also of similar usage as propositions, but they are much less common.

搭子 *dā-zi* /daq⁷tzy/ [ta?⁵tsʅ³⁴]

"Dǎ shuāng-lù" 打雙陸 [Playing backgammon] (*juàn* 1, no. 26):
姐兒窗下織白羅，情郎**搭子我裏箇人**打雙陸。
'I am weaving a white silk cloth by the window. My lover is playing backgammon **with my husband**.' (Ō&S, 98)

"Xún láng" 尋郎 [Looking for my lover] (*juàn* 1, no. 10):
搭郎好子喫郎虧，正是要緊時光弗見子渠。
'Since I became close **with my lover**, I been treated unfairly by him. At the most important times, he is not to be seen.' (Ō&S, 80)

"Fènjī" 糞箕 [The dustpan] (*juàn* 6, no. 25):
結識私情像糞箕，只沒要**搭箇苔帚**兩箇做夫妻。
'My secret love is like a dustpan, but one that didn't get married **to a broom**, the two becoming husband and wife.' (Ō&S, 244)

替 *tì* /ti⁵/ [tʻi⁴¹²] is mainly found in long songs such as in "Bí-qí cí-gū" 荸薺茨菇 [The water chestnut and the arrowhead tuber] (*juàn* 6, no. 43):

郎**替嬌娘**像荸薺，荸薺要**搭茨菇**兩箇做夫妻。
'He is **to her** like a water chestnut. The water chestnut wants to form a married couple **with the arrowhead tuber**.' (Ō&S, 258)

"Chén māma" 陳媽媽 [Mama Chén] (*juàn* 9, no. 1):
虧殺子湯家姐姐**替我**合得人緣。
'How fortunate that the young lady of the Tāng family joined fates **with me**.'

"Shāo xiāng niángniáng" 燒香娘娘 [The incense lady] (*juàn* 9, no. 5):
四個銅錢**替我**買條紅頭繩。
'Four pieces of copper have bought **for me** a length of red yarn for my hair.'

(Note that in the first example above, *tì* 替 and *dā* 搭 appear together.)

和 *hé* /hhu²/ [həu²³]

"Lěng" 冷 [Coldness] (*juàn* 3, no. 5):
我當初結識你哈裏好像寶**和**珍。
'You really looked like precious things **and** pearls when we first met.' (Ō&S, 155)

The disposal construction

In the *Shāngē*, the most commonly used preposition for the disposal construction is *zhuō* 捉, while Mandarin *bǎ* 把 is also used.

捉 *zhuō* /joq⁷/ [tsoʔ⁵] (1) A preposition that brings focus on the objects of actions. Its usage and constraints are similar to Mandarin *bǎ* 把 (for example, it is generally used with complex verb phrases), such as in "Yòu (Ā-yí)" 又 (阿姨) [Variation on "The Wife's Younger Sister"] (*juàn* 4, no. 17):

揪起子竹竿拔起子櫓，**捉**箇小阿姨推倒在後船倉。
'Having pulled the bamboo pole out of the water and drawn in the oar, he **took** his sister-in-law and pushed her down in the rear cabin.' (Ō&S, 191)

"Mén shén" 門神 [Door God] (*juàn* 9, no. 2):
記得去年大年三十夜，**捉**我千刷萬刷。
'I recall that on New Year's Eve last year, he **took** me and brushed me a thousand times over.'

"Kuíhuā" 葵花 [The sunflower] (*juàn* 6, no. 49):
郎呀，我**捉**你當子天上日頭，一心只對子你。
'My beau, I take you to be the sun in the sky; my heart turns only to you.' (Ō&S, 262)

(2) A preposition that marks the instrument or thing used in the action, as in Mandarin *ná* 拿 and *yòng* 用. For example, in "Zǒu" 走 [Passing by] (*juàn* 1, no. 17):

郎在門前走子七八遭，姐在門前只**捉**手來搖。
'The lover walks past her gate seven or eight times. She stands by the gate and simply waves **using** her hand.' (Ō&S, 88)

"Yú-chuán-fù dǎ shēng-rén xiāng-mà" 魚船婦打生人相罵 [The woman on the boat quarrels with the hunter] (*juàn* 9, no. 8):
各有道路各自做人，盡弗消得老鸛跌倒只**捉**嘴來撐。
'Each has one's own path; each conducts oneself as one wants. But none wishes to be the old crane who **uses** his beak to support himself when he falls.'

"Guāi" 乖 [Cleverness] (*juàn* 1, no. 22):
娘又乖，姐又乖，吃娘**捉**箇石灰滿房篩。
'Mother is clever, but her daughter is clever too. Mother has **taken** lime and sprinkled it throughout the room.' (Ō&S, 93)

Sometimes, a *zhuō* 捉 phrase—*zhuō* 捉 + noun—can be followed by the complement *lái* 來. This construction represents a transitional stage in the development from verb to preposition. Examples include "Zhà kùn" 詐睏 [Pretending to sleep] (*juàn* 2, no. 20):

郎做子急水裏螞蝗只**捉**腰**來**倒下去。
'He **used** his waist to **move** down, like a leech in the rapids.' (Ō&S, 137)

"Zuànzi" 鑽子 [The awl] (*juàn* 8, no. 6):
和身靠緊我來用力，一雙眼睛弗住介**捉**我**來**關關。
'With his body leaning close and tight to me, his two eyes ceaselessly take me in their gaze.'

Sometimes in rhymed verse a *zhuō* 捉 phrase can be followed by a plain, unmodified verb, as in "Xiāngxià rén" 鄉下人 [A countryman] (*juàn* 5, no. 4):

鄉下人弗識枷裏人，忽然看見只**捉**舌頭**伸**。
'A countryman didn't know that criminals are locked in cangues. On seeing one all of a sudden, he **took** his tongue and **stuck it out** [in surprise].' (Ō&S, 201)

把 *bǎ* /bo³/ [po⁵²] The book has 21 examples, 8 of which appear in *juàn* 10. See the two examples cited in Section 2 above. Six other instances are found in long songs or ancient-style poems, which are not examples of colloquial usage.

Position or existence

In *Shāngē*, basically *lái* 來 /lé²/ [lɛ²³] is one of the principal verbs indicating movement or existence (as with Mandarin *zài* 在), though *lái* 來 /laq⁸/ [laʔ²³] can also function as a preposition or complement to indicate position, and other related meanings as described below.

來 *lái* /lé²/ [lɛ²³] (1) A verb meaning 'in, at, on'. For example, in "Diū zhuān-tou" 丟磚頭 [Tossing Bricks] (*juàn* 8, no. 1):

啥個**來**個銅關口外，遠處他方？
'Who is at the Tóngguānkǒu place, far away in another land?'

來 *lái* /lé²/ [lɛ²³] (2a) As a preposition used in front of verb phrases to indicate the location of the action. For example, in "Lì qīu" 立秋 [The beginning of autumn] (*juàn* 2, no. 27):

姐兒**來**箇紅羅帳裏做風流。
'She is busy making love **inside** the red bed curtains.' (Ō&S, 142)

"Bǎi cí táng" 擺祠堂 [Making an altar to her dead lover] (*juàn* 7, no. 4):
再**來**檢妝裡面擺祠堂。
'I also place an altar to him **on** my dressing table.' (Ō&S, 272)

The preposition *lái* 來 can be confused with the verb *lái* 來, leading to ambiguity in certain contexts. For example, in "Yòu [zèng wù]" 又 (贈物) [Variation on "A Gift"] (*juàn* 1, no. 28):

再來綠紗窗下送汗巾。
'My lover also gave me a handkerchief **beside** the green screen window.'

The ambiguity allows an alternative meaning to be construed from this passage:

'My lover **came** again to the green screen window, and gave me a handkerchief.' (Ō&S, 100)

(2b) As a preposition used in front of verb phrases to introduce the places passed by in the action, meaning 'from', 'over', or 'by', similar to Mandarin *cóng* 從. For example, in "Shàng qiáo" 上橋 [Crossing the bridge] (*juàn* 7, no. 3):

若有村東頭村西頭南北兩橫頭，二十後生連垂頭，肯來小阿奴奴仙橋上過。
'No matter where, from the east, west, south or north of our village, if a twenty-year old young man is attractively dressed, please let him cross **over** my "immortal bridge."' (Ō&S, 271)

(2c) As a complement used after verbs to indicate the direction or destination of the action, meaning 'to', 'onto', or 'into', similar to Mandarin complements *zài* 在 and *dào* 到. For example, in "Lì qiū" 立秋 [The beginning of autumn] (*juàn* 2, no. 27):

一雙白腿扛來郎肩上就像橫塘人捎藕上蘇州。
'Her two white legs, she places **onto** her lover's shoulders, just as the natives of Héngtáng carry lotus roots on their shoulders to sell them in Sūzhōu.' (Ō&S, 77)

"Zhēng-lóng" 蒸籠 [Bamboo steamer tray] (*juàn* 8, no. 5):
因為你會安排，落來你箇圈套裡。
'Because you know how to arrange things, so that all falls **into** your circular trap.'

"Zhú fū-rén" 竹夫人 [The bamboo pillow] (*juàn* 8, no. 8):
挑我來十字街頭，東賣也弗要，西賣也弗成。
'Carry me **to** the four-way intersection; but no matter how you'll fail to sell any.'

(2d) As a verb complement to indicate the existence of incidents or the location and range of incidents, meaning 'in' or 'within', like Mandarin *zài* 在. Examples are in "Chūn huà" 春畫 [Erotic scenes] (*juàn* 2, no. 13):

箇樣出套風流家數儕有來奴肚裏。
'This entire set of amorous marital techniques, I have internalized **within** my belly.' (Ō&S, 133)

Note: In this example '*yǒu lái* 有來' "have within" is like '*yǒu zài* 有在', though such a construction is not grammatical in Mandarin.

"Yòu [niáng dǎ]" 又 [娘打] [Variation on "My Mother Beats Me"] (*juàn* 1, no. 24):
小阿奴奴便打殺來香房也罷休。
'In such a case I would willingly be beaten to death **within** this room.' (Ō&S, 96)

(2e) As a verb complement introducing the beneficiary—indirect object—of an action when the verb means 'to give' or 'to present'. For example, in the passive construction discussed above, "Yòu (Jiě-er shēng dé)" 又 (姐兒生得) [Variation on "Such a Beautiful Girl!"] (*juàn* 2, no. 1):

> 賣茶客人，爾弗要撥箇粗枝硬梗屑**來我**……
> 'Hey tea seller, don't you get me soiled by **giving me** the leavings of that thick branch and hard stalk of yours . . .' (Ō&S, 112)

And in "Xiézi" 鞋子 [Shoes] (*juàn* 9, no. 3):

> 拿我准**來渠**子，挑子我了行程。
> 'Give me **to him** as a trade, to carry me along the way.'

It is of interest to note that the Mandarin word *gěi* 給 never shows up in the *Shāngē* 山歌 as a verb or preposition meaning 'to give'.

(2f) As a complement introducing the person spoken to, for example, in "Shān rén" 山人 [Hill people] (*juàn* 9, no. 7):

> 若還弗信，待我唱隻《駐雲飛》**來你**聽聽。
> 'If you still do not believe it, let me sing "Zhù yún fēi" [On flying clouds] **for you** to listen to.'

> "Dìng guǐ mén" 釘鬼門 [Watch the gate of hell—stir up rumors] (*juàn* 7, no. 12):
> 咦有閒人搬**來我**裏箇聽。
> 'A troublesome man came and **told my husband** about it.' (Ō&S, 336)

來搭 *lái-dā* /lé²daq⁷/ [lɛ²³taʔ⁴], **來裏** *lái-lǐ* /lé²li⁴/ [lɛ²³li⁵²], **來呵** *lái-hē* /lé²ho¹/ [lɛ²³ho⁵²]

In this set of forms, *lái* 來 /lé²/ [lɛ²³] is an existential verb that means 'to be in/at/on', similar to Mandarin *zài* 在, while the suffixes *dā* 搭, *lǐ* 裏/裡 and *hē* 呵 reference the nearness or farness of the position. When combined, these words mean 'to be here/there'.

(1) Used as a verb to indicate 'to exist', similar to Mandarin *yǒu* 有 and *zài* 在. For example, in "Wāi chán" 歪纏 [Disputation] (*juàn* 8, no. 13):

> 姐兒便問箇釣魚箇："啥魚**來**呵？"
> 'The young girl asked the fisherman: "What fish **is** this **here**?"'

> "Yòu yǐn" 又 (引) [Variation on "Seduction"] (*juàn* 1, no. 16):
> 螢火蟲，娘**來裏**，爺**來裏**。
> 'Fireflies, mummy **is here** and daddy **is here**.' (Ō&S, 88)

> "Mén shén" 門神 [Door God] (*juàn* 9, no. 2):
> 我有介隻曲子在裡，到唱**來你**聽聽。
> 'I have this song here, to sing **here while** you listen.'

(2) Used as an adverb in front of a verb to indicate that actions are ongoing, like Mandarin *zhèngzài* 正在. For example, in "Shān rén" 山人 [Hill people] (*juàn* 9, no. 7):

咦弗**來裡**作揖畫卯，咦弗**來裡**放告投文。
'Neither **here in the midst of** bowing in greeting and reporting to work, nor **here in the midst of** making reports and submitting documents.'

"Wāi-chán" 歪纏 [Disputation] (*juàn* 8, no. 13):
正**來裡**説價錢弗了，後生看見鼻搭嘴踵趕到門前。
'Just as she was **here in the process of** ceaselessly haggling the price, seeing it, the lad rushed swaying to the door.'

"Sī-qíng bào" 私情報 [Revenge Over The Affair] (*juàn* 5, no. 27):
偷子私情轉得自家箇門，家婆再也**來搭**結私情。
'Having committed adultery and come back home, it turns out that my wife is also **having** an adulterous liaison **right here**!' (Ō&S, 220)

(3) Used as complement after verbs or adjectives to indicate the result or continuing state, similar to Mandarin *zhē* 着. For example, in "Hébāo" 荷包 [The pouch] (*juàn* 6, no. 13):

你有子銅錢銀子但憑你閣**來阿**，只沒要無錢空把布裙鬻。
'Whatever coins you have, copper or silver, you can **set it right down**;
But if you have no money, please do not roll up my skirt in vain.' (Ō&S, 234)

"Tāng pózi zhú-fū-ren xiāng mà" 湯婆子竹夫人相罵 [The hot water bottle and the bamboo pillow quarrel with each other] (*juàn* 8, no. 9):
兩箇儕跪**來搭**，直到更盡夜深。
'The two both **kneeling right there**, 'till the last watch was called in the deep of the night.'

"Yòu (wú láng)" 又 (無郎) [Variation on "Lonely"] (*juàn* 1, no. 8):
囉裏東村頭西村頭南北兩横頭二十後生閧**來搭**。
'Wherever it be, to the north or to the south, there is a twenty-year-old fellow **hanging out there**.' (Ō&S, 79)

在 *zài* /dzé⁶/ [ZE³¹] This is a Guānhuà word. There are 68 examples in *Shāngē* 山歌 [Mountain songs] in which *zài* 在 is used as a verb or a preposition. For example, in "Suō" 睃 [A glance] (*juàn* 1, no. 2):

絲網捉魚盡**在**眼上起，千丈綾羅梭裏來。
'The fishing net catches fish **in** its open-eye weave. A single shuttle, like a single glance, yields a thousand silk cloths.' (Ō&S, 67)

"Áo" 熬 [Enduring torment] (*juàn* 1, no. 9)
二十姐兒睏弗著，**在**踏床上登，一身白肉冷如冰。
'A sleepless twenty-year-old girl sits **at** the foot of her bed. Her whole body as white and frozen as ice.' (Ō&S, 80)

"Zuò shēn fèn" 做身分 [Affectation] (*juàn* 3, no. 10)
搭爛子黃蔥我箇心還**在**。
'Just as a rotten onion is still alive inside, my heart for you still **is there**.' (Ō&S, 159)

"Yòu āyí" 又[阿姨] [Variation on "The Wife's Younger Sister"] (*juàn* 4, no. 17)
小阿奴奴好像寄做**在**人家一缸頭白酒，主人未吃你先嘗。
'I am just like a jug of white spirit whose brewing has been entrusted **at** a third party's, you taste it first before the master drinks it.' (Ō&S, 191)

"Zǒu mǎ dēng" 走馬燈 [The revolving lantern] (*juàn* 6, no. 29)
一時間火發喫你騙得團團轉，如今再高閣**在**暗頭裡子弗分明。
'By cheating on me, you made me spin round and round with the air heated by the fire. Now I have been put back in the dark, **on** a high shelf where I can no longer shine.' (Ō&S, 247)

"Cāo qín" 操琴 [Playing the lute] (*juàn* 7, no. 15)
姐**在**房中織白綾，郎**來**窗外手操琴。
'She was weaving white satin **in** her room; he was playing the lute **by** the window.' (Ō&S, 283)

Note that the final example uses *zài* 在 and *lái* 來 together.

在裡 *zài-lǐ* /dzé⁶li³/ [zE²⁴li¹], **在搭** *zài-dā* /dzé⁶daq⁷/ [zE²⁴ta?¹], **在上** *zài-shàng* /dzé⁶/ [zE²⁴zã¹], **來上** *lái-shàng* /laq⁸láng⁶/ [la?²³lã⁵²]

Like *lái-dā* 來搭、*lái-lǐ* 來裡、*lái-hē* 來呵, these words are a mix of literary forms (*zài* 在, *shàng* 上) and dialect forms (*lǐ* 裡, *dā* 搭, *lái* 來). *Zài-shàng* 在上 and *lái-shàng* 來上 emphasize something is on a surface. For example, in "Mén shén" 門神 [Door God] (*juàn* 9, no. 2):

我有介隻曲子**在裡**，到唱來你聽聽。
'I have this song **here**, to sing while you listen.'

"Chén mā-mā" 陳媽媽 [Mama Chén] (*juàn* 9, no. 1):
雙膀彎裡，我常常**在搭**風流飄蕩。
'Within the curve between one's thighs, I am frequently **in there** dissolutely drifting.'

"Zuì-gōng chuáng" 醉公床 [A rocking chair] (*juàn* 2, no. 26):
等我裏情哥郎**來上**做介一箇推車勢，強如涼床口上硬彭彭。
'When my lover comes and does the push cart position with me **on it** (the rocker), it is far better than the hard bamboo bed.' (Ō&S, 142)

"Chén māma" 陳媽媽 [Mama Chén] (*juàn* 9, no. 1):
壯羅多，油碌碌，新出籠饅頭能個樣物事，**在上**游了游，到有星滋味。
'Plump and greasy, buns fresh out of the steamer are like that, **on top** they slip about so, and yet are rather flavorful.'

Other examples of *zài* 在 include, "Kùn fú zháo" 睏弗着 [Unable to sleep] (*juàn* 8, no. 12):

姐兒正**在**疑惑，只聽得窗外門敲。
'The young girl was **in the midst of** uncertainty, when she heard a knock on the door outside the window.'

"Chén māma" 陳媽媽 [Mama Chén] (*juàn* 9, no. 1):
到如今再捉我做子被頭裡個抹布，常**搭**我風流**所在**去纏綿。
'Now I'm taken to be a rag under the covers, and often **in** that sensual **spot** of mine **therein** gone tenderly entangled.'

The negative imperative

The most common forms of the negative imperative in the *Shāngē* are *méi* 沒 and *méi-yào* 沒要', which together occur 38 times. These words do not mean 'not have', but rather mean 'do not'. This form is of interest as it does not appear in modern Sūzhōu dialect or other surrounding dialects. But, as it is used frequently in the book it cannot be considered to have originated in Guānhuà.

沒 *méi* /meq^8/ [mə?^{23}], 沒要 *méi-yào* /meq^{8}iau^5/ [mə?^{23}iæ^{412}]

In "Zuàn-zi" 鑽子 [The awl] (*juàn* 8, no. 6):

上箍下箍箍緊子我，你自一家快活**沒**撥來別人鑽。
'Wrap round on top, wrap round below, wrap round me tightly. Take the thrill yourself and don't allow others to drill in.'

"Yòu liǎng láng" 又 (兩郎) [Variation on "Two Men"] (*juàn* 4, no. 10):
同結箇私情**沒要**爭，過子黃昏還有五箇更。
'If two seek illicit love with the same person, they **should not** fight about it. After dusk there are still five watches 'till morning.' (Ō&S, 355)

A few examples of *méi* 沒 in *Shāngē* use the Guānhuà meaning of 'not have, without'. The following example is a note by the editor appended to "Yú-chuán fù-nǚ dǎ shēng-rén xiāng-mà" 魚船婦女打生人相罵 [The woman on the boat quarrels with the hunter] (*juàn* 9, no. 8):

吳語謂**沒**正經曰「趙」，因曰「趙談春」云。
'In Wú dialect "to be **without** decency" is called *zhào*; hence the name Zhào Tánchūn is a play on words [meaning "indecently chat about erotica"]'.

Concluding Discussion

In the above presentation of vocabulary and grammatical forms seen in the *Shāngē* there is a clear predominance of Wú dialect types. Yet Guānhuà forms are also interspersed within the songs, sometimes even interchangeably with the dialect forms. We see this most obviously in the function words that Féng Mènglóng often adopted from Guānhuà for corresponding dialect meanings, resulting in a mix of language varieties. Clearly Féng could not fully free himself of the influence of Guānhuà when recording the Wú folk songs he collected in *Shāngē*. Hence even in a text widely recognized to be in pure dialect, the language is not a pristine version of the colloquial dialect speech of its time and place.

Yet the basic Wú dialect nature of the *Shāngē* is still remarkable when considered in light of the overall dominance of Guānhuà in other Míng vernacular texts. In most texts, where dialect forms appear they are incorporated within a broader, clearly Guānhuà base. For example:

嗄飯 *xià fàn* /hho⁶van⁶/ [ɦo¹³ᴠᴇ²¹] an Wú dialect word for 'dishes to accompany rice', which can also be written *xià-fàn* 下飯, is often used in the Wú form without being distinguished from other Guānhuà elements, as in Féng Mènglóng's *Xǐngshì héngyán* 醒世恆言 [Lasting tales to arouse the world] (*juàn* 37):

Nà jiǔjiā zhǐ dào tā shēnbiān hái yǒu tóngqián, xià fàn ànjiǔ, liúshuǐ bān lái.
那酒家只道他身邊還有銅錢，**嗄飯**案酒，流水搬來。
'The owner of the tavern presumed that he had fair bit of cash on him, and so provided him with a constant stream of **food to down his rice**, and snacks to down his wine.'

And in *Pāi'àn jīngqí* 拍案驚奇 [Tales of Table-Slapping Marvel] by Líng Méngchū 凌濛初 (1580–1644), (*juàn* 27):

Xiàn zǎi qǐng Wáng jiàoshòu yá zhōng yǐn jiǔ, chī dào zhōngjiān, xià fàn zhōng ná chū biē lái.
縣宰請王教授衙中飲酒，吃到中間，**嗄飯**中拿出鱉來。
'The county official invited Scholar Wang for a drink in the Yámen. As they ate, among the **dishes to go with rice**, a soft-shelled turtle was brought out.'

Only rarely the author might point out clearly that some words are dialect, for instance in *Wú-jiāng xuě* 吳江雪 [Snow on the Wú river] by Wúzhōng Pèihéngzǐ 吳中佩蘅子 (n.d.), (Chapter 2, *juàn* 1):

*Yuánlái **Wú zhòng de xiāngtán**, 'fùqin' jiàozuò "lǎoguān"; páoguā, páozi lǎole qiā bu rù, jiù bǎ lái zuò chēnghu fùqin de yǎhào.*
原來**吳中的鄉談**，父親叫做"老官"。匏瓜、匏子老了掐不入，就把來做稱呼父親的雅號。
'As it turns out, in **Wú vernacular** "*lǎoguān*" [venerable old official] means "father". It is difficult to nip open old bottle gourds [because they are tough]. So, people use [*lǎoguān*, close in pronunciation to *lǎoguā* "old gourd"] as a respectful address for their fathers.'

And in *Xiàolín guǎngjì* 笑林廣記 by Yóuxì Zhǔrén 遊戲主人 [The master of games] (*juàn* 1):

Bú-guò xìng Lǐ de xiǎo hú-sūn, yǒu le jǐ-gè chòu tóng-qián, yī-shí jiù Duó-Zhào qǐ-lai. Yuán zhù: Wú-sú wèi rén dāi yuē Zhào.
不過姓李的小猢猻，有了幾個臭銅錢，一時就鐸趙起來。原注：吳俗謂人呆曰趙。
'Whenever that rascally ape, whose last name is Lǐ, gets a hold of a stinking bit of money he becomes a dunderheaded Duó and Zhào type. *Note:* **Wú colloquial** refers to the dunderheaded as "Zhào."'

Sometimes an author will add notes regarding dialect pronunciation, for example in *Jiǔwěihú* 九尾狐 [Nine-Tailed Fox] by Pínghuā Zhǔrén 評花主人 (n.d.) (Chapter 14):

> *Bō **bié (dú bái)** rén kàn-jian zai, xiàng shá yàng-shì? Ā yào nán-wéi-qíng ga?*
> 撥別（讀白）人看見仔，像啥樣式？阿要難為情嘎？
> 'If you let others see you (*bié* is pronounced like *bái* /bheq⁸/ [bə?²³]), what would that be like? Wouldn't you be embarrassed?'

Both the *Shāngē* and the *Jiǔwěihú* give great emphasis to dialect pronunciation. So similar notes appear frequently in the two books.

But this is not the case in most literary materials, because most authors cannot distinguish dialects from Guānhuà. As a result, they often inadvertently insert dialect elements. The result is that it we cannot definitively tell the difference between dialect and Guānhuà in the texts. Below we look at the dialect usage of *kuài* 快 as an example to illustrate the situation in literary materials.

快 *kuài* /kua⁵/ [kuɑ⁴¹²] (1) Used after a verb or an adjective to indicate imminent change or imminent action, as in Féng Mènglóng's *Jǐngshì tōngyán* 警世通言 (*juàn* 15):

> *Lì fáng yě yǒu guǎn guò de, yě yǒu **yì mǎn kuài** de, yǐ bú zài shù nèi.*
> 吏房也有管過的，也有**役滿快**的，已不在數內。
> 'In the Ministry of Personnel, some officials have undertaken this job before. Some **will end their term of office soon** and are not included.'

It is often followed by the sentence final aspect particle *le* 了 (or *zāi* 哉), as in Féng Mènglóng's *Xǐngshì héngyán* 醒世恒言 (*juàn* 37):

> *Sān wàn yín-zi **dào shǒu kuài le**, zěn-me nèn-yàng méi fú, dào shú-shuì le qù, nòng dào zhè shí-hou!*
> 三萬銀子**到手快了**，怎麼恁樣沒福，倒熟睡了去，弄到這時候！
> 'You would **soon have** had thirty-thousand in silver in your hands. How are you so lacking in fortune, that you fell so fast asleep, and did not wake up until now!'

Shíwěiguī 十尾龜 [Ten tailed turtle] by Lù Shiè 陸士諤 (Chapter 13):

> *Lā-cháng diào-zi, chàng le yī huì. Lín-shí **zǒu kuài**, yòu zài-sān zhǔ-fu.*
> 拉長調子，唱了一會。臨時**走快**，又再三囑咐。
> 'He stretched out the melody, and sang for a bit. When about to leave, he repeatedly exhorted [the others].'

Hǎitiān hóngxuě jì 海天鴻雪記 [Tale of vast sea of heaven's snow] by Èrchūn Jūshì 二春居士 (Chapter 4):

> ●問伯颺道："阿曾吃飯勒。"伯颺道："吃仔要**餓快哉**。"
> 'He asked Bóyáng, "Have you eaten?" Bóyáng answered, "Yes, but I'll be **hungry again soon**."'

(2) Used after a verb or an adjective to indicate nearness to a certain time or a certain degree, as in *Sānxiào* 三笑 [Three laughs] published in 1803 by Wú Xìntiān 吳信天 (n.d.) (Chapter 14):

> ●先生，吾里爺是肚……肚皮大個，住立朵，天光夜**快哉**。
> 'Sir, our father is the one with the big b..be..belly, [you can] stay here as it will be dusk **soon**.'

Fùpù Xiántán 負曝閒談 [Random conversations on the burden of exposure] by Qú Yuán 蘧園 (c. 1882–1907) (Chapter 18):

> ●倪聽仔**急煞快**，尋仔俚好幾埭，尋俚勿著。
> 'After hearing it we **soon grew terribly anxious**. We looked for him many times, but could not find him.'

Èrchūn Jūshì's *Hǎitiān hóngxuě jì* (Chapter 8):

> ●二百八十銅錢一日，倪主僕兩家頭住仔有兩個月**快哉**，阿要該點介？
> 'It costs two hundred and eighty coppers a day to live here. The two of us, me and my servant, will **soon** have lived here for two months. How should we figure the total?'

The four examples above that are marked with a black dot '●' are written in Wú dialect. But the other examples, with *pīnyīn* transcriptions, are based squarely on Guānhuà, such as those from the works by Féng Mènglóng and Líng Méngchū (collectively referred to as *Sānyán èrpāi* 三言二拍).

All extant Chinese vernacular literature generally contains a complex mix of linguistic features. Yet Guānhuà is the predominant actor. As illustrated earlier, when non-Mandarin elements are found, they are generally incorporated in with Guānhuà together in the same text.[4] In sum, then:

1. There are essentially no materials written purely in dialect. Thus, while the *Shāngē* are for the most part transcribed in dialect, they nonetheless contain elements from Guānhuà. Some *chuánqí* 傳奇 type romances also have whole passages written in dialect; yet these are not in pure dialect either.
2. Written vernacular literature is based on a mix of Guānhuà and simple classical Chinese. Sometime dialect elements are mixed in; but they frequently are difficult to discern.

Overall, we are able to conclude that the *Shāngē* are written primarily in Wú dialect but contain some elements of Guānhuà. Thus, the *Shāngē* are not an entirely true picture of the spoken dialect at that time, as Féng Mènglóng unconsciously inserted many Guānhuà forms. At the same time, the situation is a clear demonstration of the powerful influence that Guānhuà had in the Míng.

---

4. For further discussion of the mix of Guānhuà, dialect, and other elements in Míng and Qīng vernacular literature see the contributions to this volume by Huáng Lín in Chapter 4 and Zhāng Huìyīng in Chapter 5.

Note: This article was presented for the first time at the *International Workshop on the History of Colloquial Chinese—Written and Spoken*, March 11–12, 2016 at Rutgers University, NJ, USA, and received kind and helpful suggestions from other participants, for which the author is grateful. Subsequently, a preliminary version of this chapter appeared in Chinese as "Féng Mènglóng biān Wúyǔ míngē jí *Shāngē* lǐ de Guānhuà 馮夢龍編吳語民歌《山歌》裏的官話," *Kumamoto gakuen daigaku bungaku gengo-gaku ronshū* 熊本学園大学 文学・言語学論集 [KGU Journal of Language and Literature] 2017: 1.2, 53–65.

References

Primary sources

Féng Mènglóng 馮夢龍 (1574–1646). 1993. *Guàzhī-er, Shāngē* 掛枝兒·山歌. In *Féng Mènglóng quánjí* 馮夢龍全集 [The complete works of Féng Mènglóng], edited by Wèi Tóngxián 魏同賢. Shànghǎi: Shànghǎi gǔjí chūbǎnshè.

Secondary sources

Chén Zhāngtài 陳章太. 1991. "Dàtián xiàn nèi de fāngyán" 大田縣內的方言 [The Dàtián county dialect]. In *Mǐnyǔ yánjiū* 閩語研究, edited by Chén Zhāngtài and Lǐ Rúlóng 李如龍, 266–303. Běijīng: Yǔwén chūbǎnshè.

Liú Jiān 劉堅, and Jiāng Lánshēng 江藍生, et. al. 1992. *Jìndài Hànyǔ xūcí yánjiū* 近代漢語虛詞研究 [A study of grammatical particles in early Mandarin]. Běijīng: Yǔwén chūbǎnshè.

Ōki Yasushi 大木康. 2003. *Fū Bōryū* Sanka *no kenkyū* 馮夢龍「山歌」の研究 [Research on Féng Mènglóng's *Shāngē*], Tokyo: Keisō shobō 勁草書房.

Shěn Chǒngsuí 沈寵綏. 1959. "Dù qǔ xū zhī" 度曲須知 [What you need to know to go through the Qǔ-type songs]. In *Zhōngguó gǔdiǎn xìqǔ lùnzhù jíchéng* 中國古典戲曲論著集成, vol. 5, edited by Zhōngguó xìqǔ yánjiūyuàn 中國戲曲研究院. Běijīng: Zhōngguó xìjù chūbǎnshè.

Shí Rǔjié 石汝杰. 1989. "Féng Mènglóng biān *Shāngē* de xūcí zhájì" 馮夢龍編《山歌》的虛詞札記 [Notes on the function words in Féng Mènglóng's *Shāngē*]. *Hanazono daigaku kenkyū kiyō* 花園大學研究紀要 20: 69–79.

Shí Rǔjié 石汝杰. "*Xiàofǔ* zhōng suǒjiàn de Míng mò Wúyǔ" 《笑府》中所見的明末吳語 [The Wú dialect in the late Ming dynasty in *Xiàofǔ*]. *Chūbun kenkyū shūkan* 中文研究集刊 3: 53–72.

Shí Rǔjié 石汝杰. 1995. "Míngqīng xiǎoshuō hé Wúyǔ de lìshǐ yǔfǎ" 明清小説和吳語的歷史語法 [The historic grammar of novels in Ming and Qing dynasties and Wú dialect]." *Yǔyán yánjiū* 語言研究 [Studies in Language] 2: 177–85.

Shí Rǔjié 石汝杰. 1996. "*Shāngē* de yǔyán fēnxī" 《山歌》的語言分析 [Analysis of the language in *Shāngē*]." *Hokuriku daigaku kiyō* 北陸大學紀要 19: 201–9.

Shí Rǔjié 石汝杰. 2006. "Féng Mènglóng biān *Shāngē* de jiàozhù wèntí" 馮夢龍編《山歌》的校注問題 [The collation and annotation in Féng Mènglóng's *Shāngē*]." *Kaigai jijō kenkyū* 海外事情研究 34 (1): 111–28.

Shí Rǔjié 石汝杰. 2009. *Wúyǔ wénxiàn zīliào yánjiū* 吳語文獻資料研究 [Literature research on Wú dialect]. Tokyo: Kohbun 好文出版.

Shí Rǔjié 石汝杰. 2015. "Míngqīng shídài běibù wúyǔ rénchēng dàicí jí xiāngguān wèntí" 明清時代北部吳語人稱代詞及相關問題 [The personal pronoun and related problems in Wú dialect in northern areas in Ming and Qing dynasties]. *Zhōngguó fāngyán xuébào* 中國方言學報 5: 25–44.

Shí Rǔjié 石汝杰, and Miyata Ichirō 宮田一郎. 2005. *Míng Qīng Wúyǔ cídiǎn* 明清吳語詞典 [A dictionary of Wú dialect in the Míng and Qīng dynasties]. Shànghǎi: Shànghǎi císhū chūbǎnshè.

Shí Rǔjié 石汝杰, and Huáng Míngmíng 黄明明. 2007–2008a. "Féng Mènglóng biān *Shāngē* jiàozhù" 馮夢龍編《山歌》校注 [Collation and annotation of Féng Mènglóng's *Shāngē*] (Chapters 1, 3, 5, and 7). *Kumamoto gakuen daigaku·bungaku gengogaku ronshū* 熊本學園大學文學·言語學論集 14 (1): 185–213, 14 (2): 147–74, 15 (1): 177–204, 15 (2): 17–30.

Shí Rǔjié 石汝杰, and Huáng Míngmíng 黄明明. 2007–2008b. "Féng Mènglóng biān *Shāngē* jiàozhù 馮夢龍編《山歌》校注 [Collation and Annotation of Féng Mènglóng's *Shāngē*] (Chapters 2, 4, and 6)." *Kaigai jijō kenkyū* 海外事情研究 35 (1): 1–24, 35 (2): 109–34, 36 (1): 1–28.

Zhāng Huìyīng 張惠英. 1992–1996. Shāngē zhù 《山歌》注 (1–4) [Notes on Shāngē (1–4)]. *Kāipiān* 開篇: *Chūgoku gogaku kenkyū* 中國語學研究 [Studies in Chinese Linguistics] 10–13.

Additional References Used by Translator

Primary sources

Féng Mènglóng 馮夢龍 (1574–1646). n.d. *Shāngē* 山歌 [Mountain songs]. Source text: Scan of edition at Peking University Library digitized by China-America Digital Academic Library and online at ctext.org and archive.org.

Féng Mènglóng 馮夢龍 (1574–1646). n.d. *Xiào fǔ* 笑府 [Treasury of laughs]. Facsimile edition included in the *Féng Mènglóng quánjí* 馮夢龍全集 [Complete works of Féng Mènglóng]. Shànghǎi: Shànghǎi gǔjí chūbǎnshè, 1993. Electronic copy at ctext.org.

Gē Zài 戈載 (1786–1856). Preface 1821 (*Dàoguāng xīnsì* 道光辛巳年). *Cílín zhèngyùn* 詞林正韻 [Correct rimes of the forest of words]. Scan of edition at Peking University Library digitized by China-America Digital Academic Library and online at ctext.org and archive.org.

Shěn Chǒngsuí 沈寵綏 (d. c. 1645). 1639 (*Chóngzhēn jǐmǎo* 崇禎己卯年). *Dùqǔ xūzhī* 度曲須知 [How to sing Qǔ-type songs]. Color scan of original edition held at Harvard College Library Harvard-Yenching Library, Harvard University. Persistent Link http://nrs.harvard.edu/urn-3:FHCL:3567635.

Secondary references

Chao, Yuen Ren [Zhào Yuánrèn 趙元任]. 1928. *Studies in Modern Wu Dialects*. Peking: Tsing Hua College Research Institute. Reprint, Běijīng: Kēxué chūbǎnshè, 1956.

Chao, Yuen Ren [Zhào Yuánrèn 趙元任]. 1956. "Wú yīn dānzì biǎo" 吳音單字表 [Common Wú Syllabary]. In reprint of Chao 1928, 159–206.

Hsu Pi-ching. 2015. *Féng Mènglóng's Treasury of Laughs: A Seventeenth-Century Anthology of Traditional Chinese Humour*. Boston: Brill.

Norman, Jerry (Luó Jiéruì 羅杰瑞). 2006. "Common Dialectal Chinese." In *The Chinese Rime Tables*, edited by David Branner, 233–54. Amsterdam: Benjamins. Chinese translation: Shǐ Hàoyuán 史皓元 [Richard VanNess Simmons] and Zhāng Yànhóng 張艷紅. 2011. "*Hànyǔ fāngyán tōngyīn*" 漢語方言通音. *Fangyan* 方言 2: 97–116.

Norman, Jerry (Luó Jiéruì 羅杰瑞). 2011. "Hànyǔ fāngyán tōngyīn" 漢語方言通音 [Common dialectal Chinese]. *Fangyan* 方言 2: 97–116. A translation and a revised version of Norman 2006, translated by Richard VanNess Simmons and Zhāng Yànhóng 張艷紅.

Ōki, Yasushi, and Paolo Santangelo. 2011. *Shan'ge, the 'Mountain Songs': Love Songs in Ming China*. Boston: Brill.

Shí Rǔjié 石汝傑, and Chén Liǔjìng 陳榴竸. 1989. Shāngē *suǒyǐn* (Sanka *sakuin*) 山歌索引 [Index to *Shāngē*]. Chūgoku gogaku kenkyū 中國語學研究 [Studies in Chinese Linguistics], *Kāi piān* 開篇, Tankan 單刊 [Monograph] no. 2. Tokyo: Kohbun 好文.

4
Changes in Language Use as Reflected in *Shuǐhǔ zhuàn* Passages Embedded in the *Jīn Píng Méi cíhuà*

Huáng Lín

Introduction

In adopting textual content from the *Shuǐhǔ zhuàn* 水滸傳, the *Jīn Píng Méi cíhuà* 金瓶梅詞話 inserted a great deal of dialect and colloquial expressions. In this way, this novel effected a transformation toward the adoption of rustic expressions in the *báihuà* 白話 colloquial of the traditional Chinese vernacular novel as the genre evolved. Among the expressions added in *Jīn Píng Méi cíhuà*, we find dialect and colloquial expressions that are characteristic of Wú dialects. Only these expressions are able truly to reflect the attributes of the dialect used by the author. This serves as a highly valuable reference for judging whether the author is a northerner or a person of the Wú region. Nonetheless, the name Yíng'ér 迎兒 [CDC Ngiang²nhi²] that is used in the first half of *Jīn Píng Méi cíhuà*, is written as Yíng'ér 蠅兒 [CDC Ying²nhi²] in the latter sections. This example raises challenging issues in determining whether the author is using Wú dialect or a northern (i.e., Mandarin) dialect.

Thirty years ago, in an article titled "*Zhōngyì shuǐhǔ zhuàn* yǔ *Jīn Píng Méi cíhuà*" 忠義水滸傳與金瓶梅詞話 [Comparing the *Water Margin* and the *Plum in the Golden Vase*], I sorted out the prose text and rhyming verse of the *Zhōngyì shuǐhǔ zhuàn* that had been embedded in *Jīn Píng Méi cíhuà* [or simply *Cíhuà* below], and in the process was able to determine the period of composition and sort out the authorship and other questions (Huáng Lín 1982). This chapter further examines embedment in the *Jīn Píng Méi cíhuà* and how additions and deletions in the text transformed the language of the *Shuǐhǔ zhuàn*. In the process we see even more clearly the wide use of dialect and colloquial expressions in *Cíhuà*, which greatly enhanced the richness and vividness of its language.

Originally, the type and degree of the "vernacular" (*báihuà* 白話) in traditional Chinese vernacular fiction varied greatly. In longer novels such as *Sānguó yǎnyì* 三國演義 [Romance of the Three Kingdoms], the language is primarily classical Chinese, not vernacular, and there is almost no use of dialect colloquialisms. Whereas the *Shuǐhǔ zhuàn* is basically composed in *báihuà*—the plain Mandarin vernacular, with some dialect elements but not many overall. In 1919, Zhāng Míngfēi 張冥飛, in discussing the differences between *wényán* 文言 'classical Chinese' and *báihuà*, and comparing the use of the terms *súyǔ* 俗語 'colloquial language' and *fāngyán* 方言 'dialect', noted that "*Báihuà* is the primary form for fiction. Though fiction written in the classical language was created before the advent of *báihuà*, its dissemination and social impact does not reach the level of the vernacular (*báihuà*) novels" (Zhāng Míngfēi 1919, 4). In establishing that vernacular fiction based on colloquial language is distinct from fiction written in the classical language, Zhāng Míngfēi understood that there is a more rustic, coarse spoken language—*súhuà* 俗話—that differs from the common written vernacular *báihuà*. What he refers to as *súhuà* 'coarse language' is not merely in reference to coarse or informal conversational forms; even more fundamentally, it connotes the use of dialect. Thus he says that

> the vernacular language can be widely adopted, while colloquial (i.e. dialect) expressions are confined to the margins. For instance, Shanghai dialect words (*súhuà*) such as *āmùlín* 阿木林 [Aʔ³³moʔ⁵⁵lin²¹] 'country bumpkin, moron', *m̥shá* 嘸啥 [ʰm̥²²sA⁴⁴] 'have no (thing or problem)', as well as truncated or cryptic similes such as *tiānguān cì* . . . *(fú)* 天官賜......(福) [tʻi⁵³kuø²¹ sʅ³⁴ . . . (foʔ⁵⁵)] 'the heavenly official bestows . . . (*good fortune*)', and *zhūtóu sān* . . . *(shēng)* 豬頭三......(牲) [tsʅ⁵⁵ʰdɤ³³sE²¹ . . . (sən⁵³)] 'pig's head and the three . . . (*beasts* [of sacrifice])', cannot be understood by people from other places [outside the Wú dialect speaking region]. (Zhāng Míngfēi 1919, 4)

Hence Zhāng Míngfēi notes that

> *Érnǚ yīngxióng zhuàn* 兒女英雄傳 [Legends of young heroes and heroines] is written entirely in *báihuà*, but has a great deal of Zhílì 直隸 (modern Héběi 河北) and Shāndōng 山東 colloquial (*súyǔ*) mixed in. . . . And although the *Jīn Píng Méi* is written in the *báihuà* vernacular style, 90% is Míng period Shāndōng earthy colloquial (*súhuà*). (Zhāng Míngfēi 1919, 6)

Clearly, when he speaks of *súhuà*, Zhāng Míngfēi essentially means dialect (*fāngyán*); whereas with *báihuà* he means what is known today as the Mandarin-based literary vernacular.

On this basis, in sorting out some of the characteristics of language use in the traditional vernacular novel, Zhāng noted that

> *Shuǐhǔ* is written in *báihuà* with an admixture of *súhuà* [because] it contains a great amount of Yuán period expressions, such as *gàn niǎo (diǎo) ma* 干鳥麼 'What are you friggin' doin'?', *gàn dāi ma* 干呆麼 'What idiocy are you up to?' [As for *Jīn Píng Méi*,] it uses *súhuà* as *báihuà*—coarse language (dialect) as the vernacular. (Zhāng Míngfēi 1919, 51)

Zhāng contrasts these with later works such as the *Hóng lóu mèng* 紅樓夢 [Dream of red mansions], which he says is "*báihuà* vernacular with classical Chinese *wényán* mixed in," and with the *Érnǚ yīngxióng zhuàn*, which he says "uses Mandarin (Guānhuà 官話) as *báihuà*" (Zhāng Míngfēi 1919, 51). Hence, the language of the *Jīn Píng Méi* is distinguished by the highly colloquial language of the characters: the entire book is chock-full of colloquial dialect language (*fāngyán súyǔ* 方言俗語). Zhāng Míngfēi's views are basically quite tenable. *Jīn Píng Méi* indeed leaves readers feeling that it verges on a true earthy colloquial novel (*súyǔ xiǎoshuō* 俗語小說)—in effect, a novel in dialect (*fāngyán xiǎoshuō* 方言小說)—and that it was quite revolutionary with regard to language use in Chinese fiction.

Comparing the *Shuǐhǔ zhuàn* and the *Jīn Píng Méi cíhuà*

The present chapter dissects and unpacks how the *Jīn Píng Méi Cíhuà* embeds passages from the *Shuǐhǔ zhuàn*. Our analysis clearly reveals that the text of *Shuǐhǔ zhuàn* as modified by the author of the *Jīn Píng Méi*, Xiàoxiào Shēng 笑笑生, results in a vivid increase in colloquial dialect coloring. Consider the below examples:[1]

1. *Shuǐhǔ* 23.350 (SH Gǔjí 1.277): 我今日就參你在本縣做個都頭，如何？
   'I am thinking of making you a constable here. How about it?' (Shapiro 1.360)
   Cíhuà 01.8b: 我今日就參你在我這縣裡做個巡捕的都頭，**專一河東水西擒拿盜賊**，你意下如何？
   'If I were to appoint you to the post of police captain here **in Ch'ing-ho, with the responsibility for maintaining law and order throughout the jurisdiction**, what would you think?' (Roy 1.24)

2. *Shuǐhǔ* 24.356 (SH Gǔjí 1.280) 原來這婦人見武大身材短矮，人物猥獕，不會風流，這婆娘倒諸般好，為頭的愛偷漢子。
   'Since nothing about her husband pleased the girl—he was short and grotesque, and had no flair or merry-making whatever—Golden Lotus was quite ready to take a lover.' (Shapiro 1.363)
   Cíhuà 01.11b: 原來金蓮自從嫁武大，見他一味老實，人物猥獕，甚是**憎嫌**，常與他**合氣**。報怨大戶："普天世界斷生了男子，何故**將奴嫁與這樣個貨？**

---

1. The edition of *Shuǐhǔ zhuàn* transcribed here for comparison is the printing based on the 1589 *Zhōngyì Shuǐhǔ zhuàn* 忠義水滸傳 edition with preface by Wāng Dàokūn 汪道昆 (1525–1593) published by *Rénmín wénxué chūbǎnshè*. For reference, the translator of the present article also consulted a 1984 edition published by *Shànghǎi gǔjí*. Here and following, the former is indicated as "*Shuǐhǔ*," with chapter (*huí* 回) and page numbers separated by a period; the latter is indicated by "SH Gǔjí" with volume and page numbers separated by a period. The edition of the *Jīn Píng Méi Cíhuà* used is the facsimile of the Míng Wànlì 萬曆 (r. 1572–1620) edition held in the Běijīng Library and published by the Gǔyì xiǎoshuō kānxínghuì in Běijīng in 1933. Here and following, passages from the *Jīn Píng Méi* are cited as "*Cíhuà*" also with chapter and page numbers separated by a period. Unless otherwise indicated, translations of the *Shuǐhǔ* passages are from Shapiro 1981, and translations of the *Cíhuà* passages are from Roy 1997–2013. Volume and page numbers, separated by periods, are provided for the English translations in reference to their sources.

Huáng Lín

每日牽著不走，打著倒退的。只是一味味 [=噇] 酒。著緊處，都是錐紮也不動。奴端的那世裡悔氣, 卻嫁了他！是好苦也！"

'It so happens that ever since Chin-lien had married Wu the Elder and had a chance to observe his guileless disposition and unsightly appearance she had **taken a violent dislike to him and quarreled with him** all the time. She resented what Mr. Chang had done to her and said to herself, "It's not as though there weren't another man in the whole wide world. **Why did he have to marry me off to the likes of this?**

If you tug him he won't move;
If you hit him he pulls back.

The only thing he can be counted on to do every day is to guzzle his wine. When you get right down to it, you could jab him with an awl without arousing him. What did I ever do in a previous incarnation to deserve such a fate? It's really intolerable."' (Roy 1.28)

3. *Shuǐhǔ* 24.357: (SH Gǔjí 1.281) 心裡尋思道："武松與他是嫡親一母兄弟，他又生的這般長大。我嫁得這等一個，也不枉了為人一世。你看我那三寸丁穀樹皮。三分相人，七分似鬼。我直恁地晦氣！據著武松，大蟲也吃他打了，他必然好氣力。說他又未曾婚娶，何不叫他搬來我家住？不想這段因緣卻在這裡。"

"'He's so big,' she thought. 'You'd never know they were born of the same mother. If I could have a man like that I wouldn't have lived in vain! With the one I've got I'm cursed for good! Three Inches of Mulberry Bark—three-tenths man and seven-tenths monster. What filthy luck! Wu Song beats up tigers. He must be very strong. . . . And I hear he's not married. Why not get him to move in? Who would have thought I was fated to meet my love here!'" (Shapiro 1.364)

Cíhuà 01.13b: 心裡尋思道："一母所生的兄弟，又這般長大，人物壯健。奴若嫁得這個，**胡亂也罷了**。你看我家那身不滿尺的丁樹，三分似人，七分似鬼。**奴那世裡遭瘟**，直到如今。據看武松又好氣力，何不交他搬來我家住？誰想這段姻緣卻在這裡。"

"'They are brothers, born of the same mother,' she thought to herself, 'and yet one of them is so big and strong. If I'd been married to him I **might have gotten by somehow or other**. But look at that Three-inch Mulberry-bark Manikin of mine! He's only:

Three parts human, and
Seven parts ghoul.

I must have been so plague-stricken in a previous incarnation that I'm still suffering the ill effects to this day. Wu Sung certainly looks manly enough to me. Why don't I see if I can get him to move in with us here? Who knows? This may turn out to be the very love-match I've been waiting for.'" (Roy 1.32)

4. *Shuǐhǔ* 24.359: (SH Gǔjí 1.283) 那婦人連聲叫道："叔叔，卻怎地這般見外？自家的骨肉，又不扶侍了別人。便撥一個土兵來使用，這廝上鍋上灶地不乾淨，奴眼裡也看不得這等人。"

"'How can you treat us like strangers?" the girl protested. "You're not just anyone, you're our own flesh and blood! With a soldier the kitchen would never be clean. I couldn't stand having that kind of lout around!"' (Shapiro 1.367)

Cíhuà 01.16a: 那婦人連聲叫道：＂叔叔，卻怎生這般計較！自家骨肉，又不服事了別人。雖然有這小丫頭迎兒，奴家見他拿東拿西，蹀裡蹀斜，也不靠他。就是撥了土兵來，那廝上鍋上灶不乾淨。奴眼裡也看不上這等人。＂

"'Brother-in-law,' the woman retorted, "how can you make so much of it? Our own flesh and blood! It's not as though I were waiting on anyone else. **It's true we've got this little chit, Ying-erh, but when I see the way she:**

Picks up this and then picks up that,

Floundering about all over the place,

there's no way I can rely on her. And even if you arrange for an orderly, he won't be any too sanitary where food is concerned. I really can't abide people like that."' (Roy 1.35)

5. *Shuǐhǔ* 24.369: (SH Gǔjí 1.293) 王婆道：＂他家賣拖蒸河漏子，熱燙溫和大辣酥。＂西門慶笑道：＂你看這婆子，只是風！＂

'[Mistress Wáng said, "Her family sells] Steaming, dripping, hot, spicy, delicious goodies." Ximen grinned. "You really are a mad woman."' (Shapiro 1.380)

Cíhuà 02.10a: 王婆道：＂他家賣的拖煎河漏子，**乾巴子肉翻包著菜肉匾食餃窩窩，蛤蜊**面熱盪溫和大辣酥。＂西門慶笑道：＂你看這風婆子，只是風！＂

"'Their stock in trade,' replied Dame Wang, 'is fried doughballs, **cured coney, stuffed patty-cake, baked buns, noodles with cockle sauce**, and hot Schlag in cider.' 'Why you crazy old crone,' laughed Hsi-men Ch'ing, 'all you can do is joke.'' (Roy 1.59)

6. *Shuǐhǔ* 24.381 (SH Gǔjí 1.305): 鄆哥叫道：＂做甚麼便打我？＂婆子罵道：＂賊猢猻，高則聲，大耳刮子打出你去！＂

"'What are you thumping me for?' yelled the boy. "Thieving ape! If you don't keep your voice down, I'll slap you right out of here!"' (Shapiro 1.395)

Cíhuà 04.7b: 鄆哥便叫道：＂你做甚麼便打我？＂婆子罵道：＂**賊合娘的小猴**！你敢高則聲，大耳刮子打出你去！＂

"'Who do you think you're hitting!' Yün-ko yelled at her. **"You lousy mother-fucking little monkey!"** the old lady cursed. "If you raise your voice again I'll drive you out of here with a couple of good boxes on the ear!"' (Roy 1.95)

7. *Shuǐhǔ* 25.395 (SH Gǔjí 1.309): 鄆哥道：＂便罵你這馬泊六，做牽頭的老狗，直甚麼屁！＂那婆子大怒，揪住鄆哥便打。

"'You're a bawd, I say, and a whore-mongering old bitch. So what!' In a fury, Mistress Wang grabbed Yunge and pummeled him.' (Shapiro 1.399).

Cíhuà 05.4a: 鄆哥道：＂便罵你這馬伯六，做牽頭的老狗肉，**直我髡髡**！＂那婆子大怒，揪住鄆哥便打。

"'If I curse you," replied Yün-ko, "for being a procuress and a pandering old bitch, **it matters about as much as my prick!**" The old lady was enraged and, grabbing hold of Yün-ko, started to beat him with her fists.' (Roy 1.100)

8. *Shuǐhǔ* 25.400 (SH Gǔjí 1.314): 這婆娘過來和西門慶說道："我的武大,今日已死。我只靠著你做主。" 西門慶道："這個何須得你說費心。"
"'Wu the Elder is dead," she said. "You're my sole support from now on." "That goes without saying."' (Shapiro 1.405).
Cíhuà 05.9a: 這婆娘過來和西門慶說道："我的武大,今日已死,我只靠著你做主。**大官人(休)是網巾圈兒打靠後。**"西門慶道："這個何須你說費心。"
'When the woman arrived she said to Hsi-men Ch'ing, "Now that Wu the Elder is dead I'm completely dependent on you, sir. **Don't put me in the position of: The rings that hold your hair net in place: always at the back of your head.**"
"What need is there for you to trouble yourself about that?" said Hsi-men Ch'ing.' (Roy 1.109)

9. *Shuǐhǔ* 26.408 (SH Gǔjí 1.320): 王婆道"都頭,卻怎地這般說!天有不測風雲,人有暫時禍福。誰保得長沒事!"
"'Now, Constable," interjected Mistress Wang, "don't you know the saying: 'The winds and clouds in the sky are unfathomable. A man's luck changes in an instant'? Who can guarantee against misfortune?"' (Shapiro 1.412).
Cíhuà 09.4b: 王婆道:"都頭卻怎的這般說!天有不測風雲,人有旦夕禍福;**今早脫下鞋和襪,未審明朝穿不穿**:誰人保得常沒事!"
"'Captain," said Dame Wang, "how can you talk that way? Weather is characterized by unexpected storms; Man is subject to unpredictable vicissitudes. **When you take off your shoes and socks today; Who knows whether you will put them on tomorrow?** Who can be sure that nothing will ever happen to him?"' (Roy 1.177)

10. *Shuǐhǔ* 26.412 (SH Gǔjí 1.324): 武松聽道:"你這話是實了?你卻不要說謊。" 鄆哥道:"便到官府,我也只是這般說。"
'[When Wǔ Sōng heard it, he said,] "You're telling the truth? You'd better not lie to me!" [Brother Yùn replied:] "I'd say the same thing in court!"' (Shapiro 1.418).
Cíhuà 09.7a: 武二聽了,便道:"你這話說是實麼?"又問道:"我的嫂子嫁與甚麼人去了?" 鄆哥道:"**你嫂子乞西門慶抬到家,待搗吊底子兒**,自還問他實也是虛!"武二道:"你休說謊。"鄆哥道:"我便官府面前,也只是這般說。"
'When Wu the Second had heard him out, he asked, "Is what you tell me really true?" Then he asked again, "And who did my sister-in-law marry herself off to?"
"Your sister-in-law," said Yün-ko, **"was carried off to his own house by Hsi-men Ch'ing, so he could knock the bottom out of her at his leisure.** And you ask me if it's true or if it's false!"

"You'd better not be lying," said Wu the Second.
"Even if I have to tell it in front of the magistrate," said Yün-ko, "I'll tell it the same way."' (Roy 1.181)

11. *Shuǐhǔ* 26.415 (SH Gǔjí 1.328): 那婦人道："叔叔，你好沒道理！你哥哥自害心疼病死了，干我什事！"
'"Brother-in-law, you're acting outrageously! Your brother died of pains in the heart. It had nothing to do with me!"' (Shapiro 1.423)
Cíhuà 87.8b: 那婦人道："叔叔，**如何冷鍋中豆兒炮**，好沒道理！你哥哥自害心疼病死了，干我甚事！"
'"Brother-in-law," the woman responded, **"why is that: The beans are popping in this cold pot?** It doesn't make any sense. The fact is your elder brother died of heart trouble. What does it have to do with me?"' (Roy 5.125)

12. *Shuǐhǔ* 45.734 (SH Gǔjí 1.566): 這一堂和尚，見了楊雄老婆這等模樣，都七顛八倒起來。但見班首輕狂……。
'The sight of the luscious Clever Cloud, piously undulating, caused the other monks to reel and stagger. [All focused on the frivolously wild head monk . . .]' (Shapiro 1.722)
Cíhuà 08.11a: 那眾和尚，見了武大這個老婆，**一個個都昏迷了佛性禪心，一個個多關不住心猿意馬**，都七顛八倒，**酥成一塊**。但見班首輕狂……。
'When the company of monks caught sight of Wu the Elder's wife: **Each and every one of them became oblivious to His Buddha nature and his meditative mind; Each and every one of them lost control of "the monkey of his mind and the horse of his will."** All at sevens and eights, **they melted into a heap**. Behold the rector becomes flippant . . .' (Roy 1.164–165)

Dialect in the *Jīn Píng Méi*

From the examples above, we can see quite clearly that the author of *Jīn Píng Méi cíhuà* intentionally added colloquial dialect expressions, sometimes in an excessively cluttered way, almost to the point of being overwrought. For instance, in Chapter 24 of the *Shuǐhǔ zhuàn*, the Mistress Wáng says to Xīmén Qìng that Pān Jīnlián and her family sell, *"tuō zhēng hélòuzi, rè-tàng wēnhé dà-làsū* 拖蒸河漏子, 熱燙溫和大辣酥 (see passage number 5 cited above). Some claim that the word *hélòuzi* 河漏子 here refers to a kind of river (freshwater) clam, used here as a figure of speech for female genitals. Others maintain that it refers to a kind of noodle dish popular in Shānxī and Shǎanxī,[2] wherein the cooking utensils and process serve as a kind of innuendo for the female genitals and sexual activity. Additionally, *làsū* 辣酥 is a

---

[2] Translator's note: Usually written *héle* 飴餎, for example Xī'ān 西安 [xuo²⁴luo⁰] (Lǐ Róng et al. 2002, 5.5194), this is a kind of buckwheat or sorghum noodle dish that is still popular today in China's northwest. In addition to *hélòu(zi)* 河漏(子), a more common alternative for writing this word is *héluò* 河洛 (Xǔ and Miyata 1999, 3.3624).

word for a long eggplant [in the Shànghǎi dialect pronounced /loʔ¹¹su²³/], which is shaped rather like the male genital organ.³ The two sentences together are a metaphor for sexual behaviour. In the *Jīn Píng Méi cíhuà* version, an additional sentence is embedded in this line: "(*tuō zhēng hélòuzi*), *gānbāzi-ròu fān bāozhe cài-ròu biǎnshí jiǎo-wōwo*, (*rè-tàng wēnhé dà-làsū*) (拖煎河漏子,) 乾巴子肉翻包著菜肉匾食, 餃窩窩, 蛤蜊麵, (熱盪溫和大辣酥). The *gānbāzi-ròu* 乾巴子肉 'meat jerky' implies the feminine sexual organ, whereas the *jiǎowōwo* 餃窩窩 'dumplings' implies the male organ. So this sentence also implies erotic activity. The word *gélí-miàn* 蛤蜊麵 'clam noodles' also implies the female sexual organ. Together with the *rè tàng wēnhé dà-làsū* 熱盪溫和大辣酥 'piping hot wine~eggplant', it is an overwrought representation of erotic sexual activity. But these additional words not only seem overly repetitive, but also leave the word *hélòuzi* dangling mid-sentence, thus muddling the entire phrase. That is why the revised Chóngzhēn 崇禎 edition of the *Jīn Píng Méi* excised many dialect expressions, especially words that were difficult to understand. Consider the following examples:⁴

1. *Shuǐhǔ* 24.369 (SH Gǔjí 1.293): 原來這個開茶坊的王婆, 也是不依本分的。
'It so happens that this Mistress Wáng, the proprietress of the teahouse, was not the sort to abide by her lot.' (Shapiro 1.380)
Cíhuà 02.9a: 原來這開茶坊的王婆子, 也不是守本分的。便是積年通殷勤, 做媒婆, 做賣婆, 做牙婆, 又會收小的, 也會抱腰, 又善放刁。**還有一件不可說：鬃髻上著綠, 陽臘灌腦袋。**端的看不出這婆子的本事來！
Chóngwén bǎn 02.15b: 原來這開茶坊的王婆子, 也不是守本分的。便是積年通殷勤, 做媒婆, 做賣婆, 做牙婆, 又會收小的, 也會抱腰又善放刁。還有 ~~一件不可說鬃髻上著綠陽臘灌腦袋。~~ 端的看不出這婆子的本事來！
'It so happens that this Dame Wang, the proprietress of the teahouse, was not the sort to abide by her lot. In fact, for years she had: Played the procuress, Made a living as a matchmaker, Peddled human flesh, Been a broker, Meddled in midwifery, Acted as accoucheur, and Revealed a knack for every sort of knavery. ~~And she had yet another accomplishment that doesn't bear mentioning: She could jab a needle through the chignon, and Inject solder into the cranial cavity.~~ Truly, this old lady's skills were such as to evade easy detection.' (Roy 1.57)

2. *Shuǐhǔ* 24.370: (SH Gǔjí 1.294) 西門慶問道："怎地叫做雜趁？" 王婆笑道："老身為頭是做媒, 又會做牙婆, 也會抱腰, 也會收小的, 也會說風情, 也會做馬泊六。"

---

3. Translator's note: But note that *dàlàsū* 大辣酥 is also a transcription of a Mongolian word for 'rice wine', *darasun* (Buell 2003, 146; Xǔ and Miyata 1999, 1.288).

4. Chóngzhēn 崇禎 edition examples from 1988 facsimile copy published by Peking University Press, *Xīn kè xiùxiàng pīpíng jīnpíngméi* 新刻繡像批評金瓶梅 [Newly engraved and illustrated, critical *Jīn Píng Méi*]. We mark the text deleted in the Chóngzhēn edition with a box in the Chinese, and mark the relevant part of the text in Roy's translation as struck out.

'[Xīmén Qìng said,] "What do you mean—'mixed market'?" [Mistress Wáng chuckled and replied,] "Mainly, I'm a match-maker. But I'm also a broker, a mid-wife, a lovers' go-between, and a bawd."' (Shapiro 1.381)

Cíhuà 02.11a: 西門慶道："乾娘，如何叫做雜趁？"王婆笑道："老身自從三十六歲沒了老公，丟下這個小廝，無得過日子。迎頭兒跟著人說媒，次後攬人家些衣服賣，又與人家抱腰、收小的，閑常也會做牽頭、做馬伯六，也會針灸看病，也會做貝戎兒。"

Chóngwén bǎn 02.18a: 西門慶道："乾娘，如何叫做雜趁？"王婆笑道："老身自從三十六歲沒了老公，丟下這個小廝，沒得過日子。迎頭兒跟著人說媒，次後攬人家些衣服賣，又與人家抱腰、收小的，閑常也會作牽頭、做馬百六，也會針灸看病，~~也會做貝戎兒~~。"

'"And what, may I ask, do you mean, Godmother, by the occasional odd job?" demanded Hsi-men Ch'ing. Dame Wang laughed. "When I was only thirty-five my old man kicked off and left me with this youngster, but without any means of livelihood. At first I tried my hand at matchmaking. Then I went round collecting people's old clothes to sell. I offered my services as an accoucheur and then as a midwife. When the occasion arises I dabble in pandering and procuring. I can also perform acupuncture, moxabustion, ~~and [t-h-i-e-v-e-r-y]~~"' (Roy 1.60)

3. *Shuǐhǔ* 24.380 (SH: Gǔjí 1.304): 王婆道："眼望旌節至，專等好消息。不要叫老身棺材出了討挽歌郎錢。"西門慶笑了去，不在話下。

'[Mistress Wáng said] "My eyes watch for the banners of royal reward, my ears are cocked for the sound of glad tidings. Don't fail me! I don't want to be 'a funeral singer demanding payment after the burial'!" Ximen laughed and departed. Of that no more need be said.' (Shapiro 1.393)

Cíhuà 04.3b: 王婆道："眼望旌節至，耳聽好消息，不要交老身棺材出了討挽歌郎錢。" **西門慶道："但得一片橘皮吃且莫忘了洞庭湖。"** 一面看街上無人，帶上眼罩，笑了去。

Chóngwén bǎn 04.5a: 王婆道："眼望旌捷旗，耳聽好消息，不要交老身棺材出了討挽歌郎錢. ~~西門慶道："但得一片橘皮吃且莫忘子洞庭湖。"~~ 一面笑著看街上無人，帶上眼紗去了。

'Dame Wang said: "My eyes are on the lookout for the flag of victory, My ears are always on the alert for good tidings. Just don't leave me in the predicament of: Trying to collect the fee for the professional mourners after the coffin has already been interred." Hsi-men Ch'ing ~~replied: "Whenever one gets so much as a tangerine peel to eat; One should never forget Tung-t'ing Lake from whence it came." Then~~, after checking to see that the coast was clear, he put on his eye shades, laughed, and departed.' (Roy 1.87)

In these examples of the textual transition from the *Shuǐhǔ zhuàn* to the Wànlì edition of *Jīn Píng Méi*, and then to the Chóngzhēn edition *Jīn Píng Méi*, we find a convoluted process of conversion from common *báihuà* vernacular to the inclusion of more colloquial dialect elements, then back to common vernacular. Subsequent

Chinese vernacular novels generally trended toward the more purely *báihuà* vernacular. Novels with heavy dialect content, such as *Hé diǎn* 何典 [Classic of what] and *Hǎishàng huā lièzhuàn* 海上花列傳 [The courtesans of Shànghǎi] are, it seems, few and far between.

The next question to ask is where exactly these colloquialisms came from. Since these embedded words reflect only the characteristic dialect of the author of *Jīn Píng Méi*, they bear crucially on the difficult matter of whether the author of *Jīn Píng Méi* was from Shāndōng or from farther south. When we consider the added words such as the ones just cited, it is very difficult to ascertain where the words originated. However, there are some that we are able to grasp. Below are a few examples:

1. *Shuǐhǔ* 23.346 (SH Gǔjí 1.273): 只聽得一聲響，簌簌地將那樹連枝帶葉劈臉打將下來，定睛看時，一棒劈不著大蟲。原來慌了，正打在枯樹上，把那條稍棒折做兩截，……
   'There was a loud crackling, and a large branch, leaves and all, tumbled past his face. In his haste, he had struck an old tree instead of the tiger, snapping the staff in two and leaving him holding only the remaining half.' (Shapiro 1.356)
   Cíhuà 1.5b: 只聽得一聲響，簌簌地將那樹枝帶葉打將下來。原來不曾打著大蟲，正打在樹枝上，磕磕把那條棒折做兩截，
   'But the only thing he heard was a loud report and a thrashing noise as the branch of a tree, with all its leaves came tumbling down in front of him. It so happens that he had not made contact with the tiger at all, but had hit the branch of a tree so hard that his quarterstaff had broken in two **[with a snap]** . . .' (Roy 1.19–20)

2. *Shuǐhǔ* 23.346 (SH Gǔjí 1.274): 武松把左手緊緊地揪住頂花皮，偷出右手來提起鐵鎚般大小拳頭，盡平生之力，只顧打。
   'Still relentlessly clutching the beast by the ruff with his left hand, Wu Song **[stealthily] freed** his right, big as an iron mallet, and with all his might began to pound.' (Shapiro 1.356)
   Cíhuà 1.6a: 武松按在坑裡，騰出右手，提起拳頭來，只顧狠打，盡平生氣力。'[Wu] Sung pressed its head down into the pit and, **freeing** his right hand **[with a thump]**, pummeled it with his fist, using all the strength at his command.' (Roy 1.20)

3. *Shuǐhǔ* 24.358 (SH Gǔjí 1.282): 武松吃他看不過，只低了頭，不怎麼理會。當日吃了十數盃酒，武松便起身。
   'Embarrassed, Wu Song kept his head down and avoided her gaze. They **finished** a dozen or so cups, and he rose to leave."' (Shapiro 1.366)
   Cíhuà 1.15a: 武松乞他看不過，只低了頭不理他。吃了一歇，酒闌了，便起身。'Wu Sung was embarrassed by the way she looked at him and merely lowered his head without responding to her. After they had been **drinking for a while** the wine ran out and he got up to go.' (Roy 1.34)

Being from Shànghǎi, it seems to me that the substitutions in these three examples all originate in Wú dialects. I discuss them below, with Shànghǎi pronunciations given to represent their Wú color.

The first example is *kèkè* 磕磕 /kʻəʔ³³kʻəʔ⁵⁵/ [apparently meaning 'knock, thump']. Generally speaking, the inlays of *Jīn Píng Méi Cíhuà* in *Shuǐhǔ zhuàn* during the tiger plot try to compress the text as much as possible so as to go straight into the story of betrayal between Pān Jīnlián and Xīmén Qìng. But the word *kèkè* is used a lot here, unexpectedly so. In my hometown Shànghǎi *jiādìng* 嘉定 dialect, *kèkè* is an adverb that means something like *qiàqià* 'just then' 恰恰, *zhèngqiǎo* 正巧 'coincidentally at that moment', or *zhènghǎo* 正好 'exactly then'. My dialect exclusively says *kèkè* for this meaning and does not use the word *qiàqià*. I have not encountered *kèkè* used in this way in other dialects.

The second example is *téng* 騰 /dfiən²⁴/ 'clear out' as used in *téng chūshǒu lái* 騰出手來 'freeing one's hand'. This word had been used earlier in traditional literature, such as in a poem by Wáng Yǔchēng 王禹偁 (954–1001): "*Biàn sì rénjiā yǎng yīngwǔ, jiù lóng téng dào rù xīn lóng*" 便似人家養鸚鵡，舊籠騰倒入新籠 'Just as when people raise parrots, the old cage is cleared out for the new' ("Liàng yí hòu zìcháo"). The meaning of the second phrase is *téng lóng huàn niǎo* 騰籠換鳥 'clear out the cage and change the bird'. Recently, a person from Qīngpǔ district in Shànghǎi characterized an economic theory with the phrase "*téng lóng huàn niǎo*", which perhaps was inspired by this poem. As for the meaning of this *téng* word, dictionaries will generally offer a simple interpretation such as *zhuǎnyí* 轉移 'transfer' or *zhuǎnhuàn* 轉換 'convert'. But these glosses do not get to the heart of the meaning. The basic meaning of *téng* here is *téngkōng* 騰空 'clear out, vacate', and only later did it come to mean *zhuǎnyí*. It thus means to first clear something away and then shift that thing to another use. In this description of Wǔ Sōng 武松 striking the tiger, Wǔ Sōng holds down the tiger in the pit with his left hand and then pulls out his right hand and uses it to ruthlessly strike the tiger. While the word *téng* in this meaning and usage does not appear to be limited to Wú dialects, there is no question that in dialects such as my hometown dialect we use *téng* for this type of situation and not words like *tōu* 偷 'steal'.

The third example is *yī-xiē* 一歇 /iʔ³³ɕiʔ⁵⁵/ 'a spell (of time)' as used in *chīle yī xiē* 吃了一歇 'ate for a spell'. It is actually also used frequently in the vernacular of *Shuǐhǔ zhuàn*. We see it, for instance, in this line from Chapter 11:

*Lín Chōng yòu bù gǎn dòngshǒu, ràng tā guòqù. Yòu **děngle yī-xiē**, kànkàn tiānsè wǎn lái, yòu bújiàn yīgè kèrén guò* 林沖又不敢動手，讓他過去。又**等了一歇**，看看天色晚來，又不見一個客人過 'Lín Chōng also did not dare to move his hands and let him pass, then **waited a bit** and watched the day turn late without seeing another guest pass by.'

and in this passage from Chapter 15:

Ruǎn Xiǎowǔ huāngmáng qù qiáo biān, jiěle xiǎochuán, tiào zài cāng lǐ, zhuōle huá jí, zhǐ yī huá, sān zhī chuán sī bìngzhe, **huále yī xiē**, *zǎo dào nàgè shuǐ gé jiǔdiàn qiá* 阮小五慌忙去橋邊，解了小船，跳在艙裡，捉了撐楫，只一撐，三隻船廝並著，**撐了一歇**，早到那個水閣酒店前 'Ruǎn Xiǎowǔ rushed to the bridge, unmoored a boat, jumped into its cabin, grabbed the oars, and with a single stroke the three boats were abreast; **then after paddling a bit**, he quickly arrived at the waterside tavern.'

This use of *yī-xiē* in the *Shuǐhǔ zhuàn* concurrently reveals something of that novel's author. I believe that the original author of *Zhōngyì shuǐhǔ zhuàn* was Shī Nàiān from Qiántáng 錢塘施耐庵. That is to say, he was from Hángzhōu, not from north of the Yangtze (Sū-*běi* 蘇北) or other such places. So it is entirely understandable that the novel has many Wú dialect turns of phrase. In the 1980s, Dài Bùfán 戴不凡 was the first to clearly point out that the author of *Jīn Píng Méi Cíhuà* was probably from a Wú dialect background. The basis for his argument was that "it can be seen in the large amount of Wú dialect used in the novel." It must be said that Dài Bùfán had a keen eye. It's a pity that he pointed to only a few examples, such as *duō* 掇 /təʔ⁵⁵/ 'carry with both hands', *chuáng* 㕭 [=噇] /zã²⁴/ 'to drink', and *shìwù* 事務 /zɿŋ²²fiu⁴⁴/ 'business, matters' (Dài Búfán 1908, 137; 1983, 140). As I have noted elsewhere, all of these were in fact actually brought into text originally from the *Zhōngyì shuǐhǔ zhuàn* (Huáng Lín 1982).

Another possible trace of Wú dialect influence that is worth considering is found in the first sentence of Chapter 6 of *Jīn Píng Méi Cíhuà*, which reads, "*Què shuō Xīmén Qìng biàn duì Hú Jiǔ shuō qù le* 卻説西門慶便對胡九説去了" 'As the story goes, Xīmén Qìng went off to speak to Hú Jiǔ'. Here the name Hé Jiǔ 何九 is written Hú Jiǔ 胡九. The homophony of Hé 何 and Hú 胡 is also a Wú dialect characteristic. Of course, it is possible that this example is simply a copy error made by a scribe who spoke the Wú dialect. But it is also possible that the author unwittingly revealed a feature of his pronunciation in error. The Chóngzhēn edition dealt with this error by entirely excising the phrase "*biàn duì Hú Jiǔ*."

Concluding Discussion

Considering the evidence so far outlined, the author of *Jīn Píng Méi Cíhuà* must have been a Wú dialect speaker. Note that I am not casually picking various words to explain the author's place of origin, which is a highly unreliable approach. Because the inclusion of text from earlier works is a characteristic of the *Jīn Píng Méi Cíhuà*, the textual sources need to be sorted out first to determine what elements predate Xiàoxiào Shēng's composition. This is the only way to be certain that the words in question were not copied from a previous work by the author of *Jīn Píng Méi Cíhuà*. The words discussed so far all occur in text of the *Jīn Píng Méi Cíhuà* where it has been modified from that of the *Shuǐhǔ zhuàn*. They thus represent the language of the author of *Jīn Píng Méi Cíhuà*, and do not originate in prior texts.

So, can we conclude definitively from this that the author of *Jīn Píng Méi Cíhuà* is employing Wú dialect in the text? I think things are more complex, and we cannot jump to a quick conclusion. There is at least one problem that has seriously puzzled me for several years and for which I have not yet found a satisfactory answer. That is the problem with the writing of the name for Yíng'ér 迎兒. The character of Yíng'ér does not exist in *Shuǐhǔ zhuàn*. She was added into the story, as the daughter of Wǔ Dà 武大, by the author of the *Jīn Píng Méi Cíhuà* during his transformation and adaptation of the episodes about Pān Jīnlián and Xīmén Qìng. She appears frequently early in *Jīn Píng Méi Cíhuà* as the illicit affair transpires between Pān Jīnlián and Xīmén Qìng, always written as Yíng'ér 迎兒. The character Yíng'ér did appear in operas and novels prior to the composition of *Jīn Píng Méi Cíhuà* and was written 迎兒. However, in the latter half of *Jīn Píng Méi Cíhuà* Chapter 87, when Wǔ Sōng returns home to kill Pān Jīnlián, the *Cíhuà* author unexpectedly writes the name Yíng'ér with the characters 蠅兒, meaning 'housefly'. The name is written 17 times as Yíng'ér 蠅兒. Only Méi Jié 梅節 has pointed out this issue (2004, 439):

> Yíng 蠅 is consistently written Yíng 迎 in the *Chóngwén* edition. But only the first ten *huí* 回 [of the Wànlì edition] write it as Yíng 迎, and the latter use of Yíng 蠅 is clearly an error for Yíng 迎. The inconsistency following Chapter 80 is evidence that more than one person had a hand in the composition.

I think that this problem is more complicated than that. First of all, this is obviously not a copy error. In such a large book as the *Jīn Píng Méi*, copy errors due to graphic or phonetic similarities are entirely possible. For example, in Chapters 25 and 28 a person named Yuè Ān 鈅安 appears. Some people think this is an error for the name Dài Ān 玳安, while others think it is another character in the novel. In my opinion it is a copy error. Méi Jié has noted that the "role and affairs this character is involved in" are closely aligned with those of Dài Ān (2004, 125). It is entirely possible that the radical 王 in *dài* 玳 in a careless cursive would look very much like a cursive rendering of the radical 金 or 钅 in *yuè* 鈅. The right halves of each graph (玳 and 鈅), *dài* 代 and *wù* 戊 are also very easy to confuse. In such a case the copyist could easily have been confused and made an error. However, such is not the case with the two graphs *yíng* 蠅 and *yíng* 迎. The difference between these two graphs is too great. So the confusion of the two graphs could not be an inadvertent copy error. It also cannot be result of the copyist's desire to take a shortcut, which would cause the resulting graph to be simpler than the original. It is not possible that the simpler *yíng* 迎 was copied as the more complicated *yíng* 蠅, with the latter's significantly greater number of strokes. Even more so, it is not possible that this kind of mistake could have been made over and over again. But the name appears written with *yíng* 蠅 17 times. That is clearly not a copy error.

It thus must have something to do with dialect of the author. Although I have not heard of using Yíng'ér 蠅兒 as a person's name, such use is not entirely inconceivable. In earlier times, using a humbling, lowly name, such as Ā-Gǒu 阿狗 'dog' or

Ā Māo 阿貓 'cat', was thought to make a child easier to raise and would help avoid death in childhood. However, the characters *yíng* 迎 'to greet' and *yíng* 蠅 'housefly' in modern Wú dialects have very different onsets in their pronunciation. The graph 迎 has an initial nasal consonant [as in Shànghǎi 上海 /ŋin²³/], while 蠅 has a zero onset [as in Shànghǎi /in⁵³/]. Does this mean that the author was a northerner who spoke a dialect that did not distinguish between the pronunciations of 迎 and 蠅? If so, how does one reconcile that with the fact that in such a great number of places the author completely naturally peppers the text with Wú dialect coloring?

Could it possibly be that the first and second halves of the book are, just as Méi Jié said, from more than one person's hand? This does not seem possible. If the former and latter portions of the book were written by two authors, it would be very easy for the new author of the latter section to miss such a minor character. The character Yíng'ér frequently appears in Chapter 6 of *Jīn Píng Méi Cíhuà*. But after Wǔdà has been killed, Yíng'ér does not appear again for more than 60 chapters. Yet while the author has clearly not forgotten her at this point, it is hard to believe he would have got her name wrong. Stepping back and considering the possibility that a new author or editor had taken over, if this new editor thought back about this character from the early chapters, he would surely not have forgotten that she was called Yíng'ér 迎兒. How could he have taken a relatively common name, that is fairly easy to write—迎兒, and replaced it with an obscure and difficult one to write—蠅兒? In her article in this volume, Professor Zhāng Huìyīng 張惠英 considers this question. She believes that the author here is playing a word game, that he intentionally made the change for effect. But it seems to me that playing a word game here is useless. This new name does not strike this reader as fun. Could another possibility be that there is some place between the Wú and more northern regions where the two syllables, *yíng* 迎 and *yíng* 蠅, have a pronunciation that differs from how they used to be pronounced?

Of course, in my opinion, the strongest possibility is still that the author used text from two different sources separately in the front and back parts of the novel. The early chapters in the book are based on a source text where the name was rendered Yíng'ér 迎兒, while the later chapters follow a source text that rendered the name Yíng'ér 蠅兒. If so, the Wú-dialect-speaking author, by the time he got to Chapter 87, was more strongly influenced by the colloquial Mandarin pronunciation and unconsciously or inadvertently did not distinguish the pronunciation of *yíng* 迎 and *yíng* 蠅. At present this seems like the most likely possibility, though it is still remote. Of course, this is all speculation. So what is the situation after all? I have thought about this for thirty years and I can still not think of a convincing reason why it is the way it is. Today, I take this opportunity to ask my respected readers to enlighten me.

References

Primary sources

Lánlíng Xiàoxiào Shēng 蘭陵笑笑生. n.d. *Jīn Píng Méi cíhuà* 金瓶梅詞話 [Words from the *Plum in the Golden Vase*]. Facsimile of the Míng Wànlì 萬曆 (r. 1572–1620) edition held in the Běijīng Library. Běijīng: Gǔyì xiǎoshuō kānxínghuì 古佚小說刊行會, 1933.

Lánlíng Xiàoxiào Shēng 蘭陵笑笑生. n.d. *Xīnkè xiùxiàng pīpíng Jīn Píng Méi* 新刻繡像批評金瓶梅 [Newly engraved and illustrated, critical *Jīn Píng Méi*]. Míng Chóngzhēn 崇禎 (r. 1628–1644) edition. Běijīng: Běijīng dàxué chūbǎnshè 北京大學出版社, 1988.

Shī Nàiān 施耐庵 (1296–1370). (1589) 1954. *Shuǐhǔ quán zhuàn* 水滸全傳 [The complete *Water Margin*]. Based on the *Zhōngyì Shuǐhǔ zhuàn* 忠義水滸傳 edition with preface by "Tiāndū wàichén" 天都外臣, i.e., Wāng Dàokūn 汪道昆 (1525–1593). Běijīng: Rénmín wénxué chūbǎn shè 人民文學出版社.

Wáng Yǔchēng 王禹偁 (954–1001). "Liàng yí hòu zìcháo" 量移後自嘲 [Taking mocking stock of myself after a move]. From *Wáng Huángzhōu xiǎoxù jí* 王黃州小畜集 [The Xiǎoxù collection of Wáng Huángzhōu]. In Sìchuān dàxué gǔjí suǒ 四川大學古籍所, ed., 2004, *Sòng jí zhēnběn cóngkān* 宋集珍本叢刊. Vol. 1, 589. Běijīng: Xiànzhuāng shūjú 線裝書局. Facsimilie of *Wáng Huángzhōu xiǎoxù jí* also in *Sìbù cóngkān* 四部叢刊, available at ctext.org; "Liàng yí hòu zìcháo" is *juàn* 9, p. 6a.

Secondary references

Dài Bùfán 戴不凡. (1980) 1983. *Xiǎoshuō Jiànwén Lù*. 小說見聞錄 [Record of things observed in traditional novels]. Zhèjiāng rénmín chūbǎnshè 浙江人民出版社. Reprint, Taipei: Mùduó chūbǎnshè 木鐸出版社.

Huáng Lín 黃霖. 1982. "*Zhōngyì Shuǐhǔ zhuàn yǔ Jīn Píng Méi cíhuà*" 忠義水滸傳與金瓶梅詞話 [*The Water Margin* and the *Plum in the Golden Vase*]. In *Shuǐhǔ zhēngmíng* 水滸爭鳴 [*Shuǐhǔ* in contention], edited by Húběi shěng Shuǐhǔ yánjiūhuì 湖北省水滸研究會 and *Shuǐhǔ* zhēngmíng biānwěihuì 水滸爭鳴編委會. Vol. 1, 222–37. Hǔběi: Chángjiāng wényì chūbǎnshè 長江文藝出版社.

Méi Jié 梅節. 2004. *Jīn Píng Méi Cíhuà Jiàodú Jì* 金瓶梅詞話校讀記 [A collation of the *Jīn Píng Méi cíhuà*]. Běijīng: Běijīng túshūguǎn chūbǎnshè 北京圖書館出版社.

Zhāng Míngfēi 張冥飛 et al. 1919. *Gǔjīn xiǎoshuō pínglín* 古今小說評林 [Collected commentary on traditional fiction]. Shànghǎi: Mínquán chūbǎn shè 民權出版社. Facsimile reprint issued in 2012 by the same publisher.

Additional References Used by Translator

Primary sources

Shī Nàiān 施耐庵. n.d. *Shuǐhǔ quán zhuàn* 水滸全傳 [The complete *Water Margin*]. 4 Vols. Reprint, Shànghǎi: Shànghǎi gǔjí chūbǎnshè 上海古籍出版社, 1984.

Secondary references

Buell, Paul D. 2003. *The A to Z of the Mongol World Empire*. Lanham, MD: Scarecrow Press.
Lǐ Róng 李榮 et al. eds. 2002. *Xiàndài Hànyǔ fāngyán dà cídiǎn* 现代漢語方言大詞典 [Unabridged dictionary of modern Chinese dialects]. 6 vols. Nánjīng: Jiāngsū jiàoyù chūbǎnshè 江蘇教育出版社.
Roy, David. 1997–2013. *The Plum in the Golden Vase or, Chin P'ing Mei*. 5 vols. Princeton: Princeton University Press.
Shapiro, Sidney. 1981. *Outlaws of the Marsh*. 2 vols. Bloomington: Indiana University Press.
Xǔ Bǎohuá 許寶華, and Miyata Ichirō 宮田一郎, eds. 1999. *Hànyǔ fāngyán dà cídiǎn* 漢語方言大詞典 [Unabridged dictionary of Chinese dialects]. 5 Vols. Běijīng: Zhōnghuá shūjú 中華書局.

5
Wordplay in *Jīn Píng Méi*

Zhāng Huìyīng

Introduction

The theme for this volume, *Colloquial Chinese and Its History: Dialect and Text*, is well chosen, as it touches upon not only the fields of linguistics, dialectology, and Chinese history, but also the history of vernacular literature. By thus combining the study of linguistics and literature, this workshop fills a great need. Outside of China, scholars working in the fields of Eastern civilizations and cultures are generally in the same department. For instance, Patrick Hanan, of the Department of East Asian Languages and Civilizations at Harvard, studied the history of Chinese vernacular literature but also addressed issues of language in vernacular literature in pertinent and thoughtful scholarly depth. In China, great importance is attached to the close reading and citation of texts and literary sources, including examples from vernacular literature, in the study of the history of Chinese and the etymology of words, particularly dialect words. At the same time, those who conduct research in the history of literature and the interpretation of literary texts, when faced with questions regarding language and dialect, must engage in discussion with linguistic specialists.

Research on *Jīn Píng Méi* 金瓶梅 [*The Plum in the Golden Vase*], for example, requires comprehensive examination from the perspectives of literature, linguistics, and folklore (and local culture). Hence our examination proceeds from two angles in the field of *Jīn Píng Méi* studies:

(1) Wordplay, particularly in the way the novel utilizes both delightful humor and angry cursing to expose the darker side of contemporary Míng 明 (1368–1644) society. It also reflects the trend of its day to seek enjoyment in punning and other forms of wordplay.

(2) Playful homophony (punning) and the mixing of northern and southern dialects are all reflective of the multi-threaded origin of Guānhuà, wherein southern Guānhuà has deeply influenced northern Guānhuà and become the base dialect of vernacular literature.

Regarding the term *wánrwénzì* 玩兒文字, which is translated as 'wordplay' in the title of this article: as a noun, *wánrwénzì* 'wordplay' refers to the employment of words and the composition of phrases in a relaxed, easygoing, pleasant, and casual manner, and not to some form of written expression that follows standards of elegance that deliberately weigh every word. The most outstanding characteristic of this kind of wordplay is that it is not constrained by graphic norms or reading standards. As an object-plus-verb term, 'wordplay' denotes the playful use of words and language and all varieties of punning. I had intended at first to use the phrase *yóuxì wénzì* 遊戲文字 'toying with words', but feared that it would be confused with the term *wénzì yóuxì* 文字遊戲 'word games', which is narrower in meaning. So I settled on *wánrwénzì* 'wordplay' for use in the title of this chapter.

Some people (such as the many authoritative linguists I am acquainted with) view the author of *Jīn Píng Méi* as an "expert" practitioner of homophonic error in Chinese, because of his frequent use of homophonic borrowing and punning. But for my part, I consider him to be a linguistic genius.

Our discussion of wordplay in *Jīn Píng Méi* begins with its author's pseudonym: Xiàoxiào Shēng 笑笑生 'Mr. Laughs-a-lot'. *Jīn Píng Méi* is a masterwork that exposes society's disgraceful and ugly side. Yet in his attitude and method, Xiàoxiào Shēng looks at human society with a smile, talks about humanity's foibles with a laugh, and writes about social phenomena with humor. His pursuit of a laugh and a smile, *xiào*, is the pursuit of entertainment and enjoyment. Just as Féng Mènglóng 馮夢龍 (1574–1646) has said, "From ancient times to the present, there is nothing that is not talk; and talk is nothing more than laughter" *Gǔ-jīn lái mò fēi huà yě; huà mò fēi xiào yě* 古今來莫非話也；話莫非笑也.

Of the works in Chinese vernacular literature written since the Sòng and Yuán dynasties, *Sānguó yǎnyì* 三國演義 [Romance of the three kingdoms] is written in a mix of vernacular and classical styles; *Shuǐhǔ zhuàn* 水滸傳 [The water margin] contains a smattering of dialect elements; and, finally, *Hónglóu mèng* 紅樓夢 [Dream of red mansions, or *Shítou jì* 石頭記 'Story of the Stone'] can be said to be a vernacular classic written with painstaking and deliberate style and polish. But the language used in *Jīn Píng Méi* belongs to a category of its own and has attracted much controversy.

In 2015, motivated by the fact that the prevailing view in the fields of linguistics and literature is that *Jīn Píng Méi* was written in the Shāndōng 山東 dialect, I took it upon myself to point out—at the annual meeting of the Dialect Society in Lánzhōu 蘭州 and the Conference on *Jīn Píng Méi* in Xúzhōu 徐州—that *Jīn Píng Méi* is a work of vernacular literature rather than a novel in the Shāndōng dialect. My hope was to bring a corrective reminder to leading scholars in the fields of literary and linguistic history. In support of my argument, I cited the findings of scholars from both China and abroad.

In a paper given at the conference on *Issues in the Standardization of Modern Chinese* organized by the Chinese Academy of Sciences in October 1955, Luó Chángpéi 羅常培 (1899–1958) and Lǚ Shūxiāng 呂叔湘 (1904–1998) noted:

> From *huàběn* 話本 'colloquial stories' to *Yuán qǔ* 元曲 'Yuán drama' to *Rúlín wàishǐ* 儒林外史 [The scholars] and *Hónglóu mèng*, vernacular literature all contains regional coloring. However, collectively, it all has a single dialect basis: Mandarin dialects [*běifānghuà* 北方話]. In addition, these works were often printed, published, and distributed in non-Mandarin speaking regions. There were also authors who did not come from north China who were writing in the same kind of vernacular Chinese. It is obvious that vernacular Chinese had come to have a broad national character to a certain extent. (Luó and Lǚ 1956, 9–10)

The American sinologist and linguist Jerry Norman also talked about this problem in his book *Chinese*:

> In Europe, since at least the end of the first millennium AD, a large number of literary languages based on local vernaculars arose and in subsequent centuries many of these early written languages became the bases of several of the most important national languages of modern times. Nothing like this seems to have happened in China. The vernacular literary language which begun to evolve in the Tang dynasty (AD 618–907) and gradually developed into the vehicle of a flourishing vernacular literature in the Song (AD 960–1279) and Yuan (AD 1271–1368) dynasties was based on a northern variety of spoken Chinese. . . . The present-day standard written language, on the other hand, is a direct continuation and development of the literary vernacular of Song and Yuan times. (1988, 2–3)

The American sinologist and scholar of Chinese vernacular literature Patrick Hanan also emphasized the issue of language in his research. The first chapter of his 1981 study, *The Chinese Vernacular Story*, titled "Language and Narrative Model," cites Féng Mènglóng regarding language use in Chinese vernacular novels:

> The Northern group included in its territory by far the greatest number of speakers as well as the capitals (and hence, usually, the cultural centers) of almost all the major dynasties. Some version of Northern had been used, at least since the Tang dynasty, as the norm for vernacular writing even by writers who, like Feng, lived outside the area. Feng's vernacular writings show some features of the southeastern variety current along the lower Yangzi [*sic*]; but since the phonemic distinctions, the dialects' main criteria, are masked by the Chinese character script, the actual differences on the page amount to mere shadings, not the clear profile. We know, moreover, that vernacular authors took some pains to avoid words and idioms with too narrow a currency and tended to choose a vocabulary intelligible within the whole Northern area. (1981, 2)

Moreover, Patrick Hanan specifically commented on the use of language in Féng Mènglóng's *Shāngē* 山歌, which was written in the Sūzhōu 蘇州 dialect, saying that "the notes and commentaries are all either in Classical or in the Northern vernacular; he can hardly be said to have practiced the Soochow dialect" (1981, 2).

Wordplay as a Characteristic of *Jīn Píng Méi*

The emphasis in the present study is on the frequent use of dialect colloquialisms, vulgar language, and non-standard characters in the *Jīn Píng Méi*. In this regard, the novel is significantly different from the colloquial *lingua franca* adopted in *Shuǐhǔ zhuàn*, *Xīyóu jì* 西遊記 [Journey to the West], and *Hónglóu mèng*, which is more widely understood. So the questions before us are:

- What are the linguistic features of the novel?
- What is their purpose?

1. In its use of language, *Jīn Píng Méi* is fond of homophonic witticisms and the use of novel Chinese characters in the playful pursuit of fun and entertainment. This is what I am referring to by the term "wordplay." The novel's wordplay interacts with the author's ribald humor, vulgar profanities, scolding curses, and vivid, colorful erotic depictions.
2. In addition to exposing the darker side of Míng society, the novel's wordplay contributed to the "table-slapping" appreciation of such major contemporary literary figures as Yuán Zhōngláng 袁中郎 (1568–1610) and Xiè Zàiháng 謝在杭 (1567–1624). Their praise must have been due to the orientation of their literary values as well as their appreciation of the use of language. I maintain that the wordplay of Xiàoxiào Shēng from Lánlíng 蘭陵 fully reveals this author's distinctive linguistic talents and is the single most outstanding linguistic feature of *Jīn Píng Méi*.
3. The wordplay in *Jīn Píng Méi* exhibits the rich and colorful depth of the vernacular literary language. This is of value to the study of both the history of Chinese as well as the history of Chinese literature. In a previous study (Zhāng Huìyīng 1979, 301–2), I noted that in the "Miùwù" 謬誤 'Corrigenda' chapter of the *Xīnjuān Xiàolín guǎngjì:* 新鐫笑林廣記 [New edition of the *Extensive Record of the Forest of Laughs*], we find the following joke under the entry for *shí è bú shè* 十惡不赦 'irredeemable in all one's evils' (Yóuxì Zhǔrén 1791, 13.8a), it says:

> 鄉人夤緣進學，與父兄叔伯暑天同走，唯新生撐傘。人問何故，答曰：'入學不曬'（原注：作鄉音'十惡不赦'讀）。
>
> A fellow villager managed to take advantage of some connections to gain entrance to school. As he headed there in the company of his father and uncles on a hot summer day, only the new student used a parasol. When someone asked the reason they replied: '*Rù xué bú shài*' 入學不曬 ('Avoid the sun when getting started in school') [Original note: This phrase is pronounced exactly like the phrase *shí è bú shè* 十惡不赦 in the local patois.]

Similar to what is noted in the editorial comment in this passage, in the Chóngmíng dialect the pronunciation of *rù xué bú shài* [szə?² ʔo?²⁻⁵ pə?⁵ so³³] is exactly the same as that of *shí è bú shè* [szə?² ʔo?⁵ pə?⁵ so³³]. Hence this anecdote illustrates some of the ways that wordplay can reflect phonology, dialects, folk customs, and other aspects of contemporary Míng society.

4. This pursuit of entertainment and delight through wordplay in the *Jīn Píng Méi* is more than an individual proclivity of the author; it also reflects a trend of his times. Féng Mènglóng, in the "Preface" he wrote to his *Xiàofǔ* 笑府 [Treasury of laughs], expressed the scorn that many contemporary scholars harbored for classical texts and standard histories, their disdain for the kind of language found in the eight-legged essay and the civil service exams, and their quest for freedom of thought and fully expressive language and writing. All of this resembled the May 4th New Culture Movement of the early twentieth century, which advocated for vernacular writing (*báihuà* 白話) and modernist poetry. This was not merely the pursuit of fashion; rather, it was a kind of revolution, both linguistic and literary. My view is that the *Jīn Píng Méi* advanced a revolution in the language of fiction and the novel.

In his Preface to the *Xiàofǔ*, Féng Mènglóng writes:

古今來莫非話也。
From ancient times to the present, there is nothing more than talk.
話莫非笑也。
Yet talk is nothing more than laughter.
兩儀之混沌開闢
The division and ordering of chaos into the polarities of *yīn* and *yáng*,
列聖之揖讓徵誅
The array of sages either deferring to each other or vying for the upper hand,
見者其誰耶
Who might be witness to it all?
其亦話之而已耳。
That would be talk, and nothing more.
後之話今亦猶今之話昔
Those of the future who talk of the present, are like those of the present who talk of the past.
話之而疑之可笑也
When talking of it and they doubt it, that is laughable.
話之而信之猶可笑也。
When talking of it and they believe it, that is laughable as well.
經書子史鬼話也而爭傳焉
The classical texts and the histories of the masters, are all talk of ghosts. Yet they vie to pass them on.
詩賦文章淡話也而爭工焉
The famous verses and renowned essays, are just idle chat. Yet they vie to labor over them.

褒譏伸抑亂話也而爭趨避焉。
Praise and ridicule, holding forth or showing restraint, are all just random chatter. Yet they vie to rush off and avoid it all.
或笑人或笑於人
There are those who laugh at others, and those who are laughed at by others.
笑人者亦復笑於人
Those who laugh at others are also the subject of ridicule.
笑於人者亦復笑人。
Those who are laughed at also ridicule others.
人之相笑寧有已時
Is it possible that this mutual ridicule will ever cease?
笑府集笑話也十三篇
This Treasury of Laughs is a collection of jokes.
猶曰薄乎雲爾。
At 13 chapters, it still can be said to be thin.
或閱之而喜請勿喜。
To those who take delight in reading it, please refrain from delight.
或閱之而嗔請勿嗔。
To those who find annoyance in reading it, please refrain from annoyance.
古今世界一大笑府
The past and present worlds are one big treasury of laughs.
我與若皆在其中供人話柄。
You and I are both in its midst. Providing fodder for talk.
不話不成人
One cannot be a person if one does not talk.
不笑不成話。
One cannot talk if one does not laugh.
不笑不話不成世界。
If there is no talk and no laughter, there is no world.
布袋和尚吾師乎？吾師乎？
Is the monk with the burlap sack my teacher? My teacher?!
墨憨齋主人題 Signed, the Master of the Inky Fool's Studio

What does Féng Mènglóng actually mean by *dànhuà* 淡話 'insipid idle chat' in this preface to his *Xiào fǔ*? Let's compare the meaning of *dàn*, as in *chědàn* 扯淡 'shoot the breeze' (homophonous with 'pulling at the balls'), and its gloss in the *Xiàndài hànyǔ cídiǎn* 現代漢語詞典 [Dictionary of modern Chinese]. *Dànhuà* and *chědàn* are both vulgarities based on homophony with the word *dàn* 蛋 'egg', which is a taboo word, for example, in the Běijīng dialect (as it also connotes 'testicles'). Hence in Běijīng the word *jīdàn* 雞蛋 was traditionally avoided for 'egg', and the synonym *jīzǐer* 雞子兒 'egg' was preferred. In 1965, the draft edition of the *Xiàndài hànyǔ cídiǎn*, edited by Dīng Shēngshù 丁聲樹, did not even include *jīdàn*, but only included *jīzǐer*, glossing that as "colloquial for *jīdàn*." [Editor/translator's note: Thus *dànhuà* 淡話 can also be understood to be more critical and vulgar than simply 'idle chat' and to mean something similar to 'bullshit'. Note also that *tán* 談 'to chat' and *dàn* 淡 'insipid' are often homophonous or almost homophonous in Wú 吳 dialects, differing only by tone, but sharing the same initial. So there are several layers of homophony and punning in this example.]

Below we examine examples of wordplay in the *Jīn Píng Méi* itself. We begin with the word *qiú* 囚 'convict', which is often used in the *Jīn Píng Méi* as an obscenity originally aimed at men; for example, the word *qiúgēnzi* 囚根子 'convict at root' is used as a euphemism for the homophonous word *qiúgēnzi* 屌根子 'cock-root' (i.e. 'prick', the male organ).[1]

1) 李瓶兒在簾外聽見，罵涎臉的**囚根子**不絕。(13.6a)
   'Lǐ Píng'ér, hearing them on the other side of the curtain, incessantly scolded him as a **shameless prick**.'
   Note: Here Lǐ Píng'ér is cursing Yīng Bójué 應伯爵 and others for continuing to drink at her home, thus keeping her from a liaison with Xīmén Qìng 西門慶.

2) 教你負心的**囚根子**，死無葬身之地。(13.10a)
   'You ungrateful **prick** ought to die and have nowhere to be buried.'
   Note: Here Pān Jīnlián 潘金蓮 is scolding Xīmén Qìng for having an illicit liaison with Lǐ Píng'ér.

3) 玳安這，'**賊囚根子**，久慣兒牢成，對著他大娘又一樣話兒，對著我又是一樣話兒。' (16.4b)
   '[Pān Jīnlián said,] "That **knave prick** Dài'ān has long been fixed in his ways; he feeds one story to me and another to his aunt."'

4) 月娘罵道，'**賊囚根子**，你不實說，教大小厮來吊拷你和平安兒,每人都是十板子。' (18.6b)
   'Auntie Yuè scolded, "You, **knave prick**, are not telling the truth. If you don't tell the truth, I'll have the elder servant boy hang you and Píng'ān'ér up for a flogging, ten strokes of the bamboo cane each."'
   Note: The use of *zéi-qiúgēnzi* 賊囚根子 'knave prick' as a vulgar castigation for a man is also seen in 26.12b, where Sòng Huìlián 宋惠蓮 curses at Lái'ān'ér 來安兒.

5) 西門慶口口聲聲只要採出**蠻囚**來，和粉頭一條繩子墩鎖在門房內。(20.15a)
   'Xīmén Qìng repeatedly declared that he wanted to gather up those **barbarous pricks** and use a length of rope in the room to bind them up with the strumpets.'
   Note: This is in reference to Xīmén Qìng cursing at Lǐ Guì'ér's 李桂兒 uncivilized johns.

---

1. Translator's note: Citations are drawn from the Míng Wànlì 萬曆 (r. 1572–1620) edition (1963 facsimile reprint published by Daian kabushiki geisha in Tokyo) unless otherwise indicated. Passages locations are identified by *huí* 回 and page number of the edition held in the Běijīng Library, a facsimile of which was published by Gǔyì xiǎoshuō kānxínghuì in 1933. We have added punctuation and bolded the words under discussion in the present article. The translation of each passage is our own.

6) 玉樓便道，**小囚兒**，你別要說嘴，這裡三兩一錢銀子，你快和來興兒替我買東西去。(21.7a)

'Yùlóu then said, "Keep your mouth shut you **little prick**. Here are three taels and a coin of silver. Hurry up and go shopping for me with Láixìng'ér."'

Note: Dài'ān is the one that Yùlóu is calling a *xiǎoqiú'ér* 小囚兒 'little cock'.

7) 金蓮罵道，'**賊囚**，猛可走來，嚇我一跳.' 金蓮怪道，'**囚根子**，唬的鬼也似的。'(26.14a).

'Jīnlián cursed, "**Knave's prick**! Walking up suddenly like that gave me a real fright." . . . Jīnlián censured him saying, "**Prick**, frightened like a ghost."'

Note: Here Jīnlián is cursing Xù'ān'ér 鈙安兒, the footboy.

8) 平白爹交我領了這**賊禿囚**來，好近遠兒，從門外寺里直走到家，路上通沒歇腳兒。走的我上氣兒接不著下氣兒。(49.14b)

'Dad Píngbái asked me to bring this **balding prick knave**. It was a fine distance, from the door of the temple straight to home, with no stopping. As I walked I could not catch my breath.'

Note: This is as Dài'ān 玳安 leading Húsēng 胡僧 to his home; he calls Húsēng a *zéitūqiú* 賊禿囚 'balding knave's prick' as he complains about the difficulty.

9) 金蓮道，**賊囚**你早不說做甚麼來。(58.21b)

'Jīnlián said, "**Knave's prick**, why didn't you say something sooner?"'

Note: This is in cursing Píng'ān 平安.

10) 春梅道，'怪小**蠻囚兒**，爹來家隨他來去，管俺每腿事。'(75.14a)

'Chūnméi said, "You creepy little **barbarous prick**. Let Dad do as he wishes at home. What business is it of ours to follow him about."'

Note: This is while cursing the footboy Chūnhóng 春鴻.

11) [韓道國]聽見胡秀口內放屁辣臊，心中大怒，走出來，踹（按：原文誤作'端'）了兩腳，罵道，'**賊野囚奴**，我有了五分銀子雇你一日，怕尋不出人來，即時趕他去。'(81.2a)

'[Hán Dàoguó] hearing Hú Xiù's farting protest, the sharp stench angered him, and he came out, kicked him, and cursed him saying, "You **wild slave to a knave's prick**. I hire you at five silver pieces a day and will have no trouble finding a replacement. Make yourself scarce and get out now!"'

12) 惠蓮道，'我早起身就往五娘屋裡，只剛才出來，你這囚在那裡來?' 平安道，'我聽見五娘教你醃螃蟹，說你會劈的好腿兒。' 嗔道，'五娘使你門首看著旋簸箕的，說你會哑的好舌頭。'把老婆說的急了，拿起條門拴來，趕著平安兒繞院子，罵道，'**賊汗邪囚根子**看我到明日對他說不說。'(23.8b).

'Huìlián said, "I got up early and went right to Wǔniáng's [the Fifth Mistress'] room. I have only just come out. Where'd you come from, you **prick**?" Píng'ān said, "I heard Wǔniáng telling you to pickle some crabs. She said you split [their/your] legs really well"; then crossly added "Wǔniáng wants you have a look at how those at the doorway wield their winnow baskets so you'll know how to wield your tongue for a satisfying suck." Fully rattled, the woman [Huìlián] pulled open the door bolt and chased Píng'ān'ér around the courtyard, saying, "See if I don't tell her about this tomorrow you wicked **prick of a sweating knave!**"'

Note: Here we see Huìlián cursing Píng'ān, first as *qiú* 'prick', then as *qiúgēnzi* 'cock-root'.

In annotations and commentaries, the syllable *qiú* 囚 is usually glossed as that of *zuìqiú* 罪囚 'guilty prisoner' or *qiúfàn* 囚犯 'prisoner' in the words *qiú* 囚, *qiúgēnzi* 囚根子 '*qiú* root', *xiǎo-qiú'ér* 小囚兒 'little *qiú*', *zéi-qiú* 'knave's *qiú*', *zéi-tūqiú* 'knave's bald *qiú*', *xiǎo mán qiú* 小蠻囚 'tiny uncivilized *qiú*', *yě qiú nú* 野囚奴 'wild slave to a *qiú*'. That is clearly understandable and easily apprehensible at first encounter. But we argue here that in *Jīn Píng Méi*, where the syllable *qiú* is used in expletives and curses, the character 囚 represents the word (or morpheme) otherwise written with the homophonous graph *qiú* 屌 'male organ', used as an obscenity to scold boys and men.

In the *Hànyǔ fāngyán dà cídiǎn* 漢語方言大詞典 'The Unabridged Dictionary of Chinese Dialects' (Xǔ and Miyata 1999, 4.5207), we find the word *qiú* 屌 for 'male organ' in a great many dialects, including: Xúzhōu in Jiāngsū 江蘇; Xī'ān 西安 in Shǎanxī 陝西; Tǔlǔfān 吐魯番 in Xīnjiāng 新疆; Zhèngzhōu 鄭州 in Hénán 河南; Tàiyuán 太原, Xīnzhōu 忻州, Wènshuǐ 汶水, and Yángqū 陽曲 in Shānxī 山西; Xīshuǐ 浠水 in Húběi 湖北; Qīngzhèn 清鎮 in Guìzhōu 貴州; and Chéngdū 成都 in Sìchuān 四川. For example, we find *qiú* 屌, glossed in this dictionary in reference to male genitals and as an obscenity to curse others, in the following dialect examples:

a. In Xúzhōu dialect *qiú* 屌 is pronounced [tɕʻiou⁵⁵], in phrases such as *gǔn dàn qù qiú* 滾蛋去屌 'get your balls out of here and go away you prick!' and *shuō-de guài hǎo, qiú!* 說得怪好，屌！ 'Said freaky right, prick!'

b. In Qīngzhèn in Guìzhōu 貴州, *qiú* 屌 is pronounced [tɕʻiou²¹], in phrases such as *bù xiǎo qiú dé* 不曉屌得 'don't friggin-prick know' and 屌二哥才幹那種事 'Only the prick second eldest brother would do that sort of thing'.

c. Mandarin dialects in Ürümqi (Wūlǔmùqí 烏魯木齊) and Turpan (Tǔlǔfān 吐魯番) in Xīnjiāng 新疆 have the word *qiúbǎzi* 屌把子 'the male genitals, penis', pronounced [tɕʻiəu²¹⁴⁻²³pɑ⁰tsɿ⁰] and [tɕʻiəu⁵¹⁻⁵³pɑ⁴⁴tsɿ⁰], respectively.

d. Xīnzhōu 忻州 dialect in Shānxī 山西 has the curse word *qiúpī* 屌坯 [tɕʻiəu³¹pʻei³¹³] 'fledging prick'.

Also, Lǐ Zhǔn 李準 uses the word and the graph *qiú* 毬 in a dialogue in his novel *Huánghé dōng liú qù* 黃河東流去 [The Yellow River flows on eastwards] (Chapter 14, Part 3; 1979, 180 and 2005, 166): "*Sì Quān shuō: 'Qiú!' Tā yòu kàn dǎ shāobǐng.*" 四圈説：'毬！' 他又看打燒餅. 'Sì Quān said, "Prick!" and went again to watch the making of the biscuits.'

The use of the graph *qiú* 囚 to write the homophone *qiú* 尿 is an ingenious stroke on the part of the author of the *Jīn Píng Méi*. It has baffled and misled countless numbers of readers, who have all taken it straightforwardly to mean *qiúfàn* 囚犯 'prisoner, jail-bird'.

Let us now turn to examine confusion over the writing of the name Yíng'ér in *Jīn Píng Méi*. Huáng lín 黃霖 has pointed out that in the novel, this single name is written with the graphs 迎兒 in some places and the graphs 蠅兒 in others. In his article in this volume, he notes that while the graphs *yíng* 迎 'to greet' and *yíng* 蠅 'housefly' are homophones in northern dialects, in modern Wú dialects they have very different onsets in their pronunciation: a nasal initial in the former and a zero initial in the latter, as Shànghǎi 上海 /n̠in²³/ vs /in⁵³/, respectively. He argues that a Wú speaker would not confuse the two and suggests that the author of the *Jīn Píng Méi* must have been a northerner who spoke a dialect that does not distinguish between the pronunciations of 迎 and 蠅. But for those who engage in language research, and especially for those who do research in dialects, this issue is really no problem at all. Writing Yíng'ér 迎兒 as 'Yíng'ér 蠅兒' is just an amusing use of near-homophony, and nothing more. Since the Wǔ Sōng story is set in the Shāndōng region and since Yíng'ér is a northern girl, it is perfectly natural to use northern homophony in this case. Pān Jīnlián hates this girl. So to write the name with characters that evoke a detestable pest, *yíng'ér* 蠅兒 'housefly', is perhaps even more delightful and amusing.

Perhaps the case of writing Yíng'ér 迎兒 as Yíng'ér 蠅兒 is similar to writing *pāi-shǒu* 拍手 'to clap one's hands' as *pái-shǒu* 排手 'to line up one's hands', as in the following examples:

13) 那婦人哽咽了一回大放聲**排手**拍掌哭起來 (26.11b).
    'That woman choked away tears for a while, then let out a loud sob, **put her hands together**, clapped, and began to cry.'

14) [Hǎiyán 海鹽] 子弟**排手**唱道 (49.5b).
    '[Hǎiyán's] troupe members **clapped** and sang.'
    Note: Here *pái-shǒu* 排手 is used to write *pāi-shǒu* 拍手 'clap'. Two other graphs that are similar to 排, 擵 and 石扉, are also used to represent 拍 in *Jīn Píng Méi*.

15) 你休只顧**石扉打**到幾時 (8.12a)
    'Stop being so absorbed in **banging** on with no end in sight.'
    Note: *Pāidǎ* '石扉打' is also written *pāidǎ* '擵打', the first graph in both words being similar in structure. This word *pāidǎ* 石扉打 and other similar words in *Jīn Píng Méi*, including *pāidǎ* 擵打, *pāigàn* 擵幹, and *pāipèng* 擵 硼, are vulgarities [for sexual acts], probably extensions of a basic meaning of 'slap' or 'bang on'.

Another case that is similar to writing Yíng'ér 迎兒 as 'Yíng'ér 蠅兒', is seen in *Jīn Píng Méi*, where *jiǎnzhuāng* 揀妝 'toiletry case' is sometimes written '*jiǎnzhuāng*

減妝' or 'jiǎnzhuāng 鑒妝'. Examples include the following (all writing 妝 with the alternative graph 粧):

16) 李瓶兒道，也罷，銀姐不吃飯，拿個盒蓋兒，我**揀粧**裡有果餡餅兒，拾四個兒來與銀娘吃吧。(44.7b)
'Lǐ Píng'ér said, "Ok, if sister Yín is not eating a rice meal, take a box lid and grab four of the pastries with fruit and nut filling that I have in my **toiletry case** to give to her to eat instead."'

17) 〔潘金蓮〕用纖手向**減粧**磁盒兒內，傾了些顫聲嬌藥末兒。(73.1b)
'[Pān Jīnlián] with her delicate hands sprinkled out some "Trembling Voice Charm" medicinal powder from the porcelain box that was in her **toiletry case**.'

18) 西門慶又替他買了半嫁粧描金箱籠、**鑑粧**、鏡架、盒礶、銅錫盆、淨桶、火架等件。(37.5a)
'Xīmén Qìng also bought half a trousseau of stuff in a filigree trunk for her [containing] a **toiletry case**, a mirror stand, box-shaped jars, a brass basin, a washing bucket, a brazier, and other things.'

In each of the three preceding examples, 'toiletry case' is written 'jiǎnzhuāng 揀粧', 'jiǎnzhuāng 減粧', and 'jiànzhuāng 鑑粧', respectively. The three variants are the same or similar in pronunciation and in fact indicate the same thing.

The Important Position of Southern Mandarin in Vernacular Literature

In this section, I briefly discuss the significant and pivotal position that southern Mandarin played in the evolution of *báihuà* vernacular literature.

In his *Yǒnglè dàdiǎn xìwén sān zhǒng jiàozhù* 永樂大典戲文三種校注, Qián Nányáng 錢南揚 (1899–1987) provides notes on regional cultural phenomena that are worth examining. The three operas he annotates in the volume, *Zhāng Xié zhuàngyuán* 張協狀元 [Top scholar Zhāng Xié], *Huànmén zǐdì cuòlìshēn* 宦門子弟錯立身 [The mistaken careers of the sons of officials], and *Xiǎo sūn tú* 小孫屠 [Little butcher Sūn], are among the oldest *xìwén* 戲文 and were created by talents who belonged to literary societies (*shūhuì* 書會) in Wēnzhōu 溫州 and Hángzhōu 杭州. *Zhāng Xié zhuàngyuán* was issued by the *Jiǔshān shūhuì* 九山書會 'Nine mountain literary society' in Yǒngjiā 永嘉 county, in what is today Wēnzhōu; *Xiǎo sūn tú* was "compiled by the literary society of ancient Hángzhōu" 古杭書會編撰; and *Huànmén zǐdì cuòlìshēn* was a "new compilation by the talents of old Hángzhōu 古杭才人新編." Additionally, several *nánqǔ* 南曲 'southern song' singing styles (*qiāng* 腔), including Yúyáo *qiāng* 余姚腔, Yìyáng *qiāng* 弋陽腔, Hǎiyán *qiāng* 海鹽腔, and Kūnshān *qiāng* 崑山腔, were also prevalent in the northern and southern reaches of the Yangtze watershed region. The northern drama (*běifāng zájù* 北方雜劇) of the Yuán 元 period (1271–1368) had decreased by the Míng dynasty, while *nánxì* 南戲

'southern drama' and *nánqǔ* were beginning to flourish. The frequent performances by Hǎiyán's troupe in *Jīn Píng Méi* reflect the rise of southern drama in the novel's time.

During the Jiājìng 嘉靖 period (1522–1566), Lǐ Kāixiān 李開先 (1502–1568), in the *Cí yuè piān* 詞樂篇 'Music of the lyric chapter' of his *Cí xuè* 詞謔 [Joy of the lyric], wrote:

> 如余姚董鸞、……錢塘毛士光、……崑山陶九官、……皆長於歌而劣於彈……北西廂擊木魚唱徹，無一曲不穩者。〔余姚董〕鸞則粧生做手猶高。(Yáng Jiāluò edition, 1974, 354)
> 'Like Dǒng Luán of Yú Yáo, . . . Máo Shìguāng of Qiántáng, . . . Táo Jiǔguān of Kūnshān, . . . all were better at singing and less talented at playing instruments. . . . In the *Northern and Western Wing*, in striking the wooden fish and singing straight through there was not a single note at which they were not able to hit perfectly. [Dǒng] Luán was especially good at playing the part of the *shēng* male lead.'

By the late Ming dynasty, the vocal instructor for the theatrical troupe of the southern opera writer Ruǎn Dàchéng 阮大鋮 (1587–1646) was Zāng Yìjiā 臧亦嘉 from Yúyáo 余姚 (near the area of modern Níngbō 寧波); at the time, the famous courtesans of the Qínhuáihé 秦淮河 district of Nánjīng 南京 included Kòu Báimén 寇白門, Gù Méi 顧眉, Lǐ Shíniáng 李十娘, Lǐ Xiāngjūn 李香君, Dǒng Xiǎowǎn 董小宛, Chén Yuányuán 陳圓圓, and Yáng Wǎnshū 楊宛叔, all of whom, besides singing Kūnqǔ 崑曲, also studied Yúyáo *qiāng* style singing with Zāng Yìjiā.

So it is easy to conceive the impact that the prevalence of the southern style *nánxì* and *nánqǔ* dramatic opera forms had on the written vernacular and how deeply the northern and southern types of Mandarin would have intertwined themselves in the process. To illustrate, next we consider the variants of a term referring to a 'busybody matchmaker of illicit liaisons, procuress': Mǎ Bāliù 馬八六, Mǎ Bóliù 馬泊六, Mǎ Bóliù 馬伯六, and Mǎ Bǎiliù 馬百六.

1) *Zhāng xié zhuàngyuán*, which is generally considered to be the earliest *nánxì* from the Sòng (960–1279) and Yuán periods, writes the name as 'Mǎ Bāliù 馬八六' in Act 45:

> （丑白）我勝花娘子，見報街道者：（唱）〔太子游四門〕，撞見**馬八六**。(Qián 2009, 190)
> '*The clown says* "I triumphed over the strumpet," *and seeing a crier announcing an arrival, sings to the tune of* The Crown Prince Tours the Four Gates: "I have run into **Mǎ Bāliù**."'

Qián Nányáng's annotation explains that "'Mǎ Bāliù' refers to someone who sets up illicit liaisons" (2009, 193, no. 15).

2) In Chapter 25 of the *Shuǐhǔ quán zhuàn* it is written 'Mǎ Bóliù 馬泊六', due to the near homophony of *bā* 八 and *bó* 泊:

便罵你這馬泊六，做牽頭的老狗。(Shànghǎi gǔjí edition 1984, 309)
'I'll curse you, you **Mǎ Bóliù**, for acting the go-between, you old dog'.

Another *Shuǐhǔ quán zhuàn* 'Mǎ Bóliù 馬泊六' example is found in Chapter 24:

王婆笑道： "老身為頭是做媒，又會做牙婆，也會抱腰，也會收小的，也會說風情，也會做馬泊六。" (Shànghǎi gǔjí edition 1984, 294)
'Old lady Wáng laughed and said, "My main occupation is as matchmaker; but I also am a procuress, and a midwife; I can assist with births; I can also assist in seductions, and can serve as a **Mǎ Bóliù**."'

3) In the Míng Wànlì 萬曆 (r. 1572–1620) edition of *Jīn Píng Méi*, we find the term written 'Mǎ Bóliù 馬伯六':

閑常也會做牽頭，做馬伯六，也會針灸看病，也會做貝戎兒。(2.11a)
'Usually in my idle time I also serve as a go-between and a **Mǎ Bóliù**; I can also provide medical advice and do acupuncture and moxabustion; and I am able to do "t-h-i-e-v-e-r-y."'

[Translator's note: *bèi-róng-ér* 貝戎兒 is a kind of anagram based on the elements in the graph *zéi* 賊, hence it means 'thief'.]

4) In the Míng Chóngzhēn 崇禎 (1628–1644) edition of *Jīn Píng Méi*, an abridged version of the sentence appears, but with 'Mǎ Bǎiliù 馬百六' (2.18a):

閑常也會作牽頭，做馬百六，也會針灸，看病。

5) Shěn Jǐng 沈璟 (1553–1610), of the Míng period, was from Wújiāng 吳江 in Jiāngsū. He also writes the word 'Mǎ Bǎiliù 馬百六' in Act Seven (*Dì qī chū* 第七齣), titled "Shèfú" 設伏 [Setting an ambush], in his *Yì xiá jì* 義俠記 [Records of the chivalrous] (1991, 405):

"你若有好親事，與我説一頭兒。若會做馬百六，我便費些錢也罷。"
'If you have marriage prospects, tell me something about it. If you can serve as **Mǎ Bǎiliù**, I can go ahead and spend a bit of cash.'

All understand what is meant by the four different ways of writing this appellation for a procuress of illicit liaisons that we see in the above examples—Mǎ Bāliù 馬八六, Mǎ Bóliù 馬泊六, Mǎ Bóliù 馬伯六, and Mǎ Bǎiliù 馬百六. But as for the source of the term, speculation varies widely.

The Qīng scholar Chǔ Rénhuò 褚人獲 (1635–1682), who was from Sūzhōu, in the Guǎng jí 廣集 [Broad collection] chapter of his *Jiānhù jí* 堅瓠集 [The 'Hard Gourd' Collection], has the following note:

俗呼撮合者曰馬伯六，不解其義。偶見《群碎錄》：北地馬群，每一牡將十餘牝而行，牝皆隨牡，不入他群……愚合計之，亦每伯［佰］牝馬用牡馬六匹，故稱馬伯六。(6.30a)

'A customary term for a go-between is Mǎ Bóliù, I found difficult to understand. Then I happened to see the following account in *Qún suì lù* 群碎錄 [Record of gathered fragments]: "In the horse herds of the northern lands, a stallion moves about in the lead of ten or so mares. The mares all follow the stallions and do not enter other herds. . . . I made my own humble accounting and found that for every hundred mares there are six stallions. Thus the phrase *mǎ-bó-liù* 馬伯六 means 'six out of a hundred horses'."[2]

An even wilder interpretation explains the term as derived from *mǎ-bó-* (or *pō*) *-liú* 馬伯(泊)留 'horse resting areas', in the following passage attributed to the *Hòu Hàn shū* 後漢書:[3]

"秦人居隴地時驅逐土人，對俘者男則奴之，女則留於馬槽而伯（泊）以供兵士，故兵士皆以馬伯留為樂。"

'When the Qín dwelled in the Lǒng territories [modern Gānsù 甘肅], they expelled the natives. From among the prisoners, men were put to slavery and women were left at the horse feeding troughs, where they stayed for the benefit of the soldiers. The soldiers thus all considered the "horse rest-stops [*mǎ-bó-*(= *pō*)-*liú*]" as enjoyment.'

It is our opinion that these various ways of writing are all due to the influences of the southern varieties of Mandarin. This is because the different graphs in the middle syllable—*bā* 八, *bó*~*pō* 泊, *bó* 伯, and *bǎ* 百—all represent *rù* 入 tone syllables that have the same or highly similar pronunciations in southern Mandarin. Because northern Mandarin dialects do not have a *rù* tone, the four syllables have diverged in pronunciation, are not homophones, and are not interchangeable in those dialects. Moreover, in most dialects in and around the Wú-speaking region [including much of southern Mandarin there], the syllables *lè* 樂 and *liù* 六 are homonyms, while in northern Mandarin dialects they are distinct in pronunciation. Thus, Mǎ Bāliù 馬八六, Mǎ Bóliù 馬泊六, Mǎ Bóliù 馬伯六, and Mǎ Bǎiliù 馬百六 are all most likely derived from *Mǎ Bó Lè* 馬伯樂 '"Horse Bó Lè"', which is in turn a reference to the legendary Bó Lè 伯樂, who was skilled at appraising horses by sight and at training and handling them. The term *Mǎ Bó Lè* 馬伯樂 was then extended to refer to a person who can size up and manage prospects for illicit relationships. In Wú and the Southern Mandarin dialects, all the variations on 'Mǎ Bóliù 馬伯六' are essentially homophonous with *Mǎ Bó Lè* 馬伯樂.

As we noted earlier, the earliest occurring use, and variant, of the term was as 'Mǎ Bāliù 馬八六' in the edition of *Zhāng Xié zhuàngyuán* issued by the *Jiǔshān shūhuì* in Yǒngjiā county, Wēnzhōu. In the modern Wēnzhōu dialect, *bā* 八 [bo³¹³] and *bǎi* 百 [pa³¹³] are different (Zhèngzhāng 2008), but we know that in the Jiāngshān

---

2. Translator's note: Extant copies of Chén Jìrú's 陳繼儒 (1518–1639) *Qún suì lù* 群碎錄 [Record of gathered fragments] do not have this passage. So Chǔ Rénhuò's citation is the only record of this account.

3. Translator's note: This passage can be found cited, for example, via Bǎidù 百度 at https://zhidao.baidu.com/question/78340567.html as well as at http://www.baike.com/wiki/馬伯六. But it is obviously an apocryphal internet folk etymology based on a false, phantom citation attributed to the *Hòu Hàn shū* 後漢書, in which it is in fact not found anywhere.

江山 dialect in the Zhèjiāng 浙江, and the Hǎimén 海門 and Qǐdōng 啟東 dialects in Jiāngsū 江蘇, as well as in many other Wú dialects, *bā* 八 and *bǎi* 百 (*bó* 伯) are homophones.[4] In the 'Mǎ Bóliù 馬泊六' variant of the term seen in *Shuǐhǔ zhuàn*, the syllables *bó* 泊 and the *bó* 伯 as in Bó Lè 伯樂 are homonyms in the Běijīng dialect and other northern Mandarin dialects.

In summary, through the various playful ways of writing names and words like the 'Yíng-ér 迎兒/蠅兒' pair, and the 'Mǎ Bóliù 馬伯六' varieties, we hope gradually to come to understand the splendid depth of the Chinese written culture, its character based wordplay, and the richness and complexity of *báihuà* vernacular literature.

We end with a double entendre from *Jīn Píng Méi*. Consider the word *niē* 捏 'pinch, squeeze, knead' in the following passage:

> 月娘道,"怪不的人說怪浪肉,平白教人家漢子**捏了捏**手,今日好了,頭也不疼,心口也不發脹了.。"玉樓笑道,"大娘你原來只少他一**捏兒**。"連大姊子也笑了。
>
> 'Yuèniáng said, "It's little wonder that folks say the wildly licentious wenches of the flesh often immodestly have fellows give their hand **a squeeze**. I'm better today. My headache is over and my stomach is no longer bloated." Yùlóu chuckled and replied, "So, Elder Auntie, it turns out that all you had lacked was a **kneading squeeze** from him." At that, even Elder Sister-in-Law let out a laugh.' (76.10b)

In Wēnlǐng, the syllables *rì* 日, *rè* 熱, *niè* 聶, *niè* 涅, *yè* 業, and *nüè* 虐 are all homophones and pronounced [ŋiəʔ²], in the *yángrù* 陽入 tone, while *niē* 捏 [ʔŋiəʔ⁵] is in the *yīnrù* 陰入 tone (Ruǎn 2014: 54).[5] Thus, *niē* 捏 would have been homophonous, or nearly homophonous, with *rì* 日 'day, daytime' and *rì* 㐹 'fuck'. A modern instance of this homophony is seen in a joke that circulated on WeChat social media during the winter solstice of December 21, 2016. Written in Níngbō 寧波 dialect and titled "*Dōngzhì*" 冬至 'winter solstice', the joke uses *niē* 捏 as a double entendre for *rì* 日: "*Kùn kùn dōngzhì yè, zuò zuò xiàzhì niē.* 困困冬至夜,坐坐夏至捏 [kʻuəŋ⁵-kʻuəŋ⁵ toŋ¹tsŋ⁵ ɦia⁶, zəu⁶-zəu⁶ ɦioʻtsŋ⁵ ŋiɪʔ⁸]' 'sleeping through the night of the winter solstice, sitting through the day of the summer solstice'.[6] In this line, the graph 困 writes the Wú dialect word *kùn* 睏 'sleep'; while *niē* 捏 [ŋiɪʔ⁸] stands in for the counterpart of *yè* 夜 [ɦia⁴] 'night'. That is to say, *niè* represents *rì* 日 [ŋiɪʔ⁸] 'daytime'.[7] As *rì* 日 and

---

4. Translator's note: For example, *bā* 八 'eight', *bǎi* 百 'hundred', *bó* 伯 'uncle' are all [pAʔ⁵] in Shànghǎi 上海 and [paʔ⁵] in Níngbō 寧波 (Xǔ and Tāng 1988; Zhū Zhāngnián 1990).
5. Translator's note: The two syllables *niè* 涅 and *niè* 捏 are homophonous in origin, both are CDC *niat⁸. The regular reflex in Wēnlǐng should be [ŋiəʔ²]. Ruǎn Yǒngméi notes that the altered tone in the syllable *niè* 捏 is likely due to Mandarin influence (personal communication).
6. Translator's note: The Níngō phonetic glosses are from Tāng Zhēnzhū 湯珍珠 et al. (1997). Níngbō homophony of *rì* 日 [ŋiɪʔ⁸] and *niē* 捏 [ŋiɪʔ⁸] confirmed in Zhū Zhāngnián et al. (1990). Our transcription gives only tone categories for the syllables (1 is *yīnpíng* 陰平, 5 is *yīnqù* 陰去, 6 is *yángqù* 陽去, and 8 is *yángrù* 陽入) and does not indicate the pitch contour or tone sandhi.
7. Note also that the Níngbō syllable *kùn* 睏 [kʻuəŋ⁵] can refer to sexual intercourse (Zhū Zhāngnián et al. 1990, 397). So in this WeChat line, *rì* 日 [ŋieʔ⁸] by extension refers to *rì* 㐹. Thus, the vulgar, erotic implication of the line is 'banging through the night of the winter solstice, sitting through the summer solstice and shagging'.

rì 日 are homonyms, and since niè 捏 can also be homophonous with them, this joke from Chapter 76 of *Jīn Píng Méi* is a play on words that follows the same phonetic realities as the WeChat joke.

The southern Wú pronunciation of *niè* 捏 (CDC *niat^8) [in its initial, final stop consonant, and tone category] reflects a preservation of an older pronunciation also seen in *rì* 日 (CDC *nhit^8) and *rì* 合 (CDC *nhit^8). This in turn reflects the dialect background of the above joke from the *Jīn Píng Méi*.

References

Primary sources

Chén Jìrú 陳繼儒 (1518–1639). *Qún suì lù* 群碎錄 [Record of gathered fragments]. Available at ctext.org.

Chǔ Rénhuò 褚人獲 (1635–1682). 2007. *Jiānhù jí* 堅瓠集 [The 'hard gourd' collection]. Shànghǎi: Shànghǎi gǔjí chūbǎnshè. A facsimile scan of an edition held by the Běijīng Library is also available at ctext.org and archive.org.

Féng Mènglóng 馮夢龍 (1574–1646). 1999. *Xiàofǔ* 笑府 [Treasury of laughs]. Běijīng: Zhōngguó xìjù chūbǎnshè.

Lánlíng Xiàoxiào Shēng 蘭陵笑笑生 (n.d.). 1963. *Jīnpíngméi cíhuà* 金瓶梅詞話 [Story of the Plum in the Golden Vase]. Facsimile reprint. Tokyo: Daian kabushiki gaisha 大安株式会社.

Lánlíng Xiàoxiào Shēng 蘭陵笑笑生 (n.d.). 1933. *Jīn Píng Méi cíhuà* 金瓶梅詞話 [Words from the *Plum in the Golden Vase*]. Facsimile of the Míng Wànlì 萬曆 (r. 1572–1620) edition held in the Běijīng Library. Běijīng: Gǔyì xiǎoshuō kānxínghuì 古佚小説刊行會.

Lánlíng Xiào Xiào shēng 蘭陵笑笑生 (n.d.). 1988. *Xīnkè xiùxiàng pīpíng Jīn Píng Méi* 新刻繡像批評金瓶梅 [Newly engraved and illustrated, critical *Jīn Píng Méi*]. Míng Chóngzhēn 崇禎 (r. 1628–1644) edition. Běijīng: Běijīng dàxué chūbǎnshè.

Lǐ Kāixiān 李開先 (1502–1568). 1937. *Cí xuè* 詞謔 [Joy of the lyric]. Běijīng: Zhōnghuá shūjú 中華書局. Also in Yáng Jiāluò 楊家駱, ed. 1974. *Lìdài shī shǐ chángbiān èrjí* 歷代詩史長編二輯 [Second collection of extended histories of poetry across the ages]. Vol. 3, 257–418. Taipei: Dǐngwén shūjú 鼎文書局.

Lǐ Zhǔn 李準. (1979) 2005. *Huánghé dōngliú qù* 黃河東流去 [The Yellow River flows on eastward]. Běijīng: Běijīng chūbǎnshè. Reprint, Běijīng: Rénmín wénxué chūbǎnshè.

Shěn Jǐng 沈璟 (1553–1610). 1991. *Shěn Jǐng jí* 沈璟集 [Collected works of Shěn Jǐng]. Shànghǎi: Shànghǎi gǔjí chūbǎnshè.

Shī Nàiān 施耐庵 (1296–1370). 1984. *Shuǐhǔ quán zhuàn* 水滸全傳 [The complete *Water Margin*]. 4 Vols. Shànghǎi: Shànghǎi gǔjí chūbǎnshè.

Yóuxì Zhǔrén 遊戲主人 [Master of play]. 1791. *Xīn juān Xiàolín guǎngjì: miùwù* 新鐫笑林廣記・謬誤 [Corrigenda chapter of the New Edition of the *Extensive Record of the Forest of Laughs*]. *Juàn* 卷 13. N.p.: Sāndétáng 三德堂 [Three Virtues Hall], Qiánlóng shíliù nián 乾隆十六年.

Secondary sources

Hanan, Patrick. 1981. *The Chinese Vernacular Story*. Cambridge, MA: Harvard University Press.

Luó Chángpéi 羅常培, and Lǚ Shūxiāng 呂叔湘. 1956. "Xiàndài Hànyǔ guīfàn wèntí" 現代漢語規範問題 [Issues in the standardization of modern Chinese]. In *Xiàndài Hànyǔ guīfàn wèntí xuéshù huìyì wénjiàn huìbiān* 現代漢語規範問題學術會議文件匯編 [Collected papers from the conference on issues in the standardization of modern Chinese]. Compiled by Xiàndài Hànyǔ guīfàn wèntí xuéshù huìyì mì chù 現代漢語規範問題學術會議秘處. Běijīng: Kēxué chūbǎnshè.

Norman, Jerry. 1988. *Chinese*. Cambridge, UK: Cambridge University Press.

Qián Nányáng 錢南揚 (1899–1987). 2009. *Yǒnglè dàdiǎn xìwén sān zhǒng jiàozhù* 永樂大典戲文三種校注 [Annotations for three plays preserved in the Yǒnglè encyclopedia]. Běijīng: Zhōnghuá shūjú.

Ruǎn Yǒngméi 阮咏梅. 2014. *Wēnlǐng fāngyán yánjiū* 溫嶺方言研究 [Research on the Wēnlǐng dialect]. Běijīng: Zhōngguó shèhuì kēxué chūbǎn shè.

Tāng Zhēnzhū 湯珍珠 et al., comp. 1997. *Níngbō fāngyán cídiǎn* 寧波方言詞典 [Níngbō dialect dictionary]. Lǐ Róng 李榮, ed. Nánjīng 南京: Jiāngsū jiàoyù chūbǎnshè, 1997.

Xǔ Bǎohuá 許寶華, and Miyata Ichirō 宮田一郎, eds. 1999. *Hànyǔ fāngyán dà cídiǎn* 漢語方言大詞典 [Unabridged dictionary of Chinese dialects]. 5 Vols. Běijīng: Zhōnghuá shūjú.

Xǔ Bǎohuá 許寶華, and Tāng Zhēnzhū 湯珍珠, comp. 1988. *Shànghǎi shìqū fāngyán zhì* 上海市區方言志 [Record of the Shanghai dialect in the city district]. Shànghǎi: Shànghǎi jiàoyù chūbǎnshè.

Zhāng Huìyīng 張惠英. 1979. "崇明方言的連讀變調" [Tone sandhi in the Chōngmíng dialect]. *Fāngyán* 方言 [Dialect] 4: 284–302.

Zhèngzhāng Shàngfāng 鄭張尚芳. 2008. *Wēnzhōu fāngyán zhì* 溫州方言志 [Record of the Wēnzhōu dialect]. Běijīng: Zhōnghuá shūjú.

Zhū Zhāngnián 朱彰年 et al., comp. 1990. *Níngbō fāngyán cídiǎn* 寧波方言詞典 [Dictionary of the Níngbō dialect]. Shànghǎi: Hànyǔ dàcídiǎn chūbǎnshè.

6
Division of Old and New Shànghǎi Dialects
A Comparative Study of Tǔhuà zhǐnán *and* Hùyǔ zhǐnán

Zhāng Měilán

Introduction

Compiled in the late Qīng, *Tǔhuà zhǐnán* 土話指南 [Guide to the Local Dialect (of Shànghǎi)] and *Hùyǔ zhǐnán* 滬語指南 [Guide to the Shànghǎi Dialect], which were both modeled on *Guānhuà zhǐnán* 官話指南 [Guide to Guānhuà], are remarkably accurate records of the state of the old and new Shànghǎi dialects of their day. Our study of their vocabulary indicates that at the time, although a large number of texts recorded the common characteristics of these varieties of the Shànghǎi dialect, the differences between the new and the old dialects have existed since the early nineteenth century. Scholars have previously explored some of these differences in lexicon, grammar, and phonetics. For example, *dìfāng* 地方 'place' replaced *hù dàng* 戶蕩 and *chǎnghuà* 場化; *wàitou* 外頭 'outside' and *wàimiàn* 外面 replaced *wàishì* 外勢 and *wàishǒu* 外首; *zuǒmiàn* 左面 replaced *zuǒbànpán* 左半爿; *ná* 拿 replaced *dān* 擔; *huíqù* 回去 replaced *guī qù* 歸去; and *nánwéiqíng* 難為情 replaced *tānchòng* 坍銃. The 1940s is recognized as the dividing boundary,[1] but we find that differences between the new and the old have existed since the late nineteenth century.

After Shànghǎi opened to foreign trade in 1843, the city quickly expanded and the population dramatically increased. With these circumstances, the Shànghǎi dialect began to take on greater regional prestige. The dialect gradually obtained the status of a regional standard to the extent that it came to be seen as the most representative Wú dialect. In our efforts to understand the Shànghǎi dialect of that time, we are fortunate that missionaries from France, Britain, Germany, and America compiled a large number of textbooks, dictionaries, and syllable tables of the Shànghǎi dialect immediately after Shànghǎi opened. In doing so, they provided us with material to trace the path of changes of the Shànghǎi dialect. The Mandarin textbook *Guānhuà zhǐnán* (1881) was compiled by Wú Qǐtài 吳啟太 and Zhèng Yǒngbāng

---

1. Shào Jìngmǐn (2014) states that Shànghǎi dialect of the past 100 years can be divided into three groups: the old group, the middle group, and the new group. Old Shànghǎi mainly refers to the people who were born before the 1940s; the middle group refers to the people born between the 1940s and the 1970s; and the new group refers to those who were born after the 1980s.

鄭永邦 from Nagasaki, Japan, who were stationed at Japan's Běijīng embassy. They were instructed and encouraged by the Chinese intellectuals Huáng Yùshòu 黃裕壽 and Jīn Guópú 金國璞. They later translated that textbook into a Shànghǎi dialect edition, the *Tǔhuà zhǐnán* (1889) to address the needs of missionaries in Shànghǎi. Later, *Hùyǔ zhǐnán* (1896) was compiled on the basis of *Tǔhuà zhǐnán*. Below is a list of the editions of these books used in the present study:

- A. ***Guānhuà zhǐnán*** in Mandarin (4 volumes), 1881, Tokyo: Bunkyūdō. (Below simply referred to as *Guide*.)
- B. ***Tǔhuà zhǐnán*** in Shànghǎi dialect (3 volumes), 1889/1908, Shànghǎi Tǔshānwān Címǔtáng. (Below simply referred to as *Tǔhuà*.)
- C. ***Hùyǔ zhǐnán*** in Shànghǎi dialect (2 volumes), 1908, Shànghǎi: American Presbyterian Mission Press. (Below simply referred to as *Hùyǔ*.)

The preface of *Tǔhuà zhǐnán* notes: "*Guānhuà zhǐnán* was originally written by Wú from Japan. It has categories like everyday conversations, the talk of diplomats, and the utterances of officials and businessmen. It is of great help to the beginners learning Mandarin. However, it is a pity that the missionaries in Sōng (Sōngjiāng 松江) cannot utilize it. So I translated it into the dialect for the sake of the many." Thus, we see that *Tǔhuà zhǐnán* is in Sōngjiāng dialect. The "Fāngyán" 方言 [Dialect] section of the *Shànghǎi xiànzhì* 上海縣志 [Shànghǎi County Annals] (1868) states: "Huátíng 華亭 pronunciation is the most prestigious among the dialects." Huátíng is the capital of Sōngjiāng township. Hence the Sōngjiāng dialect was the prestige dialect of the time.

Although the *Hùyǔ* translation was compiled eleven years after *Tǔhuà*, most of the lexicon remains the same, especially the common words. But it also reflects many differences. In this article, we mainly focus on differences in the lexicon. The data cited in the discussion that follows are drawn from the first two volumes of each text. The location of each set of examples is indicated by the volume number (in Roman numerals) and chapter number (in Arabic numerals following a colon) in parentheses following the English translation at the head of each set.

Discussion

Old Shànghǎi dialect uses dān 擔 'take' where the New Shànghǎi uses ná 拿

This phenomenon has been noted by Qián Nǎiróng 錢乃榮 (2003, 82). It appears in *Tǔhuà* and *Hùyǔ* when the words are verbs meaning 'to take'. Later the words grammaticalized to form the disposal marker.

As verbs with the meaning 'ask for', Volumes 1 and 2 of *Guānhuà* have four instances of *qǔ* 取. In *Tǔhuà* they are reflected by *dān* 擔 and in *Hùyǔ* by *ná* 拿:[2]

1) 'I will come back again here in a few days and fetch them.' (II:18)
   A. *Guide*: *Guò jǐ tiān wǒ zài shàng nín zhè'er **qǔ**-lái bà.*
      過幾天我再上您這兒**取**來罷。
   B. *Tǔhuà*: *Gé jǐ rì wǒ zàilái **dān** bà.*
      隔幾日我再來**擔**罷。
   C. *Hùyǔ*: *Xiē jǐ rì wǒ zài dào nóng cǐdì lái **ná** mò zāi.*
      歇幾日我再到儂此地來**拿**末哉。

As verbs meaning 'fetch', *ná* 拿 is used 69 times in the first two volumes of *Guānhuà*. *Tǔhuà* primarily uses *dān* 擔, 44 tokens; but we also found 9 instances of *ná*. *Hùyǔ* tends to use *ná*, with 59 tokens overall.

2) 'My master told me to bring this set of volumes'. (II:18)
   A. *Guide*: *Wǒmen lǎoyé dǎfā wǒ **ná** zhè tào shū lái.*
      我們老爺打發我**拿**這套書來。
   B. *Tǔhuà*: *Nì lǎoyé jiào wǒ **dān** gè bù shū lái.*
      伲老爺教我**擔**箇部書來。
   C. *Hùyǔ*: *Wǒ nì lǎoyé dǎfā wǒ **ná** dì bù shū lái.*
      我伲老爺打發我**拿**第部書來。

3) 'What's that man sitting in the compound with the bundle want?' (II:7)
   A. *Guide*: *Yuànzi lǐ zuòzhe dì nàgè **ná** zhe bāofú de rén, shì gàn shénme de?*
      院子裏坐着的那個**拿**着包袱的人，是幹甚麼的？
   B. *Tǔhuà*: *Tīngtáng shàng yīgè rénshǒu lǐ **dān** zhī yīgè bāoguǒ lǎo zuò lā, zuò shà gè?*
      廳堂上一個人手裏**擔**之一個包裹咾坐拉，做啥個？
   C. *Hùyǔ*: *Tiānjǐng lǐ zuò lā gè yī gè **ná** bāofú gèrén, shì zuò shà gè?*
      天井裏坐拉個伊個**拿**包袱個人，是做啥個？

Old Shànghǎi uses *dān* 擔 as the disposal particle while New Shànghǎi uses *na* 拿.

The prepositions indicating disposition *dān* 擔 and *ná* 拿 are derived from verbs *dān* and *ná*. Volumes 1 and 2 of *Guānhuà* have 135 tokens of the Mandarin preposition *bǎ* 把. *Tǔhuà* mostly uses sentences with patient subjects, while it also has 62 tokens

---

[2]. The three texts were originally written entirely in Chinese characters and included no Romanization. For the convenience and reference of the readers of this study we have transcribed all examples in modern standard Chinese pronunciation with *pīnyīn*. But it should be kept in mind that the *pīnyīn* represents neither the Guānhuà pronunciation nor the Shànghǎi pronunciation of the time. As the focus of this study is on the lexicon and not the phonology of the Shànghǎi dialect, this does not obscure the findings in any way. The morpheme under discussion is highlighted in bold in both *pīnyīn* and the Chinese character text.

of *dān* and 2 tokens of *ná*. *Hùyǔ* exclusively uses *ná*. It is obvious that *Hùyǔ* was influenced by the new group and the common language.

    4) 'Anyhow, please don't on any account divulge it, as it's a secret'. (I:16)
        A. *Guide*: Bùguǎn zěnme yàng, wǒ qiú nǐ qiān wàn bié **bǎ** zhège shì gěi xièlòule.
            不管怎麼樣，我求你千萬別**把**這個事給泄漏了。
        B. *Tǔhuà*: Wù yào guǎn yī nà néng, wǒ qiān wàn qiú géxià zǒng wù yào **dān** dì gè shì tǐ huà chūqù.
            勿要管伊那能，我千萬求閣下總勿要**擔**第個事體話出去。
        C. *Hùyǔ*: Wù guǎn nà néng, wǒ qiú nóng qiè bùkě **ná** dì gè shì tǐ huà kāi lái.
            勿管那能，我求儂切不可**拿**第個事體話開來。

    5) 'All of a sudden he pushed me backwards, and I nearly had a very bad fall'. (I:45)
        A. *Guide*: Tā chōulěngzǐ **bǎ** wǒ wàng hòu yī tuī, jīhū méi zāile gè dà jīndǒu.
            他抽冷子**把**我望後一推，幾乎沒栽了個大觔斗。
        B. *Tǔhuà*: Yī lěng mòshēng tóu li, hòumiàn **dān** wǒ yī tuī, wǒ jǐ jīhū diē xiàqù, dǎ yīgè jīndǒu.
            伊冷陌生頭裏，後面**擔**我一推，我幾幾乎跌下去，打一個觔斗。
        C. *Hùyǔ*: Wù fáng yī lěng shēng lǐ **ná** wǒ cháo hòu yī tuī, jīhū diē yīgè jīndǒu.
            勿防伊冷生裏**拿**我朝後一推，幾乎跌一個觔斗。

    6) 'Well, he was going to take back the Note itself'. (II:6)
        A. *Guide*: Zhèmezhe tā yào **bǎ** nà zhāngyuányín piào ná huíqù.
            這麼着他要**把**那張原銀票拿回去。
        B. *Tǔhuà*: Yī yào **dān** yuánpiào zi **ná** qù.
            伊要**擔**原票子**拿**去。
        C. *Hùyǔ*: Shí gài mò yī yào **ná** yī zhāng yín piào dài zhuàn qù.
            實蓋末伊要**拿**伊張銀票帶轉去。

Old Shànghǎi uses *tǎo* 討 'ask for', and now *yào* 要 is common usage

The first two volumes of *Guānhuà* have four tokens of *yào* 要, while *Tǔhuà* has two tokens of *tǎo* 討 and one token of *yào*. *Hùyǔ* has three tokens of *yào*.

    7) '(He) asked for this several taels of silver, whereupon Zǐyuán denied having any'. (II:16)
        A. *Guide*: Kě jiù hé tā **yào** nà jǐ qiān liǎng yínzi, Zǐyuán jiù bù rènle.
            可就和他**要**那幾千兩銀子，子園就不認了。
        B. *Tǔhuà*: Jiù tì yī **tǎo** gè jǐ qiān liǎng yínzi, Zǐyuán dào wù rèn zhě.
            就替伊**討**個幾千兩銀子，子園倒勿認者。
        C. *Hùyǔ*: Dào jiù dā yī **yào** yī gè jǐ qiān liǎng yínzi, zi yuán jiù wù rèn zāi.
            倒就搭伊**要**伊個幾千兩銀子，子園就勿認哉。

8) 'Every day there were always two or three men coming to my house wanting the amount of my gambling debt'. (II:26)

   A. *Guide: Jiàn tiān zǒng yǒu liǎng sān gèrén, dào wǒ jiālǐ qù **yào** dǔ zhàng.*
       見天總有兩三個人，到我家裏去**要**賭帳。

   B. *Tǔhuà: Rìzhú zǒng yǒu èrsān gèrén, dào wǒ wū li lái **tǎo** dǔ zhàng.*
       日逐總有二三個人，到我屋裏來**討**賭帳。

   C. *Hùyǔ: Měi rì zǒng yǒu liǎng sān gèrén, dào wǒ wū li lái **yào** dǔ zhàng.*
       每日總有兩三個人，到我屋裏來**要**賭帳。

Tǎo 'to ask for' appeared in the Northern and Southern Dynasties (420–589). In the late Táng Dynasty, *tǎo* meant 'asking for.' and was more commonly used in the Sòng and Yuán dynasties. In the Míng Dynasty, the usage of *yào* 要 began to become popular. This continued until the Qīng Dynasty when *tǎo* was completely replaced by *yào* 要. *Guānhuà* uses *yào*; *Hùyǔ* uses the new word; and *Tǔhuà* used the older common word of the Yuán and Míng periods.

Old Shànghǎi uses *huà* 話 'talk', and now *jiǎng* 講 is used

This change has been noted by Qián Nǎiróng (2003, 83). Volumes 1 and 2 of *Guānhuà* use nine tokens of *shuō hé* 說合 'manage a dispute'. *Tǔhuà* uses both *huàlǒng* 話攏 and *huà* 話. *Hùyǔ* uses *jiǎnghé* 講和 and *jiǎngshūqí* 講舒齊. The nuclear morpheme is *huà* 話 in the older examples and *jiǎng* 講 in the newer.

9) 'I have been managing a dispute. And what was the dispute you have been managing?' (II:19)

   A. *Guide: Wǒ shì gěi rén shuōhé shìqíngle. Nín shì gěi rén shuōhé shénme shìqíng láizhe?*
       我是給人**說合**事情了。您是給人**說合**甚麼事情來着？

   B. *Tǔhuà: Wǒ lā tì biérénjiā huàlǒng yī zhuāng shìtǐ. Tì shà rén huà yī zhuāng shà shìtǐ yé?*
       我拉替別人家**話攏**一莊事體。替啥人**話**一莊啥事體耶？

   C. *Hùyǔ: Wǒ shì dā rén huà jiàn shìtǐ. Nóng shì dā rén huà shà shìtǐ ne?*
       我是搭人**話**件事體。儂是搭人**話**啥事體呢？

10) '[I] directed them to go out of court and get someone, before going farther, to try and effect an arrangement. If none was possible, further pleas to be put in, and another hearing to be held'. (II:19)

   A. *Guide: Jiù fēnfù jiào tāmen xiàqù zhǎo rén xiān **shuōhé**; ruòshì **hé** bù liǎo, zài bǔ yī zhāng chéngcí, zài **shuō** jiùshìle.*
       就吩咐叫他們下去找人先**說合**，若是**合**不了，再補一張呈詞，再**說**就是了。

   B. *Tǔhuà: Jiù jiào yī lā xiàqù jiào rén **huàlǒng** lái; **huà** wù **lǒng** wèi, zài xiě zhuàngzhǐ lái lǎo, zài shěn.*
       就教伊拉下去教人**話攏**來，**話**勿**攏**咪，再寫狀紙來咾，再審。

C. *Hùyǔ*: *Jiù fēnfù jiào yī lā xiàqù xún rén xiān **jiǎnghé**; ruòshì **hé** wù hǎo, zài bǔ yī zhāng zhuàngzi, zài huà jiùshì zāi.*
就吩咐伊拉下去尋人先**講和**，若是**和**勿好，再補一張狀子，再**話**就是哉。

Old Shànghǎi uses the verb *hǎn* 喊 'to rent a cart' or 'to invite someone', and now *jiào* 叫 is used

Guānhuà uses *gù* 僱 to rent (a cart). *Hùyǔ* has nine tokens of the old *hǎn* 喊, and two tokens of *qǐng* 請. But *Tǔhuà* has eight tokens of the new *jiào* 叫, two tokens of *jiào* 教, and one token of *xún* 尋.

11) 'The people in our hotel had hired a wheel-barrow for a visitor, to carry his baggage'. (II:21)
    A. *Guide*: *Wǒmen zhàn lǐ gěi yīgè kèrén **gù** xiǎo chēzi yùn xínglǐ láizhe.*
    我們棧裏給一個客人**僱**小車子運行李來着。
    B. *Tǔhuà*: *Nì zhàn lǐ **jiào** xiǎo chēzi tì kèrén lābān xínglǐ.*
    伲棧裏**叫**小車子替客人拉搬行李。
    C. *Hùyǔ*: *Wǒ nì zhàn lǐ dā yīgè kèrén **hǎn** zhī xiǎo chēzi zhuāng zhī xínglǐ lái.*
    我伲棧裏搭一個客人**喊**之小車子裝之行李來。

Old Shànghǎi uses *lù qǐlái* 跺起來 'to get up', and now *qǐlái* 起來 is used

This change has been noted by Qián Nǎiróng (2003, 83). *Tǔhuà* has two tokens of *lù qǐlái* 跺起來, eleven tokens of *qǐshēn* 起身, and three tokens of *qǐlái* 起床. *Hùyǔ* uses only (*pá*)*qǐlái* 爬起來. *Lùqǐlái* 跺起來 is the old lexeme of Shànghǎi dialect. *Tǔhuà* uses both old and new words; *Hùyǔ* only uses the new expression.

12) 'I got up and walked out in the dawn, and I see the frost on the tiles is very thick'. (I:25)
    A. *Guide*: *Zǎoqǐ tiāncái liàng, wǒ **qǐlái** chūqù zǒudòng, kànjiàn wǎ shàng de shuāng hòu de hěn.*
    早起天才亮，我**起來**出去走動，看見瓦上的霜厚的很。
    B. *Tǔhuà*: *Zǎochén tóu tiānliàng zhī, wǒ **lùqǐlái**, wài shì qù kàn kàn. Wǎ shàng shuāng hòu lái jiāo guān.*
    早辰頭天亮之，我**跺起來**，外勢去看看。瓦上霜厚來交關。
    C. *Hùyǔ*: *Zǎochén tiāncái liàng, wǒ **qǐlái** chūqù zǒuzǒu, kànjiàn wǎshàng gè shuāng hòu dé jí.*
    早晨天纔亮，我**起來**出去走走，看見瓦上個霜厚得極。

13) 'I was just up, and when I heard of this I made haste and washed my face'.
    (II:21)
    A. *Guide*: *Wǒ cái **qǐlái**, tīngjiàn zhège shìqíng, wǒ jiù gǎnjǐn de xǐle liǎn.*
       我才**起來**，聽見這個事情，我就趕緊的洗了臉。
    B. *Tǔhuà*: *Wǒ kèkè **lùqǐlái**, tīngjiàn zhī dì gè shìtǐ, jiù mángshā néng kāi zhī yī bǎ miàn.*
       我刻刻**踣起來**，聽見之第個事體，就忙煞能揩之一把面。
    C. *Hùyǔ*: *Wǒ cái **qǐlái**, tīngjiàn dì gè shìtǐ, wǒ jiù gǎnjǐn gè kāi zhī miàn.*
       我才**起來**，聽見第個事體，我就趕緊個揩之面。

Old Shànghǎi uses *xiāngbāng* 相幫 'to help', while *zhàoyìng* 照應 and *bāng* 幫 are used today.

This change has been noted by Qián Nǎiróng (2003, 85). *Guānhuà* has eight tokens of *xiàoláo* 效勞, *bāng* 幫, and *wéilì* 為力. But *Tǔyǔ* solely uses the old *xiāngbāng* 相幫. *Hùyǔ* uses the new *zhàoyìng* 照應, *wéilì* 為力, *bāng* 幫, and *xiàoláo* 效勞, maintaining a consistency with Mandarin.

14) 'My relative asked me to come forward and reconcile them'. (II:19)
    A. *Guide*: *Wǒmen qīnqi zhǎo wǒ **bāngzhe** tā, chūqù gěi tāmen shuōhé.*
       我們親戚找我**幫著**他，出去給他們説合。
    B. *Tǔhuà*: *Nì shèqīn wèi jiào wǒ **xiāngbāng** yī lā, qù tì yī lāhuà-lónglái.*
       伲舍親味教我**相幫**伊拉，去替伊拉話攏來。
    C. *Hùyǔ*: *Wǒ nì qīnjuàn xún wǒ **bāng** yī, chūqù tì yī lājiǎnghé.*
       我伲親眷尋我**幫**伊，出去替伊拉講和。
15) 'He has never helped anyone, nor given any money to charity'. (II:30)
    A. *Guide*: *Xiànglái tā bù bāng rén, bùzuò hǎoshì.*
       向來他不幫人，不作好事。
    B. *Tǔhuà*: *Wù kěn **xiāngbāng** biérén, wù kěn zuò hǎoshì gè.*
       勿肯**相幫**別人，勿肯做好事個。
    C. *Hùyǔ*: *Xiànglái yī wù zhàoyìng rén, wù zuò hǎoshì.*
       向來伊勿照應人，勿做好事。

Old Shànghǎi uses *xiāngbāngrén* 相幫人 'servant'; now *yòngrén* 用人 and *dǐxiàrén* 底下人 are preferred

Volumes 1 and 2 of *Guānhuà* have fourteen tokens of *dǐxiàrén* 底下人 for the word 'servant' and eight tokens of *gēnrén* 跟人. *Tǔhuà* uses *xiāngbāngrén* 相幫人 sixteen times, and has two tokens of *gēnbān* 跟班, one token of *dǐxiàtóurén* 低下頭人,

and one token of *yònglāgèrén* 用拉個人. Meanwhile, *Hùyŭ* has fourteen tokens of *dĭxiarén* and seven tokens of *yòngrén* 用人.[3]

16) 'Some time afterwards one of the merchant's servants let out the story'. (II:31)

    A. *Guide: Hòulái háishì nàgè măimài kèrén de yīgè **gēnrén** xièlòu chū de.*
       後來還是那個買賣客人的一個跟人泄漏出的。

    B. *Tŭhuà: Hòulái zuò shēngyì kèrén gè **xiāngbāngrén** huà chūlái gè.*
       後來做生意客人個相幫人話出來個。

    C. *Hùyŭ: Hòulái háishì yīgè shēngyì kèrén gè yī gè **yòngrén** huà chūlái gè.*
       後來還是伊個生意客人個一個用人話出來個。

17) 'Then he asked his two servants how it was that two boxes had been taken wrong. It wasn't their fault, they said'. (II:21)

    A. *Guide: Tā jiù wèn tā nà liă **dĭxiarén**, zěnme huì yùn cuòle liăng zhī xiāngzi ní? Nà liă **gēnrén** shuō, bùshì tāmen de cuò.*
       他就問他那倆底下人，怎麼會運錯了兩隻箱子呢？那倆跟人説，不是他們的錯。

    B. *Tŭhuà: Jiù wèn liăng gè **gēnbān** lăo huà, nà néng nòng cuò zhī liăng zhī xiāngzi gè ne? Yī lā liăng jiā tóu huà, wù shì yī lā nòng cuò gè.*
       就問兩個跟班咾話，那能弄錯之兩隻箱子個呢？伊拉兩家頭話，勿是伊拉弄錯個。

    C. *Hùyŭ: Yī jiù wèn yī gè **dĭxiarén**, nà néng huì nòng cuò zhī liăng zhī xiāngzi ní? Yī liăng gè **yòngrén** huà, wù shì yī lā gè cuò.*
       伊就問伊個底下人，那能會弄錯之兩隻箱子呢？伊兩個用人話，勿是伊拉個錯。

Volumes 1 and 2 of *Guānhuà* also use four tokens of *gēnbānde* 跟班的. *Tŭhuà* uses two tokens of *xiāngbāngrén* and two tokens of *gēnbān*. *Hùyŭ* uses four tokens of *gēnbān*. Wade (1886/2000) mentions *gēnbān('er) de* 跟班兒的, and states that only southern dialects used *gēnbān*.

For 'embarrassed', the old expression is *tānchòng* 坍坉/坍銃, while *wúmiànkŏng* 無面孔 is now more frequently used. (Qián Năiróng 2003, 86)

Guānhuà uses *diūliăn* 丟臉. *Tŭhuà* uses the old word *tānchòng*, which is still in use in some suburbs. *Hùyŭ* uses the old word *wúmiànkŏng*.

---

3. *Yuèyīn zhĭnán*, the Cantonese edition of *The Guide to Guānhuà* mainly uses '(dĭ)xiarén 底下人 or *gēnrén*. Another Cantonese edition of *The Guide to Guānhuà*, *Dīngzhèng yuèyīn zhĭnán* 訂正粵音指南, mainly uses *huŏjì* 夥計 or *gēnbān* 跟班.

18) 'He himself would be embarrassed'. (I:11)
    A. *Guide: Zìjǐ yě **diūliǎn**.*
       自己也丟臉。
    B. *Tǔhuà: Zìjiā **tānchōng**.*
       自家坍埫。
    C. *Hùyǔ: Zìjiā yě **wúmiànkǒng** gè.*
       自家也**無面孔**個。
19) 'If you find a place for him, he will certainly do you no credit'. (II:17)
    A. *Guide: Ruòshì gěi tā zhǎoshì, tā bì **bù néng** gěi nín **zuòliǎn**.*
       若是給他找事，他必**不能**給您作臉。
    B. *Tǔhuà: Tì yī xún chāishǐ, yī bǎn yào **tānchōng** gè.*
       替伊尋差使，伊板要**坍埫**個。
    C. *Hùyǔ: Ruòshì tì yī xún shì tǐ, yī yīdìng **wù néng** tì nóng **liú shà miànkǒng**.*
       若是替伊尋事體，伊一定**勿能**替儂**留啥面孔**。
20) 'He couldn't hide his embarrassment, and took away the money, looking very much confused'. (II:33)
    A. *Guide: Tā liǎn shàng hěn mò bu kāi, jiù **xiūxiūcáncánde**, bǎ yínzi ná huíqùle.*
       他臉上很磨不開，就**羞羞慚慚的**，把銀子拿回去了。
    B. *Tǔhuà: Miànkǒng shàng wù hǎoyìsi, **tāntānchōngchōng**, dān zhī yínzi lǎo zhuàn qù gè.*
       面孔上勿好意思，**坍坍埫埫**，擔之銀子咾轉去個。
    C. *Hùyǔ: Yī miànkǒng shàng jíqí fàng wù kāi, jiù **tāntānchòngchòng**, ná yínzi ná zhuàn qù zāi.*
       伊面孔上極其放勿開，就**坍坍埫埫**，拿銀子拿轉去哉。

The old expression for 'everyday' is *rìzhú* 日逐, and the new one is *měirì* 每日. (Xǔ Bǎohuá and Táo Huán 1995)

For 'everyday', *Guānhuà* uses four tokens of *jiàntiān* 見天 showing a feature of Běijīng Dialect. *Rìzhú* 日逐 is a Wú dialect word and is only seen in *Tǔhuà*. It was still in use in the 1930s, while the new expression *měirì* 每日 is used in *Hùyǔ*.

21) 'You take some medicine according to the directions'. (II:25)
    A. *Guide: **Jiàntiān** nǐ jiù àn-zhe nàgè fāngzi chī yào.*
       見天你就按着那個方子吃藥。
    B. *Tǔhuà: **Rìzhú** zhàozhī fāngzi lǎo chī yào.*
       日逐照之方子咾吃藥。
    C. *Hùyǔ: **Měirì** nóng zhào zhī yī zhāng fāngzi lǎo chī yào.*
       每日儂照之伊張方子咾吃藥。

22) '(He) used to receive several dozens of patients every forenoon'. (II:37)
   A. *Guide:* **Jiàntiān** *zǎoqǐ qiáo ménmài de zǒngyǒu jǐshí hào.*
      見天早起瞧門脈的總有幾十號。
   B. *Tǔhuà:* **Rìzhú** *zǎochéntou ménshàng kànbìng ge zǒngyǒu jǐshí hào.*
      日逐早辰頭門上看病個總有幾十號。
   C. *Hùyǔ:* **Měirì** *zǎochen shàngmén kàn zhěn ge zǒngyǒu jǐshí hào.*
      每日早晨上門看診個總有幾十號。

The old expression for '*outside*' is wàishì 外勢, and the new one is wàitou 外頭. (Qián Nǎiróng 2003, 181)

Guānhuà uses 12 tokens of *wài* and *wàitou* for the location 'outside'. *Hùyǔ* all uses the new *wàitou*. *Tǔhuà* uses more *wàishi* (8 tokens) and less *wàimian* (1) or *wàitou* (3).

23) 'How have things gone with you since you've been away?' (II:24)
   A. *Guide:* *Nǐ zhè jǐ nián zài* **wàitou**, *shìqing zěnmeyang?*
      你這幾年在**外頭**，事情怎麼樣？
   B. *Tǔhuà: Jǐ nián la* **wàishì**, *shìtǐ nànéng?*
      幾年拉**外勢**，事體那能？
   C. *Hùyǔ: Nóng dì ge jǐ nián la* **wàitou** *ge shìtǐ nànéng?*
      儂第個幾年拉**外頭**個事體那能？

For the first-person plural pronoun, the old expression is *nì* 伲 (colloquial), and the new expression is *wǒni* 我伲 (formal) (Xǔ Bǎohuá and Táo Huán 1995)

Wǒmen 我們 is used in *Guānhuà*, and *Tǔhuà* uses more *nì* 伲 and sometimes *zìnì* 自伲 (6 tokens) but no *wǒnì* 我伲. *Hùyǔ* mainly uses *wǒnì* 我伲 (170 tokens) and sometimes *nì*.

24) 'We are both out of employment at present; What's to be done?' (I:13)
   A. *Guide:* **Wǒmen** *liǎ rújīn dōu xiánzhe, kě zuò shénme hǎo ne?*
      我們倆如今都閑着，可作甚麼好呢？
   B. *Tǔhuà:* **Nì** *liǎng jiātóu xiànzài dàjiāchái wú shá zuò, kěyǐ zuòzuò shàmo hǎo ne?*
      伲兩家頭現在大家儕無啥做，可以做做啥末好呢？
   C. *Hùyǔ:* **Wǒnì** *liǎng jiātou xiànzài quán wú shìtǐ, zuò shàmo hǎo ne?*
      我伲兩家頭現在全無事體，做啥末好呢？

Old Shànghǎi uses *ā* 阿 *VP* construction for repetition questions and the new group uses VP *fǒu* 否

The pattern "*ā* 阿 + VP" forms choice-type questions in Wú dialects. *Tǔhuà* has 28 tokens using this pattern (21 tokens of *āshì* 阿是 . . . ? 4 tokens of *āyào* 阿要 . . . ? and 3 tokens of *ā* 阿 VP . . . ?). *Hùyǔ* only has 6 tokens (5 tokens of *āshì* 阿是 . . . ? and 1 token of *ā* 阿 *VP* . . . ?). *Ā* 阿 + VP examples in the sources correspond sentences with *shì* 是, which reveals that this pattern forms "yes–no" questions. The questions in the *ā* 阿 + VP form were most likely influenced by the Wú Dialect of Sūzhōu and the adjacent area. The pattern was common in the old Shànghǎi dialect but rare in the dialect after the first half of the twentieth century. This construction is a counterpart of the "yes–no" questions seen in *The Guide to Guānhuà*.

25) 'Has he filled the vacancy?' (II:3)
   A. *Guide*: **Shì** *bǔ-guo shíquē de ma?*
      是補過實缺的麼？
   B. *Tǔhuà*: **Ā céng** *bǔ-guo xiē shíquē ge?*
      阿曾補過歇實缺個？
   C. *Hùyǔ*: **Shì** *bǔ-guo shíquē ge* **fǒu***?*
      是補過實缺個否？

26) 'Do you have to sign a written agreement?' (II:14)
   A. *Guide*: **Shì** *hái děi xiě ge zìjù ma?*
      是還得寫個字據麼？
   B. *Tǔhuà*: **Āyào** *xiě shà zhǐzhāng ge?*
      阿要寫啥紙張個？
   C. *Hùyǔ*: **Shì** *hái yào xiě yī-ge guānyuē* **fǒu***?*
      是還要寫一個關約否？

27) 'Do you know how much the rent is a month?' (II:1)
   A. *Guide*: **Kěshì** *nín zhīdao yī yuē shi duōshāo fángqián ma?*
      可是您知道一月是多少房錢麼？
   B. *Tǔhuà*: **Gēmo** *géxià xiǎode yī ge yuè jǐhuà fángqián?*
      格味閣下曉得一個月幾化房錢？
   C. *Hùyǔ*: *Nóng* **ā xiǎode** *yī ge yuē yào jǐhuà fángqián?*
      儂阿曉得一個月要幾化房租？

Old Shànghǎi uses *chái* 儕, *zǒng* 總, and *tū* 秃 for 'all' while the more recent expression is *quán* 全

Guānhuà uses the adverb *dōu* 都 and *Hùyǔ* uses the newer *quán* 全. The expressions in *Tǔhuà* are complex: it has 80 zero forms, while the remainder have 44 tokens of *chái* 儕, a Shànghǎinese word, 7 tokens of *zǒng* 總, and 5 tokens of *tū* 秃, as well as some tokens of *wánquán* 完全 (2), *yīqí* 一齊 (2), *yītāo* 一淘 (2), *yīgài* 一概 (1) and *hái* 還 (1).

28) 'The two cart pushers are unfamiliar with the road'. (II:29)
   A. *Guide: Nà liǎng gǎnchēde lù **dōu** bù shóu.*
      那倆趕車的路**都**不熟。
   B. *Tǔhuà: Liǎng ge tuīchēzige lù **chái** wù rènde ge lao.*
      兩個推車子個路**儕**勿認得個咾。
   C. *Hùyǔ: Yī liǎng ge tuīchēzige lù **quán** wù shú.*
      伊兩個推車子個路**全**勿熟。

Old Shànghǎi uses *shēngla* 生拉 (*shēnglai* 生來) for 'naturally' as an adverb, and the new group uses *zìrán* 自然 (Qián Nǎiróng 2003, 87)

29) 'If you take the contract, of course you must offer better terms than the others'. (II:10)
   A. *Guide: Nàme ruòshì nǐ bāo nàge huó, **zìrán** zǒng bǐ biéren piányi diǎnr a.*
      那麼若是你包那個活，**自然**總比別人便宜點兒啊。
   B. *Tǔhuà: Gè zhuāng shēnghuó bāo-bō zìnóng, **shēngla** bǐ biéren piányi diǎn.*
      個妝生活包撥自儂，**生拉**比別人便宜點。
   C. *Hùyǔ: Gàimo ruòshi nóng bāo yī ge shēnghuo, **zìrán** zǒng bǐ biéren piányi diǎn.*
      蓋末若是儂包伊個生活，**自然**總比別人便宜點。

30) 'Dr. Fang said, "of course the wife will be examined first"'. (II:37)
   A. *Guide: Fāng dàifu shuō, nà **zìrán** shì tàitai xiān qiáo.*
      方大夫説，那**自然**是太太先瞧。
   B. *Tǔhuà: Fāng xiānsheng huà, **shēngla** tàitai xiān kàn.*
      方先生話，**生拉**太太先看。
   C. *Hùyǔ: Fāng lángzhōng huà, **zìrán** tàitai xiān kàn.*
      方郎中話，**自然**太太先看。

The old expression for 'just, in the midst of' is *tiēzhèng* 貼正. The new expression is *zhènghǎo* 正好 and *wánquán* 完全 (Qián Nǎiróng 2014, 326)

Tǔhuà has 11 tokens of expressions meaning 'just'. *Hùyǔ* has 2 tokens of *tiēzhèng* and 2 tokens of *tiēzhǔn* 貼准.

31) 'Right while I was sitting there, drinking my tea, Yú Pèi came back'. (II:35)
   A. *Guide: Xiǎode **zhèng** zuò-zai wūli hē chá le, zhè ge gōngfū-r, Yú Pèi jiā-qù le.*
      小的**正**坐在屋裏喝茶了，這個工夫兒，俞配家去了。

B. *Tǔhuà: Xiǎode **tiēzhèng** zuò la wūli, chī chá ge chénguāng, Yú Pèi dào zhe.*
小的**貼正**坐拉屋裏，吃茶個辰光，俞配到者。

C. *Hùyǔ: Xiǎode **tiēzhǔn** zuò la fángli chī chá, dìge shíhou, Yú Pèi jiù zhuǎn-lai zai.*
小的**貼准**坐拉房裏吃茶，第個時候，俞配就轉來哉。

16. The old group uses *chángzhuāng* 常莊 for 'usually' and the new group uses *zǒng* 總 (Qián Nǎiróng 2014, 319)

Tǔhuà and *Hùyǔ* both use *zǒng* 總, but in *Tǔhuà* there are 6 tokens of *chángzhuāng* 常莊, the feature word of the Shànghǎi dialect; that is more than those in *Hùyǔ* (3 tokens). It seems that *Tǔhuà* tends to use the old expressions.

32) 'I suppose for these few days you remain at home, don't you? I do, yes'. (II:3)
A. *Guide: Lǎodì zhè jǐtiān **zǒng** zàijiā bà? Shì, zhè liǎngtiān **zǒng** zàijiā.*
老弟這幾天**總**在家罷？是，這兩天**總**在家。
B. *Tǔhuà: Dì gèjǐ rìli lǎodì **chángzhuāng** lā wūlǐ fǒu? Hā, dì gèliǎng rìli **chángzhuāng** lā wūlǐ.*
第個幾日裏老弟**常莊**拉屋裏否？哈，第個兩日裏**常莊**拉屋裏。
C. *Hùyǔ: Lǎodì dì liǎngrì **zǒng** lā wūlǐ ge zāi? Shì gè, dì liǎngrì **zǒng** lāwū lǐ.*
老弟第兩日**總**拉屋裏個哉？是個，第兩日**總**拉屋裏。

33) 'How is it you've been not at home every time I've come to see you?' (II:19)
A. *Guide: Zěnme wǒ lái zhǎo nín hǎojǐ dàng, nín **dōu** méi zàijiā.*
怎麼我來找您好幾蕩，您**都**沒在家。
B. *Tǔhuà: Wǒ lái xún duōhuí zhe, **chángzhuāng** wù lā wūlǐ.*
我來尋多回者，**常莊**勿拉屋裏。
C. *Hùyǔ: Nànéng wǒ lái xún nóng hǎojǐ dàng, nóng **zǒng** wù lā wūlǐ.*
那能我來尋儂好幾蕩，儂**總**勿拉屋裏。

The old expression for proximal demonstrative is *gè* 個 (used in Sōngjiāngfǔ) and the new one is *dì* 第 (used in the city of Shànghǎi) (Xǔ Bǎohuá and Táo Huán 1995)

Guānhuà uses *zhè* 這 as the proximal demonstrative. *Tǔhuà* mostly uses *ge* 個, with 4 tokens of *dì* 第. *Hùyǔ* only uses *dì* 第 and *cǐ* 此. Examples of these are seen in sets #1, #2, #4, and #13 above and #36 below. As a counterpart of *zhèchéngzi* 這程子 'these days' in *Guānhuà*, *gèyīshí* 個一時 is used in *Tǔhuà*, while *Hùyǔ* uses *dìliǎngrì* 第兩

日. For 'here', *Tǔhuà* uses *gèdā* 個搭 'this place', while *Guānhuà* uses *zhèr* 這兒 and *Hùyǔ* uses *cǐdì* 此地 or *dìge* 第個, as seen in examples in sets #1 and #4 above.

The old expression is *wúde* 無得 (used in Sōngjiāng) for 'not/not have/there is no', and the new is *wúméi* 無沒 (used in the city of Shànghǎi)

Guānhuà uses *méiyǒu* 沒有 as a verb and an adverb. *Tǔhuà* mainly uses *wúde* 無得 (15 tokens), and also *wúmé* 無咊 (6 tokens), *wúméi* 無沒 (2 tokens), *méiyǒu* 沒有 (1 token), *wúcéngyǒu* 無曾有 (1 token), *wú* 無 (2 tokens), *wúyǒu* 無有 (1 tokens), *wú* 無 (3 tokens) and zero forms (3 tokens). The new group all uses *wúméi* 無沒 (30 tokens).

34) 'As he must go off on service and has no brothers or relations to look after the business, he is obliged to sell the goodwill'. (II:9)
    A. *Guide*: Tā yòu **méiyǒu** dìxiōng běnjiā kěyǐ zhàoyìng mǎimài, suǒyǐ děi dào chūqù.
    他又**沒有**弟兄本家可以照應買賣，所以得倒出去。
    B. *Tǔhuà*: Yī **wúde** dìxiōng yòu **wúde** zìzúlǐ ge rén kěyǐ zhàoyìng gège shēngyì, suǒyǐ mài-tuō lā ge.
    伊**無得**弟兄又**無得**自族裏個人可以照應個個生意，所以賣脫拉個。
    C. *Hùyǔ*: Yī yòu **wúméi** dìxiōnglǎo běnjiā kěyǐ zhàoyìng shēngyì, suǒyǐ yào pán chūqù.
    伊又**無沒**弟兄咾本家可以照應生意，所以要盤出去。

35) 'I made inquiries for you at all the shops in the city here, and there were none'. (II:14)
    A. *Guide*: Wǒ zài zhè chéng lǐtóu gè pùzi lǐ dōu gěi nín zhǎo le, **méiyǒu**.
    我在這城裏頭各鋪子裏都給您找了，**沒有**。
    B. *Tǔhuà*: Chéng lǐxiàng gè diànjiā wǒ chái wèn dào gè, **wúme**.
    城裏向各店家我儕問到個，**無咊**。
    C. *Hùyǔ*: Wǒ lā cǐdì chénglǐxiàng gè pàn diàn lǐ quán tì nóng xún guò, **wúméi**.
    我拉此地城裏向各爿店裏全替儂尋過，**無沒**。

36) 'He denied the whole story, and said, "he has no evidence whatever"'. (II:16)
    A. *Guide*: Bìng **méi** zhème jiàn shì. ⋯⋯ rújīn tā yīdiǎn'er píngjù **méiyǒu**.
    並**沒**這麼件事。⋯⋯如今他一點兒憑據**沒有**。
    B. *Tǔhuà*: Bìng **wúyǒu** gè jiàn shìtǐ ⋯⋯ xiànzài wú píng wú jù.
    並**勿有**個件事體。⋯⋯現在無憑無據。
    C. *Hùyǔ*: Bìng **wúméi** dì jiàn shìtǐ ⋯⋯ xiànzài yīdiǎn píngjù **wúméi**.
    並**無沒**第件事體。⋯⋯現在一點憑據**無沒**。

Concluding Summary

In conclusion, *Tǔhuà zhǐnán* basically reflects the state of the Shànghǎi dialect, while *Hùyǔ zhǐnán* is a more strictly faithful translation of *Guānhuà zhǐnán* and is thus more influenced by Mandarin. That is perhaps a factor that accounts for the new features of *Hùyǔ zhǐnán*. Maybe our research is restricted in that our texts are translations. We hope that further exploration of other texts in the Shànghǎi dialect of the period will give us a better grasp of that dialect in the late Qīng dynasty.

Note: The research for this study was supported by funding from The Major Research Project of the National Social Science for a project titled "Studies on the Contemporary Shanghai Urban Dialect, Its Histocial Development and Database Construction" (Approval No. 19ZDA303, China).

References

Primary sources

Hùyǔ zhǐnán 滬語指南 [Guide to the Shànghǎi dialect]. 1908. Shànghǎi: The American Presbyterian Mission Press美華書館.

Wú Qǐtài 吳啟太 and Zhèng Yǒngbāng 鄭永邦. (1881) 1893. *Guānhuà zhǐnán* 官話指南 [Guide to Guānhuà (in Mandarin)]. Tokyo: Bunkyudou. Reprint, Jiǔjiāng Yìnshūjú 九江印書局.

Wú Qǐtài 吳啟太 and Zhèng Yǒngbāng 鄭永邦. 1889/1908. *Tǔhuà zhǐnán* 土話指南 [Local colloquial (in the Shànghǎi dialect)]. Second edition. Shànghǎi: Tǔshānwān címǔ tang 土山灣慈母堂.

Yuèyīn zhǐnán 粵音指南 [Guide to the Cantonese dialect]. 1910/1930. Hong Kong: Biézìguǎn 別字館. Revised edition, *Dīngzhèng yuèyīn zhǐnán* 訂正粵音指南 [The revised guide to the Cantonese dialect]. Hong Kong: Wing Fat and Company.

Secondary sources

Qián Nǎiróng 錢乃榮. 2003. *Shànghǎi yǔyán fāzhǎn shǐ* 上海語言發展史 [A history of the evolution of the Shànghǎi dialect]. Shànghǎi: Shànghǎi rénmín chūbǎnshè.

Qián Nǎiróng 錢乃榮. 2014. *Xīfāng chuánjiào shì Shànghǎi fāngyán zhùzuò yánjiū: 1847–1950 nián de shànghǎi huà* 西方傳教士上海方言著作研究：1847–1950年的上海話 [On studies of the Shànghǎi dialect by Western missionaries: The Shànghǎi dialect from 1847 to 1950]. Shànghǎi: Shànghǎi dàxué chūbǎnshè.

Shào Jìngmǐn 邵敬敏. 2014. *Xiàndài hànyǔ yíwènjù yánjīu* 現代漢語疑問句研究 [Interrogative sentences in modern Chinese]. Běijīng: Shāngwù yìnshūguǎn.

Wade, T. Francis, ed. (1886) 2000. *Yü-yen Tzŭ-êrh Chi: A Progressive Course Designed to Assist the Student of Colloquial Chinese, as Spoken in the Capital and the Metropolitan Department. Yǔyán zìěrjí* 語言自邇集. Translated by Zhāng Wèidōng 張衛東. Běijīng: Běijīng dàxué chūbǎnshè [Peking University Press].

Xǔ Bǎohuá 許寶華, and Táo Huán 陶寰. (1995) 1997. "Shànghǎi fāngyán cídiǎn yǐnlùn" 上海方言詞典引論 [Introduction to the dictionary of the Shànghǎi dialect]. *Fāngyán* 方言 [Dialect] 4: 257–75. Also in *Shànghǎi fāngyán cídiǎn* 上海方言詞典 [Dictionary of the Shànghǎi dialect], edited by Lǐ Róng, Xǔ Bǎohuá, and Táo Huán 李榮、許寶華、陶寰, 3–28. Nánjīng: Jiāngsū jiàoyù chūbǎnshè.

7
The Origin and Evolution of the Dialect Word *yá* 伢 'Child'*

Ní Zhìjiā

Introduction

As the word for 'child', *yá* 伢 is found in Chinese dialects such as Wǔhàn 武漢 [(ɕiau⁴²] ŋa²¹³] (小)伢, Héféi 合肥 [(ɕiɔ²⁴⁻³³) ia⁵⁵tsə⁰] (小)伢子, Chángshā 長沙 [ɕi⁴⁵ŋa¹³tsɿ⁰] 細伢子 and [ŋa¹³mei²¹tsɿ⁰] 伢妹子, and Nánchāng 南昌 [ɕi⁴⁵ŋa⁴⁵tsɿ⁰] 細伢子 (Běijīng Dàxué 1995, 272). To date, there have been few studies of the origin and historical development of *yá* 伢. The present discussion examines the etymon of *yá* 伢 and how its evolution and development are reflected in early texts and in the Chinese dialects.

Previous studies that have focused on the origin of the word *yá* 伢 have come to two possible conclusions (Zhāng Bǐnglín 1919; Zhèngzhāng Shàngfāng 2008; Xiāo Xù 2014): one, the word is derived from the word *yá* 牙 'tooth' as the growth of teeth is an important part of the early physical development of children; two, *yá* represents an onomatopoeia for the babbling or cry of a child, which is a common origin of words meaning 'child'. Both explanations are viable and not necessarily mutually exclusive. In addition, it has been pointed out that *yá* 牙 and other graphs, such as *wú* 吾, *yù* 禦, and *yǎ* 雅, are found used for 'child' in texts of pre-Qin and Han dynasties (Ní Zhìjiā 2019). But these examples are historically remote in relation to the words with *yá* 伢 in modern dialects, making a connection difficult to draw. We can be more certain about the relationship of the dialect words to the Sòng word *yá'ér* 牙兒, which is the focus of the present discussion.

Yá'ér in the Sòng

In Sòng 宋 period (960–1279) texts with a more colloquial cast it is possible to find examples of *yá'ér* with the meaning related to 'child'. This word is not seen in earlier records and is also rarely seen in later texts. Thus it can almost be said to be an

---

* This study was undertaken with the support from the China State Scholarship Fund, for which the author is deeply grateful.

exclusively Sòng period word. Examples include the following (arranged according to their dates of appearance):

(1) *Diēdie lái Mìzhōu, zài suì dé liǎng zǐ.* **Yá'ér** *xiù qiě hòu, Zhèngzhèng yǐ shēng chǐ. Wēngwēng shàng wèi jiàn, jì jiàn xiǎng huānxǐ* 爹爹來密州，再歲得兩子。**牙兒**秀且厚，鄭鄭已生齒。翁翁尚未見，既見想歡喜 'One year after father came to Mìzhōu, he had had two sons. The **baby** is beautiful and strong, and Zhèngzhèng has already grown teeth. Grandfather has not seen them yet and [I] think you will be delighted when you do'. (Kǒng Píngzhòng 孔平仲 [1044–1111], "Dài xiǎozǐ Guǎngsūn jì wēngwēng 代小子廣孫寄翁翁," in Kǒng, Kǒng, and Kǒng 2002, 364.)

(2) *Dé shū, zhī tóng zhū xīnfù shìfèng, bù quē zǐ zhí,* **yá'ér** *zhǎng mào* 得書，知同諸新婦侍奉，不闕子職，**牙兒**長茂 'Having received your letter, I know that you and all the daughters-in-law are looking after your parents with no neglect of you filial duties, and the **children** are all doing well'. (Huáng Tíngjiān 黃庭堅 [1045–1105], "Yǔ Shēngshū liù zhí shū 與聲叔六姪書," in *Huáng Tíngjiān quánjí* 黃庭堅全集 2001, 1875.)

(3) *Shūláng xiàngqián dú shū shí hǎo-è, Hè'niáng,* **yá'ér** *jì ān*? 樞郎向前讀書識好惡，賀娘、**牙兒**計安？ 'Young Shū, [my son,] in your studies you have learned the distinction between good and bad. [Your sister] Hè, and [my] youngest **child** are doing well I presume?' (Zhèng Gāngzhōng 鄭剛中 [1088–1154], *Běishān wénjí* 北山文集 1985, *juàn* 卷 29, 361.)

(4) *Fán yùnfù rùyuè, yú chūyī rì……bìng* **yá'ér** *yīwù, bēngjiè děng, wèi zhī 'cuīshēng'…….Zhì mǎnyuè,……yù ér bì, luò tāifà, biàn xiè zuòkè, bào* **yá'ér** *rù tārén fáng, wèi zhī 'yí kē'* 凡孕婦入月，於初一日……並**牙兒**衣物、襁藉等，謂之"催生"。……至滿月，……浴兒畢，落胎髮，遍謝坐客，抱**牙兒**入他人房，謂之"移窠" 'When an expectant mother enters the last month, on the first day. . . . Her parents send her the **baby**'s clothing and the baby carrier wrap, which is referred to as "hastening birth". After the baby's first month, . . . after the infant is bathed and it has lost its fetal hair, thanks are given to all those in attendance, and the **baby** will be brought into other's room, which is referred to as "moving the nest"'. (Mèng Yuánlǎo 孟元老 [n.d.; of the N. Sòng], *Dōngjīng mèng huá lù [jiānzhù]* 東京夢華錄〔箋注〕2006, *juàn* 5, 503–4.)

(5) *Fán shēngxià yī qī zhì qiǎngbǎo nèi jí yī suì jiē wèi zhī* **yá'ér***, èr suì yuē yīng'ér, sān suì yuē nǎitóng, sì suì yuē nǎixīng, wǔ suì yuē hái'ér, liù suì yuē xiǎo'ér* 凡生下一七至繈褓內及一歲皆謂之**牙兒**，二歲曰嬰兒，三歲曰奶童，四歲曰奶腥，五歲曰孩兒，六歲曰小兒 'From the first seven days after birth, till the time of swaddling clothing and through the first *suì* [*before* the Chinese New Year] the newborn is called **yá'ér** '**infant**'; at the second *suì* [beginning just *after* the child's first Chinese New Year] it is called *yīng'ér* 'baby'; at the third *suì* [after the second Chinese New Year] it is called *nǎitóng* 'babe at the breast'; at the fourth *suì* [after its third Chinese New Year] it is called *nǎixīng* 'smelling of breastmilk'; at the fifth *suì* [after its fourth Chinese New Year] it is called *hái'ér*

'toddler'; at the sixth *suì* [after its fifth Chinese New Year] it is called *xiǎo'ér* 'child'. (Liú Fǎng 劉昉 [*jìnshì* 1124], *Yòuyòu xīnshū* 幼幼新書 1987, *juàn* 2, 20, citing *Huì yǎn guān zhèng* 惠眼觀證.)

(6) *Yīngshān xiàn wài Dàguī shān,......chǎn yī zhǒng yú, xíngmú yǔ cháng yì, míng yuē 'yá'ér yú'. Yǒu sì zú, néng dēng àn shēng mù, zuò shēng yīyōu, quán rú yīnghái* 應山縣外大龜山，……產一種魚，形模與常異，名曰"**牙兒**魚"。有四足，能登岸升木，作聲咿嚘，全如嬰孩 'At Dàguī Mountain outside Yìngshān County, . . . a kind of fish is produced with an unusual shape and is called "**baby** fish". It has four legs and can climb onto the bank and up trees; it makes a sound that goes "*yīyōu*", all just like an infant'. (Hóng Mài 洪邁 [1123–1202], *Yíjiān zhì* 夷堅志 1981, zhī zhì 支志, "jǐng 景" *juàn* 2, 895.)

(7) *Zhōu Wǔshí Niáng xì yīn chǎn xià sǐ yá'ér, yǐzhì shēn sǐ, shīshǒu biàndòng, bù yuàn jiǎnyàn* 周五十娘係因產下死**牙兒**，以致身死，屍首變動，不願檢驗 'Zhōu Wǔshí Niáng died giving birth to a dead **baby**, and because the corpse was altered, her husband does not want an autopsy'. (Wēng Fǔ 翁甫 [*jìnshì* 1226], "Zǐ wàng sù mèi shēn sǐ bù míng, ér qí fū yuàn miǎn jiǎnyàn 姊妄訴妹身死不明，而其夫願免檢驗," cited in Zhāng Sìwéi 張四維 [1526–1585] *Mínggōng shūpàn qīngmíng jí* 名公書判清明集 1987, *juàn* 13, 501.)

(8) *Liúqì yǐn,......rú yá'ér yǒu huàn, zhǐ lìng rǔmǔ fú zhī* 流氣飲，……如**牙兒**有患，只令乳母服之 'Drink to Free the Breath [an herbal medicine], . . . to be taken by a nursing mother when her **baby** is ill'. (Tàipíng huìmín héjì jú 太平惠民和劑局 [The Sòng Pharmaceutical Bureau] 1985, *juàn* 7, 214.)

Examples 1 and 2 are the earliest examples that can be confirmed at present. Kǒng Píngzhòng and Huáng Tíngjiān are contemporaries of similar age. Both were born in the mid-eleventh century, which was the middle period of the Northern Sòng.[1] Thus the word *yá'ér* would have appeared no later than that.

In addition, in many of the above examples *yá'ér* refers to an infant who has been born recently: in (4) the *yá'ér* is one month old; example (5) reveals that *yá'ér* is an infant in the first few months of life; the "fish" referred to in (6) is actually the Chinese giant salamander, which matches the description given—"just like an infant"; in example (7) the *yá'ér* is clearly a newborn; in example (8) the *yá'ér* is still nursing and must be very young. Why would infants be called *yá'ér*? The examples give credence to both possible origins: it could indeed be related to the fact that very young children are just beginning to teeth, or it could be derived from the onomatopoeia effect of the word in its resemblance to the cry of a baby. It is not possible at this time to decide the most likely origin between these two possibilities.

While *yá'ér* referred to infants in the Sòng, the shift to the meaning of 'child' would have been relatively simple. The word *hái* 孩 in Chinese and the word *child* in English both went through a similar process of change in meaning (Ní Zhìjiā 2019).

---

1. Kǒng Píngzhòng is thought to have been born either in 1044 (Huáng Jiànbǎo 1998) or in 1046 or 1047 (Chén Liánxiāng 2005). Huáng Tíngjiān was born in 1045 (Zhèng Yǒngxiào 1997, 1).

The types of texts in which *yá'ér* appears generally have a more colloquial tone and include letters, notes, medical texts, and legal texts. This is strong evidence that *yá'ér* was an actual colloquial word used in the spoken language of the time. Thus we can conclude that the Sòng word *yá'ér* is a direct ancestor of the word *yá* in modern dialects, transmitted orally down to the present.[2]

Yá 牙/伢/伢 in the Post-Sòng Period

In texts after the Sòng, *yá'ér* rarely appears with the meaning of 'infant'. The small number of relatively reliable examples are found mainly in local gazetteers, in which *yá* is more commonly written with the graph 伢 but not 牙. Examples include the following:

(9) *Chìzǐ yuē '**yá'ér**'* 赤子曰 "**伢兒**" 'An infant is called "*yá'ér*"'. (Chén Shìyuán 陳士元 [1516–1597], *Sú yòng zázì* 俗用雜字, in his *Gǔ sú zì lüè* 古俗字略 1996, 165–66.)

(10) *Fán yānzhī, zān-ěr, yáchǐ, jiǎndāo, yǐzhì jīngdiǎn, mùyú,* ***yá'ér*** *xījù zhīlèi, wú bù jí* 凡臙赤、簪珥、牙尺、剪刀、以至經典、木魚、**伢兒**嬉具之類，無不集 'Every sort of thing is gathered [there], such as rouge, hairpins and earrings, ivory rulers, scissors, as well as classics, wooden clappers in a fish shape, and **baby's/child's** toys'. (Zhāng Dài 張岱 [1597–1684], "Xīhú xiāngshì 西湖香市," in *Táo'ān mèng yì* 陶庵夢憶 2007, *juàn* 7, 82.)

(11) *Xiǎo'ér yuē '**yá'ér**'* 小兒曰 "**伢兒**" 'Children are called "*yá'ér*"'. (Wáng Gōngxiān 王恭先 [*jìnshì* 1659], comp., *Línjìn xiàn zhì* 臨晉縣志 1686, *juàn* 3, 23a. [Note: Línjìn 臨晉 is in the area of modern Línyī 臨猗 in Shānxī 山西.])

(12) *Fán hū niányòu yuē '**yá'ér**', yòu yuē 'làizǎi'* 凡呼年幼曰 "**牙兒**"，又曰"賴崽" 'Children are called "*yá'ér*" or "*làizǎi*"'. (Zōng Jìchén 宗續辰 [nd.], comp., *Yǒngzhōu fǔ zhì* 永州府志 1828, *juàn* 5b, 2a.)

The earliest appearance of the graph *yá* 伢 is in the *Jíyùn* 集韻, under the *píng* 平 tone in the *má* 麻 rime, with the pronunciation gloss *nga*[2] (牛加切) and the meaning gloss "the people of the Wú region call newborns *yāyá* 亞伢". Homophonous and synonymous with *yá* 牙, *yá* 伢 is a popular (non-standard) alternative for that graph. In the above, *yá* 牙/伢 still means 'infant' in example (9); but in examples (11) and (12) it has clearly already come to mean 'child'; while in example (10) it is ambiguous and could have either meaning. We see in these examples that *yá'ér* had gradually evolved from the earlier meaning of 'infant' and come to mean 'child'.

---

2. In the dialects *yá* most commonly means 'child'. But it can also mean 'infant' in some dialects. Examples include *yárénzi* 伢人子 [ŋa⁴⁴⁻⁴² ɲiẽ⁴⁴ tsʅ⁰] and *máoyázi* 毛伢子 [mɔ³¹ ŋa⁴⁴ tsʅ⁰] in Yúdū 于都, Jiāngxī 江西 (Xiè Liúwén 1998, 50); *yázǎi* 伢仔 [ŋa⁵⁵ tsiɛ²¹] in Jiàn'ōu 建甌, Fújiàn 福建 (Lǐ Rúlóng and Pān Wèishuǐ 1998, 57), *yá* 伢 being an alternate graph for the same word (see below).

In addition to *yá'ér*, in the Míng (1368–1644) and the Qīng (1644–1912) we also find examples meaning 'child', or even the young of animals, with the suffix *zǐ* 子 and those with the single syllable *yá*, for example:

(13) *Zhè sī cóng xiǎo'er yě bù zhī tōu le rénjiā duōshǎo* **zhū yázi**, *yánggāo'er chī le* 這廝從小兒也不知偷了人家多少**豬牙子**、羊羔兒吃了 'Who knows how many peoples' **piglets** and lambs this fellow has stolen and eaten since he was young'. (Wú Chéng'ēn 吳承恩 [c. 1500–c. 1582], Chapter 86 in *Xī yóu jì* 西遊記 2011, 1006.)

(14) *Xiǎo'ér wèi zhī* '*yázi*' 小兒謂之"犽子" 'Children are referred to as *yázi*'. (Cài Fùwǔ 蔡復午 [n.d.], comp., *Dōngtái xiàn zhì* 東台縣志 1817, *juàn* 15, 9a.)

(15) *Yá, súzì* 犽, 俗字 '*Yá* 犽 is a non-standard graph'. *Wú rén wèi chìzǐ yuē* '*yá*' 吳人謂赤子曰"犽" 'The people of the Wú region call newborn babies *yá*'. *Jīn sú hū sītóng tōng yuē* '*yá*', *yì zuò* '*yá*' 今俗呼廝童通曰"犽", 亦作"牙" 'Nowadays servant children are generally popularly called *yá* 犽, which is also written with the graph 牙'. (Zhāng Zìliè 張自烈 [1597–1673], "Yá bù 牙部," in *Zhèngzì tōng* 正字通 1996, 648.)

(16) *Yá, xiǎo'ér yě* 犽, 小兒也 '*Yá* means "child"'.... *Wúzhōng hū ér yuē* '*yá*' 吳中呼兒曰"犽" 'In the Wú region children are called *yá*'. (Hú Wényīng 胡文英 [1723–1790], *Wúxià fāngyán kǎo* [*jiàoyì*] 吳下方言考〔校議〕 2012, *juàn* 4, 45.)

In example (13), *zhū yázi* 豬牙子 'piglet' and *yánggāo'er* 羊羔兒 'lamb' are mentioned in parallel. This serves both to confirm the meaning of the word for 'piglet' and to reveal that *zǐ* 子, like *ér* 兒, is a suffix, while also demonstrating that *zhū yá* 豬牙 and *yánggāo* 羊羔 are both pairs of root morphemes of the words. Hence, *yá* 牙 here means 'whelp, young animal' itself, in contrast with the Sòng *yá* 牙, which must be combined with *ér* to mean 'infant'. The meaning of 'whelp, young animal' must in origin have been derived from the meaning of 'child', therefore it can be inferred that *yá* 牙 itself could earlier have served to mean 'child'. With *zhū yázi* 豬牙子 'piglet' as our referent, we can see that *yázi* 犽子 in example (14) as well as *yá'ér* 牙/犽兒 in the earlier examples (9) to (12) all have the same 'root + suffix' structure, with the meaning determined by the root *yá* 牙/犽.[3] In examples (15) and (16), *yá* 犽 is used as a single syllable, which is a direct indication that the morpheme *yá* 牙/犽 had clearly come to mean 'child' as a free, unbound, morpheme. The above examples reveal further evolution of the morpheme *yá* in meaning and usage that had taken place after the Sòng period.

Later the graph *yá* 伢 replaced *yá* 牙 and *yá* 犽. This newer graph *yá* 伢 is not found in early lexical texts or rime books. One of the earliest reliable examples of the

---

3. In example (5) in Part Two above, *yá'ér* 牙兒, *yīng'ér* 嬰兒, *hái'ér* 孩兒, and *xiǎo'ér* 小兒 are also raised in parallel, revealing that *ér* 兒 has the lexical meaning of 'child'. Thus it is reasonable to analyze the structure of the word *yá'ér* 牙兒 in the Sòng period as 'root + root'. From there, the meaning of *yá'ér* 牙兒 'infant' is comprised of *yá* 牙 and *ér* 兒, while the single morpheme *yá* 牙 cannot mean that.

graph is its use in the names of the characters Pān Sānyá 潘三伢 and Liú Chángyá 劉長伢 in Hán Shìqí's 韓世琦 (d. 1686) *Fǔ Wú shū cǎo* 撫吳疏草. This book was published in 1666, and the names appear in *juàn* 卷 7 (p. 57a) and *juàn* 25 (p. 79a), respectively. In light of the common tradition to use words denoting children in names (especially in nicknames, where *wá* 娃 'child' and *zǎi* 仔 'young boy' are also used), it can be inferred that *yá* 伢 in these names is derived from *yá* 伢 meaning 'child'. *Yá* 伢 used in names is not frequently seen in early and mid-Qīng period texts and only becomes common in late Qīng sources, especially in local gazetteers (see Part Four below). By the Republican period in the early twentieth century, the *yá* directly meaning 'child' also begins to be written with the graph *yá* 伢. For example, we see it in *Zhōngxiáng xiàn zhì* 鍾祥縣志 *juàn* 12 (p. 27a): *Yá, yázi, háizi yě* 伢，伢子，孩子也 '*yá* as in *yázi* means "child"'. After that, *yá* 伢 gradually fully replaced *yá* 牙 and *yá* 犽, becoming the graph most commonly used in the present day for *yá* 'child'.

To sum up, in light of the rare occurrence of *yá'ér* in post-Sòng texts, the word was probably no longer in the koine, but still existed in the living dialects of the time. The meaning of *yá'ér* 牙兒 changed from 'infant' to 'child' and gradually shifted to simply *yá* 牙, that is, the single syllable came to mean 'child', which concurrently led to a greater diversity of usages. At the same time, the graph for *yá* 'child' was eventually replaced by the newer graph *yá* 伢. Through this process, the character for the morpheme *yá*, from its use in the Sòng word *yá'ér*, became the form and use of *yá* 伢 that we find in modern Chinese dialects today.

The Distribution of Words with the Morpheme *yá* 伢 in Modern Dialects in Comparison to the Historical Situation

Map 40 in the volume on lexicon (*Cíhuì juàn* 詞彙卷) in the *Hànyǔ fāngyán dìtú jí* 漢語方言地圖集 [Linguistic atlas of Chinese dialects] (Cáo Zhìyún 2008, below referred to as LACDL040) provides a relatively comprehensive presentation of the distribution of words for 'child' in the modern Chinese dialects. In that map, the words that are based on the morpheme *yá* 伢 are distributed as shown in Map 7.1.[4]

Map 7.1 reveals that modern dialects having words with the morpheme *yá* 伢 are distributed primarily in the central and lower reaches of the Yangtze watershed (excluding Zhèjiāng 浙江). In addition, they are found in a small region in southern Jiāngxī, and occasionally in some dialects in Shǎanxī, Shānxī, Zhèjiāng, Fújiàn,

---

4. The map is adapted from LACDL040. Place names, listed in the appendix, cannot be indicated on it due to space limitations. We have drawn on additional sources to add several dialect sites on the map, including Hánchéng 韓城 and Héyáng 合陽 in Shǎanxī 陝西; Yǒngjì 永濟 in Shānxī 山西 (from Xíng Xiàngdōng et al. 2012, 452); in Jiāngsū 江蘇: Lìshuǐ 溧水, Gāochún 高淳, Zhènjiāng 鎮江, Liyáng 溧陽, Yíxīng 宜興, Jiāngyīn 江陰 (from Editorial board of *Jiāngsū yǔyán zīyuán zīliào huìbiān* 2015, 427–32), Jīntán 金壇 (from Mèng Jìyuán 1993, 761), and Jùróng 句容 (from Zhōu Yún 2007, 105); Yúdū 于都 in Jiāngxī 江西 (from Xiè Liúwén 1998, 50); in Fújiàn 福建: Jiànníng 建寧, Pǔchéng 浦城 (from Lǐ Rúlóng 2001, 416, 513), and Jiàn'ōu 建甌 (from Lǐ and Pān 1998, 57); Guǎngzhōu 廣州 in Guǎngdōng 廣東 (from Bái Wǎnrú 1998, 15). Note that in these additional dialects *yá* 伢 is not always used in words for 'child'; in some it is only used in words for 'infant' or 'boy'.

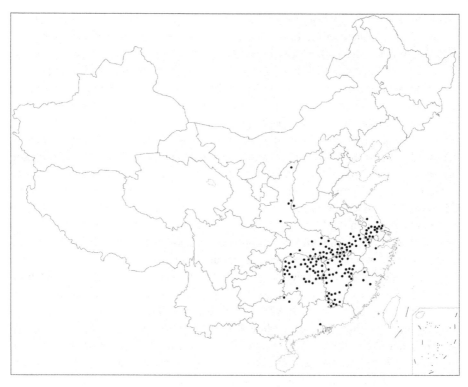

Map 7.1: Distribution of words with the morpheme *yá* 伢 in modern dialects

Guǎngdōng, and Guǎngxī 廣西. In terms of dialect type or classification, words with the morpheme *yá* 伢 are generally used in Jiāng-Huái 江淮 Mandarin, in the Gàn 贛 and Xiāng 湘 dialects, partly in Southwestern Mandarin (in Húběi 湖北 and Hú'nán 湖南), and in Hakka (in southern Jiāngxī), as well as occasionally in Central Mandarin, the Jìn 晉, Wú 吳, Mǐn 閩, and Yuè 粵 dialects, and Pínghuà 平話.

Now let us consider the geographical distribution of words concerning 'child' with *yá* 牙/伢 in earlier texts, focusing on the Sòng, the late Qīng, and the Republican period, which are periods with the largest number of textual witnesses:

A. **Sòng *yá'ér* 牙兒**. Looking at the examples in Part Two above: Kǒng Píngzhòng, the author of example (1), was from Xīngàn 新淦 in Línjiāng 臨江 (in the area of modern Xíajiāng 峽江 in Jiāngxī). The author of example (2), Huáng Tíngjiān, was from Fēnníng 分寧 in Hóngzhōu 洪州 (modern Xiūshuǐ 修水 in Jiāngxī). Zhèng Gāngzhōng, who authored example (3), was from Jīnhuá 金華 in Wùzhōu 婺州 (modern Jīnhuá in Zhèjiāng). The native place of Mèng Yuánlǎo, who penned example (4), is unknown; but he moved to Biànliáng 汴梁 (modern Kāifēng 開封 in Hénán 河南) in his youth, where he later lived for more than twenty years. The descriptions of life in the capital, Biànliáng, during the last years of the N. Sòng that Mèng records in his *Dōngjīng mèng huá lù* are replete with dialect colloquialisms in the city's language of the time. Example (6) is clearly identified with Yìngshān County (modern Guǎngshuǐ 廣水 in Húběi). Wēng Fǔ 翁甫, the author of example (7), was from Chóng'ān 崇安 in Jiànníng 建寧 (modern Wǔyíshān 武夷山 in Fújiàn). The example is from records of cases he presided over during his tenure as an official in Zhèjiāng.[5] (The geographical information for the other examples is not clear.)

Clearly *yá'ér* had a broad geographic distribution; though it was still primarily centered in the lower and mid-Yangtze River watershed. Notably, example (4) reveals that *yá'ér* was used in the Northern Song capital of Biànliáng. The Biànliáng dialect (or more broadly the dialect of the Central Plains, Zhōngyuán 中原), was without doubt the prevailing prestige dialect of the Northern Sòng. Consequently, *yá'ér* would have had an even wider range than that reflected in the texts. Indeed, it was likely a word in the Mandarin koine, or lingua franca, of the time.

B. *Yá* 伢 in late Qīng and the Republican period. The gazetteers of this period contain a large number of examples of *yá* in personal names. From this we can infer that the locales where they originated would likely have had the word *yá* for 'child' (see Part Three above). A survey of the *Erudition Database of Chinese Local Records* (*Àirúshēng Zhōngguó fāngzhì kù* 愛如生中國方志庫) I and II, revealed this phenomenon in the following counties: Lìshuǐ 溧水, Gāochún 高淳, Dāntú 丹徒, Jùróng 句容, Dānyáng 丹陽, Jīntán 金壇, Wǔjìn 武進, Yánghú 陽湖 (in modern Wǔjìn 武進), Lìyáng 溧陽, Fèngyáng 鳳陽, Jiànpíng 建平 (modern Lángxī 郎溪), Guǎngdé 廣德, Huánggāng 黃岡, Huáng'ān 黃安 (modern Hóng'ān 紅安), Máchéng 麻城, Luótián 羅田, Jiāngxià 江夏, Fèngxīn 奉新, Lè'ān 樂安, Nánfēng 南豐, Guāngzé 光澤, Shàowǔ 邵武, Zhǐjiāng 芷江, and Huìtóng 會同.

There is no great overall difference in geographic distribution of the Sòng *yá'ér* and the *yá* of the late Qīng and Republican periods. The largest differences are seen in the absence of *yá* in personal names in the area of Zhèjiāng and the Central Plains region (primarily Hénán and nearby), which appear to have no longer used the word *yá* 牙/伢 for 'child'. This situation is clearly revealed in the LACDL040 map, which shows that these two regions generally use other forms for 'child'. In Zhèjiāng, there is a great variety of words (with the morpheme of *rén* 人, *nóng* 農, *mèi* 妹, etc.); while in the Central Plains, *hái* 孩 prevails. Yet *yá* 牙/伢 does show up in a few places, for example, in Hángzhōu 杭州 and Wǔyì 武義 in Zhèjiāng, Hánchéng and Héyáng in Shǎnxī, and Yǒngjì in Shǎnxī. These places can thus be seen to maintain remnants of the *yá* 牙-type words from when they had a wider distribution in Zhèjiāng and in the Central Plains in earlier times.

The distribution of *yá* from the late Qīng and the Republican period down to the present (reflected in Map 7.1) has basically remained the same.

---

5. Our sources for these authors' backgrounds are: Huáng Hóng 2005 for Kǒng Píngzhòng; the *Sòngshǐ* 宋史 biographies of Huáng Tíngjiān and Zhèng Gāngzhōng (Toqto'a 1977, 13109, 11512); Mèng Yuánlǎo's preface to *Dōngjīng mèng huá lù* (p. 1); and Chén Zhìchāo 1987 for Wēng Fǔ.

The historical progression of the geographic distribution of *yá* that is reflected in the modern dialects in light of the textual evidence of earlier periods tells us that *yá* 伢 is directly derived from the Sòng period word for 'infant', *yá'ér* 牙兒. The latter word was likely common in the Northern Sòng Mandarin koine and was prevalent in the Central Plains and the lower and mid-Yangtze watershed. After the Jìngkāng exodus (*Jìngkāng zhī nàn* 靖康之難, the Jurchens had besieged and sacked Biànliáng in early 1127), the Sòng court moved south, accompanied by great numbers of ordinary citizens, who brought the word *yá'ér* even further southward. It thus made its way to Zhèjiāng and southern Jiāngxī, and even into places in Fújiàn, Guǎngdōng, and Guǎngxī.[6] After the Sòng, *yá'ér* disappeared from the Mandarin koine but remained alive in many dialects, within which the morpheme *yá* further extended its semantic range, and variant words developed from it. The morpheme has been steadily distributed primarily in the lower and mid-Yangtze watershed region; though in contrast to the Sòng, in the Central Plains and Zhèjiāng it has for the most part been replaced by other words, except in a few places where it continues to be used.

Concluding Thoughts

Regarding the evolution of the Mandarin dialects, Lǚ Shūxiāng (1985, 58) surmised that

> the modern Mandarin dialect area can for the most part be divided into a northern region (the Yellow River basin and Manchuria in the northeast) and a southern region (the Yangtze River basin and the southwest). We can probably surmise that in the Sòng-Yuán period these two dialectal systems were already considerably differentiated. In the northern region *měi* 每 was used [as a plural marker] and in the south *men* 們 was used [as a plural marker]. In the Northern Sòng period the dialects of the Central Plains 中原 still belonged to the southern dialect system. The ancestor of the present Northern Mandarin dialects was the dialect of a small region around Yānjīng 燕京. When the Jīn and Yuán dynasties occupied the Central Plain, the population moved away en masse; only at that time did Northern Mandarin come to be spoken to the north and south of the great river [i.e., the Yellow River], and Southern Mandarin retreated southward. (translation from Norman 1997, 21)

Jerry Norman moved forward along this line of argument, noting that

> the dialect map of north China underwent a radical transformation between the 10th and 13th centuries. A highly innovative form of Mandarin, formed in northeastern

---

6. Today, in Zhèjiāng Hángzhōu and Wǔyì still have *yá* in their words for 'child'. In the notes on yá 伢 in the *Jíyùn* (see Part Three), the Wú dialect region in the Northern Sòng already had the word *yāyá* 亞伢, meaning 'infant'. But in light of its form and the history of Hángzhōu, the word [ɕiɔ^{53}iɑ$^{213>31}$ɹə$^{213>21}$] 小伢兒 'child' in the Hángzhōu dialect (Simmons 1992, 503; Bào Shìjié 1998, 121) is clearly descended from *yá'ér* of the Northern Sòng Central Plains dialect—perhaps even directly from the Biànliáng dialect of the time, and is not a preservation of *yāyá* 亞伢. The origin of the Wǔyì word [ɕiɑ^{445}uɑ^{53}kuen^{53}] 細伢鬼兒 'child' (collected in Cáo Zhìyún, et al. 2016, 471) is inconclusive. It could be derived either from the Wú *yāyá* or from the Central Plains *yá'ér* both in the Northern Sòng period.

China, spread southward and westward displacing and forcing further south the older type of Mandarin found in the Central Plains. A more conservative variety of Mandarin survived in the mountainous areas of Shānxī province giving rise to what Lǐ Róng has called the Jìn dialects.... The old Mandarin of the Zhōngyuán region became ensconced south of the Huái River and in Hángzhōu. It also profoundly influenced the Wú dialect of the Jiāngsū and northern Zhèjiāng regions. (Norman 1997, 24, 27)

The conclusions drawn by the present article entirely support the argument of Lǚ Shūxiāng and Jerry Norman summarized above. As we noted, the Northern Sòng *yá'ér* was in the lexicon of the contemporary koine, that is to say that it belonged to the common vocabulary of Southern Mandarin. The word originally had a wide distribution, but it lost its foothold in the Central Plains as Northern Mandarin pushed in, and was replaced by the northern word *hái* 孩. Yet it was able to continue to exist in the relatively remote areas of Shānxī and Shǎanxī and also traveled with Southern Mandarin as it spread southward—Hángzhōu is a clear case in point. It can be said that the word *yá'ér* provides significant lexical proof of the Lǚ-Norman view of Mandarin history.

Recent research into dialect phonology often points to matters of historical strata in the analysis. The present study demonstrates that the concept of historical strata is also operative in research on dialect lexicon. The result of our investigation into both early texts and modern dialects confirms that the words with the morpheme *yá* 伢 most certainly belong to the Southern Mandarin stratum rooted in the Sòng. If future research uncovers more words of this type, we will have a much clearer picture of the historical strata and evolutionary process of the Chinese dialects.

Appendix: Chinese Dialect Sites Where the Morpheme *yá* 伢 Is Found

Note: (1) Sites are listed alphabetically under each province. (2) Places listed twice have sites representing different dialect types, which are identified within following parentheses. (3) Sites in italics are additional to those listed in the LACDL040 Map.

Shǎanxī 陕西: *Hánchéng* 韓城, *Héyáng* 合陽, Shénmù 神木, Zhèn'ān 鎮安

Shānxī 山西: *Yǒngjì* 永濟

Jiāngsū 江蘇: Bǎoyìng 寶應, Dōngtái 東台, *Gāochún* 高淳, *Jiāngyīn* 江陰, *Jīntán* 金壇, Jìngjiāng 靖江 (Mandarin), Jìngjiāng 靖江 (Wú), *Jùróng* 句容, *Lìshuǐ* 溧水, *Lìyáng* 溧陽, Nántōng 南通, Rúdōng 如東, Rúgāo 如皋, Tàixīng 泰興, Yángzhōng 揚中, *Yíxīng* 宜興, *Zhènjiāng* 鎮江

Ānhuī 安徽: Ānqìng 安慶, Cháohú 巢湖, Dōngzhì 東至, Guǎngdé 廣德, Héféi 合肥, Héxiàn 和縣, Huáiníng 懷寧, Lángxī 郎溪, Níngguó 寧國, Qiánshān 潛山, Qīngyáng 青陽, Sùsōng 宿松, Tàihú 太湖, Tóngchéng 桐城, Wàngjiāng 望江, Wúhú (city) 蕪湖市, Wúwéi 無為, Xuānchéng 宣城, Yuèxī 岳西, Zōngyáng 樅陽

Húběi 湖北: Chìbì 赤壁, Chóngyáng 崇陽, Dàyě 大冶, Èzhōu 鄂州, Guǎngshuǐ 廣水, Hèfēng 鶴峰, Hóng'ān 紅安, Hónghú 洪湖, Huángméi 黃梅, Huángshí 黃石, Jiāyú 嘉魚, Jiānlì 監利, Qíchūn 蘄春, Qiánjiāng 潛江, Shíshǒu 石首, Wǔhàn 武漢, Wǔxué 武穴, Xiánníng 咸寧, Yángxīn 陽新, Yídū 宜都, Yīngshān 英山, Yìngchéng 應城, Zhōngxiáng 鍾祥

Jiāngxī 江西: Ānyuán 安遠, Chóngrén 崇仁, Chóngyì 崇義, Dàyú 大余, Dìngnán 定南, Dōngxiāng 東鄉, Fēnyí 分宜, Fǔzhōu 撫州, Gànxiàn 贛縣, Guǎngchāng 廣昌, Guìxī 貴溪, Húkǒu 湖口, Jí'ān (county) 吉安縣, Jīnxī 金溪, Jiǔjiāng (county) 九江縣, Líchuān 黎川, Lóngnán 龍南, Lúxī 蘆溪, Nánchāng (city) 南昌市, Nánchéng 南城, Nánkāng 南康, Píngxiāng 萍鄉, Póyáng 鄱陽, Quánnán 全南, Ruìchāng 瑞昌, Shànglì 上栗, Shàngyóu 上猶, Wànzǎi 萬載, Wǔníng 武寧, Xīnjiàn 新建, Xīnyú 新余, Xìnfēng 信豐, Xīngzǐ 星子, Xiūshuǐ 修水, Yìyáng 弋陽, Yīngtán 鷹潭, Yǒngxīn 永新, Yǒngxiū 永修, *Yúdū* 于都, Zhāngshù 樟樹, Zīxī 資溪

Hú'nán 湖南: Ānxiāng 安鄉, Bǎojìng 保靖, Chángdé 常德, Chángshā (city) 長沙市, Chángshā (county) 長沙縣, Chénxī 辰溪 (Xiāng 湘), Fènghuáng 鳳凰, Gǔzhàng 古丈, Hànshòu 漢壽, Héngyáng (county) 衡陽縣, Huāyuán 花垣, Huáróng 華容, Jíshǒu 吉首, Lǐlíng 醴陵, Línlǐ 臨澧, Línxiāng 臨湘, Liúyáng 瀏陽, Lóngshān 龍山, Lúxī 瀘溪 (Xiāng 湘), Mìluó 汨羅, Nánxiàn 南縣, Píngjiāng 平江, Shàodōng 邵東, Shàoyáng (city) 邵陽市, Táojiāng 桃江, Táoyuán 桃源, Wàngchéng 望城, Xiāngtán (county) 湘潭縣, Xiāngyīn 湘陰, Xīnhuǎng 新晃, Xīnníng 新寧, Xīnshào 新邵, Yìyáng 益陽, Yǒngshùn 永順, Yuánlíng 沅陵, Yuèyáng (city) 岳陽市, Yuèyáng (county) 岳陽縣, Zhāngjiājiè 張家界, Zhūzhōu 株洲

Zhèjiāng 浙江: Hángzhōu 杭州, Wǔyì 武義

Fújiàn 福建: Gǔtián 古田, *Jiànníng* 建寧, *Jiàn'ōu* 建甌, *Pǔchéng* 浦城

Guǎngdōng 廣東: *Guǎngzhōu* 廣州, Nánxióng 南雄

Guǎngxī 廣西: Línguì 臨桂, Sānjiāng 三江

Note: A previous version of this chapter appeared in Chinese as "Hànyǔ fāngyán cí 'yá' de láiyuán yǔ yǎnbiàn 漢語方言詞 '伢' 的來源與演變," *Yǔyánxué lùncóng* 語言學論叢 2019 (59): 166–90.

References

Historical sources

Northern Sòng (960–1127) texts

Dīng Dù 丁度 (990–1053) et al., comp. 2005. *Jíyùn* 集韻. Běijīng: Zhōnghuá shūjú.
Huáng Tíngjiān 黃庭堅 (1045–1105). 2001. *Huáng Tíngjiān quánjí* 黃庭堅全集. Edited by Liú Lín 劉琳 et al. Chéngdū: Sìchuān Dàxué chūbǎnshè.

Kǒng Wénzhòng 孔文仲 (1038–1088), Kǒng Wǔzhòng 孔武仲 (1042–1097), and Kǒng Píngzhòng 孔平仲 (1044–1111). 2002. *Qīngjiāng sān Kǒng jí* 清江三孔集. Edited by Sūn Yǒngxuǎn 孫永選. Jǐnán: Qílǔ shūshè.

Liú Fǎng 劉昉 (*jìnshì* 進士 1124). 1987. *Yòuyòu xīnshū* 幼幼新書. Punctuated edition. Běijīng: Rénmín wèishēng chūbǎnshè.

Mèng Yuánlǎo 孟元老 (n.d.). 2006. *Dōngjīng mèng huá lù jiānzhù* 東京夢華錄箋注. Annotated by Yī Yǒngwén 伊永文. Běijīng: Zhōnghuá shūjú.

Zhèng Gāngzhōng 鄭剛中 (1088–1154). 1985. *Běishān wénjí* 北山文集. Běijīng: Zhōnghuá shūjú.

Southern Sòng (1127–1279) texts

Hóng Mài 洪邁 (1123–1202). 1981. *Yíjiān zhì* 夷堅志. Edited by Hé Zhuó 何卓. Běijīng: Zhōnghuá shūjú.

Tàipíng huìmín héjì jú 太平惠民和劑局 [The Sòng Pharmaceutical Bureau], comp. 1985. *Zēngguǎng Tàipíng huìmín héjì jú fāng* 增廣太平惠民和劑局方. Běijīng: Zhōnghuá shūjú.

Yuán (1279–1368) texts

Toqto'a [脱脱 Tuōtuō] (1314–1356) et al. 1977. *Sòng shǐ* 宋史. Běijīng: Zhōnghuá shūjú.

Míng (1368–1644) texts

Chén Shìyuán 陳士元 (1516–1597). 1996. *Gǔ sú zì lüè* 古俗字略. With appended *Sú yòng zázì* 俗用雜字. *Xù xiū Sìkù Quánshū* 續修四庫全書 edition, vol. 238, 1–166. Shànghǎi: Shànghǎi gǔjí chūbǎnshè.

Wú Chéng'ēn 吳承恩 (c. 1500–c. 1582). 2011. *Xī yóu jì* 西遊記. Běijīng: Rénmín wénxué chūbǎnshè.

Zhāng Dài 張岱 (1597–1684). 2007. *Táo'ān mèng yì* 陶庵夢憶. Edited by Mǎ Xīngróng 馬興榮. Běijīng: Zhōnghuá shūjú.

Zhāng Sìwéi 張四維 (1526–1585), comp. 1987. *Mínggōng shūpàn qīngmíng jí* 名公書判清明集. Edited by Zhōngguó Shèhuì Kēxuéyuàn lìshǐ yánjiūsuǒ Sòng Liáo Jīn Yuán shǐ yánjiūshì 中國社會科學院歷史研究所宋遼金元史研究室. Běijīng: Zhōnghuá shūjú.

Zhāng Zìliè 張自烈 (1597–1673). 1996. *Zhèngzì tōng* 正字通. Běijīng: Zhōngguó gōngrén chūbǎnshè.

Qīng (1644–1912) texts

Cài Fùwǔ 蔡復午 (n.d.), comp. *Dōngtái xiàn zhì* 東台縣志. Jiāqìng èrshí'èr nián kèběn 嘉慶二十二年刻本 [Blockprint edition of 1817].

Hán Shìqí 韓世琦 (d. 1686). *Fǔ Wú shū cǎo* 撫吳疏草. Kāngxī wǔ nián kèběn 康熙五年刻本 [Blockprint edition of 1666].

Hú Wényīng 胡文英 (1723–1790). 2012. *Wúxià fāngyán kǎo jiàoyì* 吳下方言考校議. Edited and annotated by Xú Fù 徐復. Nánjīng: Fènghuáng chūbǎnshè.

Wáng Gōngxiān 王恭先 (*jìnshì* 1659), comp. *Línjìn xiàn zhì* 臨晉縣志. Kāngxī èrshíwǔ nián kèběn 康熙二十五年刻本 [Blockprint edition of 1686].

Zōng Jìchén 宗續辰 (n.d.), comp. *Yǒngzhōu fǔ zhì* 永州府志. Dàoguāng bā nián kèběn 道光八年刻本 [Blockprint edition of 1828].

Republican Period (1912–1949) texts

Lǐ Quán 李權 (1868–1947), comp. *Zhōngxiáng xiàn zhì* 鍾祥縣志. Mínguó èrshíliù nián qiānyìnběn 民國二十六年鉛印本 [Typeset edition of 1937].

Modern sources

Bái Wǎnrú 白宛如. 1998. *Guǎngzhōu fāngyán cídiǎn* 廣州方言詞典. Nánjīng: Jiāngsū jiàoyù chūbǎnshè.

Bào Shìjié 鮑士杰. 1998. *Hángzhōu fāngyán cídiǎn* 杭州方言詞典. Nánjīng: Jiāngsū jiàoyù chūbǎnshè.

Běijīng Dàxué Zhōngguó yǔyán wénxué xì yǔyánxué jiàoyánshì 北京大學中國語言文學系語言學教研室, eds. 1995. *Hànyǔ fāngyán cíhuì* 漢語方言詞彙. 2nd ed. Běijīng: Yǔwén chūbǎnshè.

Cáo Zhìyún 曹志耘, ed. 2008. *Hànyǔ fāngyán dìtú jí* 漢語方言地圖集. "Lexicon" volume 詞彙卷. Běijīng: Shāngwù yìnshūguǎn.

Cáo Zhìyún 曹志耘 et al. 2016. *Wúyǔ Wùzhōu fāngyán yánjiū* 吳語婺州方言研究. Běijīng: Shāngwù yìnshūguǎn.

Chén Liánxiāng 陳蓮香. 2005. "Jiāngxī 'Línjiāng sān Kǒng' shēng-zú nián kǎo" 江西"臨江三孔"生卒年考. *Xīnyú Gāozhuān xuébào* 新余高專學報 3: 29–30.

Chén Zhìchāo 陳智超. 1987. "Sòng shǐ yánjiū de zhēnguì shǐliào—Míng kèběn *Mínggōng shūpàn qīngmíng jí* jièshào" 宋史研究的珍貴史料——明刻本《名公書判清明集》介紹. In *Mínggōng shūpàn qīngmíng jí* 名公書判清明集, compiled by Zhāng Sìwéi 張四維 (1526–1585), 645–86. Běijīng: Zhōnghuá shūjú.

Editorial board of *Jiāngsū yǔyán zīyuán zīliào huìbiān* 《江蘇語言資源資料匯編》編委會, eds. 2015. *Jiāngsū yǔyán zīyuán zīliào huìbiān* 江蘇語言資源資料匯編. "Lexicon" Vol. A 詞彙卷（上）. Nánjīng: Fènghuáng chūbǎnshè.

Huáng Hóng 黃宏. 2005. "Běi Sòng 'sān Kǒng' jíguàn xīn kǎo" 北宋"三孔"籍貫新考. *Dōngnán Dàxué xuébào* 東南大學學報. "Zhéxué shèhuì kēxué bǎn" 哲學社會科學版 6: 64–66.

Huáng Jiànbǎo 黃健保. 1998. "Guānyú 'sān Kǒng'" 關於"三孔". *Xīnyú Gāozhuān xuébào* 新余高專學報 1: 10–13.

Lǐ Rúlóng 李如龍. 2001. *Fújiàn xiàn-shì fāngyán zhì 12 zhǒng* 福建縣市方言志12種. Fúzhōu: Fújiàn jiàoyù chūbǎnshè.

Lǐ Rúlóng 李如龍 and Pān Wèishuǐ 潘渭水. 1998. *Jiàn'ōu fāngyán cídiǎn* 建甌方言詞典. Nánjīng: Jiāngsū jiàoyù chūbǎnshè.

Lǚ Shūxiāng 呂叔湘. 1985. *Jìndài Hànyǔ zhǐdàicí* 近代漢語指代詞. Shànghǎi: Xuélín chūbǎnshè.

Mèng Jìyuán 孟濟元, ed. 1993. *Jīntán xiàn zhì* 金壇縣志. Nánjīng: Jiāngsū rénmín chūbǎnshè.

Ní Zhìjiā 倪志佳. 2019. "Hànyǔ fāngyán cí 'yá' de láiyuán yǔ yǎnbiàn" 漢語方言詞"伢"的來源與演變. *Yǔyánxué lùncóng* 語言學論叢 59: 166–90.

Norman, Jerry (Luó Jiéruì 羅杰瑞). (1997) 2004. "Some Thoughts on the Early Development of Mandarin." In *Hashimoto Mantarō kinen chūgoku gogaku ronshū* 橋本萬太郎紀念中國語學論集, edited by Anne O. Yue 余靄芹 and Endō Mitsuaki 遠藤光曉, 21–28. Tokyo: Uchiyama shoten 內山書店. Chinese translation by Tsu-lin Mei 梅祖麟, "Guānyú Guānhuà fāngyán zǎoqī fāzhǎn de yīxiē xiǎngfǎ" 關於官話方言早期發展的一些想法. *Fāngyán* 方言 4: 295–300.

Simmons, Richard VanNess. 1992. "The Hangzhou Dialect." PhD diss., University of Washington, Seattle.

Xiāo Xù 蕭旭. 2014. "'Yīng'ér' yǔyuán kǎo" "嬰兒"語源考. In *Qúnshū jiàobǔ xù* 群書校補續, 2065–84. Taipei: Huā Mùlán wénhuà chūbǎnshè.

Xiè Liúwén 謝留文. 1998. *Yúdū fāngyán cídiǎn* 于都方言詞典. Nánjīng: Jiāngsū jiàoyù chūbǎnshè.

Xíng Xiàngdōng 邢向東 et al. 2012. *Qín-Jìn liǎng shěng yánhé fāngyán bǐjiào yánjiū* 秦晉兩省沿河方言比較研究. Běijīng: Shāngwù yìnshūguǎn.

Zhāng Bǐnglín 章炳麟. 1919. *Xīn fāngyán* 新方言. Hángzhōu: Zhèjiāng túshūguǎn.

Zhèng Yǒngxiǎo 鄭永曉. 1997. *Huáng Tíngjiān niánpǔ xīnbiān* 黃庭堅年譜新編. Běijīng: Shèhuì kēxué wénxiàn chūbǎnshè.

Zhèngzhāng Shàngfāng 鄭張尚芳. 2008. "Hànyǔ fāngyán biǎo 'háizi' yì de qī gè cígēn de yǔyuán" 漢語方言表"孩子"義的七個詞根的語源. *Yǔwén yánjiū* 語文研究 1: 32–34.

Zhōu Yún 周芸. 2007. "Jùróng fāngyán yánjiū" 句容方言研究. Master's thesis. Guǎngxī Dàxué 廣西大學, Nánníng 南寧.

II. Chinese Dialects and Their History

8
The Demarcation of Western Mandarin and the Designation of the Chéngdū Dialect as Its Standard Form in Modern China*

Kengo Chiba

Introduction

One of the most striking events in the history of colloquial Chinese was the emergence of Guānhuà 官話 (Mandarin),[1] which was used by the upper social classes and was the *lingua franca* in the Míng–Qīng era. No one can contest that Mandarin provided the foundation for China's modern national languages, which were later called Guóyǔ 國語 and Pǔtōnghuà 普通話. Most previous studies have analyzed how Mandarin came to be the national language—in particular, how the Běijīng dialect came to be identified as the basis of the national language—from the perspective of social history and sociolinguistics (Murata and Lamarre 2005, esp. pts. 1 and 2; Kaske 2008; Hirata 2016). Yet in spite of the accumulated studies on this topic, little is known about the process whereby a dialect came to be regarded as the dominant form in a specific region in China. Chiba (2007a), for example, analyzed Western Mandarin and pointed out that the establishment of a regional typical language involved nearly the same mechanism as the establishment of a national standard language. However, the process of creation of a typical dialect requires further research.

In the present day, it would be sensible to assume that the language of Shànghǎi should be the representative of the Wú 吳 dialects, that of Chángshā 長沙 of the Xiāng 湘 dialects, and that of Hong Kong or Guǎngzhōu of the Yuè 粵 dialects.[2] However, taking the Wú dialects as an example, the political and economic heartland of Wú, which overlapped with half of Jiāngsū 江蘇 and most of Zhèjiāng 浙江 province, was not Shànghǎi but Sūzhōu 蘇州 until the middle of the nineteenth century.

---

* This work is supported by the Japan Society for the Promotion of Science (JSPS) Grant-in-Aid for Scientific Research (Type C, #26370509) and the Chuo University Overseas Research Program.
1. Mandarin has at least three different meanings from the view of sociolinguistics: (1) the language that civil officers used during the Ming-Qing period; (2) China-proper dialects that encompass most of the territory of Greater China; and (3) the language that became the matrix of development of the standard national language in the twentieth century. See Yoshikawa (2015, 53–54). In this chapter, the term *Mandarin* as defined in the first instance is used.
2. Two of the most basic books on Chinese dialectology, Běijīng dàxué (1989) and Yuán (2001), indirectly support this point of view by referring to these dialects in order to describe the features of the dialect groups in which they are included.

Thus, the prestige of the Shànghǎi dialect must be due to Shànghǎi's improved political and economic presence in that period: to be more exact, it must have been due to research, learning, and the unconscious codification of the dialect by Westerners who came to the city after 1842. Here, it is worth pointing out that there were some deliberate attempts by foreigners to demarcate dialect areas and choose typical dialect forms in China during the nineteenth and twentieth centuries.

In Western Mandarin, the dialect of Chéngdū 成都, which has been the capital of Sìchuān 四川 province for more than 300 years, is usually considered the representative dialect.[3] Many previous studies that have argued for the internal demarcation of Western Mandarin list the Chéngdū dialect among its subdivisions (Sìchuān shěng fāngyán diàochá zhǐdǎozǔ 1960; Huáng 1986; Zhōngguó shèhuì Kēxuéyuàn et al. 2012). Yet there seems to be little agreement on how the Chéngdū dialect gained this position. There are several other major cities in the western provinces, such as Chóngqìng 重慶, Wǔhàn 武漢, Guìyáng 貴陽, and Kūnmíng 昆明, which would have rivaled Chéngdū. So it is difficult to insist on the political and economic dominance of Chéngdū in the twentieth century.

In this chapter, I demonstrate that research on the Chinese language, as well as the language education of Western Mandarin led by foreigners (including missionary scholars in China), influenced the development of the Chéngdū dialect as the dominant form of Western Mandarin. Historical research on colloquial Chinese shows that what we often considered to be the dominant dialect of an area was not consciously selected due to its representative linguistic features, but rather was adopted because of historical circumstances.

Mandarin(s) in the Míng-Qīng Period and Its Traditional Classification

In the Míng–Qīng period, Mandarin was spoken among people above a certain social position and was regarded as the *lingua franca*. Since Mandarin held social prestige because of its use by officials and was understood by a large portion of the population, missionaries coming to China were often obliged to study Mandarin before learning the dialect of the region to which they had been appointed. Thus, the missionaries compiled quite a few linguistic works in Mandarin.

According to the accounts of these foreigners, Mandarin was the language spoken at court, where mandarins and literati gathered from all over the empire. For example, American missionary scholar and diplomat Samuel Wells Williams referred to Mandarin as "the court dialect," using this term in one of his works (Williams 1844). Thirty years later, Williams wrote about the social status of Nánjīng 南京 Mandarin in the late nineteenth century as follows: "In this wide area, the Nanking, called 南京官話 [Nánjīng Guānhuà] or 正音 [Zhèngyīn] or true pronunciation, is

---

3. See Běijīng dàxué (1989) and Yuán (2001).

probably the most used, and described as 通行的話 [*tōngxíng de huà*], or the speech everywhere understood" (Williams 1874, xxxii).

In spite of these claims, it was the Běijīng dialect that rose gradually in sociolinguistic status to become the fashionable and/or official language of the empire.[4] The Běijīng dialect gained prominence because of Běijīng's position as the capital of the empire. Williams underpinned this fact by referring to the Běijīng dialect as follows: "The Peking, however, also known as 北京話 [Běijīnghuà] or 京話 [Jīnghuà] is now most fashionable and courtly, and like the English spoken in London, or the French in Paris, is regarded as the accredited court language of the empire" (Williams 1874, xxxii). His observation aptly reflected the Běijīng dialect's rising position.

According to Takata (2001), from the mid-nineteenth century on, as modern diplomatic relationships, characterized by treaties and exchanges of legations, were established between China and Western nations, the legitimacy of the Běijīng dialect greatly strengthened. Takata hypothesized that Thomas Francis Wade's monumental textbook on the Běijīng dialect, *A Progressive Course* (1867), helped Běijīng Mandarin rise to the status of China's national language. Thus, the rise of the Běijīng dialect was first realized through diplomatic discourse. Yoshikawa Masayuki accepted this view and revealed the genealogy of the "Běijīng school" of British diplomats that traced back to Thomas Taylor Meadows and John Francis Davis. Meadows was an interpreter at the British consulate in Canton and later in Shànghǎi, and taught Wade basic Chinese in his younger days.[5] Davis was the second governor of Hong Kong (1844–1848) and had such a high regard for Wade that he made Wade Vice Chinese interpreter in 1847. Yoshikawa elucidated that the Běijīng school stressed the importance of studying the Běijīng dialect as early as the 1840s. For instance, Meadows invented the Romanization system for the Běijīng dialect, which Wade followed in his famous system of Romanization for the Běijīng dialect[6] (Yoshikawa 2015). Twenty years after the dawning of the Běijīng school era, Wade made a famous declaration in his book: "Pekinese is the dialect an official interpreter ought to learn. Since the establishment of foreign legations with their corps of students at Peking, it has become next to impossible that any other should take precedence" (Wade 1867, vi).

Nánjīng Mandarin and the Běijīng dialect were mutually intelligible; even so, the difference between the two gradually became apparent to intellectuals. First, from the aspect of phonology, apart from the palatalization of initials before high-front vowels in syllables of the *jiàn* 見 (velar) and *jīng* 精 (dental sibilant) series,

---

4. Nakamura Masayuki points out that no materials show the phonetic features of "Běijīng Mandarin" that marks a clear distinction from the Běijīng dialect, thus, proposing a hypothesis that there was only the Běijīng dialect, Běijīng *Mandarin* never existed (Nakamura 2006, 1–4). This chapter supports Nakamura's idea. For more discussion, see Chiba (2019, 51–56).
5. Wade dedicated his first published textbook of the Běijīng dialect titled *The Book of Experiments* 尋津錄 [*Xún jīn lù*] (1859) to Meadows. Though Meadows had incurred the Foreign Ministry's displeasure for years due to the gaps in opinion on diplomatic policy toward China, Wade did not avoid Meadows and acknowledged his contributions in public. See Kwan (2013, 29–47).
6. Meadows (1847, 48). He invented the spelling *hs* for the unvoiced alveolo-palatal fricative [ɕ].

the major indexes for distinguishing one variety from the other were as follows: (a) the *rù* 入 tone was an independent tone in Nánjīng Mandarin, while it merged into the other three tones in the Běijīng dialect; (b) from the mid-Qīng period onward, the *jiàn* and *jīng* series initials were distinguished in Nánjīng Mandarin before high-front vowels,[7] whereas they were mixed and confused in the Běijīng dialect; (c) syllables belonging to *rùshēng*, especially those ending in *-k* in Middle Chinese, had diphthongs or triphthongs in the Běijīng dialect, but not in Nánjīng Mandarin; for example, according to Wade's Romanization system, which is based on the Běijīng dialect, *bái* 白 'white' is read as *pai²* and *duó* 鐸 'bell' as *tuo²*, while these characters are pronounced as *pe* and *to*, respectively, in Williams (1874), a typical dictionary of Nánjīng Mandarin; (d) the Běijīng dialect clearly distinguished the finals *-o* and *-uo* of the traditional *Guǒshè* 果攝 rhyme group (i.e. those traditionally ascribed to *kāikǒu* 開口 and *hékǒu* 合口 syllables of Division I [*yī děng* 一等]), for example *gè* 個 [a measure word] and *hé* 河 'river' in contrast to *guò* 過 'pass' and *huò* 貨 'commodity', while Nánjīng Mandarin did not. Consider the examples of 河 *ho* and 過 *kuo*, found in Wade (1867), compared to *ho* 河 and *ko* 過 in Williams (1874).[8]

Second, from the aspect of lexicon, it will be helpful to refer to the materials compiled by Westerners, especially those focused on the phrasal differences between Nánjīng Mandarin and the Běijīng dialect. For example, American missionary Calvin Wilson Mateer's *A Course of Mandarin Lessons* (1892), which concerns the three variations of Mandarin—Běijīng, Jǐnán 濟南, and Nánjīng—indicated the words employed by each language with three lines.[9] However, as Jǐnán is often dropped in the book, lines may be reduced from three to two. These two lines then show the contrast between Nánjīng and Běijīng variations. In examples (1) and (2) below, a slash differentiates between the Nánjīng and Běijīng expressions, in that order, from left to right. Hence, Nánjīng Mandarin uses *dìfang* 地方, while the Běijīng dialect employs *luòdì* 落地 for 'place' in (1). In (2), Nánjīng Mandarin uses *jǐduō* 幾多, while the Běijīng dialect employs *duōme* 多麽 in 'how far'.

---

7. See the discussion on Table 8.1. This is the so-called *jiān-tuán* 尖團 'sharp-round' distinction, the diagnostic significance of which is also touched upon by Zēng Xiǎoyú and Simmons in their contributions to this volume.
8. Some materials do not follow this tendency. For example, though Prémare's *Notitia Linguae Sinicae* (ca. 1728) shows Nánjīng Mandarin-like features as defined in indexes (a) to (c), his Romanization of *hé* 河 and *guò* 過 are *ho* (*kāikǒu*) and *kouo* (*hékǒu*), respectively (Prémare ca.1728/1831). Also, Edkins states as follows: "In the mandarin dictionaries another final is made by inserting u before o. Thus 歌 [gē], 戈 [gē], are pronounced ko, kwo respectively, and 賀 [hè], 禍 [huò], ho, hwo, but the w after h appears to be now falling into disuse" (Edkins 1857, 49).
9. Though Mateer recognizes that these three dialects are all mutually cognate Mandarins, I have an opposite viewpoint. See note 4.

(1) 那 // 個 // [地方/落地] // 不 // 好
Nà // ge // [dìfang/luòdì] // bù // hǎo
that // CL[10] // place // NEG // good
"That place is not good." (Mateer 1892, 1)[11]

(2) 府上 // 到 // 這裏 // [幾多/多麼] // 遠
Fǔshàng // dào // zhèli // [jǐduō/duōme] // yuǎn
your.house // to // here // how.much // distant
"How far is it from your house to this place?" (Mateer 1892, 49)

The Third Mandarin

According to the currently accepted subdivision, the dialect of Mandarin spoken in southwestern China is called Western Mandarin or *Xīnán Guānhuà* 西南官話. However, the term "Western Mandarin" is of fairly recent origin. It was first used by Joseph Edkins, an outstanding British missionary-scholar in the field of linguistics, as follows: "The finals wan and wang coincide in the Nanking dialect, where 光 [guāng] and 官 [guān] are both pronounced kwan. They are kept clearly separate in northern and western mandarin" (Edkins 1857, 47).

Edkins first divided Mandarin into three regional variations. He wrote: "Accordingly a third Mandarin system must here be introduced. The Nanking and Peking dialects are at least as wide apart, as that of Sï-c'huwen [i.e., Sìchuān] is from either of them. In fact, the three are varieties of the same great dialect" (Edkins 1857, 8). The phonetic features of the three variants are illustrated in Table 8.1.[12] The plus sign '+' means that the feature is applicable for that variation, the minus sign '–' indicates that it is not applicable, and the plus-minus sign '±' means that it is irregular depending on the documents.

Table 8.1: Phonological features of regional variants of Mandarin

	Southern (Nánjīng)	Northern (Běijīng)	Western (Chéngdū)
(a) The *rù* tone is an independent tone	+	–	±
(b) *Jiān* and *tuán* type initials are distinct	+	–	+
(c) Finals in *rù* tone syllables are diphthongs or triphthongs	–	+	–
(d) Finals -*o* and -*uo* of *Guǒshè* 果攝 are distinct	±	+	–

---

10. Abbreviations used here and/or below in this chapter are: CAUS = causative; CL = classifier; CONT = continuous; IMP = imperative; NEG = negation; PASS = passive; PERF = perfective; PROG = progressive; PRT = sentence-final particle.
11. Romanizations in examples (1) and (2) employ the *pīnyīn* system. The English translations are extracted from the text of Mateer (1900, 5, 225).
12. Besides these four features, Western Mandarin generally makes no distinction between initials /n/ and /l/, and between /n/ and /ŋ/ at the end of a syllable when preceded by the vowels /i/ and /ə/. Although the former feature is shared by the Nánjīng *dialect*, most of the materials on Nánjīng *Mandarin* make a clear distinction between these two initials.

As for feature (a), Edkins (1857, 8) pointed out that Nánjīng Mandarin retained the *rù* 入 tone as an independent tone, while Western Mandarin generally merged it into *yángpíng* 陽平.[13] Thus, it seems likely that the *rù* tone in Western Mandarin was in the process of disappearing. However, this claim varies according to the available materials. For example, Kilborn (1917), which will be mentioned in the next section as one of the major materials of Western Mandarin, did not include the *rù* tone as an independent tone, while Plusieurs missionnaires (1893) retained it. Thus, it cannot be asserted that the *rù* tone had completely lost its independence by the end of the nineteenth century.

As for (b), Western Mandarin unambiguously distinguished *jiān* 尖 'sharp' initials (dental sibilants) from *tuán* 團 'round' initials (palatals) before high-front vowels. For example, sin^4 姓 'surname' is distinct from $shin^4$ 幸 'luck' and $tsie^5$ 節 'joint' is distinct from $chie^5$ 結 'tie' in Grainger (1900).[14]

With regard to (c), Western Mandarin did not employ diphthongs or triphthongs in some syllables in the *rù* tone, as was often done by Northern Mandarin. A table in Edkins (1857, 62–64) that compares the five sound systems of Nánjīng, Běijīng, Jǐnán, Chéngdū, and the reconstructed sounds of the fourteenth century 中原音韻 *Zhōngyuán yīnyùn*, shows *peh* (Nanking), *pai* (Běijīng), and *pe* (Chéngdū) for *bǎi* 百 'hundred'; *yoh* (Nánjīng), *yau* (Běijīng), and *yo* (Chéngdū) for *yào* 藥 'medicine'; and *kioh* (Nánjīng), *tsiau* (Běijīng), and *tsio* (Chéngdū) for *jiǎo* 脚 'foot'. Western Mandarin thus displayed some features similar to Southern Mandarin in this respect.

As for (d), Northern Mandarin, the Běijīng dialect clearly distinguished the finals -*o* and -*uo* of the traditional *Guǒshè* 果攝 rhyme group. In contrast, both are rendered -o in Western Mandarin, such as *ho* 河 [hé] 'river' and *ko* 過 [guò] 'pass' in Grainger (1900). Hence, Western Mandarin is similar to Southern Mandarin in this regard.

Based on points (a) to (d), it is evident that Western Mandarin was not only distinguishable from the Běijīng dialect, but also was different from Nánjīng Mandarin because of the reduced *rù* tone.

Another important contribution of Edkins was that he considered the Chéngdū dialect to be the typical dialect of Western Mandarin: "In Western mandarin, taking C'heng-tu-fu [i.e., Chéngdūfǔ 成都府] the capital of Sï-c'hwen as the standard, there are four tone-classes" (Edkins 1857, 8). He made another similar remark in his book: "For the pronunciation of C'hengtu [i.e., Chéngdū], the best standard of western mandarin" (48). Accordingly, the Western Mandarin that he defined was based not on the dialect of other cities but on that of Chéngdū.

---

13. There exist some exceptions among contemporary Sìchuān dialects: the *rù* tone merges into *yīnpíng* 陰平 in the Yǎ'ān 雅安 and Shímián 石棉 dialects, and into the *qù* 去 tone in Zìgòng 自貢 and Rénshòu 仁壽 dialects. See Yáng (1984) and Zhōngguó shèhuì kēxuéyuàn et al. (2012).
14. The superscript numbers at the top right of the Romanized text designate the tone. Number 1 stands for *yīnpíng*, 2 for *yángpíng*, 3 for *shǎng* 上 tone, 4 for *qù* tone, and 5 for *rù* tone.

Edkins's point of view was widely accepted among Westerners in China. Let us consider a French–Chinese dictionary compiled by French Catholic missionaries as an example:

> Le présent Dictionnaire, composé par des Missionnaires ayant vécu de longues années dans le *Sé tch'ouān*, et en collaboration avec des prêtres indigènes, contient le language parlé couramment par le peuple des villes et des campagnes dans le *Sé tch'ouān*, et à peu de chose près dans le *Yûn nân* et le *Koúi tcheōu*. Il diffère peu de ce que l'on est convenu d'appeler *la langue mandarine*.
>
> [The present dictionary, compiled by the missionaries who resided in Sìchuān for years, in collaboration with the native priests, contains the language spoken generally by the people in the cities and countryside of Sìchuān, which has little difference from those of Yúnnán and Guìzhōu. It differs little from the language known as Mandarin.]
>
> (Plusieurs missionnaires 1893, iii)

This statement shows that the notion that the language spoken in Southeast China was independent of other variations of Mandarin was supported beyond the nationality and denomination of the missionaries. Another French–Chinese dictionary also supports Edkins's opinion:

> La langue mandarine est la langue familière non-seulement des officiers du gouvernement et de toutes les personnes instruites, mais aussi des quatre cinquièmes de la population. Elle se divise en trois dialectes principaux: le dialecte de Tch'eng tou fou dans le Seu tch'oen, le dialecte de Napkin et le dialect de Pékin.
>
> [The Mandarin language is familiar not only to the officers of government and educated literati, but also to four-fifths of the population. It is basically divided into three dialects: the dialect of Chéngdūfū 成都府 of Sichuan province, the dialect of Nanking, and the dialect of Peking.]
>
> (Couvreur 1892, préface)

This citation implies that the base of Western Mandarin should be considered the Chéngdū dialect.

Edkins's grammar became so widespread that it influenced the research of both that age and later generations.[15] For example, Prussian diplomat and sinologist Paul Georg von Möllendorff divided Mandarin into three groups as follows: "The *Kuanhua* [i.e. *Guānhuà*] may be divided into three regions: a northern, a central and a western" (Möllendorff 1896, 56). Thirty years later, in 1925, Chinese scholar 毛坤 Máo Kūn translated Möllendorff's paper into Chinese. In Máo's translation, the three variations of Mandarin were *Běibù* 北部 'Northern', *Zhōngbù* 中部 'Central', and *Xībù* 西部 'Western', respectively (Máo 1925, 2–6). After Máo, Lǐ Fānggùi 李方桂 attempted a demarcation of Chinese dialects (Lǐ Fānggùi 1937) and divided

---

15. The fact that Edkins's grammar had a second edition (1864), when most works of that nature were printed only once, shows that the book was popular at that time.

Mandarin into the three types: "The Northern, the Eastern, and the Southwestern." Yuen Ren Chao [Zhào Yuánrèn 趙元任] published a similar classification (Chao 1948, 6). So it can be safely asserted that Edkins's subdivision was followed by Chinese scholars as well as Western researchers.

Publication and Education of Western Mandarin

Materials

Until the mid-nineteenth century, there did not appear any analysis of Western Mandarin in materials by Protestant missionary-scholars. It was the China Inland Mission (CIM) that first sent a missionary to Sìchuān; he was followed by other missions such as those of the Methodist Church of Canada (MCC) and the American Baptists. However, at the beginning of their evangelization in Sìchuān, they suffered from a shortage of language teaching materials and the lack of an established language-learning system. Frederic Stephenson in his history of MCC's China Mission described the missionaries' plight at the time as follows: "When our Mission was founded twenty-five years ago, we had no course of study in the language, nor was there such a profusion of books—primers, readers, dictionaries, etc.—as are to be had now, to aid one in the mastery of Chinese" (Stephenson 1920, 40).

Here, "the language" is understood to be Western Mandarin, since there already existed at the time a plethora of learning materials for Nánjīng Mandarin. Accordingly, missions such as the MCC were driven to compile dictionaries and conversation textbooks by themselves, specializing in the acquisition of Western Mandarin. In the following lines, some of the better-known works on Western Mandarin will be introduced; after that, some of the features of Western Mandarin in the early twentieth century as evidenced by these sources will be discussed.

i. *Dictionnaire Chinois–Français de la langue Mandarine parlée* (1893)

This is one of the earliest materials on Western Mandarin compiled in the form of a book by Westerners. The authors are anonymous and are only indicated as "Plusieurs missionnaires du Sé-tch'oūan Méridional" [some missionaries in Southern Sìchuān] on the front page.

The dictionary was considered an important source of Western Mandarin during the Republic of China era. Luó Chángpéi 羅常培 rated this dictionary highly: "There are outstanding dictionaries on other dialects, for instance . . . the Sichuan dialect has *Dictionnaire Chinois-Français* by the Northern [*sic*] Sichuan Church. These books can provide us with plenty of research sources" (Luó 1934, 149–50).[16]

---

16. "至於其餘的方言也有特別好的字典，例如……四川話有川北教會的《漢法中國西部官話字典》等。這些部書都供給我們不少的材料。" The authors of this dictionary were in fact missionaries – not in Chuānběi 川北 (Northern Sìchuān), however, but rather in southern Sìchuān, and thus the reference here should be to Chuānnán 川南: the Southern Sìchuān Church.

ii. *Western Mandarin* 西蜀方言 [*Xī Shǔ Fāngyán*] (1900)

This thick dictionary compiled by Adam Grainger has more than 800 pages, 3,786 characters, and 13,484 entries, as well as 401 proverbs. Grainger made a point of registering colloquial words and idioms in this work, writing that "many phrases used by scholars have been rejected as too 'bookish,' but, on the other hand, nothing has been regarded as too common for insertion" (Grainger 1900, i).

It seems that more colloquial phraseology is present in Grainger (1900) than in Plusieurs missionnaires (1893). This is evident in the fact that the Grainger (1900) includes 191 words with no characters. These words are represented in the dictionary using similar sounding characters with the radical 口 *kǒu* added, such as "[口+昭] chao³" [marker of the passive]: *Fēng bǎ wǒ chuī zhǎo le* 風把我吹昭了 'I have been affected by the wind; caught cold' (Grainger 1900, 597).[17] Besides serving as a Chinese–English dictionary, Grainger (1900) has a 94-page segment that covers about 6,000 English words with their Chinese equivalents; hence, it can be used not only as a comprehensive Chinese–English dictionary but also as an English–Chinese glossary.

iii. *A Course of Lessons in Spoken Mandarin, based on the Gouin Method* 華英聯珠分類集成 [*Huá-Yīng Liánzhū Fēnlèi Jíchéng*] (1908)

This medium-length textbook was compiled by Canadian missionary James Endicott, who came to China in 1895 and engaged in evangelical work there for fifteen years. Endicott (1908) includes 100 lessons spread across 201 pages: Western Mandarin sentences and their translations in English are presented on facing pages and include vocabulary and phrases for practical daily use. No Romanization is given in the text—perhaps Endicott expected students to use the textbook in the presence of a Chinese teacher. Nor are any phonetic, grammatical, or lexical interpretations given, as it was likely assumed that learners would be listening to and repeating the sounds uttered by the Chinese teacher.

iv. *Chinese Lessons for First Year Students in West China* (1917)

This textbook was compiled by MCC missionary Omar Leslie Kilborn. He was a medical missionary and one of the pillars of the MCC China Mission in the early twentieth century, along with Endicott.

As the title implies, this textbook was a medium-length study tool for beginner Western Mandarin students. The book specifically focused on speaking and listening, elucidating conversational language for the missionaries' daily needs, with topics such as "hiring a coolie," "sedan chair riding," and "changing dollars."

This textbook has 278 pages, containing 1,008 short sentences organized under 32 topics. Kilborn recommends a quite unique approach to his book: "There has

---

17. Originally the radical "口" was added on the left side of the character "昭", forming a single graph; due to font limitations we could not represent it that way in this chapter.

been no attempt to put easier lessons first; you are at perfect liberty to begin literally anywhere, even in the middle of a lesson, if you wish. You will find, however, that the first hundred sentences have not only the romanisation [*sic*], but also complete literal translation. The second hundred have dropped the literal translation, and the two hundredth sentence is the last to have the complete romanisation" (Kilborn 1917, IX).

Linguistic features

The above-mentioned works clearly reflect the features of Western Mandarin, especially the Chéngdū dialect. Here are some examples that represent the syntactical, lexicological, and phonological characteristics of Western Mandarin.

Syntactical features treated here are the verb-suffix *tao*³ 倒, the complement *ch'i*³ 起, the serial verb 拿跟 *la²ken*¹, the causative verb 着 *cho*⁵, and the disjunctive question particle 嗎 *ma*¹.¹⁸ First, an example of the verb-suffix *tao*³, which chiefly means continuous or imperative in Western Mandarin, is shared below: (3a) is an example of the former (continuous), while (3b) is an example of the latter (imperative).

(3) a. 先生 // 在 // 書房-裏 // 坐-倒
*sien*¹*sen*¹ // *tsai*⁴ // *shu*¹*fang*²*-li*³ // *tso*⁴*-tao*³
teacher // in // study-inside // sit-CONT
'The teacher is sitting in his study'. (Endicott 1908, 2–3)¹⁹
b. 放-倒
*fang*⁴*-tao*³
put-IMP
'Put it down'. (Kilborn 1917, 92)

*Tao*³ in example (3) is more of a suffix than a complement, and according to Furuya (1997). This type of grammaticalized *tao*³ was attested in the late Ming period.

Second, in Western Mandarin, *ch'i*³ is often the marker of a continuous action or state as well as a directional complement, as is the case in *Pǔtōnghuà*. As seen in example (4), *ch'i*³ is often used in the construction of "V1 *ch'i*³ V2," which means "V2 while V1."

(4) 涼轎 // 的 // 坐位 // 要 // 拱-起 // 編
*Liang*²*chiao*⁴ // *ti*⁵ // *tso*⁴*ue*⁴ // *iao*⁴ // *kong*³*-ch'i*³ // *pien*¹
cool.chair // DE // seat // should // arch-CONT // braid
'The seat of the open chair is to be plaited in a convex shape'. (Kilborn 1917, 111)

---

18. All Romanizations of Western Mandarin and the examples (3) to (10) are adopted from Grainger (1900).
19. English translations in examples (3), (4), (6), and (10) are taken from their original text. However, for examples including French sources, i.e., (5), (7), (8), and (9), English translations were made by the author.

Third, the serial verb *la²ken¹* functions as a marker indicating passivity as in (5), especially in the context of someone or something suffering from mischief or damage, which may correspond to 被 *bèi* in *Pǔtōnghuà* to some extent.[20] *La²gen¹* would originally have been a benefactive serial verb, which means 'to confer' or 'to give', and would have served the role of a marker of the passive voice. In the modern Chéngdū dialect, the word form slightly changes to 拿給 *na²gei³*.

(5) 拿跟 // 人家 // 哄-倒 // 了
    La²ken¹ // ren²chia¹ // hong³-tao³ // la³
    PASS // person // deceive-PERF // PRT
    'He was deceived by a person' (Plusieurs missionnaires 1893, 117)

The verb *cho⁵* in Western Mandarin served as a passive or causative marker. In the modern Chéngdū dialect, *cho⁵* is still used as a passive marker, such as in the sentence *Yīfu zháo yǔ lín-shī le* 衣服着雨淋濕了 'The clothes got soaked in the rain'.[21] In contrast, *cho⁵* as a causative marker as in (6) is no longer in use today; instead, *hǎn* 喊 is commonly used in the modern language.

(6) 着 // 一 // 個 // 人 // 去
    cho⁵ // i⁵ // ko⁴ // ren² // ch'ü⁴
    CAUS // one // CL // person // go
    'Send a man'. (Grainger 1900, 418)

The connector *ma* in disjunctive questions as in (7) seems quite unique. As Zhāng, Zhāng, and Dèng (2001) did not refer to this marker, it does not seem to be in use today in Chéngdū, although it is still spoken in several pockets surrounding the city, such as 南充 Nánchōng.[22]

(7) 這 // 個 // 月 // 大 // 嗎 // 小
    che⁴ // ko⁴ // üe⁵ // ta⁴ // ma¹ // siao³
    this // CL // month // large // or // small
    'Is this month thirty days or twenty-nine days?' (Plusieurs missionnaires 1893, 345)

For lexical features, see examples (8) and (9). The word *wūtou* 屋頭 originally meant 'room' or 'house', while in (8), it means 'wife'. The verb *guòjiǔ* 過酒 (9)

---

20. French missionaries state: "Voir les particules 被, *pí*, 拿跟, *lâ kēn*, qui peuvent donner un sens passif à quelques verbes" [see the particles 被, *pí*, 拿跟, *lâ kēn*, which are able to give the passive meaning to some verbs] (Plusieurs missionnaires 1893, x).
21. See Xióng (2006, 40). This doctoral thesis is one of the earliest historical studies on the Chéngdū dialect in the form of one cohesive volume.
22. Mǎ et al. (1986) is one of the few textbooks on Western Mandarin in the twentieth century focusing on the Nánchōng dialect, which takes up this type of interrogative construction with the word 嘜 *me* instead of *ma*, for example, *Shì huí fàndiàn me háishi dào bié de dìfang qù* 是回飯店嘜還是到別的地方去? 'Are you going back to the hotel or another place?' and *Zhèzhèn jiù chī me háishi láng mén* 這陣就吃嘜還是郎門? 'Do we eat now or what do we do?' (Mǎ et al. 1986, [1] 249).

originally meant 'to drink liquor'; here it has evolved to mean 'to have a wedding party' or 'to get married'.

(8) 你 // 的 // 屋頭 // 好 // 了 // 沒有
ni³ // ti⁵ // u⁵t'ou² // hao³ // liao³ // mo⁵iu³
you // DE // house // good // PERF // NEG
'Did your wife get over her cold?' (Plusieurs missionnaires 1893, 376)

(9) 他 // 過 // 了 // 酒 // 沒有
T'a¹ // ko⁴ // liao³ // tsiu³ // mo⁵iu³
he // drink // PERF // liquor // NEG
'Is he married?' (Plusieurs missionnaires 1893, 640)

A phonological feature we will look at here is the tone sandhi in reduplicated words. In example (10) below, the words *chio²chio¹* 腳腳 'legs', *k'uan⁴k'uan¹* 橫橫 'crosspiece', and *fung⁴fung¹* 縫縫 'crevice' are common in Western Mandarin. What is noteworthy here is the Romanization in the original text. For example, *chiao²chiao¹* is Romanized as *GIO²GIO¹* in Kilborn (1917, 84), with the tone category of every syllable indicated by a number at the top right of the Romanized syllable (the convention also followed in this chapter). In *GIO²GIO¹*, the tone of the second syllable is indicated as 1 or *yīnpíng*, which should originally be 2 (*yángpíng* originating in the *rù* tone) as with the first syllable. Similarly, *k'uan⁴k'uan¹* is indicated as *KWAN⁴KWAN¹* and *fung⁴fung¹* as *FUNG⁴FUNG¹*. For both Romanized forms, the first syllable is *qù* tone, while the second is *yīnpíng* tone due to the tone sandhi. This type of tone sandhi is a feature of reduplicated words in the dialect.[23]

(10) 椅子 // 的 // 腳腳 // 橫橫 // 靠背 // 各 // 處 // 縫縫 // 都 // 要 // 抹²⁴-乾淨
i³tsi³ // ti⁵ // chio²~chio¹ // k'uan⁴~k'uan¹ // k'ao⁴pe⁴ // ko⁵ // ch'u⁴ // fung⁴~fung¹ // tu¹ // iao⁴ // ma¹-kan¹chin⁴
chair // DE // legs // crosspiece // back // every // point // crevice // all // should // wipe-clean
'The legs, crosspieces, and backs of the chairs, together with all the crevices, must be dusted clean'. (Kilborn 1917, 84)

Codification

Generally speaking, codification propels the standardization of the language prevalent in a certain region. A dialect that has characters that can be used to transcribe it usually prevails over dialects without them.

---

23. The phenomena in which the tone of the second character changes to *yīnpíng* is also attested in Fù Chóngjǔ's *Chéngdū Tōnglǎn* (1909), which was published in the same age as Kilborn (1917). The Chéngdū dialect today also maintains the same pattern of tone sandhi. See Chiba et al. (2005, 47).

24. Due to font limitations the graph *mā* 抹 is used for what the source writes as [扌+麻].

The compilation of dialect materials such as dictionaries, textbooks, and grammars was a pivotal event in the history of Chinese dialects.[25] In the case of Western Mandarin, the ability to transcribe the Chéngdū dialect with Chinese characters and the Latin alphabet seems to have had a significant importance. Foreigners in Sìchuān practiced transcription to reduce Western Mandarin to a written form, as seen in the works mentioned above. They even created a series of new Chinese characters with the radical 口 *kǒu* to mark colloquial words and morphemes in the dialect that had no conventional characters with which to write them, as attested in Grainger (1900). The codification of the Chéngdū dialect contributed to the rise of its legitimacy as the dominant dialect of Western Mandarin.[26] In fact, transcription of the Chéngdū dialect with Chinese characters has a rather long tradition. Dating back to the Ming period, Lǐ Shí's (1597–1674) comprehensive glossary *Shǔyǔ* 蜀語 collected words and phrases of the Sichuan dialect along with explanations and pronunciation guidelines. However, the codification by Westerners in the late nineteenth and the early twentieth centuries was much more organized and vigorous.

It should be stressed that it is mainly because of the MCC that we can benefit from works on Western Mandarin of that period. The MCC valued publishing as well as medical service during its Sìchuān mission. According to Bond, Endicott had been the chief of the printing office of the MCC since 1902, when he took charge of the Lèshān 樂山 church (Bond 1909, 90). He promoted publishing vehemently; in 1902 alone, he printed 100 million pages of religious tracts in Chinese. During his term as director at the Canadian Methodist Mission Press (CMMP), the printing office was relocated from Lèshān to Chéngdū and became the largest of its kind in Western China (Bond 1909, 90; Chiba et al. 2005, 7–12). As a part of the publishing enterprise, learning materials on Chinese language went to print proactively. These materials would play a crucial role in the codification of the Chéngdū dialect.

On the whole, linguistic works that might serve as tools for transcribing were rarely formally published during the late nineteenth and the early twentieth centuries, and educational materials on Chinese dialects for Westerners were basically just drafts compiled by the Western teachers themselves with the aid of native scholars. For instance, according to the preface by Endicott, his textbook expanded from a draft. Compared to the Chéngdū dialect, the other dialects of Western Mandarin such as Chóngqìng and Wǔhàn were less codified. These dialects did not have as many linguistic materials as the Chéngdū dialect. To my knowledge, there are merely a few syllabaries and textbooks on the Wǔhàn and Kūnmíng dialects published by Western institutions, such as James Addison Ingle's *The Hankow Syllabary* (1899) for the Hànkǒu dialect, and *Short Cut to Western Mandarin* (1910) for the Kūnmíng dialect,

---

25. This is also the case with Chinese dialects other than Western Mandarin. For the Hakka dialects, for example, see Lamarre (2005).
26. Although not published as a single volume, one of the earliest works on the grammar of Western Mandarin is Plusieurs missionnaires (1893, VIII–X).

edited by a Norwegian missionary, Edward Amundsen.[27] Even though many groups of missionaries resided and evangelized in Chóngqìng, the lack of published dialect materials on the Chóngqìng dialect is worth noting.[28]

West China Union University

The codification of the Chéngdū dialect was proactively carried out in Sìchuān province. Western Mandarin education for Westerners in the colleges in Chéngdū was one important driver of the compilation of materials. Protestant missions in Chéngdū were basically cooperative, and some of them—the American Baptist Foreign Missionary Society (ABFMS), MCC, the Friends' Foreign Mission (FFM), and the Methodist Episcopal Mission (MEM)—agreed to establish a union church university in Chéngdū. This led to the birth of the West China Union University (WCUU) Huáxī Xiéhé Dàxué 華西協合大學 in 1914.[29] According to the *China Mission Year Book*, WCUU was a conglomeritic university that had a medical school, a pharmacy school, and attached normal schools for men and women, as well as a middle school. The Union Language School for New Missionaries, a special affiliated facility, was established around the same time. (The Editor 1914, 201). We cannot disregard the language schools affiliated with the church universities in China, as they accumulated know-how on methods of Western Mandarin education for half a century.

The two textbooks, Endicott (1908) and Kilborn (1917), were prepared for this language school, as was clearly stated by Walmsley: "Both Dr. Kilborn and Dr. Endicott wrote textbooks for the guidance of young missionaries when learning the language" (Walmsley 1974, 140). An article in a contemporary periodical also highlighted this fact: "In the language school in Chengtu [*sic*] it has been in use for several years, though they do not use it to the exclusion of other methods. The text they use is called *Mandarin Lessons*, is written by Mr. Endicott, and is published by the Canadian Methodist Press, Chengtu." (Pettus 1914, 773).[30] Here "the language school" designates the one affiliated to the WCUU, hence these statements clearly show that the language taught at the university was Western Mandarin, and in particular, the Chéngdū dialect.

Behind the well-organized Chéngdū dialect education lay the emphatic beliefs of Kilborn, who insisted that new missionaries should have plenty of time to acquire the language. To this effect, Kilborn wrote: "The first business of the missionary on

---

27. For more details on the phonetic system of Ingle (1899), see Chiba (2018). Also see Chiba (2007b) for preliminary remarks on Amundsen (1910).
28. An exception is the works of Edward Harper Parker, who made some trailblazing observations on various Chinese dialects, including the Sìchuān dialects (Parker 1882). However, he did not compile a comprehensive book of his miscellaneous papers on dialects, which were mainly published in the *Journal of the North-China Branch of the Asiatic Society* and the *China Review*.
29. It is incorrect to write 協和 *xiéhé* instead of 協合 *xiéhé*, which are homonyms in *Pǔtōnghuà*. This mistake may be due to a confusion originating with Fújiàn Xiéhé Dàxué 福建協和大學 Fujian Christian University, which existed in Fúzhōu 福州 during 1915–1951.
30. In the quotation, *Mandarin Lessons* should be understood as *A Course of Lessons*.

arrival in China is to 'get the language'. And most missions now allow the first two years for language study. We might better avoid that word 'allow'; saying rather that a minimum of two years is required by most missions for language study, during which period no other responsibility is put upon the new worker. I believe that we shall soon come to the point when no new worker will be given more than partial responsibility during his third and perhaps his fourth years, so that he may have large freedom for perfecting himself in the language, and in methods and principles of work" (Kilborn 1917, I). Kilborn repeatedly insisted on a "minimum of two years" duration to acquire the language. To secure ample time to "get the language," he established a small language class in 1912. Consistent with the beliefs of Kilborn, the MCC conducted its own language classes in Chéngdū before the founding of WCUU. It is worth noting that the classes of the MCC were open to all Westerners who wished to study the language, even if they belonged to other denominations. The language school of WCUU was actually the reorganized and expanded "Missionaries' Training School" of the MCC. At the language school, the newly arrived missionaries were taught a two- or three-year course to acquire basic proficiency in the local language. James Livingstone Stewart, the Vice President of the university at the time, had described the course as follows: "Union Language School, three years course, the first year in residence, for students of the Chinese language" (Stewart 1915, 195).

The establishment of the language school highlights WCUU's emphasis on dialect education. MCC's policy was unique in that many other missions could not afford to give the same level of language education due to a lack of supplies and funds, and thus, newcomers were often obliged to enroll in daily services as soon as they arrived in China.[31] Kilborn explained the advantage of studying at the language school as follows:

> Sometimes a new worker will spend hours in the effort to satisfy his teacher on a sound. He believes that he reproduces the sound accurately, but is really unable to catch the fine distinctions that are heard and spoken by his Chinese teacher. Unfortunately, the teacher is unable to explain just what is wrong, or if he does, we do not understand him. And so in some instances the teacher gives up in despair, and allows his pupil to continue his mispronunciation. Here is one of the times where the help of a fellow-missionary has already met and conquered the difficulty referred to. Here is one of the many advantages of the language school, or "Missionaries' Training School", such as is carried on as a department of the Union University at Chentu. (Kilborn 1917, VI–VII)

Surprisingly, the Chéngdū dialect was the sole target language taught in the school, as is evident from the teaching materials used. The supervisors from the committee of Protestant missions, who visited the school in Chéngdū, also clearly stated this fact: "The work in the schools is all done in the dialect of the place where

---

31. Such busyness was seen in many places where missionaries came to evangelize. For example, Ingle was engaged in service as soon as he arrived in China, with poor proficiency in Chinese. See Chiba (2018, 45–46).

the school is located. The schools visited, therefore, are all one dialect schools. This is also true of the school in Canton and the one in West China" (Commission of the C. C. C. 1915, 405).

Conclusion

In this chapter, I have analyzed the mechanisms of how a dialect emerges as a "representative" dialect in a demarcated dialect region through an examination of the Chéngdū dialect and Western Mandarin during the nineteenth and twentieth centuries. The findings can be summarized as follows: First, Joseph Edkins identified Western Mandarin and distinguished it from Nánjīng Mandarin and the Běijīng dialect. He selected the Chéngdū dialect as the representative dialect of Western Mandarin, and his view was treated as the established theory for several decades. Regardless of who authored the works on Western Mandarin, their linguistic framework, including the terms, was established by Edkins. Thus, it was natural for them that the Western Mandarin to which they referred to was based on the Chéngdū dialect.

Second, in Sìchuān, a variety of dictionaries and textbooks on Western Mandarin were published by Westerners. This prolific publishing activity of materials on Western Mandarin was, however, seen only in Chéngdū. This aided the augmentation of the legitimacy of the Chéngdū dialect as the typical form of Western Mandarin, as a greater amount of material existing on a topic leads to a greater chance of it being studied and considered worthy of study.

Third, the motivation for active publishing was dialect education at the WCUU. The language school affiliated with WCUU required a variety of teaching materials specializing in the local dialect to teach the local language to newly arrived missionaries. This is why the dialects in western provinces such as Chóngqìng, Wǔhàn, and Kūnmíng could not become the standard form of Western Mandarin. Although few studies have focused on the language schools attached to the Christian universities in China and their Chinese-language education programs, this chapter attempted to elucidate the process of the codification of the Chéngdū dialect through, at least in part, these institutions.

We must pay close attention to the huge impact and the authority of the Western education system newly introduced to China in that period, because the imperial examination system was abolished in 1905 and new, Western-style schools quickly replaced the traditional private schools. After 1905, a bachelor from a Western-style college was regarded as the equivalent of a traditional degree of *xiùcái* 秀才 under the old examination system. Moreover, WCUU was the only church university west of Wǔhàn. Elites from every corner of southwestern China learned from Western professors in the Chéngdū dialect.[32] As those who received higher education at the

---

32. WCUU had almost 200 Western professors in the twentieth century. For famous alumni and professors, see Zhāng (2000, 41–85).

WCUU came to share the same Chéngdū dialect, its legitimacy as the intellectual and academic language in southwestern China would have been greatly augmented.[33] As a consequence of these historical developments, before the birth of modern dialectology in China, the paradigm of Western Mandarin and the Chéngdū dialect as the standard had been set by Westerners, and this has been maintained since then. The Chéngdū dialect "triumphed"—borrowing Takata's term—within the range of Western Mandarin through codification and language education and obtained the position of the standard dialect in the region. However, it could not develop any further because the path from being a regional standard to the national language was blocked by "the triumph of Běijīng" as described in Takata (2001). Compared with Nánjīng Mandarin or the Běijīng dialect that had been reduced to writing for several centuries and had an extensive literature, the start of codification of the Chéngdū dialect came too late to be of lasting consequence.[34]

References

Amundsen, Edward. 1910. *Short Cut to Western Mandarin*. Hong Kong: Kelly & Walsh.
Běijīng dàxué Zhōngguó yǔyán wénxué xì yǔyánxué jiàoyánshì 北京大學中國語言文學系語言學教研室. 1989. *Hànyǔ fāngyīn zìhuì* 漢語方音字彙 [An index of readings in Chinese dialects]. Beijing: Wenzi gaige chubanshe.
Bond, Geo J. 1909. *Our Share in China and What We Are Doing with It*. Toronto: The Missionary Society for the Methodist Church.
Chao, Yuen Ren 趙元任. 1948. *Mandarin Primer*. Cambridge, MA: Harvard University Press.
Chiba, Kengo 千葉謙悟. 2007a. "Shinmatsu ni okeru zenkoku kyōtsūgo oyobi chihō kyōtsūgo no settei: Western Mandarin to no kanren kara" 清末における全国共通語および地方共通語の設定—Western Mandarin との関連から [Demarcation of national language and regional standard language in the late Qing period: In the focus of Western Mandarin]. In *Jūkyū seiki chūgokugo no shosō: shūenshiryō (ōbei, nihon, ryūkyū, chōsen) kara no approach* 19世紀中国語の諸相—周縁資料（欧米・日本・琉球・朝鮮）からのアプローチ [Aspects of Chinese language in the nineteenth century: Approaches from the marginal (Europe, America, Japan, Ryukyu, and Korea)], edited by Uchida Keiichi and Shěn Guówěi, 61–82. Tōkyō: Yūshōdō.
Chiba, Kengo 千葉謙悟. 2007b. "*Kaei shōkei* onsetsuhyō" 『華英捷徑』音節表 [A syllabary of the *Huáyīng jiéjìng*]. *Kāipiān* 開篇 26: 186–98.
Chiba, Kengo 千葉謙悟. 2018. "J. A. Ingle *Kan'on shūji* (1899) to kindai Kankō hōgen" J. A. イングル『漢音集字』(1899) と近代漢口方言 [J. A. Ingle's *The Hankow Syllabary* and the modern Hankou dialect]. *Chūgoku bungaku kenkyū* 中國文學研究 44: 45–65.

---

33. In general, the language in colleges increases its legitimacy. For instance, for the case of Xhosa in South Africa, see Kamiya (1998, 17–18).
34. John Livingstone Nevius, an American missionary-scholar at Shandong, accurately made an observation on the supremacy of Mandarin as early as the end of the 1860s. He stated: "[M]andarin is simply one of the many spoken languages of China, and bears the same relation to the classical language, or language of books, that the other spoken dialects do. It owes its prominence to the three facts stated above, viz., that it is spoken over a wider region of country, it is the common medium of communication between officials throughout the empire, and is reduced to writing and has an extensive literature" (Nevius 1869, 203).

Chiba, Kengo 千葉謙悟. 2019. "Xīwén zīliào yǔ guānhuà yánjiū: jiān lùn Guānhuà guān zhī chāyì yǐjí nán-běi Guānhuà de gàiniàn" 西文資料與官話研究—兼論官話觀之差異以及南北官話的概念 [Examining the Mandarin phonetic system through western materials: An analysis of the differences in views of the Mandarin language and the concept of southern and northern Mandarin]. *Chūgoku gogaku* 中國語學 266: 44–62.

Chiba, Kengo 千葉謙悟, Xióng Jìn 熊進, and Takahashi Keita 高橋慶太. 2005. *Hyakunen mae no Shisen hōgen: Kaei renju bunrui shūsei to Seishoku hōgen* 百年前の四川方言—『華英聯珠分類集成』と『西蜀方言』—[Sìchuān dialect of one hundred years ago: *Huáyīng liánzhū fēnlèi jíchéng* and *Xīshǔ fāngyán*]. Tōkyō: Chūgoku koseki bunka kenkyūsho.

Commission of the C. C. C. [Chinese Continuation Committee]. 1915. "Summary of the reports of the schools visited by the language study commission of the C. C. C." *China Mission Year Book* 6: 404–10.

Couvreur, Séraphim. 1892. *Dictionnaire français-chinois contenant les expressions les plus usitées de la langue mandarine*. Ho Kien Fou: Imprimerie de la Mission Catholique.

The Editor. 1914. "Union and co-operation." *China Mission Year Book* 5: 200–10.

Edkins, Joseph. 1857/1864. *A Grammar of the Chinese Colloquial Language, commonly called the Mandarin Dialect*. Shanghai: American Presbyterian Mission Press.

Endicott, James. 1908. *A Course of Lessons in Spoken Mandarin: Based on the Gouin Method*. Chentu [sic]: Canadian Methodist Mission Press.

Fù Chóngjǔ 傅崇矩. 1909. *Chéngdū tōnglǎn* 成都通覽 [A guidebook to Chéngdū]. Chengdu: Bashu shushe, 1987.

Furuya, Akihiro 古屋昭弘. 1997. "Mindai no "V dao" ni tsuite" 明代の"V倒"について [On "V dao" in the late Ming Chinese]. *Kāipiān* 開篇 16: 99–102.

Grainger, Adam. 1900. *Western Mandarin, or the Spoken Language of Western China*. Shanghai: American Presbyterian Mission Press.

Hirata, Shōji 平田昌司. 2016. *Wénhuà zhìdù hé Hànyǔ shǐ* 文化制度和漢語史 [Cultural structure and the history of the Chinese language]. Beijing: Beijing daxue chubanshe.

Huáng Xuězhēn 黃雪貞. 1986. "Xī'nán guānhuà de fēnqū (gǎo)" 西南官話的分區（稿）[Classification of Western Mandarin (draft)]. *Fāngyán* 方言 4: 262–72.

Ingle, James Addison. 1899. *The Hankow Syllabary, with References to Giles' Dictionary, Prepared for the Use in the American Church Mission*. Hankow: N. B. S. S. Mission Press.

Kamiya, Toshio 神谷俊郎. 1998. Seijiteki tan'i to shite no "buzoku" no sōshutsu to kirisutokyō senkyōshi no yakuwari—Minami Afurika 'Kōsa zoku' to iu wakugumi no shiisei ni tsuite (1)—政治的単位としての「部族」の創出とキリスト教宣教師の役割—南アフリカ「コーサ族」という枠組みの恣意性について (1)—[Creation of "tribe" as political unit and the role of Christian preachers—Arbitrariness of the framework of Xhosa in South Africa (1)]. http://www.aa.tufs.ac.jp/~tkamiya/Xhosa_ethn.html.

Kaske, Elisabeth. 2008. *The Politics of Language in Chinese Education, 1895–1919*. Leiden: Brill.

Kilborn, Omar Leslie. 1917. *Chinese Lessons for First Year-Students in West China*. [s.l.]: The Union University.

Kwan, Uganda Sze Pui 關詩珮 [Guān Shīpèi]. 2013. "Fānyì zhèngzhì jí Hànxué zhīshi de shēngchǎn: Wēi Tuǒmǎ yǔ Yīngguó wàijiāobù de Zhōngguó xuésheng yìyuán jìhuà (1843–1870)" 翻譯政治及漢學知識的生產：威妥瑪與英國外交部的中國學生譯員計畫 (1843–1870) [Translating politics and production of knowledge on Chinese studies:

Thomas Wade and the student interpreter project by the ministry of foreign affairs of the United Kingdom]. *Zhōngyáng yánjiūyuàn jìndàishǐ yánjiūsuǒ jíkān* 81: 1–52.

Lamarre, Christine. 2005. "Chiikigo de kaku koto—Hakkago no kēsu (1860–1910)" 地域語で書くこと—客家語のケース（1860–1910） [Writing in a regional language—A case of Hakka (1860–1910)]. In *Kanjiken no Kindai: Kotoba to Kokka* 漢字圏の近代：ことばと国家 [Modern times in Chinese civilization: Language and nation], edited by Murata Yūjirō and Christine Lamarre, 169–92. Tōkyō: Tōkyō daigaku shuppankai.

Li, Fang-Kuei 李方桂. 1937. "Languages and Dialects." In *The Chinese Year Book*, edited by Kuei Chung-shu 桂中樞, 59–65. Shanghai: The Commercial Press.

Lǐ Shí 李實. 1990. *Shǔyǔ jiàozhù* 蜀語校注 [Annotation of *Shǔyǔ*]. Annotations by Huáng Rénshòu 黃仁壽. Chéngdū: Bashu shushe.

Luó Chángpéi 羅常培. 1934. "Zhōngguó fāngyīn yánjiū xiǎoshǐ" 中國方音研究小史 [Brief description of research on Chinese dialects]. *Dōngfāng zázhì* 東方雜誌 31 (7): 141–53.

Mǎ, Zhēn 馬真, Hashimoto Mantarō 橋本萬太郎, Imai Keiko 今井敬子, Kitayama Sachiko 喜多山幸子, Ōta Itsuku 太田斎, and Research Institute for Language and Cultures of Asia and Africa, Tokyo University of Foreign Studies 東京外国語大学アジア・アフリカ言語文化研究所. 1986. *Seinan kanwa kyōhon* 西南官話教本 [A textbook of Western Mandarin]. Tōkyō: Research Institute for Language and Cultures of Asia and Africa, Tokyo University of Foreign Studies.

Máo Kūn 毛坤. 1925. "Xiànxíng Zhōngguó yìzú yǔ jí Zhōngguó fāngyán zhī fēnlèi" 現行中國異族語及中國方言之分類 [Current classification of Non-Chinese languages and Chinese dialects]. *Gēyáo* 歌謠 89: 2–6.

Mateer, Calvin Wilson. 1892/1900. *A Course of Mandarin Lessons*. Shanghai: American Presbyterian Mission Press.

Meadows, Thomas Taylor. 1847. *Desultory Notes on the Government and People of China, and on the Chinese Language*. London: William H. Allen & Co.

Möllendorff, Paul Georg von. 1896. "On the foreign languages spoken in China and the classification of the Chinese dialects." *China Mission Hand-Book* 1: 46–57.

Murata, Yūjirō 村田雄二郎, and Christine Lamarre. 2005. *Kanjiken no kindai: kotoba to kokka* 漢字圏の近代：ことばと国家 [Modern times in Chinese civilization: Language and nation]. Tōkyō: Tōkyō daigaku shuppankai.

Nakamura, Masakyuki 中村雅之. 2006. "Edkins no shirushita 19 seiki no kanwaon" Edkins の記した19世紀の官話音 [Mandarin phonetic system in the nineteenth century recorded by Edkins]. *KOTONOHA* 38: 1–4.

Nevius, John Livingstone. 1869. *China and the Chinese*. London: Sampson Low, Son, and Marson.

Parker, Edward Harper. 1882. "The dialect of Eastern Sz Ch'uan." *China Review* 11: 112–20.

Pettus, W. B. 1914. "Language Study." *The Chinese Recorder* 45: 771–74.

Plusieurs missionnaires du Sé-tch'oūan Méridional. 1893. *Dictionnaire Chinois-Français de la langue Mandarine parlée dans l'ouest de la Chine avec un vocabulaire Français-Chinois*. Hong Kong: Imprimerie de la Société des Missions Étrangères.

Prémare, Joseph Henri Marie de. c. 1728/1831 *Notitia Linguae Sinicae*. Malaccae: Cura Academiae Anglo-Sinensis.

Sìchuān shěng fāngyán diàochá zhǐdǎozǔ 四川省方言調查指導組. 1960. "Sìchuān fāngyán yīnxì" 四川方言音系 [Phonological system of the Sìchuān dialect], *Sìchuān dàxué xuébào (shèhuì kēxué)* 四川大學學報 (社會科學) 3: 1–123.

Stephenson, Frederic Clarke. 1920. *Our West China Mission*. Toronto: The Missionary Society of the Methodist Church.

Stewart, James Livingstone. 1915. "West China Union University" 協合大學校 [Xiéhé dàxuéxiào], Chengtu, West China. *China Mission Year Book* 6: 193–97.

Takata, Tokio 高田時雄. 2001. "Thomas Wade to Pikingo no shōri" トマス・ウエイドと北京語の勝利 [Thomas Wade and the triumph of Běijīng dialect]. In *Seiyō kindai bunmei to Chūka sekai* 西洋近代文明と中華世界 [Western modern civilization and the sphere of Chinese civilization], edited by Hazama Naoki, 127–42. Kyōto: Kyōto Daigaku gakujutsu shuppankai.

Wade, Thomas Francis. 1867. *A Progressive Course Designed to Assist the Student of Colloquial Chinese*. London: Trübner & Co.

Walmsley, Lewis C. 1974. *West China Union University*. New York: United Board for Christian Higher Education in Asia.

Williams, Samuel Wells. 1844. *An English and Chinese Vocabulary in the Court Dialect*. Macao: The Office of the Chinese Repository.

Williams, Samuel Wells. 1874. *A Syllabic Dictionary of the Chinese Language*. Shanghai: American Presbyterian Mission Press.

Xióng, Jìn 熊進. 2006. "Seito hōgen no bunpō kenkyū: bunpōka no approach" 成都方言の文法研究—文法化のアプローチ [Research on grammar of the Chéngdū dialect: An approach from grammaticalization]. PhD diss., Waseda University.

Yáng Shíféng 楊時逢. 1984. *Sìchuān fāngyán diàochá bàogào* 四川方言調查報告 [Report on the Sìchuān dialects]. Taipei: Zhongyang yanjiuyuan lishi yuyan yanjiusuo.

Yoshikawa, Masayuki 吉川雅之. 2015. "Jūkyū seiki zaika ōbeijin no kanwazō" 十九世紀在華欧米人の官話像 [On the images of Mandarin from the Westerners' view in the nineteenth century]. *Kotoba to shakai* ことばと社会 17: 51–80.

Yuán Jiāhuá 袁家驊. 2001. *Hànyǔ fāngyán gàiyào* 漢語方言概要 [An outline of Chinese dialects]. Beijing: Yuwen chubanshe.

Zhāng Lìpíng 張麗萍. 2000. *Xiāngsī Huáxība: Huáxī xiéhé dàxué* 相思華西坝：華西協合大學 [Reminiscences of Huáxība: West China Union University]. Shijiazhuang: Hebei Jiaoyu Chubanshe.

Zhāng Yīzhōu 張一舟, Zhāng Qīngyuán 張清源, and Dèng Yīngshù 鄧英樹. 2001. *Chéngdū fāngyán yǔfǎ yánjiū* 成都方言語法研究 [Research on the grammar of the Chéngdū dialect]. Chéngdū: Bashu shushe.

Zhōngguó shèhuì kēxuéyuàn yǔyán yánjiūsuǒ 中國社會科學院語言研究所, Zhōngguó shèhuì kēxuéyuàn mínzúxué yǔ rénlèixué yánjiūsuǒ 中國社會科學院民族學與人類學研究所, and Xiānggǎng chéngshì dàxué yǔyán zīxùn yánjiū zhōngxīn 香港城市大學語言資訊研究中心. 2012. *Zhōngguó yǔyán dìtújí (Hànyǔ fāngyán juàn)* 中國語言地圖集（漢語方言卷）[Linguistic Atlas of China (volume on Chinese dialects)]. Beijing: Shangwu Yinshuguan.

9
A Question in the Final Systems of Míng-Time Guānhuà

W. South Coblin

Introduction

The fifteenth-century Korean sinologist Sin Sukchu申叔舟 (1417–1475) recorded in a specially modified version of the Han'gûl alphabet two different types of pronunciation for the early Míng 明 koiné, Guānhuà 官話. One of these was known as the *zhèngyīn* 正音 ("Standard Readings"; SR) and is probably to be attributed to one Ní Qiān 倪謙 (1415–1479), a Chinese official from Nanking who spent time in Korea in 1450.[1] The readings elicited from Ní Qiān by Sin Sukchu were based on the government-sponsored dictionary, *Hóngwǔ zhèngyùn* 洪武正韻, published in 1375. They probably represent the formal reading pronunciation of that time.

A second type of pronunciation recorded by Sin was known as the *súyīn* 俗音 ("Popular Readings"; hereafter PR). These are probably to be attributed to Huáng Zàn 黃瓚 (1413?–1438?), a southern court official living in exile in Liáodōng 遼東, who was visited by and consulted on a number of occasions by Sin during his Chinese-language researches.[2] They are thought to represent Huáng's standard spoken Guānhuà pronunciation of the time. In many instances the two pronunciation systems, Standard Reading and Popular Reading, are in fundamental agreement. But in some cases there are significant differences. The present study will deal with one of these divergences.[3]

The Question

In the following set of examples, a difference in syllable finals is found between the readings of Sin's Standard Reading and Popular Reading systems. The Korean

---

1. On the life of this man, see Goodridge (1976: Vol. II, 1088–1090). For a discussion of his probable role as Sin's chief informant, see Yùchí (1990).
2. For a biographical study of this individual, see Ledyard (1965). Further useful information on him is given by Yùchí (1990), who postulates his role as Sin's primary *súyīn* informant.
3. For more detailed discussion of these and other source materials to be mentioned below, see Coblin (2007) and (2009).

transcriptional forms follow the transliteration of Kim (1991). For each example, a *Qièyùn* 切韻 System (QYS) spelling is cited in the orthography of Bernhard Karlgren, as emended by F. K. Li (1971). QYS forms are given for convenience of reference to the traditional phonological framework, and no assumptions are made about the historicity or phonetic reality of that framework.

QYS	SR	PR
莊，裝，妝 (tṣjang)	tṣaŋ (平)	tṣwaŋ
樁 (ṭång)	tṣaŋ (平)	tṣwaŋ
壯 (tṣjang-)	tṣaŋ (去)	tṣwaŋ
撞 (ḍång-)	tṣaŋ (去)	tṣwaŋ
創，瘡 (tṣhjang)	tṣ'aŋ (平)	tṣ'waŋ
窗 (tṣ'ång)	tṣ'aŋ (平)	tṣ'waŋ
創，愴，滄 (tṣhjang-)	tṣ'aŋ (去)	tṣ'waŋ
床 (dẓjang)	dẓaŋ (平)	dẓwaŋ
撞，幢 (ḍång)	dẓaŋ (平)	dẓwaŋ
狀 (dẓjang-)	dẓaŋ (去)	dẓwaŋ
霜，孀 (ṣjang)	ṣaŋ (平)	ṣwaŋ
雙 (ṣång)	ṣaŋ (平)	ṣwaŋ
爽 (ṣjang:)	ṣaŋ (上)	ṣwaŋ

In these examples the Standard Reading forms end in -aŋ, while the Popular Reading forms have final -waŋ. It is the latter final type that is typical of today's Northern Mandarin dialects as a whole, and of Modern Standard Chinese in particular. Discrepancies of this type have led some authorities to question the reality or factuality of the Standard Reading forms. For example, K. Kim (1991, 37) remarks rather cautiously that "some standard readings could be archaic or idealized constructs." Y. Kim (1989, 36), on the other hand, is far more unequivocal in this regard. He remarks:

> the Correct Pronunciation [i.e., our Standard Readings; *WSC*] was arrived at mainly by examining rhyme books rather than by direct description of speech sounds. Thus, we may also question the degree of accuracy of the Correct Pronunciation in representing the sound system underlying *Hongwu zhengyun*.

That the Standard Readings are tied to the *Hóngwǔ zhèngyùn* is of course common knowledge, since the original historical sources specifically confirm the link. To wit, the Standard Readings are patently the supposedly correct reading pronunciations of characters in the dictionary. The basic question is, rather, how did Sin Sukchu arrive at his Standard Reading orthographic forms? Did he simply look up *fǎnqiè* formulae in rime books and create the Standard Readings as a philological exercise, assigning abstract spelling forms to the initial and final categories distinguished in those lexicographical works? Or did he actually sit down with Ní Qiān and ask him to pronounce the head characters of each homophone group in the *Hóngwǔ zhèngyùn*, and then record what he had heard alphabetically? That the two men became good friends and spent a considerable amount of time together is known from the sources, but this does not in and of itself answer our question, for the fact remains that there is no actual step-by-step description of how Sin pursued his transcriptional work on the Standard Readings. The only recourse here is therefore to examine actual cases of differences between the Standard Readings and the Popular Readings, to see what they may be able to tell us. And the instance of Sin's contrasting Standard Reading -*aŋ* vs. Popular Reading -*waŋ* variants for the same characters provides an appropriate case in point.

The Evidence

In considering this question it is interesting to note variant readings of the type cited below, which are taken from the Guānhuà syllabary, *Xīrú ěrmùzī* 西儒耳目資 (XREMZ; published in 1626) of the Jesuit missionary, Nicolas Trigault (1577–1628). The *Xīrú ěrmùzī* forms are given in Trigault's orthography followed by phonetic interpretations in square brackets.[4]

QYS	SR	XREMZ
滄 (tṣhjang-)	tṣ'aŋ (去)	ch'ām, ç'ām [tṣ'aŋ ~ ts'aŋ]
愴 (tṣhjang-)	tṣ'aŋ (去)	ch'oám, ch'uám, ch'ām, ç'ām [tṣ'uaŋ ~ tṣ'aŋ ~ ts'aŋ]
創, 瘡 (tṣhjang)	tṣ'aŋ (平)	ch'oām, ch'uām, ch'ām, ç'ām [tṣ'uaŋ ~ tṣ'aŋ ~ ts'aŋ]
奘 (dzjang:, dzâng:, dzâng-)	dzaŋ (上, 去)	choàm, çàm [tṣuaŋ ~ tsaŋ]

Here we see that variant forms in final -*aŋ* were actually in use in the Guānhuà variety recorded by Trigault two centuries after Sin Sukchu's time. And in the first example, for *chuàng* 滄, only -*aŋ* readings were known to Trigault.

We now descend several decades to the "Vocabulario de la Letra China," a Guānhuà character dictionary compiled by the Dominican missionary Francisco Diaz (1606–1646), around 1640. In this work, most forms that are of interest to us are transcribed with final -*uam* or -*oam*, indicating that he read these syllables with Chinese final -*uaŋ*. However, there are two interesting exceptions to this:

---

4. Note that, following Portuguese missionary convention, Trigault rendered Chinese final [ŋ] as -m.

QYS	SR	Diaz
奘 (dzjang:, dzâng:, dzâng-)	dzaŋ (上,去)	choàm, çàm [tṣuaŋ ~ ts'aŋ]
瘡 (tṣhjang)	tṣ'aŋ (平)	çām', choām' [tsaŋ ~ tṣ'uaŋ]

In these two cases, Diaz knew variant readings in -*aŋ* which contrasted with those in -*uaŋ*.

A similar phenomenon is observable in the somewhat later material recorded by the Dominican friar Francisco Varo (1627–1687) in his manuscript Spanish–Chinese dictionary of Guānhuà, completed in 1679 (see Coblin 2006). At one point in this text (2006, 111) the word *chuāng* 瘡 "ulcer" occurs a number of times, spelled as *choāng'* [tṣ'uaŋ].[5] But Varo adds the note "nota que *choāng'* y *çhāng'* est idem" ['note that *choāng'* and *çhāng'* is (> are) the same']. And, interestingly, in the 1670 Portuguese–Guānhuà predecessor version of the 1679 dictionary, *chuāng* 瘡 is indeed usually spelled *çhāng'* rather than *choāng'*. A similar orthographic note occurs later in the 1679 text (2006, 172), and a number of instances of the spelling *çhāng'* for 瘡 appear there (e.g., 2006, 13 and 177). Elsewhere (2006, 296) the word *chuāng* 創 "to wound" is written *çhāng'*; and for *zhuāng* 椿, classifier for *shì* 事 'thing, affair', we find the spelling *chāng* rather than *choāng*. For *zhuǎng/zàng* 奘 "stout" we find the spelling *çhāng'* (2006, 498). And, most interestingly, for *zhuàng* 壯 "robust" we find *çhiáng* (2006, 562). What is most significant here is Varo's view that pronunciations in -*aŋ* and -*uaŋ* were "the same," that is, equally valid in the Guānhuà of his time. Finally, we come to the French Jesuit missionary, Joseph Prémare (1666–1736) and his *Notitia Linguae Sinicae*, a grammar of Guānhuà completed ca. 1730. Our data are derived from the printed version of 1893 and secondarily from an earlier edition of 1831.[6] Like Francisco Diaz, Prémare normally rendered the finals that interest us as -*oang* [*uaŋ*]. However, we find in his grammar the following interesting variant pair:

QYS	SR	Prémare
窗 (tṣ'ång)	tṣ'aŋ (平)	t'chouāng, ts'ang [tṣ'uaŋ ~ ts'aŋ]

What we have seen in the later Guānhuà data of Trigault, Diaz, Varo, and Prémare are occasional or stray cases of final -*aŋ*, with dominant -*uaŋ* serving as the more usual reading for the syllable types that concern us. However, in the late sixteenth century Portuguese–Chinese dictionary manuscript (PDC), an early Guānhuà lexicon attributed to the Jesuits Michele Ruggieri (1543–1607) and Matteo Ricci (1552–1610), and probably compiled in Guǎngdōng 廣東, we find quite a different picture (Ruggieri and Ricci 2001). Consider the following:[7]

---

5. By Varo's time missionary linguists felt free to follow the orthographic conventions of their individual languages rather than earlier Portuguese practice. Consequently, Varo rendered Chinese -ŋ as Spanish -ng.
6. I am grateful to Professor Richard Bodman for allowing me to use his copy of this rather rare work.
7. At this period there was no established transcription for Guānhuà among the European missionaries. Consequently, the authors of this manuscript used a rather erratic system based on mixed Portuguese and Italian spelling conventions. For discussion, see Yang (1989).

QYS	SR	PC
撞 (ḍång-)	tṣaŋ (去)	cia', can, ciam, zan [tṣaŋ ~ tṣan ~ tsan]
妝 (tṣjang)	tṣaŋ (平)	za', zan [tsaŋ ~ tsan]
壯 (tṣjang-)	tṣaŋ (去)	za', zan [tsaŋ ~ tsan]
瘡 (tṣhjang)	tṣ'aŋ (平)	zan, za', cia' [tsan ~ tsaŋ ~ tṣaŋ]
床 (dẓjang)	dẓaŋ (平)	za', zan [ts'aŋ ~ ts'an]
裝 (tṣjang)	tṣaŋ (平)	za', zan [tsaŋ ~ tsan]
窗 (tṣ'ång)	tṣ'aŋ (平)	za', zan [ts'aŋ ~ ts'an]
創 (tṣhjang)	tṣ'aŋ (平)	cia' [tṣ'aŋ]
狀 (dẓjang-)	dẓaŋ (去)	zan, cia' [tsan ~ tṣaŋ]
雙 (ṣång)	ṣaŋ (平)	san [san]

Here we see that all attested syllables of this type have the vowel -*a*- rather than the diphthong -*ua*-. The Portuguese–Chinese Dictionary is therefore in complete agreement with Sin's Standard Reading system on this point.

Conclusions

In the material examined here we have found traces of Standard Reading-like vocalism in all the late Míng and early Qīng 清 vernacular Guānhuà sources we have consulted. And the Portuguese–Chinese Dictionary data go even further in agreeing completely with the Standard Reading system. This suggests that on this point the Standard Reading corpus reflects actual spoken forms of Guānhuà and was not simply a fanciful artificial or dictionary-based pronunciation system. Why a southern regional type Guānhuà sound system like that found in the Portuguese–Chinese Dictionary should agree so well with Sin's Standard Reading forms at such a late date remains a topic for future investigation. But, whatever else it means, it establishes beyond question that Standard Reading-type vocalism was still present in actual spoken varieties of Guānhuà long after the time of Sin Sukchu. There is no reason to assume that Sin's spellings were artificial or fictitious.

References

Coblin, W. South. 2006. *Francisco Varo's Glossary of the Mandarin Language*. Monumenta Serica Monograph Series, Vols. LIII/1 and LIII/2, Nettetal: Steyler Verlag.

Coblin, W. South. 2007. *Modern Chinese Phonology: From Guānhuà to Mandarin. Collection des cahiers linguistique Asie Orientale*, no. 11. Paris: Ècole des Hautes Études en Sciences Sociales.

Coblin, W. South. 2009. "Retroflex Initials in the History of Southern Guanhua Phonology." *Cahiers de linguistique Asie Orientale* 38 (1): 125–62.

Diaz, Francisco. c. 1640. "Vocabulario de la letra China con la explicacion hecho con gran propriedad y abundancia de palabras por el Padre F. Francisco Diaz de la orden de Predicatores ministro inconsable in esto Reyno de China." Manuscript held by the Biblioteka Jagiellonska, Krakow.

Goodrich, L. Carrington, ed. 1976. *Dictionary of Ming Biography*. New York: Columbia University Press.

Kim, Youngman. 1989. *Middle Mandarin Phonology: A Study Based on Korean Data*. Ann Arbor: UMI Dissertation Services.

Kim, Kwangjo. 1991. *A Phonological Study of Middle Mandarin: Reflected in Korean Sources of the Mid-15th and Early 16th Centuries*. Ann Arbor: UMI Dissertation Services.

Ledyard, Gari. 1965. "Biographical Notes on Huang Tsan." *Asea yŏn'gu* 亞細亞研究 8 (1): 129–37.

Li, Fang Kuei 李方桂. 1971. "Shànggŭyīn yánjiù" 上古音研究 [A study of Archaic Chinese phonology]. *Tsinghua Journal of Chinese Studies* 清華學報, New Series IX: 1–61.

Prémare, Joseph. c. 1730. *Notitia Linguae Sinicae*. First circulated in manuscript; then published: Malacca, 1831: Academiæ Anglo-Sinensis; Hong Kong 1893: Société des Missions-Etrangères.

Ruggieri, Michele, and Matteo Ricci. 2001. *Dicionário Português-Chinés*/葡漢辭典 *Pú-Hàn cídiǎn/Portuguese-Chinese Dictionary*. Edited by John W. Witek, SJ. San Francisco: Ricci Institute for Chinese-Western Cultural History (University of San Francisco) and Lisbon: Biblioteca Nacional Portugal, Instituto Português do Oriente.

Yang, Paul F. M. 1989. "The Portuguese-Chinese Dictionary of Matteo Ricci: A Historical and Linguistic Introduction." In *Proceedings of the Second International Conference on Sinology, Section on Linguistics and Paleography*, Vol. I, 191–241. Taipei: Academia Sinica. (Also reprinted in Ruggieri and Ricci 2001.)

Yùchí, Zhìpíng 尉遲治平. 1990. "Lǎo Qǐdà Piáo tōngshì yànjiě Hànzìyīn de yŭyīn jīchǔ" 老乞大、朴通事諺解漢字音的語音基楚 [The phonological basis for the Chinese character readings in the Han'gul alphabet spellings found in the *Lǎo Qǐdà* and the *Piáo tōngshì*]. *Yŭyán yánjiù* 語言研究 1: 11–24.

10
The Hénán Xìnyáng Dialect of 150 Years Ago
Evidence from Dialect Islands in Jiāngsū, Zhèjiāng, and Ānhuī

Huáng Xiǎodōng

Introduction

As dialect islands preserve a number of ancient characteristics, they are of great significance in historical linguistic research. For example, we can use them to reconstruct the features of proto- or ancestral dialects as well as deduce the period in which earlier dialects underwent phonological changes. This chapter considers the Hénán 河南 dialect islands in Jiāngsū 江蘇, Zhèjiāng 浙江, and Ānhuī 安徽 in comparison to the Hénán dialect of modern Xìnyáng 信陽, and reconstructs the characteristics of the ancestral dialects of 150 years ago.

Pang-hsin Ting [Dīng Bāngxīn] 丁邦新 once pointed out that "China having a vast landscape, there are likely a great many isolated dialect islands in existence. Such dialect islands often preserve various features of historical pronunciation" (1998, 168–69). Other scholars have also pointed out the significance of dialect islands in this regard. Some have even begun to utilize them in reconstruction. For example, Lǐ Rúlóng 李如龍 and others discovered in their research on the Mǐnnán 閩南 dialect island of the Shāchéng 沙埕 township in Fúdǐng 福鼎 that the *jī* 雞 rime in the Quánzhōu 泉州 dialect rime book *Huìyīn miàowù* 彙音妙悟 (published in 1800) is preserved in that dialect island and can be reconstructed as [ue] (Lǐ, Zhuāng, and Yán 1995, 63, 119–33). Though in Quánzhōu 泉州 itself, the pronunciation has already merged with the *guā* 瓜 rime [ue]. Additionally, the pronunciation is also still preserved in the [ɤe] rime of the dialect island of Wǎnyáo 碗窰 in Níngdé 寧德 (Lǐ and Chén 1982). Qiū Xuéqiáng 丘學強 researched in detail the linguistic characteristics of the Jūnhuà 軍話 dialect islands in Guǎngdōng 廣東 and Hǎinán 海南. He pointed out that Jūnhuà dialects have a strong connection to Míng dynasty Guānhuà: "Perhaps, we can even say that the Jūnhuà dialects are living fossils that preserve the Míng dynasty koine [*tōngyǔ* 通語] (including its reading pronunciation, in both southern and northern varieties) . . . In-depth research on Jūnhuà dialects will be greatly beneficial in reconstructing the features of the Guānhuà of the Míng dynasty in its various stages" (Qiū 2002, 62).

We can reconstruct a proto-dialect using a single dialect island; we can also use several dialect islands with the similar origins in different places for a reconstruction. Relatively speaking, the latter approach is sounder and more reliable. This chapter examines the Hénán dialect islands found in Jiāngsū, Zhèjiāng, and Ānhuī and attempts to reconstruct their historical characteristics through a comparison with the dialects of Guāngshān 光山, Xīnxiàn 新縣, and Luóshān 羅山 in modern Xìnyáng.

The Origin and Distribution of the Hénán Dialect Islands in Jiāngsū, Zhèjiāng, and Ānhuī

Due to historical immigration movements, many Hénán dialect islands formed in the junction areas of Jiāngsū, Zhèjiāng, and Ānhuī. According to *Zhōngguó yǔyán dìtú jí* 中國語言地圖集 (Chinese Academy of Social Sciences 1988), there are many Hénán dialects in six counties along the boundary between Ānhuī and Zhèjiāng, including Guǎngdé, Lángxī 郎溪, Xuānchéng 宣城, Níngguó 寧國, Ānjí 安吉, and Chángxīng 長興. The total Hénán dialect–speaking population is about 400,000. Additionally, according to Guō Xī 郭熙 (1995), there are many Hénán dialect islands in Jùróng 句容, Lìshuǐ 溧水, Lìyáng 溧陽, Jīntán 金壇, Gāochún 高淳, Yíxīng 宜興, Dānyáng 丹陽, Dāntú 丹徒, Wújiāng 吳江, and other counties in the southern Jiāngsū area. The population of these islands exceed 100,000. Thus, the population of Hénán speakers in the Jiāngsū, Zhèjiāng, and Ānhuī area is over 500,000.[1]

How did the Hénán dialect islands of Jiāngsū, Zhèjiāng, and Ānhuī form? According to Bào Shìjié 鮑士杰 (1988), Gě Qìnghuá 葛慶華 (2000, 60–61), and Cáo Shùjī 曹樹基 (1997, 414–71), the migrant dialects of the communities at the junction of the three provinces of Jiāngsū, Zhèjiāng, and Ānhuī originated with speakers who arrived after the Tàipíng 太平 Rebellion. In the wake of that rebellion, the originally dense population of the Jiāngsū, Zhèjiāng, and Ānhuī region had dramatically decreased; thousands of people had fled or died during the rebellion, and their farmland was left abandoned. To rectify this situation, the Qīng 清 government implemented policies to attract farmers, reducing military service and taxes for those who moved into the area. Migrants from Hénán, Húběi 湖北, and other areas moved in to resettle and farm the deserted lands. As noted in the *Chángxīng xiànzhì shíyí* 長興縣志拾遺 [Supplement to the Chángxīng county gazette] (1875), "The greatest numbers of people from other areas who came to resettle and farm the land were from Hénán and Húběi, with those from southern and central Zhèjiāng following

---

1. The population may in fact be even larger. According to Bào Shìjié 鮑士杰 (1988), more than 170,000 settlers from Hénán settled in Chángxīng county 長興縣, accounting for more than one third of the population there. In Ānjí county 安吉縣 there are more than 100,000 people of Hénán origin. Southern Ānhuī has an even larger population originating in Hénán, most of whom live in Guǎngdé county 廣德縣. According to the *Ānhuī shěngzhì fāngyánzhì* 安徽省志·方言志 (1997, 570), people of Hénán origin account for over half of the population in Guǎngdé county. (At the end of 1998, 505,600 people lived in Guǎngdé county; more than 250,000 of those came from Hénán.)

in slightly lesser numbers."[2] Hénán immigrants mainly came from the southern regions of Guāngzhōu 光州 and Rǔníng 汝寧 prefectures, including the counties of Guāngshān, Luóshān, Shāngchéng 商城, Gùshǐ 固始, and Huángchuān 潢川. These areas had long been densely populated, and during the rebellion the population there had been less affected by loss to draft into compulsory military service because the place was so remote.[3] Consequently the region was a primary source of outward migration following the Tàipíng Rebellion. During the years between the late Qīng dynasty and the Republic of China, millions of immigrants moved into the Jiāngsū, Zhèjiāng, Ānhuī, and Jiāngxī provinces from Guāngshān county alone.[4]

During the Guāngxù 光緒 reign (1871–1908) of the Qīng dynasty, the *Xùzuǎn Jùróng xiànzhì* 續纂句容縣志 [Continuation of the Jùróng county records] reported that "ten years after the war-torn turmoil of the Xiánfēng 咸豐 reign period (1850–1861), the registered population of the southern counties [of Jiāngsū] have greatly diminished, and are only 20% or 30% of normal times, with the fields and mountains mostly abandoned." It also recorded: "In the fourteenth year of the Guāngxù reign, the migrants from Húběi and Hénán (Jīng-Yù 荊豫) completely resettled and opened up the region" (Guō Xī 1995). The Hénán immigrants in the southern Jiāngsū region came primarily from Guāngshān, Luóshān, Shāngchéng, and other places near the southeast part of Hénán. The wave of immigration began in the mid-nineteenth century and continued until the beginning of the twentieth century.

During the Tàipíng Rebellion, Guǎngdézhōu 廣德州 and Níngguófǔ 寧國府 in southern Ānhuī served as the outer screen for the Tàipíng capital "Tiānjīng 天京" (Nánjīng), and that screen had to be traversed when traveling to Jiāngsū and Zhèjiāng. Thus it became a primary front in the battles between the Tàipíng rebels and imperial troops. Consequently, it was heavily battered during the rebellion, and after the war was one of the most attractive and obvious places for migration and settlement. According to Zhèng-Zhāng Shàngfāng 鄭張尚芳 (1986), among the migrants to southern Ānhuī, immigrants from Hénán were principally from the Xìnyáng areas of Guāngshān, Gùshǐ and Luóshān. There were also those from farther afield in Xíngyáng 滎陽 in Hénán. Guǎngdé county in Ānhuī was a central destination of Hénán immigrants and earned the nickname "Xiǎo Hénán 小河南" [Little Henan].

Guō Xī (2000) has pointed out that "the Hénán type dialects spoken in southern Jiāngsū developed from the mixing of the Hénán dialects of Guāngshān, Luóshān, and Shāngchéng, ... while the Guāngshān dialect can be considered to be representative of the Hénán dialects that formed the base of the Hénán type dialects of the southern Jiāngsū region." Huáng Xiǎodōng 黃曉東 (2004, 2006) noted that the

---

2. Cited in Bào Shìjié 鮑士杰 1988.
3. As noted in the "Yìwénzhì" 藝文志 [Arts and Literature] section [*juàn* 卷 4] of the *Guāngshān xiànzhì yuēgǎo* 光山縣志約稿 [Manuscript for the Guangshan County Gazette], published in the Republican period, and cited in Gě Qìnghuá 葛慶華 (2000, 60).
4. As noted in the "Dìlǐ zhì - hùkǒu" 地理志·户口 [Geography and Household Registration] section [*juàn* 卷 1] of the *Guāngshān xiànzhì yuēgǎo*, and cited by Gě Qìnghuá 葛慶華 (2000, 60).

situation with the Hénán dialects in Ānjí of Zhèjiāng is similar to that of southern Jiāngsū. They also have a set of base dialects, including Guāngshān, Xīnxiàn, and areas of southern Luóshān.[5]

The above discussion reveals that the Hénán dialect islands in Jiāngsū, Zhèjiāng, and Ānhuī share a common origin and that the causes and processes of their formation are similar. So we can treat them as dialects with a shared origin for the purposes of a comparative reconstruction of the features of their common ancestor: proto- [or common] Xìnyáng of Hénán (by which we are referring to the ancestor of the dialects of Guāngshān, Xīnxiàn, and the southern Luóshān area).

Reconstruction of the Common Phonology of the Hénán Dialect Islands in Jiāngsū, Zhèjiāng, and Ānhuī

In this article, the representative Hénán dialect islands of Jiāngsū, Zhèjiāng, and Ānhuī are Mòpán 磨盤 township of Jùróng in Jiāngsū, the villages of Āncháng 安城 and Héngtáng 橫塘 in Zhèjiāng's Ānjí county (and originally within Āncháng township, which is now incorporated into Dìpù 遞鋪 township), and Guǎngdé 廣德 county of Ānhuī.[6] In addition, we make reference to the Hénán dialect of Xiānshān 仙山 in Chángxīng county of Zhèjiāng. Our data for these dialects is most detailed for Mòpán, Āncháng, and Héngtáng, with that for Guǎngdé somewhat less detailed, while the material we have on Xiānshān is extremely sketchy. Our comparative data for the Hénán source dialects primarily includes Guāngshān (Shílǐ 十里), Xīnxiàn (Hǔwān 滸灣), and Luóshān (with Zhānghé 張河 representing the northern area, and Zhōudǎng 周黨 representing the southern area). For convenience, in the following discussion we simply refer to the dialect sites by name.

---

5. Xīnxiàn was separated into Guāngshān, Máchéng 麻城, and Huángān 黃安 in 1932. Most of the counties, including the county seat, belong to Guāngshān. Surveys by Yán Déliàng 閆德亮 (2004) and the author revealed that the Luóshān dialect is split into southern and northern types. The boundary between the two types falls along National Highway No. 312. The present study refers to the whole of Luóshān, except when the southern or northern regions are explicitly indicated.
6. In fact, "Āncháng Hénán dialect" includes the nearby Wāncháng 灣長 village Hénán dialect, as the Hénán dialects in these two areas are basically the same.

Comparison of initial constants

Pronunciation of common dialectal Chinese (CDC) alveopalatals (zhīxì 知系)[7]

Table 10.1: Alveopalatals in the Hénán dialect islands of Jiāngsū, Zhèjiāng, and Ānhuī

English	'poetry'	'fan'	'water'	'spring'	'strong'	'bed'	'insect'	'pig'	'book'
Examples/ Dialects	詩 shī	扇 shàn	水 shuǐ	春 chūn	壯 zhuàng	床 chuáng	蟲 chóng	豬 zhū	書 shū
Mòpán 磨盤	s	s	s	tɕʰ	ts	tsʰ	tsʰ	ts	s
Ānchéng 安城	s	s	s	tɕʰ	ts	tsʰ	tsʰ	tɕ	ɕ
Héngtáng 橫塘	時ʂ	ʂ	s	tʂʰ	ts	tsʰ	tʂʰ	tʂ	ʂ
Guǎngdé 廣德	知ts	閃s	s	-	-	tsʰ	tsʰ	ts	s
Guāngshān 光山	ʂ	ʂ	s	tʂʰ	ts	tsʰ	tʂʰ	tʂ	ʂ
CDC	*shi[1]	*shian[5]	*shui[3]	*chiun[1]	*cong[5]	*jong[2]	*jiung[2]	*cie[1]	*shie[1]

The CDC alveopalatals are not pronounced as retroflex [tʂ tʂʰ ʂ] in Mòpán, Ānchéng, and Guǎngdé, which differs from the source dialects. We speculate that these three Hénán dialects originally had retroflex pronunciations, but due to influence from surrounding dialects in which retroflex and dental sibilants are not distinguished, the [tʂ] set of initials was merged with the [ts] set. Afterwards, outside the island areas, regardless of dialect influence, the consonant [tʂ] disappears and only [ts] remains. Evidence for the earlier situation is found in the pronunciation of some Ānchéng speakers where traces of the initial [tʂ] are preserved in certain words. This is probably the remnant of an earlier distinction between [tʂ] and [ts] initials.

In contrast to the three dialect islands of Mòpán, Ānchéng, and Guǎngdé, in Héngtáng and the Hénán dialects, initial [tʂ] is very common. Though Héngtáng and Ānchéng are only a few miles apart, the pronunciations of CDC alveopalatals fall into two different types. This is because the Héngtáng village is a more purely Hénán-type dialect with little influence from other dialects. So it more easily retains earlier phonological characteristics. Whereas in the vicinity of Ānchéng we find Wú, Ānqìng, and northern Jiāngsū-type dialects, which do not distinguish [ts] and [tʂ] initials and have a greater influence on the Hénán dialect in Ānchéng.

Mòpán, Ānchéng, Héngtáng, and Guǎngdé are the same as Guāngshān, Xīnxiàn, and Luóshān in the way they distinguish the CDC alveopalatals and velars. In yù shè 遇攝, shān shè 山攝, and zhēn shè 臻攝, before high-front vowels (third division, hékǒu 合口), CDC alveopalatals (the zhī 知 and zhāng 章 sets) are merged

---

7. (1) Here and following, Guāngshān is included for comparison. (2) Some of our data are missing cited syllables. So here and below, for the time being, we include syllables from the same or nearby traditional phonological category. (3) In our Héngtáng data shàn 扇 'fan' is recorded with the initial [ʂ], but in the Dānzì yīn 單字音 [Syllable pronunciation glossary] table it is recorded as [s]. The latter is an error. (4) CDC forms (starred '*') are based on Norman 2006 and 2011. The correspondences indicated for initials, finals, and shè 攝 between CDC and the traditional Qièyùn 切韻 categories also follow Norman 2006 and 2011.

with velars (*jiàn* 見 initial set) but are distinguished elsewhere (except for *yù shè* in Mòpán). Examples in Mòpán include: *zhuān* 專 'expressly' CDC *cion¹ and *juān* 捐 'donate' CDC *kion¹ are both [tɕyɛn¹]; *chuán* 船 'boat' CDC *jion² and *quán* 權 'authority' CDC *gion² are both [tɕʰyɛn²]; *zhūn* 肫 'gizzard' CDC *ciun¹ and *jūn* 均 'uniform' CDC *kiun¹ are both [tɕyn¹].

Pronunciation of the initial *rì* 日 (CDC alveopalatal initial *nh)

Table 10.2: **Pronunciation of the initial *rì* in Hénán, Jiāngsū, Zhèjiāng and Ānhuī dialect islands (with *róng* 榮 and *yòng* 用 included for comparison)**

English	'such as'	'and'	'two'	'day'	'heat'	'soft'	'recognize'	'meat'	'glory'	'use'
Examples/ Dialects	如 *rú*	而 *ér*	二 *èr*	日 *rì*	熱 *rè*	軟 *ruǎn*	認 *rèn*	肉 *ròu*	榮 *róng*	用 *yòng*
Mòpán	乳 ʮ	ər	ər	ər	ye	yɛn	zən	zəu	容 zoŋ	zoŋ
Ānchéng	y	ɚ	ɚ	ɚ	yE	yɛ̃	ʐən	ʐəu	ʐoŋ	ʐoŋ
Héngtáng	儒 ʮ	—	ər	ər	ʐɥɛ	—	ʐen	ʐou	永 ɥen	ʐoŋ
Guǎngdé	—	—	ɚ	ʐɿ	ʐɥe	—	ʐ	ʐ	—	ɥəŋ
Guǎngshān	ʮ	—	ɚ	ɚ	ɥE	ɥɛ̃	ʐən	ʐəu	ʐəŋ	ʐəŋ
CDC	*nhie²	*nhi²	*nhi⁶	*nhit⁸	*nhiat⁸	*nhion⁴	*nhin⁶	*nhiuk⁸	*yung²	*yung⁶

The pronunciation of the *rì* initial varies greatly within the Hénán dialect islands we have been discussing: in Mòpán it is realized separately as [z] and [Ø] (zero) initials; in Guǎngdé it is realized as allophones [ʐ] and [z] (note *rèn* 認 and *ròu* 肉 lack finals); in Ānchéng and Héngtáng it is realized separately as retroflex [ʐ] and zero [Ø] initials. Among the dialect islands we have been discussing, Ānchéng and Héngtáng adhere most closely to their Hénnán origin, followed by Guǎngdé, with Mòpán changing the most rapidly. The pronunciations of the *rì* initial in these dialects closely reflect the path of the developments:

From [ʐ] and [Ø] in Guǎngshān, Ānchéng, and Héngtáng →
   To [ʐ] and [z] in Guǎngdé →
      To [z] and [Ø] in Mòpán

There is a set of syllables that are reflexes of CDC *iung (擁雍癰 with zero initial in the upper register) and *yung (融榮永泳咏容蓉熔庸甬勇湧用 with zero initial in the lower register), and which Zhāng Shìfāng 張世方 (2002, 32) refers to as the "*róng* 榮 syllable class" ('榮' 類字), that have developed fricative initials that parallel the reflexes of the *rì* initial in many of these dialects: in the Ānchéng and Héngtáng dialects all are initial [ʐ]; in the Mòpán dialect they are initial [z]. (The Guǎngdé dialect has too few examples for us to include it here.) We can see that this development is essentially shared across the Hénán dialect islands, which reveals that it was probably a feature of the earlier dialect of Xìnyáng.

Pronunciation of the initials *ní* 泥 and *lái* 來 (CDC initials *n and *l)

In the Hénán type dialects of Mòpán, Ānchéng, and Guǎngdé, syllables reflecting CDC *n and *l initials in the rime *yú* 魚 (CDC *ie) have developed zero initial. Examples in Mòpán include: *nǚ* 女 'woman' CDC *nie⁴ and *lǚ* 旅 'travel' CDC *lie⁴ are both [ʮ³], and *lǘ* 驢 'donkey' CDC *lie² and *Lǚ* 呂 (the surname Lǚ) CDC *lie⁴ are both [ʮ²]. Guāngshān and Xīnxiàn also exhibit this phenomenon. For instance, in Guāngshān *lǘ* 驢 is [ʮ²] and *Lǚ* 呂 is [ʮ³]. So we can see that the Hénán dialect islands preserve this particular merger of CDC *n and *l in the *yú* rime from their source dialect.

Pronunciation of the initials *yǐng* 影 and *yí* 疑 (CDC *zero [upper register] and *ng initials)

In the Hénán dialect islands of Mòpán, Ānchéng, Héngtáng, Guǎngdé, CDC zero *Ø initial in upper register tones (corresponding to the traditional *yǐng* 影 initial category) and CDC initial *ng (in lower register tones, corresponding to the traditional *yí* 疑 initial) before unrounded vowels (corresponding to traditional *kāikǒu* 開口 in first and second division *yī èr děng* 一二等 categories) are generally merged as initial [ŋ]. For example, in Ānchéng, *yǎo* 咬 'to bite' CDC *ngau⁴ is [ŋɑo³]; *ān* 安 'at ease, quiet' CDC *on¹ is [ŋɛ̃¹]; *ēn* 恩 'compassion' *en¹ is [ŋən¹]; *yìng* 硬 'hard' CDC *ngang⁶ is [ŋən⁵]. As this matches a similar situation in the dialects of Guāngshān, Xīnxiàn, and Luóshān, it is clear that the earlier source Xìnyáng dialect(s) had initial [ŋ] in this set of words.

Pronunciation of the initials *wéi* 微 (CDC *mv), *yí* 疑 (CDC *ng), *yǐng* 影 and *yù* 喻 (both CDC *zero initial)

Syllables with CDC initials *mv (traditional *wéi* 微 initial), *ng (traditional *yí* 疑 initial), and zero *Ø initial (traditional *yǐng* 影 and *yù* 喻 initials in upper and lower registers, respectively) before rounded vowels (corresponding to traditional *hékǒu* 合口), in the Mòpán dialect all have labiodental voiced fricative initial consonant [v]; in Ānchéng it is generally zero [Ø] initial, though individual speakers pronounce them with initial [v] or bilabial fricative initial [ʋ]; and in Héngtáng all have zero [Ø] initial.

In Xiānshān, some of the corresponding syllables are pronounced with initial [ʋ], while others have zero initial, for example: *wén* 聞 'smell' CDC *mvun² is [uən²]; *wèn* 問 'ask' CDC *mvun⁶ is [uən⁵]; *wèi* 味 'flavor' CDC *mvui⁶ is [ʋei⁵]; *wěi* 尾 'tail' CDC *mvui⁴ is [ʋei³]; and *wán* 玩 'play' CDC *nguon² is [uan²].

In Guǎngdé in the words *wū* 屋 'room' CDC *uk⁷ [vu¹], *wēi* 威 'threat' CDC *ui¹ [vei¹], and *wěn* 穩 'sturdy, solid' CDC *un³ [vən³] usually have the voiced labiodental fricative [v], whereas *wài* 外 'outside' CDC *nguai⁶ [uɛ⁵], *wǎn* 晚 'late' CDC *mvan⁴ [uã³], and *wáng* 王 'king' CDC *wong² [uã²] have no labiodental element in the initial.

Within the source language(s) of the dialects (those of common Hénán), Luóshān pronounces these syllables with initial [v], but Guāngshān and Xīnxiàn both have zero [Ø] initial. Neither situation is matched by the above-mentioned dialect islands. We think that there are two possibilities to explain this situation. The first is that the Guāngshān and Xīnxiàn dialects originally had initial [v] and it was subsequently lost. The second possibility is that the Guāngshān and Xīnxiàn dialects never had initial [v] in these syllables. In the latter case, the Hénán dialect islands in Jiāngsū, Zhèjiāng, and Ānhuī would have inherited the characteristic from the Luóshān dialect. But since the dialect islands all seem to share an original [v] initial, we are more inclined to accept the first hypothesis.

Pronunciation of the *xiǎo* 曉 (CDC voiceless velar fricative *x) and *xiá* 匣 (CDC voiced velar fricative *h) initials and the *fēi* 非 set of initials (CDC labiodentals) before rounded vowels (*hékǒu* 合口)

Table 10.3: The distinction between velar fricatives and labiodental fricatives in the Hénán dialect islands of Jiāngsū, Zhèjiāng, and Ānhuī

English	'flower'	'hair'	'gray'	'fly'	'tiger'	'house'	'red'	'wind'	'fire'	'live'
Examples/ Dialects	花 *huā*	發 *fā*	灰 *huī*	飛 *fēi*	虎 *hǔ*	府 *fǔ*	紅 *hóng*	風 *fēng*	火 *huǒ*	活 *huó*
Mòpán		fa		fei		fu	xoŋ	foŋ	xo	xo
Ānchéng		fa		fei		fu	xoŋ	foŋ	xɔ	xɔ
Héngtáng	畫 xua	fa	—	肺 fei	呼 fu	fu	弘 xoŋ	foŋ	xo	xo
Guǎngdé		fa		fei		fu	—	—	xo	xo
Guāngshān		fa		fei		fu	xəŋ	fəŋ	xɔ	xɔ
CDC	*xua¹	*fat⁷	*xuoi¹	*fui¹	*xu³	*fu³	*hung²	*fung¹	*xuo³	*huot⁸

In the three Hénán dialect islands of Mòpán, Ānchéng, and Guǎngdé, CDC velar fricatives (corresponding to traditional *xiǎo* 曉 and *xiá* 匣 initials) and labiodentals (corresponding to the traditional *fēi* 非 set of initials) are merged as initial [f] in certain syllables—that is, where CDC *x is followed by high/close back rounded *u as main vowel or medial—a situation that is also seen in Xīnxiàn and that is basically matched in Guāngshān as well. In Héngtáng the merger is only found before the final [u] and not in other finals, which contrasts somewhat with the other dialect islands and their source dialect. The factors behind these developments are unclear. But we can be sure that this merger is a feature of the common Xìnyáng source dialects.

Comparison of the finals

Maintenance or loss of the *rù* 入 tone

The three Hénán dialect islands of Ānchéng, Héngtáng, and Guǎngdé do not have *rù* tone finals, which is consistent with their source dialects. Guō Xī 郭熙 (1997) notes that in Mòpán "some syllables reflecting Middle Chinese [or CDC] *rù* tone finals have a short, abrupt enunciation, and in addition have a slight glottal stop ending. But they do not form a contrastive tone category. Our speaker considers them to be essentially similar to non-*rù* syllables in a corresponding final category." According to *Jiāngsū shěngzhì fāngyán zhì* 江蘇省志方言志 (1998, 59–61, 146–48), in the region surrounding Mòpán—Jùróng to the north, Jīntán to the east, Lìyáng to the south, and Lìshuǐ to the west—all have a *rù* tone category and contrasting *rù* tone finals. So the *rù* tone-like pronunciation of certain *rù* syllables in the Mòpán dialect is probably due to influence from the surrounding dialects rather than a preservation of features of the source dialects.

Loss of rounding in final vocalism

Table 10.4: Presence or absence of rounded main vowels and medials in the Hénán dialect islands of Jiāngsū, Zhèjiāng, and Ānhuī

English	'song'	'early'	'crime'	'mouth'	'to blow'	'tear'	'water'
Examples/ Dialects	歌歌 *gē*$_{gē}$	初魚 *chū*$_{yú}$	罪灰 *zuì*$_{huī}$	嘴支 *zuǐ*$_{zhī}$	吹支 *chuī*$_{zhī}$	淚脂 *lèi*$_{zhī}$	水脂 *shuǐ*$_{zhī}$
Mòpán	ko	tsʰəu	tsei	tsei	tsʰei	li	sei
Ānchén	kɔ	tsʰəu	tsei	tsei	tsʰei	li	sei
Héngtáng	哥 ko	tsʰou	tsei	tsei	tsʰei	li	sei
Guǎngdé	—	tsʰəu	—	tsei	tsʰei	—	sei
Guāngshān	kɔ	tsʰəu	tsei	tsei	tsʰei	lei	sei
CDC	*ko[1]	*che[1]	*dzuoi[4]	*tsui[3]	*chui[1]	*lui[6]	*shui[3]

English	'to carry'	'sour'	'brush'	'inch'	'spring'	'strong'	'window'
Examples/ Dialects	端桓 *duān*$_{huán}$	酸桓 *suān*$_{huán}$	刷鎋 *shuā*$_{xiá}$	寸魂 *cùn*$_{hún}$	春諄 *chūn*$_{zhūn}$	壯陽 *zhuàng*$_{yáng}$	窗江 *chuāng*$_{jiāng}$
Mòpán	tɛn	sɛn	sa	tsʰən	tɕʰyn	tsaŋ	tsʰaŋ
Ānchén	tɛ̃	sɛ̃	sa	tsʰən	tɕʰyən	tsã	tsʰã
Héngtáng	tan	蒜 san	sa	tsʰen	tʂʰyn	tsaŋ	tsʰaŋ
Guǎngdé	tã	—	sa	—	—	床 tsʰã	tsʰã
Guāngshān	tɛ̃	sɛ̃	sɑ	tsʰən	tsʰyən	tsã	tsʰã
CDC	*ton[1]	*son[1]	*shuat[7]	*tshun[5]	*chiun[1]	*cong[5]	*chong[1]

We discuss these by *shè* rime category:

(1) *Guǒ shè* 果攝 syllables are all *kāikǒu* and have no medial -u- or -y- in both the dialect islands and the source dialects (with the exception of a small number of words with *yǐng* and *yí* initials [CDC *ng and *zero respectively]).

(2) *Yù shè* 遇攝 syllables (in CDC rimes *u and *e) corresponding to *hékǒu* syllables in the first division (合口一等) with dental sibilant initials (*duān* set 端系, *jīng* subset 精組), and those corresponding to *hékǒu* syllables in the third division (合口三等) with alveopalatal initials (*zhuāng* subset 莊組) merge with syllables in *liú shè* 流攝 (CDC *eu and *ieu), and are all pronounced with no medial -u- (i.e. all in *kāikǒu*) in both the dialect islands and the source dialects. For example, in Mòpán, *zǔ* 組 'group' (CDC *tsu³, in *Qièyùn* [Qy] rime *mú* 模), *zǔ* 阻 'obstruct' (CDC *ce³, in Qy rime *yú* 魚), and *zǒu* 走 'walk' (CDC *tseu³, in Qy rime *hóu* 侯) are all merged as [tsəu³]; *cū* 粗 'coarse' (CDC *tshu¹, in Qy rime *mú* 模), *chū* 初 'beginning' (CDC *che¹, in Qy rime *yú* 魚), and *chōu* 抽 'take out' (CDC *chieu¹, in Qy rime *yóu* 尤), are all merged as [tsʻəu¹]; *sū* 蘇 'revive' (CDC *su¹, in Qy rime *mú* 模), *shū* 梳 'to comb' (CDC *she¹, in Qy rime *yú* 魚), and *sōu* 搜 'to search' (CDC *sheu¹/seu¹, in Qy rime *yóu* 尤), are all merged as [səu¹].

(3) *Xiè* 蟹 *shè* and *zhǐ* 止 *shè* syllables (in CDC rimes *ui and *uoi) from the traditional *hékǒu* category (corresponding to CDC syllables having back, round medials or main vowels) have non-round *kāikǒu* pronunciations following dentals and alveopalatals in both the dialect islands and the source dialects. In Mòpán, Ānchéng, and Héngtáng some syllables with CDC initials *n and *l (traditional *ní* 泥 and *lái* 來 initials) have developed a high front medial or main vowel (becoming *qíchǐ hū* 齊齒呼), for example, *lèi* 淚 'tears' as seen in Table 10.4 above. While in Guāngshān these syllables have final [ei] and thus belong to modern *kāikǒu hū* 開口呼 (having no rounded medial or main vowel). The present author has found that these syllables also have final [i] in *both* Xīnxiàn and Luóshān.

(4) *Shān* 山 *shè* syllables from the traditional *hékǒu* category (corresponding to CDC *on) in the first and second division (*yī*, *èr děng* 一二等) in dentals and alveopalatals (*duān* 端 and *zhī* 知 sets), as well as *zhēn* 臻 *shè* syllables from the traditional *hékǒu* category (corresponding to CDC *un) in the first and third division (*yī*, *sān děng* 一三等) in dentals (*duān* 端 set) are also in *kāikǒu hū* (having no rounded medial or main vowel) in all the dialect islands, a situation that is consistent with the source dialects.

(5) *Dàng* 宕 and *jiāng* 江 *shè* syllables (corresponding to CDC *ong) derived from alveopalatals (*zhī* set) are in *kāikǒu hū* in all the dialect islands, a situation that is again consistent with the source dialects.

In general, then, the dialect islands are consistent with the source dialects with regard to the loss of rounding in the vocalism of finals in the Hénán dialect islands of Jiāngsū, Zhèjiāng, and Ānhuī.

Shēn, zhēn, zēng, and gěng shè 深臻曾梗攝

Traditional *shēn* 深, *zhēn* 臻, *zēng* 曾, and *gěng* 梗 *shè* in non-*rù* tone syllables (having only nasal consonant endings, and no oral stop endings and corresponding to CDC *em, *im, *in, *un, *iun, *ing, *iang, and *ang) are merged into finals sharing the same main vowel and consonant ending. The Hénán dialects in Mòpán, Ānchéng, Héngtáng and Guǎngdé have corresponding finals such as [ən], [iən], [uən], or [yən] (the latter corresponding to CDC *iun in *zhēn shè* syllables in traditional *hékǒu sān, sì děng* 三四等). For example, in Ānchéng, *shēn* 參 'ginseng' (CDC *shem¹ in *shēn shè*), *shēn* 身 'body' (CDC *shin¹ in *zhēn shè*), *shēng* 升 'ascend' (CDC *shing¹ in *zēng shè*), and *shēng* 生 'give birth' (CDC *shang¹ in *gěng shè*) are all [sən¹]; *jīn* 金 'gold' (CDC *kim¹ in *shēn shè*), *jīn* 巾 'kerchief' (CDC *kin¹ in *zhēn shè*), and *jīng* 京 'capital' (CDC *kiang¹ in *gěng shè*) are all [tɕin¹]; while *gǔn* 滾 'roll' (CDC *kun³ in *zhēn shè*) is [kuən³] and *jūn* 軍 'military' (CDC *kiun¹ in *zhēn shè*) is [tɕyən¹]. These pronunciations are the same as in Guāngshān, Xīnxiàn and Luóshān. Clearly this situation has not changed in over one hundred and fifty years.

Comparison of the tones

Tone category

The Hénán dialect islands (including Xiānshān) all have four tone categories: (1) *yīnpíng* 陰平 tone (containing syllables from CDC *píng* tone having voiceless initials, and from *rù* tone having voiceless and sonorant initials), (2) *yángpíng* 陽平 tone (containing syllables from CDC *píng* tone having voiced initials, and *rù* tone having voiced obstruent initials), (3) *shǎng* 上 tone (including syllables from CDC *shǎng* tone having voiceless and sonorant initials), and (4) *qù* 去 tone (including syllables from CDC *qù* tone, of all initial types, and *shǎng* tone in voiced obstruent initial types). The above tone correspondences are the same as those in Guāngshān and northern Luóshān, but differ from southern Luóshān and some areas of Xīnxiàn.

Our research has found that southern Luóshān has a *rù* tone (which does not however have separate rime categories). Also, some places in Xīnxiàn have a register distinction in the *qù* tone—distinguishing *yīnqù* 陰去 and *yángqù* 陽去. We believe that while these phenomena reflect characteristics of older dialects, they are not principal features in the source dialects. As a result, the dialect islands do not show these characteristics.

Tone pitch-contour

Table 10.5: Comparison of tone contours in the Hénán dialect islands of Jiāngsū, Zhèjiāng, and Ānhuī

Tone category	Dialect islands					Source dialects	
	Mòpán	Ānchéng	Héngtáng	Xiānshān 仙山	Guǎngdé	Guāngshān	Northern Luóshān
Yīnpíng 陰平	41	53略低	53	42	42	53略低	42
Yángpíng 陽平	44	55	55	55	55	55近445	55
Shǎngshēng 上聲	224	35近325	24	325	35	35近325	35近325
Qùshēng 去聲	312	312近313	214	213	312	31	312

As can be seen in Table 10.5, the pitch-contours of the four tones are similar to those in the source dialects, especially to those of northern Luóshān.

Conclusions

Through comparison of the Hénán island dialects of Jiāngsū, Zhèjiāng, and Ānhuī, we have been able to roughly outline the early common characteristics and features of the Hénán dialects in Guāngshān, Xīnxiàn, and southern Luóshān. Below we summarize those features.

Initials

(1) CDC dental and retroflex affricates, [ts] and [tʂ] sets, contrast; and CDC alveopalatals (the *zhī* 知 set) before high-front *hékǒu* finals are merged with velars (*jiàn* 見 initial set). (2) The pronunciation of the CDC *rì* initial is generally [z], while the "*róng* 榮 syllable class" parallel the reflexes of the *rì* initial. (3) Some CDC syllables with initials *n and *l (*ní* 泥 and *lái* 來) in the CDC rime *ie (*yú* 魚) are pronounced with zero initial. (4) Syllables with CDC *zero [upper register] (*yǐng* 影) and *ng initials (*yí* 疑) before unrounded vowels have a velar nasal initial [ŋ]. (5) Syllables with CDC initials *mv (*wéi* 微), *ng (*yí* 疑), and *zero (*yǐng* 影 and *yù* 喻) have voiced labiodental initial [v] before rounded vowels. (6) Syllables with CDC voiceless velar fricative *x (*xiǎo* 曉) and voiced velar fricative *h (*xiá* 匣) initials and a set of syllables with labiodental initials (*fēi* 非) before rounded vowels (*hékǒu* 合口) are partly or fully merged.

Finals

(1) CDC *rù* tone is lost. (2) *Guǒ* 果 *shè* syllables are *kāikǒu*. (3) *Xiè* 蟹 *shè* and *zhǐ* 止 *shè* syllables (in CDC rimes *ui and *uoi) from the traditional *hékǒu* category (corresponding to CDC syllables having back, round medials or main vowels) have non-round *kāikǒu* pronunciations; within that a subset of syllables with CDC initials *n and *l (*ní* 泥 and *lái* 來) have developed a high front medial or main vowel. (4) *Shān* 山 *shè* syllables from the traditional *hékǒu* category (corresponding to CDC *on) in the first and second division in dentals and alveopalatals (*duān* 端 and *zhī* 知 sets), as well as *zhēn* 臻 *shè* syllables from the traditional *hékǒu* category (corresponding to CDC *un) in the first and third division in dentals (*duān* 端 set) are also *kāikǒu*. (5) *Dàng* 宕 and *jiāng* 江 *shè* syllables (corresponding to CDC *ong) derived from alveopalatals are all *kāikǒu*. (6) *Yù shè* 遇攝 syllables (in CDC rimes *u and *e) corresponding to *hékǒu* syllables in the first division with dental sibilant initials (*jīng* 精 set), and those corresponding to *hékǒu* syllables in the third division with alveopalatal initials (*zhuāng* 莊 subset) merge with syllables in *liú shè* 流攝 (CDC *eu and *ieu), and are all *kāikǒu*. (7) Traditional *shēn* 深, *zhēn* 臻, *zēng* 曾, and *gěng* 梗 *shè* in non-*rù* tone syllables are generally merged.

Tones

1) Tone categories and tone contrasts match those in the Guāngshān dialect: there is a register (*yīn* and *yáng*) distinction only in *píng* tone; CDC *shǎng* tone syllables with *cìzhuó* 次濁 (sonorant) initials are in the upper register (*yīn*) *shǎng* tone; CDC *shǎng* tone syllables with *quánzhuó* 全濁 (voiced obstruent) initials have merged with the *qù* tone; CDC *rù* tone syllables having *qīng* 清 (voiceless) or *cìzhuó* (sonorant) initials are in *yīnpíng*, while those derived from *quánzhuó* (voiced obstruent) initials are in *yángpíng*. (2) The pitch-contour of the four tones is as follows: *yīnpíng* is roughly [42], mid-falling; *yángpíng* is roughly [55], high-level; *shǎng* is roughly [35], high-rising; and *qù* is roughly [312], falling-rising.

Dialect Data Sources

The data for Ānjí 安吉 (specifically the Hénán dialect spoken in Ānchéng 安城), Luóshān (Zhānghé 張河 and Zhōudǎng 周黨), Guāngshān (Shílǐ 十里), and Xīnxiàn (Hǔwān 滸灣) are based on surveys conducted by the author. Data for Xìnyáng 信陽, Shāngchéng 商城, Huángchuān 潢川, Gùshǐ 固始, Xīxiàn 息縣, Zhèngyáng 正陽, Huáibīn 淮濱, and Tóngbǎi 桐柏 are from Zhāng Qǐhuàn 張啟煥 (1993) as well as county gazettes (*xiànzhì* 縣志). Data for the Mòpán 磨盤 Hénán dialect in Jùróng 句容 are from Guō Xī 郭熙 (1996, 1997). The Hénán dialect data for Guǎngdé 廣德 county are from *Ānhuī shěngzhì—fāngyán zhì* 安徽省志·方言志. Those for the Hénán dialect of Héngtáng 橫塘 in Ānjí 安吉 come from *Ānjí xiànzhì* 安吉縣志.

Data for the Hénān dialect in Xiānshān仙山 of Chángxīng county 長興縣 are from Bào Shìjié 鮑士杰 (1988).

Note: A previous version of this chapter appeared in Chinese as "Yī-bǎi wǔshí niánqián de Hénán Xìnyáng huà 一百五十年前的河南信陽話," *Huázhōng xuéshù* 華中學術 2017 (3) [19]: 129–136.

References

Primary sources

Bào Shìjié 鮑士杰. 1988. "Zhèjiāng xīběibù Wúyǔ yǔ Guānhuà dē biānjiè 浙江西北部吳語與官話的邊界" [The Wú dialect and Guānhuà boundary in northwest Zhèjiāng]. *Fāngyán* 方言 [Dialect] 1: 25–30.

Cáo Shùjī 曹樹基. 1997. *Zhōngguó yímín shǐ* 中國移民史 [A history of internal Chinese migration]. Volumes (i.e., *juàn* 卷) 5 and 6. Fúzhōu: Fújiàn rénmín chūbǎnshè.

Chinese Academy of Social Sciences and Australian Academy of the Humanities 中國社會科學院和澳大利亞人文科學院. 1988. *Zhōngguó yǔyán dìtú jí* 中國語言地圖集 [Language atlas of China]. Hong Kong: Longman.

Dīng Bāngxīn 丁邦新. 1998. *Dīng Bāngxīn yǔyánxué lùnwén jí* 丁邦新語言學論文集 [Collected papers of Dīng Bāngxīn in linguistics]. Běijīng: Shāngwù yìnshūguǎn.

Gě Qìnghuá 葛慶華. 2000. "Jìndài Sū Zhè Wǎn jiāojiè dìqū rénkǒu qiānyí yánjiū" 近代蘇浙皖交界地區人口遷移研究:1853–1911 [Research on migration in the border region of Jiāngsū, Zhèjiāng, and Ānhuī between 1853 and 1911]. PhD diss., Fudan University.

Guō Xī 郭熙. 1995. "Sūnán dìqū dē Hénán fāngyán dǎo qún" 蘇南地區的河南方言島群 [Hénán dialect island clusters in the southern Jiāngsū region]. *Nánjīng dàxué xuébào* 南京大學學報 [Journal of Nanjing University] 4: 120–25 and 136.

Guō Xī 郭熙. 1996. "Mòpánhuà tóngyīn zìhuì" 磨盤話同音字彙 [Syllabary of the Mòpán dialect]. *Zhènjiāng shīzhuān xuébào* 鎮江師專學報 [Journal of Zhenjiang Teachers College] (Social Science) 4: 72–80.

Guō Xī 郭熙. 1997. "Mòpánhuà yīnxì" 磨盤話音系 [Mòpán dialect phonology]. *Nánjīng dàxué xuébào* 南京大學學報 [Journal of Nanjing University] (Social Science) 4: 52–61.

Guō Xī 郭熙. 2000. "Sūnán dìqū hénánhuà dē guīshǔ wèntí" 蘇南地區河南話的歸屬問題 [The origin of Hénán dialect islands in the southern Jiāngsū area]. *Dōngnán dàxué xuébào* 東南大學學報 [Journal of Southeast University] 4: 95–101.

Huáng Xiǎodōng 黃曉東. 2004. "Zhèjiāng Ānjí xiàn Guānhuà fāngyándǎo yánjiū" 浙江安吉縣官話方言島研究 [Research on Mandarin dialect islands in Ānjí county in Zhèjiāng]. PhD diss., Beijing Language and Culture University.

Huáng Xiǎodōng 黃曉東. 2006. "Zhèjiāng Ānjí xiàn Hénán fāngyándǎo dē nèibù jiēchù yǔ rónghé" 浙江安吉縣河南方言島的內部接觸與融合 [Internal contact and convergence in the Hénán dialect islands of Ānjí county in Zhèjiāng]. *Yǔyán kēxué* 語言科學 [Linguistic Science] 3: 61–71.

Lǐ Rúlóng 李如龍, and Chén Zhāngtài 陳章太. 1982. "Wǎnyáo Mǐnnán fāngyándǎo èrbǎi duō nián jiān dē biànhuà" 碗窰閩南方言島二百多年間的變化 [Changes in the Wǎnyáo Mǐnnán dialect island(s) across two centuries]. *Zhōngguó yǔwén* 中國語文 [Chinese Language] 5: 354–64.

Lǐ Rúlóng 李如龍, Zhuāng Chūshēng 莊初升, and Yán Xiūhóng 嚴修鴻. 1995. *Fújiàn shuāng fāngyán yánjiū* 福建雙方言研究 [Research on the bi-dialect situation in Fújiàn]. Hong Kong: Hànxué chūbǎn shè 漢學出版社.

Norman, Jerry. 2006. "Common Dialectal Chinese." In *The Chinese Rime Tables*, edited by David Branner, 233–54. Amsterdam: John Benjamins.

Norman, Jerry (Luó Jiéruì 罗杰瑞). 2011. "Hànyǔ fāngyán tōngyīn" 漢語方言通音 [Common dialectal Chinese]. A translation and a revised version of Norman 2006; translated by Shǐ Hàoyuán 史皓元 [Richard VanNess Simmons] and Zhāng Yànhóng 張艷紅. *Fangyan* 方言 2: 97–116.

Qīu Xuéqiáng 丘學強. 2002. "Yuè, Qióng jūnhuà yánjiū" 粵、瓊軍話研究 [Jūnhuà in Guǎngdōng and Hǎinán]. PhD diss., Jìnán University 暨南大學.

Yán Déliàng 閏德亮. 2004. "Luóshān fāngyīn gàishù" 羅山方音概述 [Overview of Luóshān dialect pronunciation]. *Xìnyáng shīfàn xuéyuàn xuébào (zhé shè bǎn)* 信陽師範學院學報 (哲社版) [Journal of Xinyang Normal University (Philosophy and Social Science)] 3: 93–97.

Zhāng Qǐhuàn 張啟煥, Chén Tiānfú 陳天福, and Chén Yí 程儀. 1993. *Hénán fāngyán yánjiū* 河南方言研究 [Research on the Hénán dialects]. Kāifēng: Hénán dàxué chūbǎnshè.

Zhāng Shìfāng 張世方. 2002. "Běijīng Guānhuà yǔyīn yánjiū" 北京官話語音研究 [Research on the pronunciation of Beijing Mandarin]. PhD diss., Beijing Language and Culture University.

Zhèng-Zhāng Shàngfāng 鄭張尚芳. 1986. "Wǎnnán fāngyán dē fēnqū (gǎo)" 皖南方言的分區（稿）[Classification of the dialects of southern Ānhuī (draft)]. *Fāngyán* 方言 [Dialect] 1: 8–18.

Local gazetteers (*dìfāngzhì* 地方志)

Ānhuī shěng dìfāngzhì biānzuǎn wěiyuánhuì 安徽省地方志編纂委員會. 1997. *Ānhuī shěngzhì: fāngyánzhì* 安徽省志·方言志. Běijīng: Fāngzhì chūbǎnshè.

Ānjí xiàn dìfāngzhì biānzuǎn wěiyuánhuì 安吉縣地方志編纂委員會. 1994. *Ānjí xiànzhì* 安吉縣志. Hángzhōu: Zhèjiāng rénmín chūbǎnshè.

Gùshǐ xiànzhì biānzuǎn wěiyuánhuì 固始縣志編纂委員會. 1994. *Gùshǐ xiànzhì* 固始縣志. Zhèngzhōu: Zhōngzhōu gǔjí chūbǎnshè.

Huángchuān xiànzhì biānzuǎn wěiyuánhuì 潢川縣志編纂委員會. 1992. *Huángchuān xiànzhì* 潢川縣志. Běijīng: Sānlián shūdiàn.

Jiāngsū shěng dìfāngzhì biānzuǎn wěiyuánhuì 江蘇省地方志編纂委員會. 1998. *Jiāngsū shěngzhì: fāngyánzhì* 江蘇省志·方言志. Nánjīng: Nánjīng dàxué chūbǎn shè.

Shāngchéng xiànzhì biānzuǎn wěiyuánhuì 商城縣志編纂委員會. 1991. *Shāngchéng xiànzhì* 商城縣志. Zhèngzhōu: Zhōngzhōu gǔjí chūbǎn shè.

Xīnxiàn zhì biānzuǎn wěiyuánhuì 新縣志編纂委員會. 1990. *Xīnxiàn zhì* 新縣志. Zhèngzhōu: Hénán rénmín chūbǎnshè.

Xìnyáng dìqū dìfāng shǐzhì biānzuǎn wěiyuánhuì 信陽地區地方史志編纂委員會. 1992. *Xìnyáng dìqū zhì* 信陽地區志. Běijīng: Sānlián shūdiàn.

11
An Exploration of the Nature of Nánjīng Mandarin in the Míng Dynasty

Zēng Xiǎoyú

Introduction

In the study of the history of Mandarin, the term 'Nánjīng Mandarin' (Nánjīng Guānhuà 南京官話) is key and is related to the underlying dialect source of Mandarin in the Míng. At present, there are two very different viewpoints regarding the standard speech of Mandarin in the Míng dynasty. One point of view is that the standard language in the Míng was based on the Nánjīng dialect (Lǔ 2007; Zhāng 2014a). Another is that the Nánjīng dialect could not be the source dialect of the standard language in the Míng, but was instead a southern (Jiāng-Huái) regional variant of the reading pronunciation of the Central Plains dialects (Mài and Zhū 2012).

In all fairness, both sides of the debate are well supported in the literary record and historical data. So why are the two sides at odds? The controversy between the two different points of view can be analyzed as follows:

(1) The exact reference of 'Nánjīng' during the Míng dynasty varies. In a broad sense it refers to Nánzhílì 南直隸 'the Southern Garrison Command District' (which is inclusive of Ānhuī, Jiāngsū, and the Shànghǎi region). However, in a narrower sense, it refers strictly to the city of Nánjīng.
(2) There are different meanings for Nánjīnghuà 南京話 'Nankingese, Nánjīng dialect' in the Míng dynasty itself. It can more generally refer to the Míng Mandarin koine, Southern Mandarin, or the Mandarin of Nánzhílì. In a more restricted sense it refers only to the Nánjīng dialect of the Jiāng-Huái Mandarin type.
(3) How strict was the distinction between Central Plains pronunciation and Nánjīng pronunciation in the phonology of the Nánjīng Mandarin koine, Guānhuà?
(4) Not enough attention has been given to discovering evidence from textual sources. Also, evidence from various phonetic transliterations and Romanized materials remains insufficiently known.

In short, the fundamental problem centers on the *name* as opposed to the *real linguistic nature* of Nánjīng Mandarin. A key area of dispute is whether or not the Nánjīng Mandarin of the Míng dynasty contains elements of Central Plains phonology.

With this in mind, this chapter focuses on investigating phonetic transliterations and Romanizations of Nánjīng Mandarin from historical times. We seek to explain the nature of Míng period Nánjīng Mandarin through an analysis of the phonological features these materials reveal.

Analysis of Textual Sources Regarding Mandarin from the Míng Dynasty

The textual sources and the phonological features they represent

The sources we consulted for an overview of the Mandarin of the Míng period and the relevant phonological features of each are listed and discussed below.

Rhyme books and rhyme tables

a) Xú Xiào's 徐孝 *Chóngdìng Sīmǎ Wēngōng děngyùntú jīng* 重訂司馬溫公等韻圖經 (1602): Reflects Míng period Běijīng dialect phonology, including the distribution of the *rù* tone syllables into non-*rù* tones, the merger of lower register *shǎng* tone syllables (i.e., those that had voiced initials) with *qù* tone, and a clear distinction between syllable finals /-n/ and /-ŋ/ (Guō Lì 2003).

b) Lǚ Kūn's 呂坤 *Jiāo tài yùn* 交泰韻 (1603): Reflects Míng period Central Plains dialect phonology, including loss of the *rù* tone, wherein *rù* syllables with voiceless or voiced sonorant initials merged with the *yīnpíng* tone, a clear distinction between syllable finals /-n/ and /-ŋ/, a partial merger of lower register *shǎng* tone syllables with the *qù* tone (Nìng Jìfú 2009, 205–24); may specifically reflect the Luòyáng dialect of Hénán (Lǐ Xīnkuí and Mài Yún 1993, 240; Gěng Zhènshēng 1992, 185–86; Nìng Jìfú 2009, 509; Zhāng 2014b).

c) Fāng Yǐzhì's 方以智 *Qièyùn shēngyuán* 切韻聲原 (1641): Reflects Míng period Jiāng-Huái dialect phonology, including a *rù* tone category with glottal stop ʔ ending, a merger of a set of syllables derived from Middle Chinese (MC) alveopalatals (*zhuāngzǔ nèizhuǎn* 莊組內轉) with the dental sibilant (*jīngzǔ* 精組) set, no distinction between syllable finals /-n/ and /-ŋ/ (Sūn Yízhì 2005).

Phonetic transliterations and Romanizations

d) Nicholas Trigault's *Xīrú ěrmùzī* 西儒耳目資 (1626): Reflects Míng Nánjīng Mandarin phonology, including a *rù* tone, a distinction between final /-n/ and /-ŋ/, the maintenance of a distinct lower register *shǎng* tone (though these syllables are marked with a circle to distinguish them from the other *shǎng* syllables), and the merger of a set of syllables derived from MC alveopalatals with the dental sibilant set (Zēng 1989, 2014a); here classified as transliteration because it is a transcription of Mandarin using the Roman alphabet.

e) *Băiyí guăn yìyŭ* 百夷館譯語 (1407, 1573) [Mandarin-Dai phonetic transcriptions]: Reflects Míng Nánjīng Mandarin phonology, with a *rù* tone category, and no distinction between MC syllable final nasals *-m, *-n, and *-ŋ (Zēng 2014b; Sarashina 2003).

f) *Riukyu guăn yìyŭ* 琉球館譯語 (1401–1535) [Mandarin-Ryukyu phonetic transcriptions]: Reflects Míng period Běijīng dialect phonology, including a general loss of the *rù* tone, but has lack of distinction between MC syllable final nasals *-m, *-n, and *-ŋ, and shows the merger of a set of syllables derived from MC alveopalatals with the dental sibilant set, while other MC alveopalatals (the *zhī* 知 and *zhāng* 章 groups) are merged (Ding 1995, 91–126); also seen by some to reflect Míng Nánjīng Mandarin phonology with a distinct *rù* tone (Endo 2001, 307).

g) Ryukyu Mandarin textbooks from the Míng and Qīng, including *Guānhuà wèndá biànyŭ* 官話問答便語 and *Xué Guānhuà* 學官話: Reflect Southern Mandarin phonology, with a *rù* tone, merger of MC *yángshăng* with the *qù* tone, no distinction between final /-n/ and /-ŋ/, *zhī* and *zhāng* groups in the MC alveopalatals are merged; there is a partial palatalization of MC velar initials before high front vowels (Setoguchi 1994, 24–35).

h) Ch'we Sejin's 崔世珍 *Pŏnyŏk No Gŏlae Pak Tongsa* 翻譯老乞大·朴通事 (early sixteenth century) [Korean transcription of Míng Mandarin]: Reflects a form of Nánjīng Mandarin used in Běijīng, has a *rù* tone and distinction between syllable finals /-n/ and /-ŋ/ (Endo [1984] 2001, 256–66).

i) Okajima Kanzan's 岡島冠山 *Tō-on gazoku gorui* 唐音雅俗語類 (1726) [Japanese transcription of a Mandarin pronunciation known as Tō-on 唐音]: Reflects "Nánjīng Mandarin" phonology, voiceless reflexes of MC voiced obstruents, MC alveopalatals are distinct from the dental sibilants, has a *rù* tone (Xiè Yùxīn 2010, 14, 68–70).

j) *Ō Baku Tō-on* 黄檗唐音 and *Ō Baku shingi* 黄檗清規 (seventeenth to eighteenth centuries) [Japanese transcriptions of Mandarin]: Primarily reflects Míng Nánjīng Mandarin phonology, but initials are quite similar to those of Běijīng, shows the merger of a set of syllables derived from MC alveopalatals with the dental sibilant set, has a *rù* tone (Lĭ Wúwèi 2005, 159–65).

Note that although some of the Japanese transliterations in the above sources are from the early Qīng or before, Nánjīng Mandarin was the primary language taught in Japan from the Edo (1603–1867) through the early Meiji (1868–1912) periods and Běijīng Mandarin only began to be taught in 1876 (Rokkaku 1988, 122; Chén Xiăo 2014, 63–64). Hence we can include the Qīng materials as representatives of Míng Mandarin.

Comparative analysis of the phonological features in these sources

The salient phonological features found in some or all of the sources can be enumerated by initial, final, and tone features, or contrasts, as outlined below.

Features of the initials

(1) devoicing of MC voiced obstruents;
(2) reflection of the *jiān-tuán* 尖團 'sharp-round' contrast;
(3) distinction between initials [l-] and [n-];
(4) lack of distinction within MC alveopalatals (the traditional *zhī*, *zhuāng* and *zhāng* 知莊章 initial groups are merged for the most part);
(5) merger of the set of syllables derived from Middle Chinese (MC) alveopalatals (*zhuāngzǔ nèizhuǎn* 莊組內轉) with the dental sibilant (*jīngzǔ* 精組) set.

Features of the finals

(1) merger of MC syllable finals *m and *n;
(2) distinction between final nasals /n/ and /ŋ/;
(3) presence of the *rù* tone.

Features of the tones

(1) a register (*yīn-yáng* 陰陽) distinction in the *píng* 平 tone;
(2) merger of MC *shǎng* 上 tone syllables reflecting MC voiced initials with the *qù* 去 tone;
(3) merger of *rù* 入 tone syllables reflecting MC voiced initials with lower (*yáng*) *píng* tone;
(4) merger of *rù* tone syllables reflecting MC sonorant initials with *qù* tone, while *rù* tone syllables reflecting MC voiceless initials are variously merged into all 4 tones; *or*
(5) *rù* tone syllables reflecting MC entering tones with voiceless initial and sonorants all merge with the upper (*yīn*) *píng* tone; *or*
(6) the *rù* tone is preserved.

We can compare the salient phonological features of each of the sources. This is done in Table 11.1, identifying the features as we have numbered them above. We use a plus-sign '+' where the source reflects a feature, a minus-sign '-' when the feature is not reflected, and a blank when the feature cannot be determined in the source. Examining the features as they are comparatively arrayed in Table 11.1, we find the following points of note.

Shared across all the sources, the common phonological features of the Běijīng dialect, the Zhōngyuán dialect type, and the Jiāng-Huái dialect type are:[1]

In the initials,

(1) MC voiced obstruents have become voiceless
(2) the 'sharp-round' contrast is preserved

---

1. As noted above regarding *Riukyu guǎn yìyǔ* (1401–1535), Dīng (1995, 91–126) considers that it reflects Běijīng dialect phonology in the Míng, but because of the presence of the *rù* tone, Endo (2001, 307) considers that it perhaps reflects Nánjīng Mandarin phonology in the Míng.

(3) distinction between initials [l-] and [n-] is preserved
(4) the *zhī-zhuāng-zhāng* 知莊章 initial groups are merged in to a single group, corresponding to the MC alveopalatals.

In the finals,

(1) Middle Chinese syllable coda -m is merged with -n.

In the tones,

(1) there is a register distinction in the *píng* tone
(2) MC *shǎng* tone syllables reflecting MC voiced initials are merged with the *qù* tone.

Table 11.1: Phonological features found in the texts

Dialect type and sources	Features of the initials ① ② ③ ④ ⑤	Features of the finals ① ② ③	Features of the tones ① ② ③ ④ ⑤ ⑥
Běijīng dialect Xú Xiào (1602)	+ + + + -	+ + -	+ + + + - -
Zhōngyuán dialects Lǚ Kūn (1603)	+ + + + -	+ + -	+ +/- + - + -
Jiāng-Huái dialects Fāng Yǐzhì (1641)	+ + + + +	+ - +	+ + - - - +
Nánjīng Mandarin Trigault (1626)	+ + + + +	+ + -	+ +/- - - - +
Nánjīng Mandarin *Bǎiyí guǎn yìyǔ* (1407, 1573)	+ + +	+ - +/-	+
Běijīng dialect or Nánjīng Mandarin* *Ryūkyū guǎn yìyǔ* (1401~1535)	+ + + + +	+ - -	+
Southern Mandarin Ryūkyū Mandarin texts (Míng & Qīng)	+ + + +	+ - +/-	+ + - - +
Nánjīng Mandarin as used in Běijīng Cuī Shìzhén (early 16th c.)	+ + + +/- +/-	+ + +/-	+ + - - - +
Nánjīng Mandarin Okajima Kanzan (1726)	+ + + + +	+ +	- - - - - +
Běijīng dialect or Nánjīng Mandarin *Ō Baku Tō-on* (17th & 18th c.)	+ + + + +	+ - +	+

* As noted in Table 11.1 regarding *Riūkyū guǎn yìyǔ* (1401–1535), Ding (1995: 91–126) considers that it reflects Běijīng dialect phonology in the Míng, but because of the presence of the *rù* tone, Endo (2001:307) considers that it maybe reflects Nánjīng Mandarin phonology in the Míng.

Significantly, this set of shared features reveals to us that all the transliteration materials uniformly reflect features of the common Mandarin koine that was used as a *lingua franca* across all of China in the Míng (and the early Qīng), whether or not there are specific details and features reflective of Nánjīng Mandarin, Southern Mandarin or Běijīng Mandarin. The situation is clear even though the transliteration materials have some limitations. For example, the Tai language only has dental affricates [ts] and [tsʰ] and lacks retroflex affricates [tʂ tʂʰ]. Hence the *Băiyí guăn yìyǔ* cannot distinguish between Mandarin [ts tsʰ] and [tʂ tʂʰ]. Also, Japanese transcriptions cannot render the Mandarin distinction between dental nasal stop [-n] syllable endings and velar nasal stop [-ŋ] endings.

Comparing transliteration materials with the phonological features of Mandarin dialects

If we exclude the features that are shared among our sources, as listed in Table 11.1, we have the following set of features that are *not* fully shared across the Běijīng dialects, the Zhōngyuán dialects, and the Jiānghuái dialects:

(a) The syllable finals [-n] and [-ŋ] are only seen to be distinct in the Běijīng and Zhōngyuán dialects.
(b) Only the Jiāng-Huái dialects preserve the *rù* tone.
(c) In the Běijīng dialect, the *rù* tone is lost, with the *rù* syllables merging into the other four tones.
(d) In the Zhōngyuán dialects, the *rù* tone is lost but with *rù* syllables reflecting MC voiceless initials; as well, those with voiced sonorant initials merge regularly with the *yīnpíng* tone.
(e) The initials of a set of words reflecting the traditional the *zhuāngzǔ nèizhuǎn* initial group have merged with the dental sibilants (*jīngzǔ*).

Table 11.2 indicates which if any of these features are reflected in each of our transliteration sources and shows clearly that all of the transliteration materials show at least one of the features of Jiāng-Huái dialects. All retain the *rù* tone, while in most the *zhuāngzǔ nèizhuǎn* initial group set of words is seen to be merged with the dental sibilants (*jīngzǔ*). Some of them also share the distinction of syllable final [-n] and [-ŋ] with Běijīng and Zhōngyuán dialects.

Table 11.2: Comparison of the transliterations with Mandarin dialect phonology

	Běijīng and Zhōngyuán dialects	Běijīng dialect	Zhōngyuán dialects	Jiāng-Huái dialects	
	Syllable final [-n] and [-ŋ] are distinct	*rù* tone is lost with the *rù* tone syllables merging into the other 4 tones	*rù* tone syllables with MC voiceless initials or voiced sonorant initials merge with the *yīnpíng* tone	The *zhuāngzǔ nèizhuǎn* set of words have merged with the dental sibilants	*rù* tone is preserved
Xīrú ěrmùzī (Trigault 1626)	+			+	+
Bǎiyí guǎn yìyǔ (1407, 1573–)	−				+
Ryūkyū guǎn yìyǔ (1401–1535)	−			+	+
Ryūkyū guānhuà kèběn (Míng–Qīng)	−			+	+
Lǎo·Piáo (Cuī Shìzhén, early 16th c.)	+				+
Tángyīn yǔlèi (Okajima Kanzan 1726)				+	+
Huángbò tángyīn (17th and 18th c.)				+	+

Brief summary

The above review of the transliteration materials reveals that they all share features that were common across all Mandarin dialects in the Ming. At the same time, the majority of them reflect the features specifically characteristic of the Jiāng-Huái dialects, while a couple of them additionally show features specific to the Běijīng and Zhōngyuán dialects.

Significantly, previous studies of these materials (Endo 1984, 1990, 2001; Nìng 2009; Setoguchi 1994; Lǐ 2005; Xiè 2010; Zēng 1989, 2014a, 2014b), identify fully seven of the transliteration materials as Nánjīng Mandarin or Southern Mandarin (see Table 11.1 for the identifications given for each of the materials). This despite the fact that the details of the phonologies of each of the transliteration materials also differ strikingly.

Míng Period Nánjīng Mandarin from the Perspective of the Modern Dialects

Historical traces of Míng period Nánjīng Mandarin in the language of descendants in Míng garrison communities

The modern Tiānjīn 天津 dialect, the Túnbǔ 屯堡 vernacular of Guìzhōu, the Yáchéng 崖城 Garrison Mandarin (*jūnhuà* 軍話) of Hǎinán 海南, and the Mandarin dialects of Yúnnán 雲南 are all spoken by descendants of Míng dynasty Mandarin speakers who had migrated out of the Nánzhílì 南直隸 'Southern Jurisdiction' region into various military settlements (*jūntún* 軍屯) in the northeast and far south and southwest (Zēng 2013a, 2013b, 2014a). Nánzhílì encompassed the areas of modern Jiāngsū 江蘇 and Ānhuī 安徽 and comprised the Greater Nánjīng (Dà Nánjīng 大南京) region of the Míng.

In the present day, these dialects evidence features that differ from the surrounding dialects but that correspond to the Jiāng-Huái dialects or Central Plains dialects. For example, in Old Tiānjīn the reflexes of the *zhī* 知, *zhuāng* 莊, and *zhāng* 章 (MC alveopalatals) initials follow the Nánjīng type with regard to their merger and contrast with the *jīng* 精 set of initials (dental sibilants). The Túnbǔ vernacular, which is of the Southwestern Mandarin type, reflects phonological features of Zhōngyuán dialects, such as a contrast between dental and retroflex fricative and affricate initials (for example, the contrast between [ts] and [tʂ]), and the merger of *rù* tone syllables, reflecting MC voiceless initials or voiced sonorant initials, into the *yīnpíng* tone. Yúnnán Mandarin shows the phonological features of Zhōngyuán dialects on the one hand, such as preservation of the contrast between dental and retroflex sibilants, and features of the Jiāng-Huái dialects on the other, such as the loss of distinction between syllable final nasals [-n] and [-ŋ] and maintenance of the pre-posed interrogative particle in the sentence pattern 'K+VP?'. Yáchéng Mandarin also preserves the 'K+VP?' sentence pattern while also preserving the *rù* tone, both examples of how that dialect retains features of Jiāng-Huái Mandarin.

These differing arrays of features originating in either Zhōngyuán Mandarin or Jiāng-Huái Mandarin reveal that these two types of Mandarin were distinct in the Míng but coexisted in the Nánzhílì, out of which the Tiānjīn, Túnbǔ, Yáchéng, and Yúnnán Mandarin varieties originated. It is thus highly likely that the common Mandarin koine spoken in Nánzhílì in the Míng dynasty was a kind of amalgam of the two types, mixing features of both Jiāng-Huái and Zhōngyuán Mandarins.

Localized Pǔtōnghuà in Ānhuī and Jiāngsū as a reference point for the Míng Mandarin koine

In the summer of 2011, the author took students to Ānhuī to investigate the Jiāng-Huái Mandarin of Héféi 合肥 and the Zhōngyuán Mandarin of Bèngbù 蚌埠, Gùzhèn

固鎮, and Méngchéng 蒙城. When communicating with locals in Ānhuī we found the Mandarin to be quite similar across and between the Jiāng-Huái Mandarin areas and the Zhōngyuán Mandarin areas. Though it was possible to discern individual differences between the Jiāng-Huái and Zhōngyuán varieties, the communication was still fluent and smooth. All speakers of both varieties also were quite sure that they were speaking Pǔtōnghuà. Similarly, in Jiāngsū province there is also a commonly used local "Jiāngsū Pǔtōnghuà."

Labov's "uniformitarian principle" objectively supports the inference that there was indeed a Mandarin koine that was broadly spoken in the Nánzhílì jurisdiction in the Míng dynasty (Labov 1994, 21–25). It would have been quite similar to the localized varieties of Pǔtōnghuà spoken in present-day Ānhuī and Jiāngsū. This Míng koine would have had even more strongly distinctive characteristics, linguistic fluidity, and adaptability than modern varieties of localized Pǔtōnghuà. This is because the modern Pǔtōnghuà standard has been far more widely and powerfully promulgated than the more informal *lingua franca* that was Míng period Nanjing Guānhuà.

Conclusion

The above discussion leads to the following four conclusions:

One, the prestige and widespread use of the Nánjīng Guānhuà koine in the Míng is clearly illustrated and supported by the high value that missionaries of the time placed on mastery of the Nánjīng dialect (Ricci and Trigault 1983, 391), as well as by the fact that Nánjīng Guānhuà was the primary form of Mandarin taught and learned in Japan prior to 1876 (Rokkaku 1988, 122).

Two, the phonology of Nánjīng Mandarin was a flexible amalgam of the Jiāng-Huái and Zhōngyuán types of Mandarin. That is to say that these two underlying types, Jiāng-Huái and Zhōngyuán, did not function in opposition or as alternatives in serving as the foundation for Nánjīng Guānhuà and had coequal influence in its formation and evolution.

Three, the core phonology of Míng period Nánjīng Mandarin/Guānhuà was comprised of a set of shared features from the Běijīng, Zhōngyuán, and Jiāng-Huái dialects. These features included: voiceless reflexes of the Middle Chinese voice obstruent initials; preservation of the sharp-round contrast in fricative and affricate initials; preservation of the distinction between the initials [l-] and [n-]; general merger of the *zhī-zhuāng-zhāng* initials into a single group (corresponding to the MC alveopalatals); merger of MC syllable final [-m] into [-n]; a two register *píng* tone (with *yīn* and *yáng* categories); and a merger of the MC lower register *shǎng* tone (that had voiced initials) with the *qù* tone.

Four, Nánjīng Mandarin/Guānhuà was a dynamic elastic system without a rigidly fixed model. As a *lingua franca*, Míng Guānhuà was not an inflexible standard like modern Pǔtōnghuà, but was a flexibly interpreted conceptualization of a "correct pronunciation" (*zhèngyīn* 正音). The rime books and rime tables of the Míng period, as well as the various transliteration materials, were in fact each individual linguistic records that had been independently recorded and compiled at the time. As such, on the one hand, they could not avoid being influenced by the individual dialects of their compilers and/or the speakers they consulted; on the other hand, they could not escape the linguistic attitudes and preconceptions of their compilers regarding what they chose to record and how they interpreted it (such as valuing actual current usage and pronunciation or giving greater weight to adherence to tradition). Hence it is not really possible to identify a single, clearly identifiable source for the Nánjīng Guānhuà of the Míng. It is thus no surprise that there are various inconsistencies and discrepancies among and between the various representations of Nánjīng Mandarin in the historical record.

Note: The author expresses thanks to Professor Richard VanNess Simmons for his invitation to participate in the 'International Workshop on the History of Colloquial Chinese—Written and Spoken' held at Rutgers University, March 11–12, 2016, where this chapter was first presented. She also wishes to thank Professors Hóu Jīngyī and Endo Mitsuaki for their help and instruction in the process of writing this chapter. This study received generous funding as a key project of National Social Science Fund of China (number 11AZD072). A previous version of this chapter appeared in Chinese as "Míngdài Nánjīng Guānhuà xìngzhì kǎoshì 明代南京官話性質考釋," *Yǔyán Kēxué* 語言科學 2016 (2): 178–87.

References

Bào Míngwěi 鮑明煒. 2010. *Bào Míngwěi Yǔyán xué wénjí* 鮑明煒語言學文集 [Collected works on linguistics by Bào Míngwěi]. Nánjīng: Nánjīng dàxué chūbǎnshè.

Chén Xiǎo 陳曉. 2014. "Jīyú Qīng hòuqí zhì mínguó chū nián Běijīng huà wénxiàn yǔliào de gè'àn yánjiū" 基於清後期至民國初年北京話文獻語料的個案研究 [Features of the Běijīng dialect seen in documents from the late Qīng dynasty and the early Republican period]. PhD diss., Peking University.

Dīng Fēng 丁鋒. 1995. *Liúqiú duì yīn yǔ míngdài guānhuà yánjiū* 琉球對音與明代官話研究 [The Ryukyu transcriptions and Míng Mandarin]. Běijīng: Zhōngguó shèhuì kēxué chūbǎnshè.

Endo Mitsuaki 遠藤光曉. (1984) 2001. "Fānyì lǎoqǐdà·Piáo tōngshì lǐ de Hànyǔ shēngdiào" 《翻譯老乞大·朴通事》裏的漢語聲調 [The Chinese tones in the translation of *Lǎoqǐdà* and *Piáo tōngshì*]. *Yǔyán xué lùn cóng* 語言學論叢 [Essays on linguistics], vol. 13. Reprint in *Zhōngguó yīnyùn xué lùn jí* 中國音韻學論集 [Studies on Chinese Historical Phonology], 253–66. Tōkyō: Hakuteisha 白帝社.

Endo Mitsuaki 遠藤光曉. 1990. *Fānyì lǎo qǐ dà·Pǔtōng Hànzì zhùyīn suǒyǐn* 《翻譯老乞大·朴通事》漢字注音索引 [Index to the phonetic glosses for Chinese in the translation of *Lǎoqǐdà* and *Piáo tōngshì*]. Tōkyō: Kōbun shuppansha 好文出版社.

Endo Mitsuaki 遠藤光曉. 2001. *Hànyǔ fāngyán lùngǎo* 漢語方言論稿 [Studies on Chinese dialects]. Tōkyō: Kōbun shuppansha 好文出版社.

Gěng Zhènshēng 耿振生. 1992. *Míng Qīng děngyùnxué tōnglùn* 明清等韻學通論 [A study of Míng and Qīng rhyme tables]. Běijīng: Yǔwén chūbǎnshè.

Guō Lì 郭力. 2003. *Gǔ Hànyǔ yánjiū lùngǎo* 古漢語研究論稿 [Studies in old Chinese]. Běijīng: Běijīng yǔyán dàxué chūbǎnshè.

Labov, William 拉波夫. 1994. *Principles of Linguistic Change*. Vol. 1: *Internal Factors*. Oxford: Blackwell. Chinese translation: *Yǔyán biànhuà yuánlǐ nèibù yīnsù* 語言變化原理內部因素. Beijing: Peking University Press, 2007.

Lǐ Wúwèi 李無未. 2005. *Yīnyùn wénxiàn yǔ yīnyùnxué shǐ—lǐ wú wèi wén cún* 音韻文獻與音韻學史—李無未文存 [Historical phonological texts and the history of Chinese phonology—articles by Lǐ Wúwèi]. Chángchūn: Jílín wénshǐ chūbǎnshè.

Lǐ Xīnkuí 李新魁, and Mài Yún 麥耘. 1993. *Yùnxué gǔjí shùyào* 韻學古籍述要 [Overview of historical sources on Chinese phonology]. Xī'ān: Shǎanxī rénmín chūbǎnshè.

Lǚ Guóyáo 魯國堯. 2007. "Yánjiū Míng mò Qīng chū Guānhuà jīchǔ fāngyán de niàn-sān nián lìchéng—'cóng zì-fènglǐ kàn' dào 'cóng zì-miànshàng kàn'" 研究明末清初官話基礎方言的廿三年歷程—'從字縫裏看' 到 '從字面上看' [My twenty-three years of study of the base dialects for Guānhuà from late Míng to early Qīng—moving from between the words to clear evidence]. *Yǔyán kēxué* 語言科學2: 3–22.

Mài Yún 麥耘, and Zhū Xiǎonóng 朱曉農. 2012. "Nánjīng fāngyán bùshì Míng dài Guānhuà de jīchǔ" 南京方言不是明代官話的基礎 [The Nanjing dialect was not the language that underlay Guānhuà]. *Yǔyán kēxué* 語言科4: 337–58.

Nìng Jìfú 寧忌浮. 2009. *Hànyǔ yùnshū shǐ (Míngdài juàn)* 漢語韻書史（明代卷）[The history of studies of Chinese phonology (volume on the Míng dynasty)]. Shànghǎi: Shànghǎi rénmín chūbǎnshè.

Ricci, Matteo 利瑪竇, and Nicolas Trigault 金尼閣. 1983. *Lì Mǎdòu Zhōngguó zhájì* 利瑪竇中國札記 [Matteo Ricci's notes on China]. Translated by Hé Zhàowǔ 何兆武, Hé Gāojì 何高濟, Wáng Zūnzhòng 王遵仲, and Lǐ Shēn 李申. Běijīng: Zhōnghuá shūjú.

Rokkaku Tsunehiro 六角恆廣. 1988. *Chūgokugo kyōiku-shi no kenkyū* 中國語教育史の研究 [History of the teaching of Chinese language (in Japan)]. Tōkyō: Tōyō shoten.

Sarashina Shinichi 更科慎一. 2003. "*Báiyíguǎn yìyǔ* yīnyì Hànzì shēngdiào chūtàn" 《百夷館譯語》音譯漢字聲調初探 [A preliminary investigation of the Chinese tonal system in *Báiyíguǎn yìyǔ*]. Nánkāi dàxué dòng tái yǔ jí hàn zàng yǔyán xuéshù tǎolùn jiāoliú huì lùnwén 南開大學侗台語及漢藏語言學術討論交流會論文. Paper presented at the Kam-Tai and Sino-Tibetan Languages Workshop in Nánkāi University.

Setoguchi Litsuko 瀬戶口律子. 1994. *Liúqiú guānhuà kèběn yánjiū* 琉球官話課本研究 [The Ryukyu textbooks of Guānhuà]. Hong Kong: T. T. Ng Chinese Language Research Centre, Institute of Chinese Studies, Chinese University of Hong Kong.

Sūn Yízhì 孫宜志. 2005. "Fāng Yǐzhì *Qièyùn shēngyuán* yǔ Tóngchéng fāngyán" 方以智《切韻聲原》與桐城方言 [Fāng Yǐzhì's *Qièyùn shēngyuán* and the Tóngchéng dialect]. *Zhōngguó yǔwén* 中國語文 [Studies in Chinese Language] 1: 65–74.

Trigault, Nicolas 金尼閣. 1626 [1957]. *Xīrú ěrmùzī (shàng, zhōng, xià)* 西儒耳目資（上，中，下）[An audio-visual aid to Western scholars (volumes 1 to 3)]. Běijīng: Wénzì gǎigé chūbǎnshè.

Xiè Yùxīn 謝育新. 2010. "Rìběn Táng tōngshì Tángyīn yǔ shíbā shìjì de Hángzhōu huà Nánjīng guānhuà" 日本唐通事唐音與十八世紀的杭州話南京官話 [The Hángzhōu and Nánjīng dialects of the eighteenth century reflected in the Tō-on materials of Japan]. PhD diss., Běijīng University.

Zēng Xiǎoyú 曾曉渝. 1989. "*Xīrú ěrmùzī* yīnxì yánjiū" 《西儒耳目資》音系研究" [A study of the phonology of *Xīrú ěrmùzī*]. Xīnán shīfàn dàxué shuòshì xuéwèi lùnwén 西南師範大學碩士論文. MA thesis, Southwestern Normal University.

Zēng Xiǎoyú 曾曉渝. 2013a. "Tiānjīn huà yuánliú jiāodiǎn wèntí zài tàntǎo" 天津話源流焦點問題再探討 [Revisiting the source and development of the Tianjin dialect]. *Zhōngguó yǔwén* 中國語文 [Studies of Chinese Language] 2: 116–27.

Zēng Xiǎoyú 曾曉渝. 2013b. "Míngdài nán zhílì xiáqū de Guānhuà fāngyán kǎochá fēnxī" 明代南直隸轄區的官話方言考察分析 [Research on the Mandarin dialects of southern Zhílì in the Míng dynasty]. *Gǔhànyǔ yánjiū* 古漢語研究 [Studies in ancient Chinese] 4: 40–50.

Zēng Xiǎoyú 曾曉渝. 2014a. *Xīrú ěrmùzī* yīnxì jīchǔ fēi Nánjīng fāngyán bǔzhèng 《西儒耳目資》音系基礎非南京方言補正 [Additional evidence to show that the phonology of the *Xīrú ěrmùzī* is not based on the Nánjīng dialect]. *Yǔyán kēxué* 語言科學 [Language Science] 4: 423–29.

Zēng Xiǎoyú 曾曉渝. 2014b. Bǐngzhǒng běn *Bǎiyí yìyǔ* yǔyīn xiànxiàng chūtàn 丙種本《百夷譯語》語音現象初探 [Primary exploration of the phonology of the *bǐng* versions of *Bǎiyí yìyǔ*]. *Nánkāi yǔyán xué kān* 南開語言學刊 2: 13–27.

Zhāng Wèidōng 張衛東. 2014a. "Lùn yǔ Nánjīng huà, Míng dài Guānhuà lìshǐ xiāngguān de jǐ gè wèntí" 論與南京話，明代官話歷史相關的幾個問題 [Issues related to the history of the Nánjīng dialect and Guānhuà in the Míng dynasty]. *Zhōngguó yǔyán xué* 中國語言學 [Chinese Linguistics] 7: 14–18.

Zhāng Wèidōng 張衛東. 2014b. "Lùn *Jiāotàiyùn* de yīnxì xìngzhì jí nánběi Guānhuà yǔyīn de qūbié biāozhì" 論《交泰韻》的音系性質及南北官話語音的區別標誌 [The phonological nature of Jiāotàiyùn and the distinguishing characteristics of southern and northern Mandarin]. In *Chéngzétáng fāngyán lùncóng—Wáng Fútáng jiàoshòu bāzhì shòuqìng lùnwén jí* 承澤堂方言論叢—王福堂教授八秩壽慶論文集 [*Chéngzétáng* studies in dialects—Festschrift in honor of Professor Wáng Fútáng on his 80th birthday], edited by Lǐ Xiǎofán 李小凡 and Xiàng Mèngbīng 項夢冰, 34–48. Běijīng: Yǔwén chūbǎnshè.

12
Language Use in the Chinese Community of Manila in the Seventeenth Century
A Case of Occasional Diglossia?

Henning Klöter

Introduction

Research on the history of Mandarin (*guanhua* 官話) traditionally focuses on diachronic changes in the areas of phonology, lexicon and syntax (cf., *inter alia*, Coblin 2000, 2009, 2010, 2017). It is thus concerned with diachronic language changes in a stricter sense, that is, changes pertaining to language as such. In contrast, taking a sociolinguistic approach, this chapter places the spread of Mandarin in the historical context of a Chinese speech community outside China—the Chinese migrants who settled in the Philippines during the seventeenth century. The settlers are commonly referred to as *Sangleys* or *Sangleyes* in historical sources. To what extent can it be claimed that their community was characterized by societal multilingualism? Can the language situation in the Sangley speech community be described in terms of diglossia? If yes, on what grounds is it possible to identify different varieties in terms of the traditional high (H) versus low (L) dichotomy? Concretely speaking, what role did Mandarin play in the Chinese community of Manila in the early seventeenth century? This question refers to both language competences of the Chinese migrants in Manila and their language attitudes toward Mandarin as the *lingua franca* of the officials, irrespective of their own individual competences. This chapter argues that in terms of individual competences and total number of competent speakers, there are some historical traces of Mandarin as an H variety in the Chinese speech community. Although the settlers mainly spoke Hokkien, a southern Sinitic variety originating in China's southeastern Fujian province, we may assume that the recognition of the high status of Mandarin was well-established and inextricably linked with the continuity of social hierarchies across regional boundaries.

My approach to the questions raised above has received much inspiration from publications in the area of historical sociolinguistics. This interdisciplinary field at the nexus of linguistics and social history explores "the extent to which sociolinguistic theoretical models, methods, findings, and expertise can be applied to the process of reconstruction of the past of languages in order to account for diachronic linguistic changes and developments" (Conde-Silvestre and Hernández-Campoy 2012, 4). In sociolinguistics, answers to questions pertaining to language choice, language proficiency, and language attitudes can be gained through different methods, including surveys, interviews, observation, and experiments. By contrast, historical sociolinguistics relies entirely on an analysis of historical documents. As Hernández-Campoy and Schilling write, "the socio-linguistic study of historical language forms must rely on linguistic records from previous periods—most of which will be incomplete or non-representative in some way—as well as on knowledge and understanding of past sociocultural situations that can only be reconstructed rather than directly observed or experienced by the researcher" (2012, 63). As will be shown in the paragraphs that follow, the reconstruction of past sociocultural situations to a considerable extent also relies on historical sources in a wider sense, particularly on sources that cannot be considered linguistic records. It is in any case almost trivial to point out that answers provided by historical documents and linguistic records must remain sketchy. One obvious reason is that historical sociolinguistics directs questions at historical documents. These questions, however, were not on the minds of the people who wrote the documents. Research in the field of historical sociolinguistics thus faces the same challenge as historical linguistics in general, that is, to master "the art of making the best use of bad data" (Labov 1994, 11).

The Spread of Mandarin

It is a widely accepted claim that the use of Mandarin in imperial China was by and large restricted to oral communications among government officials. As Coblin points out, *guanhua* (literally 'language of officials') was "the universal standard language or koiné spoken by officials and educated people in traditional China during the Míng (1368–1644) and Qīng (1644–1912) dynasties" (2000, 537). This general explanation prompts several questions. Most importantly, social stratification is never along a clear-cut line separating the world of officials from the world of non-officials, or educated from uneducated people. In imperial China, many members of society were "uneducated" and fully illiterate. Yet there were also members of society who were educated to some degree without being members of officialdom. This leads to the question as to how far the use of Mandarin spread to different social strata. Moreover, competence in Mandarin was determined not only by social factors (degree of education, social contacts), but also by regional factors. For example, it is easily conceivable that Mandarin during the late Ming dynasty was used much more widely in the Nanjing area than in southeastern China, where mutually unintelligible Sinitic varieties are spoken. As pointed out earlier, historical documents do not provide clear answers to these questions. Instead, they provide seemingly contradictory answers. Compare the following quotations from the two Western missionaries: Matteo Ricci (1552–1610) and Walter Henry Medhurst (1796–1857). In 1615, Ricci wrote:

Besides the various dialects of the different provinces, the province vernacular so to speak, there is also a spoken language common to the whole Empire, known as the Quonhoa, an official language for civil and forensic use. . . . The Quonhua dialect is now in vogue among the cultured classes, and is used between strangers and the inhabitants of the province they may visit. With the knowledge of this common language, there really is no necessity for the members of our Society to learn the dialects of the provinces in which they work. A province dialect would not be used in polite society, although the more cultured classes might use it in their home province as a sign of neighborliness, or perhaps outside of the province from a sense of patriotism. This national, official tongue is so commonly used that even the women and children understand it. (Ricci [1615] 1953, 28–29)

The second quotation is from the Protestant missionary Walter Henry Medhurst:

The Mandarin tongue is partially understood throughout the whole Empire, by the better informed part of the inhabitants, and, in some central districts, it is said to be the current language of the people, but, in the southern provinces, the vulgar dialects differ more or less from the Court language, and in Hok-këèn, where the difference is most marked, the cultivation of the Mandarin tongue is less general. The author, having never visited China, has had little opportunity of conversing with the higher ranks of the Chinese, but from constant intercourse with the middling and lower classes who emigrate to the Eastern Islands, his uniform experience for the last fourteen years has been, that no man in five hundred knows any thing of the Mandarin tongue, or can carry on a conversation of more than ten words in it. (Medhurst 1832, v)

At first glance, Ricci's words seem diametrically opposed to Medhurst's. How should it be possible that in the early seventeenth century, Mandarin was "commonly used," even outside officialdom, and two hundred years later "no man in five hundred knows any thing of the Mandarin tongue"? To be sure, Ricci's claim concerning the widespread use of Mandarin seems to be steeped in wishful thinking, since it was an obvious attempt to legitimize the language policy of the Jesuit Order. This policy followed an explicit decision by Alessandro Valignano (1539–1606), who issued a clear order that the language to be learned was to be Mandarin (Witek 2001, 154; see also Gao 2008; Klöter 2011, 34–35). This policy was reinforced with the establishment of a formal four-year Jesuit language curriculum known as the *ratio studiorum* 'plan of studies', which likewise strengthened the position of Mandarin in the field of pronunciation (for details, see Brockey 2007, 257). When Ricci made his remarks on the widespread use of Mandarin, he had already spent some time in southeastern China. In other words, even if the linguistic setting in Nanjing during the late Ming dynasty supported his claim, his previous experience in the south should have told another story.

Mutilingualism or Min Only? The Sangley Community in Manila

In the paragraphs that follow, I will examine the spread of Mandarin in a Chinese speech community during the seventeenth century. I have chosen the "Sangley community" in Manila mainly because the use and spread of Mandarin among the Sangleys is, at least to a modest degree, documented in historical accounts.

Spain's colonization of the Philippines in 1565 provided a basis for Chinese trade and settlement (Weightman 1960, 47–64; Wickberg 1965, 3). Wickberg reports that in the early 1570s, the Spaniards "found a small settlement of about 150 Chinese" in the Manila area. Within 30 years, this number had soared to 20,000 (1965, 4–6). In the first decades of the seventeenth century, relations between the Spanish colonizers and the Chinese settlers were marked by hostility. According to Horsley, the Spaniards, less than forty years after their initial settlement, "had formed a pattern of hatred against the Chinese that persisted for more than three centuries" (1950, 1). Wickberg points out that the Chinese outnumbered the Spaniards, who lived in constant fear of an uprising, or even an invasion of troops from China (Wickberg 1999, 188). Yet from an economic perspective, the presence of both Spaniards and Sangleys in Manila was beneficial to both. Each side prospered, and moreover, the Spaniards were able to utilize the presence of Chinese to prepare for an expansion of their mission to the Chinese mainland (see Menegon 2009; Wills 1994). The Chinese migrants traded goods and provided various kinds of services. According to Chia, "the Spanish began very quickly to rely on the Chinese, or Sangleyes, not only for goods from China, but for all kinds of services in the colony. All the craftsmen, storekeepers, unskilled laborers, and most farmers, fishermen, and domestic servants were Chinese" (2006, 515). Wickman writes that the Chinese in the Philippines were "indispensable to local economies and societies" (1999, 187).

There is compelling historical and linguistic evidence that the Sangleys came from the region now known as Fujian province. As Chia points out, different regional origins within Fujian correlated with different professions:

> There was a distinction between those from the Zhangzhou area, who were poorer, more apt to get work other than as traders, and more likely to stay in the islands. In contrast, the Quanzhou area natives were more involved in the junk trade, directly or indirectly, and many of them were short-term sojourners. They could come on the junks soon after the Chinese New Year, stay on board or in the Parián for a few months while waiting for the *nao* to arrive, and then hope to leave after having finished their business (or arranged to leave it in the hands of brokers) when the south-west monsoon started blowing, at around the same time when another *nao* set sail for Acapulco. (Chia 2006, 522)

In a similar vein, Wickberg argues that in the early period of Chinese settlement in the Philippines, there was a pre-eminence of Zhangzhou people (1999, 187).

The question of regional provenance is obviously related to the question of language use. In a previous study (Klöter 2011, chapter 6), I claimed that the language spoken by the Sangleys was a contact variety displaying features from the Southern Min Quanzhou and Zhangzhou dialects, and I proposed to label this contact variety Early Manila Hokkien (EMH). My phonological sketch of EMH is based on evidence cited from grammars and dictionaries compiled by Spanish missionaries during the seventeenth century. Other scholars have emphasized the Zhangzhou affinity of the data and consequently treated EMH as a "kind of Zhāngzhōu variety" of Southern Min (Kwok 2018, 53; see also Kwok 2018, 157–59; Ang 2014). Firmer conclusions, however, have thus far not been reached due to two obvious lacunae in research: the utilization of all extant missionary linguistic sources, and a systematic comparison with native Chinese sources of the same period.

It has to be emphasized that the linguistic environment of the Sangley community was more complex than just involving two Southern Min varieties. Social factors such as intermarriage led to contact with native Philippine languages, such as Tagalog. Actually, though, traces of Min–Tagalog contact cannot be found in the grammars and dictionaries written by Spanish missionaries. Since the Sangleys also interacted with Spanish traders and missionaries, and various colonial administrators, it is reasonable to suggest that Spanish–Min language contact must have taken place as well. Except for Southern Min phonetic translations of Spanish Christian terms (cf. Loon 1967), I have not been able to spot any instances of Spanish influence on EMH.

This leads one to ask whether and to what extent Mandarin was part of the Chinese speech community in Manila. In contrast to Spanish and Tagalog, there is no obvious social or historical evidence of a Mandarin presence in a non-Mandarin speech community. To state the obvious, if a language is present in a speech community, it is present through its speakers. If Mandarin was used in Manila, there would have to be evidence today pointing to the presence of Mandarins, that is, officials, merchants, or other persons with a certain level of education. The question goes beyond the mere spread of Mandarin; it is also about the *nature* of the spread in sociolinguistic terms. If Mandarin was spoken among the Sangleys, can the functional division of Mandarin and EMH be analyzed in terms of diglossia? Concretely speaking, is there any historical evidence pointing to the fact that Mandarin was used in domains such as administration or education? This question thus calls for another kind of historical account that does more than merely point out that Mandarin-speakers were part of the Sangley community. If we want to define a historical speech community in terms of diglossia, then we need to identify domains that made a functional distribution into high and low possible, such as the presence of educational or bureaucratic institutions that were controlled by Mandarins. It must be stated from the outset that there is no compelling evidence in support of Mandarin/Hokkien diglossia in the Sangley community based on institutions associated with formal domains. Peng points out that "Chinese education [in the Philippines] did not start until the late nineteenth century" (Peng 2013, 447), and it would be reckless to assume an institutional presence of any kind of *yamen* headed by a Mandarin. Such an institutional presence of the mandarinate would have been incompatible with the Spanish colonizers' firm administrative grip on social life. There are, however, some pieces of evidence that, when combined, suggest that the language situation could have had traces of diglossia, and I provisionally refer to this type of diglossia as "occasional diglossia," to be explained presently.

Historical Accounts

The provisional term "occasional diglossia" is based on the scenario that representatives of the Chinese state bureaucracy visited the Philippines on several occasions. Their social position was clearly recognized and respected by the local Chinese settlers. During these occasional encounters, language use played a recognizable role in distinguishing between higher and lower social ranks. In the sections that follow, this scenario will be illustrated by a number of quotations from historical documents selected from the *The Philippine Islands, 1493–1898*, published in the early twentieth century in 55 volumes by Emma Blair (1851–1911) and James Alexander Robertson (1873–1939). This work (hereafter BR) is a collection of translations from Spanish sources covering the entire period of Spanish colonial rule. Although the body of translated documents has rightly been criticized for its fragmentation and inaccuracies (Cano 2008), it still provides *a few* insights into the correlation between language use and social hierarchies in the Chinese community. I emphasize "a few" because language-related phenomena are scarcely mentioned. I must also emphasize that this perspective on history is exclusively through the Spanish lens, for "hardly anything written by the Chinese has come down to us" (Bernal 1966, 66).

In 1609, the Spanish historian Bartolomé Leonardo de Argensola wrote the following account of Chinese mandarins visiting Manila in 1594:

> The vessels brought seven mandarins, some of the greatest viceroys or governors of their provinces. . . . The mandarins left their ships twice to visit Don Luis [i.e. Luis Perez Dasmariñas], attended by a great pomp and retinue. He received them kindly, and gave each mandarin a gold necklace. They told him that they had come by order of their king to get the Chinese who were wandering unsettled among those islands without his leave. But this was considered a pretext for the truth, for so many mandarins were unnecessary for it, or so many armed ships and supplies. (BR XVI, 287)

This brief description suggests how official Chinese–Spanish contacts in Manila were conducted during the early colonial period. In addition, the following quotation clearly suggests that mandarins maintained their superior positions vis-à-vis the local Chinese migrants. It describes a visit by Chinese officials to Manila in 1603 and was written by the Spanish official Geronimo de Salazar y Salcedo:

> On Friday . . . there entered into this city three infidel Sangleys, who came in the last arrived ships from the kingdom of China; and they wear the garments and caps which are usually worn in that kingdom by the great mandarins. . . . The said three

Sangleys, who claim to be mandarins, go out from their houses on their way to this city, seated in chairs upon the shoulders of four Sangleys; and, attached to their persons, on each side go six of their guards armed as archers. . . . Between these go two Sangleys each one of whom cries out in his own language from time to time, with loud shouts; and it is said that they are calling out, "Make way, for the mandarins are coming," and as soon as they come out of their houses, and until they enter them again, these cries are kept up. When the Sangleys meet the mandarins, they flee from them and hide themselves; and if they cannot do this they bend their backs very low with their arms extended upon the ground, and remain in this position while the mandarins pass, which is quite in the form and manner which is customary in the said kingdom of China. (BR XII, 94f)

Interestingly, the 55 volumes also provide some bits and pieces of Spaniards studying the Mandarin language. In a biographical footnote, the editors claim that the Augustinian friar Alonso de Alvarado (d. 1576) "was the first Spaniard in the Philippines to learn the mandarin dialect of the Chinese language, and that he ministered to the Chinese converts there" (BR VI, 115). Also, according to an account from 1640, Fray Thomas de Sierra "devoted himself to learning the mandarin language" (BR XXXII, 87). Thus, from historical documents it is evident that Mandarin was spoken on certain occasions within the Sangley community of Manila. In two respects, however, the sources do not allow for definite conclusions. First, it is unclear how often mandarins from China visited Manila and precisely how they interacted with the Chinese community. Second, it is also not known to what extent members of the Chinese merchant community had acquired a competence in Mandarin that would qualify them as bilingual at least to some degree. The implications of this lack of historical evidence will be discussed presently.

Linguistic Sources

During the first half of the seventeenth century, Western missionaries compiled the first grammars and dictionaries of the language spoken by the Sangleys. Unsurprisingly, most of these sources document the Hokkien dialect of the Sangleys, that is, EMH (see Klöter 2011). But there is one exception: the archives of the University of Santo Tomas in Manila hold a dictionary titled *Dictionario Hispanico Sinicum* (hereafter *Dictionario*). This is a bilingual Spanish–Hokkien dictionary of unknown authorship, containing around 20,000 entries on 552 double-sided folios (facsimile edition in Lee et al. 2018). The dictionary is undated but contains some textual evidence suggesting that it was written before the end of the Ming dynasty (i.e., before 1644). For example, the translation of 'China' is «大明国 | dǎy bēng côg'», the name of the Ming dynasty; no reference to the Qing dynasty (1644–1911) can be found. Moreover, it is known that the Dominicans shifted their focus of language learning from Hokkien to Mandarin when they were about to enter China in the 1630s. It seems likely that such a comprehensive Hokkien dictionary was compiled before this shift of focus occurred (Klöter 2011, 74).

In terms of its lexicographic arrangement, most parts of the dictionary have a straightforward bilingual arrangement. Spanish entries are placed in the left column, and Hokkien equivalents follow in columns two and three, the former using characters and the latter romanized transcriptions. Interestingly, the first part of the *Dictionario* contains a fourth column with romanized transcriptions different from those in the preceding column. Many of these transcriptions resemble the Mandarin transcriptions in Varo's glossaries of the late seventeenth century (in Coblin 2006). One example is <açotar> 'whip, flog', which is transcribed as <tà> in both the added column in the *Dictionario* and in Varo's glossary of the Mandarin language. For <afloxar> 'loosen', we find <fāng> in the *Dictionario* and <fáng> in Varo's glossary. The transcriptions in the fourth column are discontinued on folio 210v., the last entry being a subentry of <escriuir> 'write'. More data would be needed for us to conclude whether the fourth column is indeed Mandarin. Still, the examples provided point clearly in this direction. From the extract in Figure 12.1 it is also evident that the fourth column was written by a different scribe than wrote the first three columns, one obvious proof of this being the different shapes of the handwritten letter <t> in line 3. It is quite obvious, however, that the Mandarin column must have been part of the original compilation plan, since the space for the fourth column has been left blank in the remaining part of the dictionary (see Figure 12.2). The only explanation for this blank space is that it was supposed to be filled in at a later stage. The *Dictionario* may therefore rightly be considered an uncompleted trilingual Spanish–Hokkien–Mandarin dictionary, probably the earliest trilingual Chinese dictionary involving a European language at all.

Figure 12.1: Excerpt from the *Dictionario*, f. 87v, with permission of Archivo de la Universidad de Santo Tomás, Manila

Figure 12.2: Excerpt from the *Dictionario*, f. 213v, with permission of Archivo de la Universidad de Santo Tomás, Manila

If the claim that this document has trilingual Spanish–Hokkien–Mandarin entries turns out to be correct, it seems likely that the person who added the column had access to Mandarin informants. But who were these informants? In 1589, the Dominican Juan Cobo (c. 1546–1592) noted that "I wish to say that the people who come over are the poor, seagoing people, fishermen and laborers who come to earn a living" (in Felix 1966, 138). However, Cobo's contacts with the Chinese were not restricted to the poor. Wills notes that he also interacted with "men of substantial Confucian learning," resulting in the publication of "a remarkable work of Neo-Confucian-Christian apologetics" in 1593 (1994, 116). This publication, according to Wills, is "remarkable evidence for the presence of at least one reasonably learned Chinese scholar in Manila at this time and for the very rapid progress of Dominican dialogue with the Chinese" (1994, 117; cf. Klöter 2011, 40). Some fifty years later, around 1648, the Dominican Francisco Varo (1627–1687) reportedly studied Mandarin in Manila for one year before embarking for China in 1649 (Coblin and Levi 2000, x). There is no reason to cast doubt on this biographical detail, yet it is hard to conceive that Varo's first steps in Mandarin learning benefited from the linguistic environment of Manila. Missionary sources unambiguously state that Hokkien "is most widely spoken here" ("la que mas aqui se abla," qtd and translated in Klöter 2011, 176–77), that is, in the Chinese community of Manila. We must assume, then, that Varo received some kind of formal schooling organized by the Dominican order. Thus far, however, little research has been done on the founding of Mandarin education by Dominicans in Manila after the 1630s.

Although many questions regarding the spread of Mandarin in the Philippines remain unanswered, one thing is certain: Mandarin never replaced Hokkien as the principal language of the ethnic Chinese in the Philippines. Indeed, until recently, Hokkien (together with Northern Min dialects) has remained the main home language in the Chinese community, to be distinguished from Mandarin as a language learned in Chinese community schools (cf. Gonzalez 1998, 502). To be sure, the widespread use of Hokkien among ethnic Chinese in the Philippines today is largely due to migration from China during the 1950s and 1960s (Gonzalez 1998, 510). This, however, does not exclude the possibility of historical continuation dating back to the early history of Chinese migration in the late sixteenth century.

Mandarin in Manila: Occasional Diglossia?

To what extent can the use of Hokkien and Mandarin in the Philippines be explained in terms of diglossia? From the extant sources, we may construct the following scenario: Hokkien was the dominant language in the Chinese community of Manila. Yet at the same time the Sangleys must have been fully aware of the social status of Chinese mandarins and their language, although it seems unlikely that many Hokkien speakers had a good command of Mandarin. As a 'high' variety within the Chinese community, Mandarin comes close to Platt's notion of a Dummy High. As explained by Platt, a Dummy High "refers to speech varieties of which some of the members have a certain knowledge, and which are given prestige ratings by the speakers . . . but which are not in fact utilized extensively in any domain" (Platt 1977, 373–74, qtd in Fasold 1984, 49). Fasold adds that a Dummy High "owes its significance in the community almost exclusively to the high regard in which the people hold it; it is not used for any real communicative purpose" (1984, 49). Interestingly, Fasold uses the term in reference to Mandarin in Malaysia, a case that bears important resemblance with the Chinese speech community in the Philippines.

There is a subtle difference between the two definitions of Dummy High cited here. Platt's definition implies that some members of the speech community are at least partly bilingual. In Fishman's (1967) terms, this would be a case of diglossia with bilingualism, at least a certain degree of bilingualism. Yet theoretically speaking, Fasold's definition of Dummy High would also be applicable in the case of diglossia *without* bilingualism. The sheer perception of an external variety as High vis-à-vis the internal Low variety would suffice to create a diglossic situation. More historical data about the language competence of Chinese settlers in Manila would be needed to judge which of these definitions most aptly describes our case. Quite obviously, however, a High status for Mandarin did not rest solely on imagination. Sociolinguistic imagination was nurtured by real-life situations whenever cohorts of mandarins visited the Philippines and staged their authority and social status. Since these visits occurred only occasionally, I tentatively refer to this type of diglossia as occasional diglossia.

Concluding Remarks

My proposal to label the functional distribution of Mandarin and Hokkien in the Chinese community of Manila as occasional diglossia inevitably remains tentative and one-dimensional. It is tentative, in that a safe conclusion would require more historical data. For the time being, we may simply point out that according to some historical sources, Mandarin was spoken to some extent during the first decades of Chinese community-building in Manila. To be sure, the appearance of Mandarin language data in linguistic sources and the reference to Mandarin-speaking mandarins in historical sources do not allow us to measure the degree to which Mandarin had spread into the community of Hokkien-speaking Sangleys. The very fact that Sinitic language varieties were imported from China to Manila does not necessarily imply that the social domains of language use associated with diglossia came with them. Safer conclusions would also require a better demographic understanding of the Sangleys, notably the degrees of literacy and exposure to education in the community.

The proposal is one-dimensional, since it focuses on Mandarin and Hokkien only. As pointed out earlier, for obvious reasons, the language situation within the Sangley community was far more complex. Since the Philippines were under Spanish colonial rule and Spanish was the dominant language of the colonial administration, Mandarin and Hokkien had low status vis-à-vis Spanish. At the same time, Hokkien coexisted with various native Philippine languages. Although the Sangleys dwelled in a closed area of Manila known as Parián, it is a well-established historical fact that contact with other ethnic groups took place. In this context, it must be emphasized that the first wave of migration from China to the Philippines was restricted to males, many of whom married local Philippine women. By the mid-eighteenth century, their offspring—known as mestizos—outnumbered Chinese migrants born in China (cf. Skinner 2001, 55; see also Chu 2010). The period from the first days of Chinese settlement to the formation of a mestizo community involved complex patterns of language contact that must have added to the sociolinguistic complexity associated with the Chinese community. Such an assumption seems self-evident, yet it has not been studied systematically on the basis of historical sources. The sociolinguistic picture becomes even more complex when written languages are considered. Note in this context that in Ferguson's (1959) seminal article on diglossia, Classical Chinese as a written language is identified as H in a diglossic situation. If we included both Classical Chinese and written Hokkien (cf. Loon 1966, 11–13) in our analysis of Parián as a speech community, existing sub-definitions of diglossia would arguably fail to capture its complexity. Put simply, a historico-sociolinguistic analysis of the Chinese speech community in Manila would require safe information on the education and literacy of the Sangleys. An analysis of the sociolinguistic setting of the Sangley speech community in all its complexities must therefore be left for future research. At this point it has to be emphasized that the purpose of this chapter has been to analyze the spread of Mandarin at a certain place at a certain time in history. The intent here has been to complement studies that examine Mandarin language history from the perspective of historical changes in sounds, words, and grammar. An overseas Chinese community arguably offers an ideal testing ground for this purpose, since new patterns of diglossia and bilingualism easily evolve as speakers migrate to new environments. If, on the other hand, H versus L divisions remain intact despite migration, as seems to have been the case with Mandarin and Hokkien in the Sangley speech community during the first decades of the seventeenth century, then we can assume that this division depends on social beliefs deeply anchored in the culture of the speakers.

References

Ang Ui-jin 洪惟仁. 2014. "Shiliu, qi shiji zhijian Lüsong de Zhangzhou fangyan" 16、17世紀之間呂宋的漳州方言 [The Zhangzhou dialect of Luzon between the sixteenth and the seventeenth century]. *Lishi dili* 歷史地理 30: 215–38.

Bernal, Rafael. 1966. "The Chinese Colony in Manila, 1570–1770." In *The Chinese in the Philippines 1570–1770*, Vol. 1, edited by Alfonso Felix Jr., 40–66. Manila, Bombay, New York: Solidaridad Publishing House.

Blair, Emma Helen, and James Alexander Robertson [= BR], eds. 1903–1909. *The Philippine Islands, 1493–1898*. 55 vols. Cleveland, OH: The A. H. Clark Company.

Brockey, Liam. 2007. *Journey to the East: The Jesuit Mission to China, 1579–1724*. Cambridge, MA: Belknap Press of Harvard University Press. https://doi.org/10.4159/9780674028814.

Cano, Glòria. 2008. "Blair and Robertson's *The Philippine Islands, 1493–1898*: Scholarship or Imperialist Propaganda?" *Philippine Studies* 56 (1): 3–46.

Chia, Lucille. 2006. "The Butcher, the Baker, and the Carpenter: Chinese Sojourners in the Spanish Philippines and Their Impact on Southern Fujian (Sixteenth–Eighteenth Centuries)." *Journal of the Economic and Social History of the Orient* 49 (4): 509–33. https://doi.org/10.1163/156852006779048435.

Chu, Richard T. 2010. *Chinese and Chinese Mestizos of Manila: Family, Identity, and Culture, 1860s–1930s*. Leiden and Boston: Brill. https://doi.org/10.1163/ej.9789004173392.i-452.

Coblin, W. South. 2000. "A Brief History of Mandarin." *Journal of the American Oriental Society* 120 (4): 537–52. https://doi.org/10.2307/606615.

Coblin, W. South. 2006. *Francisco Varo's Glossary of the Mandarin Language*, 2 vols. Sankt Augustin: Monumenta Serica Institute.

Coblin, W. South. 2009. "Retroflex Initials in the History of Southern Guānhuà Phonology." *Cahiers de linguistique Asie Orientale* 38, no. 19: 125–62. https://doi.org/10.1163/1960602809X00081.

Coblin, W. South. 2010. "The Phonology of Common Yangtze Watershed Mandarin." In *Studies in Honor of Jerry Norman*, edited by W. South Coblin and Anne O. Yue, 157–83. Hong Kong: Institute of Chinese Studies, Chinese University of Hong Kong.

Coblin, W. South. 2017. "Guānhuà 官話, Historical Development." In *Encyclopedia of Chinese Language and Linguistics*, Vol. II, edited by Rint Sybesma et al., 327–33. Leiden and Boston: Brill. https://doi.org/10.1163/2210-7363_ecll_com_00000173.

Coblin, W. South, and Joseph A. Levi. 2000. "Editor's Foreword." In *Francisco Varo's Grammar of the Mandarin Language (1703): An English Translation of* Arte de la lengua Mandarina, ix–xviii. Amsterdam and Philadelphia: John Benjamins.

Conde-Silvestre, J. Camilo, and Juan M. Hernández-Campoy. 2012. "Introduction." In *The Handbook of Historical Sociolinguistics*, edited by Juan M. Hernández-Campoy and

J. Camilo Conde-Silvestre, 1–8. Malden and Oxford: Wiley-Blackwell. https://doi.org/10.1002/9781118257227.ch.
Fasold, Ralph. 1984. *The Sociolinguistics of Society*. Oxford and Cambridge, MA: Blackwell.
Felix, Alfonso. 1966. *The Chinese in the Philippines*, Vol. 1. Manila: Solidaridad Publishing House.
Ferguson, Charles A. 1959. "Diglossia". *Word* 15 (2): 325–40.
Fishman, Joshua A. 1967. "Bilingualism with and without Diglossia; Diglossia with and without Bilingualism." *Journal of Social Issues* 23 (2): 29–38. https://doi.org/10.1111/j.1540-4560.1967.tb00573.x.
Gao Yongan 高永安. 2008. "Míngmò xīfāngrén xuéxí Zhōngwén de lǐniàn hé fāngfǎ tànxī" 明末西方人學習中文的理念和方法探析 [Western concepts and methods of Chinese language learning at the end of the Ming dynasty]. *Yǔyán jiàoxué yǔ yánjiū* 語言教學與研究 2: 9–16.
Gonzalez, Andrew. 1998. "The Language Planning Situation in the Philippines." *Journal of Multilingual and Multicultural Development* 19 (5): 487–525. https://doi.org/10.21832/9781853599224-005.
Hernández-Campoy, Juan M., and Natalie Schilling. 2012. "The Application of the Quantitative Paradigm to Historical Sociolinguistics: Problems with the Generalizability Principle." In *The Handbook of Historical Sociolinguistics*, edited by Juan M. Hernández-Campoy and J. Camilo Conde-Silvestre, 63–79. Malden and Oxford: Wiley-Blackwell. https://doi.org/10.1002/9781118257227.ch4.
Horsley, Margaret Wyant. 1950. "Sangley: The Formation of Anti-Chinese Feeling in the Philippines. A Cultural Study of the Stereotypes of Prejudice." PhD diss., Columbia University.
Klöter, Henning. 2011. *The Language of the Sangleys: A Chinese Vernacular in Missionary Sources of the Seventeenth Century*. Leiden and Boston: Brill. https://doi.org/10.1163/9789004195929.
Kwok, Bit-chee. 2018. *Southern Mǐn: Comparative Phonology and Subgrouping*. London, New York: Routledge. https://doi.org/10.4324/9781315672304.
Labov, William. 1994. *Principles of Linguistic Change*, Vol. 1. Oxford and Cambridge, MA: Blackwell. https://doi.org/10.1002/9781444327496.
Lee, Fabio Yuchung, et al., eds. 2018. *Hokkien Spanish Historical Document*, Series I: *Dictionario Hispanico Sinicum, Arte de la Lengua Chio Chiu*. Hsinchu: National Tsing Hua University Press.
Loon, Piet van der. 1966. "The Manila Incunabula and Early Hokkien Studies (Part 1)." *Asia Major* 12: 1–43.
Loon, Piet van der. 1967. "The Manila Incunabula and Early Hokkien Studies (Part 2)." *Asia Major* 13: 95–186.
Medhurst, Walter Henry. 1832. *A Dictionary of the Hok-këèn Dialect of the Chinese Language, According to the Reading and Colloquial Idioms*. Macao: East India Company.
Menegon, Eugenio. 2009. *Ancestors, Virgins, and Friars: Christianity as a Local Religion in Late Imperial China*. Cambridge: Harvard University Asia Center. https://doi.org/10.2307/j.ctt1dnn8nw.
Peng, Chia Oai. 2013. "Chinese Education in Southeast Asia." In *Routledge Handbook of Chinese Diaspora*, edited by Tan Chee-Beng, 446–58. Oxford and New York: Routledge. https://doi.org/10.4324/9780203100387.ch27.

Platt, John. 1977. "A Model for Polyglossia and Multilingualism (with Special Reference to Singapore and Malaysia)." *Language in Society* 6 (3): 361–78.

Ricci, Matteo. 1615/1953. *China in the Sixteenth Century: The Journals of Matthew Ricci, 1583–1610* [De Christiana expeditione apud Sinas suscepta ab societate Jesu]. Translated by Louis J. Gallagher. New York: Random House.

Skinner, G. William. 2001. "Creolized Chinese Societies in Southeast Asia." In *Sojourners and Settlers: Histories of Southeast China and the Chinese*, edited by Anthony Reid and Kristine Alilunas-Rodgers, 51–93. Honolulu: University of Hawai'i Press.

Weightman, George Henry. 1960. "The Philippine Chinese: A Cultural History of a Marginal Trading Community." PhD diss., Cornell University.

Wickberg, Edgar. 1965. *The Chinese in Philippine Life, 1850–1898*. New Haven: Yale University Press.

Wickberg, Edgar. 1999. "The Philippines." In *Encyclopedia of the Chinese Overseas*, edited by Lynn Pan, 187–99. Cambridge, MA: Harvard University Press.

Wills, John E. 1994. "From Manila to Fuan: Asian Contexts of Dominican Mission Policy." In *The Chinese Rites Controversy: Its History and Meaning*, edited by David E. Mungello, 111–27. Nettetal: Steyler Verlag.

Witek, John W. 2001. "Introduction." In *The Portuguese-Chinese Dictionary of Michele Ruggieri and Matteo Ricci*, edited by John E. Witek, 151–67. Lisbon: Instituto Português do Oriente, National Library of Portugal.

13
Frontier Mandarins and Lán Mào's *Yùnlüè yìtōng* in the Míng*

Richard VanNess Simmons

Introduction

The prestige Mandarin koine known as Guānhuà 官話 is a descendant of the Mandarin dialects of the central plains that were pushed southward in the twelfth century when the Sòng 宋 (960–1279) court vacated the north to escape the Jurchen invasion. The result of this southern migration was that a somewhat evolved version of central plains Mandarin came to be widely spoken in the areas of modern Ānhuī 安徽 and Jiāngsū 江蘇 in the region between the Huái 淮 and Yangtze rivers, the territories from which Zhū Yuánzhāng 朱元璋 (1328–1398) eventually marched forth to expel the Mongol Yuán 元 (1271–1368) dynasty and establish the Míng 明 (1368–1644) dynasty.

Dispersed in large part through the establishment of *jūntún* 軍屯 'military villages' and *wèisuǒ* 衛所 'military garrisons,' the northern Ānhuī–southern Jiāngsū type Mandarin spread into the far reaches of Míng China's southern territories. This Jiāng-Huái Mandarin also gave rise to Southwestern Mandarin when speakers of the former flooded into Yúnnán and surrounding regions in the early years of the Míng. Much of this population movement resulted from the forced migrations instituted during the Hóngwǔ 洪武 (1368–1398) reign.

Witnesses and evidence for Mandarin in the Míng that shed light on the nature of the language that was making its way into the far reaches of the empire include:

- Long-lasting dialect islands descended from Míng times.
- Contemporary descriptions, such as rime books and rime tables compiled in the Míng on the basis of contemporary pronunciation.

---

* Earlier drafts of sections of this chapter were presented at the 225th Meeting of the American Oriental Society in New Orleans, March 13–16, 2015; at the East Asian Studies Seminar in the School of Historical Studies in the Institute for Advanced Studies (IAS) in Princeton on March 30, 2015, where the author was Starr Foundation East Asian Studies Endowment Fund Member in Spring 2015; and at the Workshop on the "History of Colloquial Chinese—Written and Spoken" held at Rutgers University, March 11–12, 2016, that was supported by a generous grant from the Chiang Ching-Kuo (CCK) Foundation. The author is deeply grateful for the support received through the IAS and the CCK Foundation and for the comments and input from colleagues at these various venues.

- Non-Chinese descriptions of Mandarin such as those of Korean scholars and Western missionaries.

Long-lasting dialect islands descended from Míng times include those that developed out of early Míng military settlements. Probably because of the prestige attached to them due to their connection to the broader Mandarin *lingua franca*, the dialects of these islands persisted over the centuries and have been observed and recorded by twentieth-century researchers. Many of the rime books and rime tables that were compiled in the Míng departed sharply from the traditional Middle Chinese *Qièyùn* 切韻 phonology and presented descriptions based on contemporary Míng pronunciation. A particularly early Míng era innovator was Lán Mào 蘭茂 (1397–1476), whose *Yùnlüè yìtōng* 韻畧易通 presents a Míng phonology that itself was probably a southwestern *jūntún* dialect and that has many features found in dialect islands descended from Míng Mandarin.

A highly salient Korean description of early Mandarin essentially contemporaneous with Lán Mào's work is that of Sin Sukcho 申叔舟 (1417–1475), who was a linguist and scholar of Chinese. His work has been extensively studied by Kim Kwangjo (1991) and Coblin (2000a, 2007). Western missionary descriptions do not show up until a century after Lán Mào. The *Xīrú ěrmùzī* 西儒耳目資 'Guide to the eyes and ears of the Western scholar,' by Nicolas Trigault (Chinese name, Jīn Nígé 金尼閣, 1577–1628), is the most thorough Míng era description of Mandarin. Coblin (1997) presents a detailed treatment. The Mandarin described in these sources shares many features with the various types of Mandarin seen in the dialect islands and the *Yùnlüè yìtōng*. Investigating all these diverse types of sources, a picture emerges of the type of Mandarin that was prevalent in the Míng as well as the extent of its reach and some of the changes and developments it went through in the course of its evolution in the fourteenth to sixteenth centuries.

In the present study, we first examine examples of the garrison Mandarin found in dialect islands that originated in the Míng, focusing on some in southeastern China where *jūnhuà* 軍話 'garrison dialect' and *zhènghuà* 正話 'correct speech' are spoken. We then look at the phonology of the Mandarin recorded in the *Yùnlüè yìtōng* in light of what we learn from the dialect islands. This allows us to sketch out the most salient features of the wide-reaching Míng *lingua franca*. At the same time, we are able to illustrate the fuzzy, flexible character of the traditional Guānhuà koine and demonstrate how it was able to achieve a long and venerable life, as well as deep and lasting influence, across China's broad territory even while surrounded by China's innumerable and vastly variant dialects.

Frontier Mandarins

Many of the long-lasting dialect islands descended from Míng times formed on the outer periphery of the empire. These can be characterized as outlying, or frontier Mandarins. They are Mandarin dialects that are found in regions of China outside the normal Mandarin territorial range, or Mandarin dialects that are found in actual border regions, or on the periphery of Chinese territory. These dialects all contain features that are generally considered to be Mandarin. They often are a kind of quasi-creole formed from the mixing of disparate dialects; and in their formation they reflect the vicissitudes of Chinese history and population movement. The characterization "quasi-creole" reflects the fact that these dialects usually originated through the mixing of two or more languages; the new mixed forms subsequently became the primary language of succeeding generations.

Having taken root, evolved, and existed in isolation, frontier Mandarins preserve many of the features of their ancestor dialects. They can thus help us better understand the early history of Mandarin and the development of Guānhuà. They confirm the validity of features that are diagnostic for Mandarin affiliation and shed light on what was considered the prestige form of speech in earlier centuries.

Frontier Mandarins include (1) Mandarin dialect islands in non-Mandarin-speaking regions, (2) whole peripheral regions transformed into Mandarin territory, and (3) a mix of the two: islands within transformed regions.

1. Mandarin dialect islands in non-Mandarin-speaking regions include those found in Guǎngdōng, Fújiàn, Hǎinán, Guǎngxī, Shāndōng, and other places. Many of the Mandarin dialect islands originate in the Míng, some even earlier, and include the dialects known as *jūnhuà* and *zhènghuà*. All have some combination of Mandarin characteristics. There are also many dialect islands that are not Mandarin that share similarities to the Mandarin islands with regard to their historical background and formation. But our investigation here focuses specifically on Mandarin dialect islands.

A dramatic example of a major Mandarin dialect island is the old Hángzhōu dialect that originated in the Southern Sòng (1127–1279). It was formed by the massive influx of northern speakers from Kāifēng and the surrounding Central Plains, when the Sòng court retreated south and established their capital in the city. Subsequently the Hángzhōu dialect served as the principal prestige Mandarin behind the rise and formation of the written vernacular known as Báihuà 白話.

2. Whole peripheral Mandarin regions include the dialects spoken in China's southwest and Dōngběi 東北 Mandarin in the northeast. The Mandarin flood into China's southwest happened primarily in the early Míng following resettlement policies instituted by the founding emperor.[1] The Mandarin takeover of the northeast took place at the end of the Qīng and in the early Republican period.[2]

3. Mandarin islands within transformed regions mix Mandarin islands into larger frontier Mandarin regions. Such a situation is found, for example, in the *zhànhuà* 站

---

1. For extensive discussion of Míng population resettlement, see Cáo Shùjī (1997), esp. pp. 267–320 regarding early Míng population resettlement in the southwest.
2. See Simmons (2016a) for details on the population movement in and out of China's northeast territories in the Míng and the Qīng.

話 'station dialect' islands that formed in the northeast and subsequently were encircled by Dōngběi Mandarin (Simmons 2016a, 61–65).

Considered in terms of their rough dates of formation, in the Sòng we find the formation of the Hángzhōu Mandarin island; in the Míng we find the development of *jūnhuà*, *zhènghuà*, and southwestern Mandarin; and in the Qīng we see the formation of *zhànhuà* and other northeastern migrant Mandarins. Below we look more closely at examples of the frontier Mandarin dialects that formed in the Míng; this provides a rough picture of the geographic range of Mandarin dialects in the dynasty as well as a sense of their shared characteristic features.

Jūnhuà 軍話 and *Zhènghuà* 正話

Jūnhuà-type dialects have been characterized in various ways. Pān Jiāyì 潘家懿 identifies them as "creole type dialects in the south that have Mandarin characteristics" (1998, 1). Qiū Xuéqiáng 丘學強 notes that they are "closely related to the garrison communities in the Míng and preserve the characteristics of the Míng koine" (2005, 154). Huáng Xiǎodōng 黃曉東 agrees that they are "dialect islands that formed in military colonies or garrisons in historical times" (2007, 21). Essentially then, the *jūnhuà* that we examine below are Mandarin creoles, *hùnhé xíng yǔyán* 混合型語言, that took form in military garrison communities: Míng garrison Mandarin creoles that formed out of, or in proximity to, the more widely spoken Guānhuà koine.[3]

Zhènghuà is a variety of *jūnhuà*, as it also arose in *wèisuǒ* 衛所 garrisons established to guard certain territories. The name is derived from the term *zhèngyīn* 正音 'proper pronunciation', as in Zhèngyīn shūguǎn 正音書館 'Mandarin Academies' that were established in the Qīng to train southern exam candidates to speak proper Guānhuà. The Qīng scholar Yú Zhèngxiè 俞正燮 (1775–1840), in his *Guǐsì cúngǎo* 癸巳存稿 [Collected writings in the *guǐsì* year (1833)], tells us that in 1729 the Yōngzhèng 雍正 emperor (r. 1723–1735) called for the establishment of schools to improve the Mandarin of those in Guǎngdōng and Fújiàn who would sit for exams.[4] These Qīng period academies did not last long and were rather unsuccessful. But the effort illustrates that there was some attempt to teach and promulgate a *zhèngyīn* in

---

3. A koine, Chinese *tōngyǔ* 通語, is a supra-regional, vernacular language that forms through contact between two or more varieties or dialects of a language that are related or mutually intelligible. Speakers of a koine use the koine language for communication across a broad region and generally do not abandon their own native vernaculars or dialects. Creoles are more geographically confined and have come to serve as the speakers' native tongue. For further discussion of koines and creoles, see Kerswill (2004); Leonhardt (2013, 26, 45, 50); McWhorter (1998); Siegel (1985); Thomason and Kaufman (1988, 147–66); and Trudgill (1986).
4. "In the sixth year of the Yōngzhèng reign (1729) it was decreed: whereas large numbers of people in Fújiàn and Guǎngdōng are not well versed in Guānhuà, local officals should tutor them; court ministers for a period of eight years are to bar from the examinations any candidates at the ranks of *jǔrén*, *shēngyuán*, *gòngjiān*, and *tóngshēng* who do not know Guānhuà; and in Fújiàn schools to teach correct pronunciation are to be established at locations in all the provincial cities 雍正六年奉：旨以福建、廣東人多不諳官話者，地方官訓導；廷臣議以八年為限，舉人、生員、貢監、童生不諳官話者不准送試；福建省城四門設立正音書館" Yú Zhèngxiè 1833, 9.29b/115.

the south at the time. In reference to southern varieties of Mandarin considered to be *zhèng* 'proper', *zhèngyīn* designated Mandarin dialects that were presumably closer to the prestige Guānhuà koine.

Earlier, in the fourteenth century, Zhū Yuánzhāng 朱元璋 (1328–1398), had driven out the Yuán dynasty Mongolian rulers and founded the Míng dynasty. He set up the empire's capital in Nánjīng in 1368. Nánjīng, and Zhū Yuánzhāng's native village Zhōnglí 鍾離—modern Fèngyáng 鳳陽 in northeastern Ānhuī—lie within territory where the older, southern type of Mandarin had taken root in the Southern Sòng. Zhū Yuánzhāng subsequently set up a military garrison, *wèisuǒ* 衛所, colony system to consolidate and preserve his command over the vast Chinese territory. In this system, 5,600 imperial troops constituted one *wèi* 衛 and 1,120 soldiers constituted a *suǒ* 所. The descendants of the military colonists had hereditary rights to the land and residences. The system lasted from 1369 to 1410. The *wèisuǒ* system thus was most prominent in the period when the Míng capital was Nánjīng, before it was moved to Běijīng in 1421 (Pān Jiāyì 1998).

The *wèisuǒ* garrison communities gave rise to dialects and creoles that evolved within the motley groups recruited as garrison troops, who were probably from a wide variety of regions and dialect backgrounds. But the officials and military leaders must have all adhered to a general understanding of the common Míng koine language: Guānhuà modeled on the Míng era Southern Mandarin prevalent in Nánjīng and Ānhuī as well as the area of southern Jiāngsū and northern Zhèjiāng. In the early period, buoyed by the prestige of association with Zhū Yuánzhāng and the ruling class, the Mandarin of troops speaking varieties of the Ānhuī and southern Jiāngsū dialects must have been dominant.

Many of the *wèisuǒ* garrison dialects developed into quasi-creoles based loosely on the Guānhuà koine but formed from the mixing of disparate northern dialects and the influence of the surrounding vernaculars. The mixing and creolization were fostered over generations as the hereditary garrison inhabitants intermarried with locals (Pān Jiāyì 1998). As the garrisons comprised discrete communities that were surrounded by other local dialects, eventually the languages spoken within them became well-established creoles and the communities formed dialect islands that were essentially Mandarin outposts.

Zhènghuà Mandarin Islands in the Huálóu Villages 華樓村

Chén Yúnlóng (2006) provides a detailed look at a cluster of *zhènghuà* Mandarin dialect islands in Guǎngdōng that originated in the Míng. The dialects that Chén studied are found along the coast of Guǎngdōng in the area of modern Diànbái *xiàn* 電白縣. In Míng times this had been a garrison community known as Shéndiàn *wèi* 神電衛 in Gāozhōu *fǔ* 高州府 that occupied a commanding spot on the Diànbái coastal bay.

Shéndiàn *wèi* was one of 24 *wèisuǒ* 衛所 'garrison outposts' established along the coast in 1394 after Huā Mào 花茂, the Military Commander of Guǎngzhōu, petitioned to set them up to divert bandits into military service (Faure 2007, 71). Huā Mào was from Cháo *xiàn* 巢縣 in the area of modern central Ānhuī 安徽 near Héféi 合肥. That region was near Zhū Yuánzhāng's hometown, and its inhabitants likely spoke a variety of Mandarin that was closely related to the Míng prestige variety. This variety must have also been dominant among Huā Mào's troops as well.

The garrison troops in the settlements established by Huā Mào may have been effective in the beginning. But over the ensuing centuries repeated encroachments by pirates and bandits caused many of the original inhabitants to flee for the hills to the north and northwest to what is now Huálóu *cūn* 華樓村. They took their language with them and it became a nativized, living language in their newly established enclaves (Chén 2006, 1–4).

The Huálóu *cūn* area has a fairly large concentration of the *zhènghuà*-speaking descendants. Chén Yúnlóng settled on the dialects of this village as most representative of the region's *jiùshí zhènghuà* 舊時正話 'old-time *zhènghuà*'. These dialects are surrounded by a variety of southern dialect types: Cantonese or Yuè, known locally as Báihuà 白話, Mǐn, known locally as Líhuà 黎話, and Hakka, known locally as Āihuà 哎話 (Chén 2006, 4–6).

The Huálóu *cūn* dialects have a number of features that set them apart from the other Chinese dialects around them, including a series of Mandarin characteristics that are not shared by the surrounding dialects. Their mix of Mandarin characteristics is an indication that the Huálóu *cūn* dialects must have been derived from Míng era Mandarin vernaculars. For example (here and below drawn from Chén Yúnlóng 2003, 2006):

1. Middle Chinese voiced initials are voiceless, becoming aspirated in *píng* 平 tones and unaspirated in non-*píng* (*zè* 仄) tones: [k'iaŋ²¹³] 強 'strong', [tsʻoi²¹³] 垂 'hang down', [kiɐu⁵⁵] 舊 'old', [ti⁵⁵] 地 'ground'.
2. Initial onset [w] in certain words (reflecting the traditional *wéi* initial category) where southern dialects have a nasal initial [m]: [waŋ³¹] 網 'net', [wɐi³¹] 尾 'tail', [wan³¹] 晚 'late', [wɐn⁵⁵] 問 'ask'.
3. The attributive particle is [ti³³] 的.
4. Initial in the word for 'five' does not have a nasal element: [wu³¹] 五. Compare the word for 'five' in the nearby dialects: Hakka [ŋ³¹], Mǐn [ŋeu³¹], and Cantonese [m²¹].
5. The third-person pronoun ('he/she/him/her') is [tʻa³³] 他 and the plural marker is [mɐn²¹³] 們. The pronoun *tā* 他 is found universally in Mandarin dialects and only found outside Mandarin in a small number of dialects in Dānyáng on the border with Jiāng-Huái Mandarin in Jiāngsū. Compare nearby: Hakka 佢 [kʻi²¹³], Mǐn 伊 [ji³³], and Cantonese 佢 [kʻɵy³⁵].
6. Disposal and passive marker is [pa³¹] 把.

There is also a wide variety of typical Mandarin vocabulary in the Huálóu *zhènghuà* dialects. In the following examples, the *zhènghuà* forms are Mandarin, while the Hakka, Mǐn, and Yuè equivalents are all non-Mandarin (adapted from Chén Yúnlóng 2003, 275):

Pǔtōnghuà	Zhènghuà	Hakka	Mǐn	Yuè
guō 鍋 'pot'	[wo³³]	[wok⁵t'ɐu²¹³]	[tia⁵³t'ɐu²²]	[wok²t'ɐu²]
zhuō 桌 'table'	[tsok²¹³]	[t'ai²¹³]	[tsʻoŋ³¹]	[t'ai¹³]
dōngxi 東西 'thing'	[tuŋ³³si³³]	[ɲia³³]	[mi⁵⁵mi⁵⁵]	[ɲie¹³]
kàn 看 'look'	[k'an⁵⁵]	[t'e³¹]	[k'am²²]	[t'ai¹³]
liǎn 臉 'face'	[len³¹]	[mien⁵³]	[min³³]	[min²²]
shuǎ 耍 'play'	[ɬa³¹]	[liau³¹]	[lam³³]	[liu³¹]
shuì 睡 'sleep'	[soi⁵⁵]	[soi³³]	[k'oi⁵⁵]	[fɐn²¹]
zhàn 站 'to stand'	[tsam⁵⁵]	[k'i³³]	[k'ia³¹]	[k'ei¹³]
gāngcái 剛才 'just now'	[tsiaŋ³³tsiaŋ³³]	[tsiŋ⁵³]	[na⁵⁵]	[ŋam³³]

Evidence of the dialect's mixed or creole nature is found in various non-Mandarin elements seen in Huálóu *cūn zhènghuà*:

1. Final consonant [m] in addition to the usual Mandarin final consonants of [n] and [ŋ] (=ng), as in [nam²¹³] 南 'south', [ɬam³³] 三 'three', and [iɐm³³] 音 'sound'.
2. The final consonants [p], [t], [k] in *rù* 入 tone words, for example in the numbers [pat²¹³] 八 'eight', [sɐp⁵⁵] 十 'ten', and [pɐk⁵⁵] 百 'hundred'.
3. The general negative and the negative imperfective are both [mou³¹] 冇.
4. The interrogative 'what' is [mɐt⁵⁵] 乜.

Non-Mandarin words in this *zhènghuà* dialect are another example of the results of mixing or creolization (adapted from Chén Yúnlóng 2003, 275):

Pǔtōnghuà	Dialect word	Zhènghuà	Hakka	Yuè	Mǐn
shān 山 'mountain'	lǐng 嶺	[liŋ³¹]	[liŋ³³]	[liaŋ⁵⁵]	[ɲia³¹]
mángguǒ 芒果 'mango'	xiāntáo 仙桃	[ɬen³³t'ou²¹³]	[ɬon³³t'o²¹³]	[ɬen⁵⁵t'ou²¹]	[ɬen³³t'o²²]
pǎo 跑 'to run'	zǒu 走	[tsɐu³¹]	[tse³¹]	[tsɐu¹³]	[tsau³¹]
dòng 動 'to move'	[no cognate]	[ɲiuk⁵]	[ɲiuk⁵]	[ɲiuk⁵]	[ɲiuk⁵]
pàng 胖 'fat'	féi 肥	[fɐi²¹³]	[fei²¹³]	[fɐi²¹]	[poi²²]
yào 要 'want to'	ài 愛	[ai⁵⁵]	[o⁵³]	[iu³³] (=要)	[ai²²]
shù 樹 'tree'	mù 木	[muk⁵]	[muk⁵]	[muk⁵]	[tsiu³³] (=樹)

With regard to tones, the Huálóu dialects have five tones and present us with a typical southern Mandarin type tone system:

Tone 1 *Yīnpíng*
Tone 2 *Yángpíng*
Tone 3 *Shǎng*
Tone 4 *Qù*
Tone 5 *Rù*

The tone contours and examples of syllables in each tone category are:

	Píng 平	*Shǎng* 上	*Qù* 去	*Rù* 入
Yīn 陰	33	31	55	(short vowel)
	東 [tuŋ]	懂 [tuŋ] 攏 [luŋ]	凍 [tuŋ]	<u>5</u> 六 [luk]
Yáng 陽	213	(*cìzhuó*)		(long vowel)
	同 [tʻuŋ]	動 [tuŋ]	= 洞 [tuŋ]	213 落 [lok]

The Mandarin characteristics of this set of tones include:

(a) a true *yīn/yáng* register split only in the *píng* tone;
(b) *shǎng* tone syllables with sonorant or resonant (*cìzhuó* 次濁) initials (m, n, ŋ, l), which remain in *shǎng*, but all other *yángshǎng* tone syllables merge with *qù*;
(c) the *rù* tone, which is preserved through the presence of the final consonants p, t, and k.

The two registers of the *rù* are conditioned by the vowel length of the syllable. From the tone contour, we can see that the *rù* tone can be analyzed phonemically as contiguous with *yángpíng* and *qù* tones. The existence of the *rù* tone category is consistent with the southern type Mandarin origin of the dialect. On the other hand, the presence of the final consonants p, t, and k, the contour parallel to non *rù* tones, and the split based on vowel quality are in contrast to the glottal stop ending more generally found in Mandarin dialects that have the *rù* tone. This might be due to the areal influence of Cantonese, where these features are common (as well as Hakka and Mǐn with regard to the final consonants), which would possibly reflect the surrounding dialects' influence on the creolized dialect.

But it also might be a preservation of a feature that was still present in the Mandarin of the early Míng. Evidence for this latter conclusion is seen in the *Yùnlüè yìtōng* 韻畧易通 that we discuss further below. Even considering the vowel conditioned nature of its split *rù* tone with consonental stop endings, the overall picture of the Huálóu tone system is fully consistent with the tonal system southern Mandarin of the Míng period Guānhuà koine, which had a similar set of five tones (Coblin 2000b, 537–43).

Pínghǎi 平海 *Jūnhuà* in Guǎngdōng

Another of the 'garrison outposts' established by Huā Mào in Guǎngdōng was that of Pínghǎi 平海 on the Rěnpíng 稔平 peninsula just east of Hong Kong. As the peninsula had been a thriving haven for pirates and bandits during the transition between the Yuán and the Míng, construction of a walled town at Pínghǎi was begun in 1385. After Huā Mào's 1394 petition, it was officially established as a major garrison: *Pínghǎi shǒuyù qúnmù qiānhù suǒ* 平海守御群牧千戶所 'A thousand household outpost for the protection of the pastureland' (Pān Jiāyì 1998, 43). The troops stationed there were drawn from China's southeastern provinces, and their leaders were all from outside the Guǎngdōng region. The heterogeneous background of the troops and their leaders created a fertile ground for the development of a Mandarin koine-based creole, similar to the situation in Huálóu *cūn*.[5]

Qiū Xuéqiáng 丘學強 (2005, 119–34) provides a detailed examination and demonstration of the Mandarin nature of the resulting Pínghǎi dialect that has survived to the present day as a dialect island, and of its commonalities with Central Plains phonology ("*Zhōngyuán yīn* 中原音"). It closely resembles the Huálóu *cūn* dialects in many ways. For example, it shares some of the same Mandarin characteristics:

1. Middle Chinese voiced initials are voiceless, becoming aspirated in *píng* 平 tones and unaspirated in non-*píng* (*zè* 仄) tones: [k'iaŋ^{13}] 強 'strong', [tʃ'ei^{13}] 搥 'pound on', [kieu^{55}] 舊 'old', [ti^{55}] 地 'ground'.
2. Initial onset [w] in certain words (reflecting the traditional *wéi* initial category) where southern dialects have a nasal initial [m]: [vaŋ^{31}] 網 'net', [vat^{13}] 襪 'sock', [van^{5531}] 萬 'ten-thousand', [vən^{55}] 問 'ask'.
3. Initials in the words for 'five' [vu^{31}] 五 and 'fish' 魚 [ju^{13}] are not nasal.
4. The third-person pronoun ('he/she/him/her') is [t'a^{33}] 他 (though the plural marker is not *men* 們).
5. The simple negative is [bet^{33}] *bù* 不.
6. The word for face is [lin^{31}] *liǎn* 臉.

But note that in the following, Pínghǎi contrasts with Huálóu *cūn*, with variant forms:

1. The interrogative 'what' is [ʃi^{55}mo^{33}] 什麼, not [mɐt^{55}] 乜.
2. Disposal marker is [paŋ^{33}] 幫, not *bǎ* 把.
3. The attributive particle (equivalent to *de* 的) has three different forms: [e^{33}], [te^{33}], and [le^{33}].

---

5. A detailed discussion of the linguistic background for Pínghǎi *jūnhuà* is provided in Qiū Xuéqiáng 丘學強 (2005, 91–118).

In addition, Pínghǎi shares some of the apparently non-Mandarin elements found in Huálóu *cūn zhènghuà*:

1. The final consonant [m], as in [nam¹³] 南 'south', [ʃam³³] 三 'three', and [əm⁵⁵] 音 'sound'.
2. The final consonants [p], [t], [k] in *rù* 入 tone words, for example, in the numbers [pat¹³] 八 'eight', [səp³³] 十 'ten', and [pek³³] 百 'hundred'.
3. The negative imperfective is [mau³¹] 冇.

The Pínghǎi dialect's tones are also close to those of Huálóu *cūn zhènghuà* dialects and, in addition to having similar contours, share the same Mandarin characteristics noted above for Huálóu *cūn*.

	Píng 平	Shǎng 上	Qù 去	Rù 入
Yīn 陰	33	31 (includes cìzhuó)	55	33
Yáng 陽	13			13

The two *rù* tones are also generally in complementary distribution depending on the final and its vowel.

The creole nature of the Pínghǎi *jūnhuà* dialect is seen in the mix of Mandarin and non-Mandarin local features. As with the Huálóu *cūn* dialects, this is most obvious in the dialect's colloquial vocabulary. Some typically Mandarin vocabulary in the dialect includes: *zhàn* 站 'to stand' [tʃan⁵⁵], *kàn* 看 'to look at' [k'an⁵⁵], *chuān* 穿 'to wear [clothing]' [tʃ'yn³³], *béng* 甭 'don't' [negative imperative] [puŋ³⁵]. Some regional non-Mandarin words include: 'to cover' [k'əm¹³] 冚, 'sleep' [k'uən⁵⁵] 睏, 'just now' [ŋam³³ŋam³³] 啱啱, 'table' [t'ai¹³] 檯.

Though Pínghǎi *jūnhuà* and Huálóu *cūn zhènghuà* have many differences, they are still closely comparable and adhere to a common Mandarin type in their overall dimensions. This is remarkable considering that these two dialect islands are separated by more than 500 kilometers. The Mandarin *lingua franca* common to China's far southern territories in Míng times most certainly had commonly accepted characteristics that were highly influential and widely modeled by speakers.

Nánpíng 南平 Mandarin in Fújiàn

A further well-established Mandarin dialect island that formed in the Míng is the Nánpíng 南平 dialect in Fújiàn, which was studied by Chung-yu Chen Chow [Chén Chóngyú 陳重瑜] (Chow 1974; Chen 1981). This dialect arose in the wake of a tenant uprising known as the Dèng Màoqī 鄧茂七 Rebellion in the mid-fifteenth century. Centered in Shāxiàn 沙縣 in Yánpíng *fǔ* 延平府 in a region west of Fúzhōu, and instigated in 1448 by Dèng Màoqī, the rebellion involved four prefectures and upwards of 20 counties, and ultimately required 50,000 troops and several expeditions over the course of a year to suppress.[6]

According to the *Míng shílù* 明實錄, those sent to suppress the rebellion were military garrisons under direct imperial control—*zhílì wèisuǒ* 直隸衛所—from Shāndōng, Hénán, and "Jiāngběi" (northern Jiāngsū).[7] At the time, these *zhílì wèisuǒ* troops were stationed or located primarily in what is now modern Jiāngsū, north of the Yangtze, though such garrisons could have been stationed in Hénán and Shāndōng as well. The imperial capital had only moved north to Běijīng in 1421, just a quarter century earlier. So there was still a substantial imperial presence in the Jiāngběi region. The troops would all have been speakers of various varieties of Mandarin. A large contingent of these troops remained stationed in Nánpíng following the rebellion. The result of their commingling is the Nánpíng dialect spoken by the descendants of these troops.

Chung-yu Chen's analysis concluded that Nánpíng is most likely a Jiāng-Huái type southern Mandarin. It has a *rù* tone with a glottal stop [ʔ] ending, just like the modern Jiāng-Huái dialects. It thus has the same system of five tones that was standard for Guānhuà in the Míng: (1) *yīnpíng* 陰平, (2) *yángpíng* 陽平, (3) *shǎng* 上, (4) *qù* 去, (5) *rù* 入:

	Píng 平	*Shǎng* 上	*Qù* 去	*Rù* 入
Yīn 陰	33	24 (includes *cìzhuó*)	35	3
Yáng 陽	11			

Note that just as we saw in Pínghǎi *jūnhuà* and Huálóu *cūn zhènghuà*, in Nánpíng *shǎng* tone syllables with sonorant or resonant (*cìzhuó* 次濁) initials (m, n, ŋ, l) remain in *shǎng*, but all other *yángshǎng* tone syllables merge with *qù*. Some examples are: *lǎo* 'old' 老 [lau³], *mǐ* 'rice' 米 [mi³], *nǔ* 'female' 女 [nü³], *mǎ* 'horse' 馬 [ma³].

Phonological characteristics of Nánpíng Mandarin include (with examples from Chow 1974; Chen 1981):

1. Middle Chinese voiced initials are voiceless, becoming aspirated in *píng* tones and unaspirated in *zè* tones.
2. Initials [n] and [l] are in free variation, similar to the Nánjīng dialect.

---

6. Troop numbers are cited in Chung-yu Chen (1981) and Brook (1998, 84). Also see Tong (1991, 185) and Lú Zēngfū (2010).
7. "The military and officials in the campaign that entered Fújiàn were mostly from Imperial Garrisons in Shāndōng, Hénán, and north of the Yangtze who had done training rounds at the capital 福建征進官軍多系山東、河南、及江北直隸衛所，赴京輪操之數。" *Míng shílù: Míng Yīngzōng ruì huángdì shílù* 明英宗睿皇帝實錄 [Veritable record of the reign of the farsighted Yīngzōng emperor (Zhū Qízhèn 朱祁鎮, r. 1427–1464)]. *Juàn* 卷 173.2a/vol. 29: 3324.

3. Syllable initials corresponding to the traditional *rì* 日 and *wéi* 微 initials are non-nasal, usually zero initial. Examples include: 'person' *rén* 人 [iŋ²], 'sun' *rìtou* 日頭 [i²təu²], 'two' *èr* 二 [e⁴], 'ear' *ěrduo* 耳朵 [e²to³], 'hot' *rè* 熱 [ie²⁵], 'kiss' *wěn* 吻 [uəŋ³], 'late' *wǎn* 晚 [uaŋ³], 'ask' *wèn* 問 [uəŋ4].
4. The words for 'five' *wǔ* 五 [u³] and 'fish' *yú* 魚 [ü²] have non-nasal initials.
5. A set of syllables belonging to the traditional *jiàn* 見 initial in the *kāikǒu* 開口 'open mouth', *èrděng* 二等 'second division' group—the so-called *jiàn-kāi-èr* 見開二 set—have medial -i- (which is not seen in non-Mandarin dialects), for example, 'river' *jiāng* 江 [kiaŋ¹], 'room' *fángjiān* 房間 [x⁽ᵘ⁾aŋ²kieŋ¹], 'say, talk' *jiǎng* 講 [kiaŋ³], 'descend' *jiàng* 降 [kiaŋ⁴], 'pleat' *jiǎn* 襇 [kieŋ³], 'simple' *jiǎn* 簡 [kieŋ³].
6. Velar initials corresponding to the initials in the larger traditional *jiànzǔ* 見組 initial set are not palatalized before high front vowels (such as the vowel 'i'), nor are dental sibilant initials corresponding to the traditional *jīngzǔ* 精組 set. Hence, we find the contrast seen between the following syllables:

Modern standard Mandarin			Nánpíng velars	in contrast to			Nánpíng dental sibilants
jiǔ	'nine'	九	[kiu³]		'wine'	酒	[tsiu³]
qì	'sob'	泣	[k'i²⁵]		'seven'	七	[ts'i²⁵]
jiāo	'to water'	澆	[kiau¹]		'pepper'	椒	[tsiau¹]
jìn	'near'	近	[kiŋ⁴]		'clean'	淨	[tsiŋ⁴]
xiàng	'toward'	向	[xiaŋ⁴]		'resemble'	像	[siaŋ⁴]
jiāng	'river'	江	[kiaŋ¹]		'starch'	漿	[tsiaŋ¹]

The contrast listed under item number 6 above is a precursor to the so-called *jiān-tuán* 尖團 'sharp–round' distinction that developed as an intermediate stage in other Mandarin dialects wherein the velars palatalized before high front vowels (k becoming tɕ, k' becoming tɕ', and x becoming ɕ) while the sibilants remained unpalatalized. The distinction disappeared altogether when the sibilants later also palatalized before high front vowels (ts becoming tɕ, ts' becoming tɕ', and s becoming ɕ), as illustrated by the modern standard Mandarin in which the contrast is not seen.

Distinguishing lexical characteristics of Nánpíng Mandarin include (Chung-yu Chen 1981, 186):

1. The third person pronoun is *tā* 他 [t'a¹].
2. The personal plural marker is *men* 們 [məŋ²].
3. The simple negative is *bù* 不 [pu²].
4. The demonstrative is *zhè* 這 [tsi⁴].
5. The attributive particle is *de* 的 [ti²].
6. Disposal marker is *bǎ* 把 [pa³].

7. The word for 'face' is *liǎn* 臉 [lien³].

Items 1, 3, and 5 are especially useful identifiers. Jerry Norman characterized the Mandarin dialects as "the *tā, bù, de* 他、不、的 dialects" highlighting these three lexical items diagnostic power.⁸ The Nánpíng dialect fits such a characterization quite well.

The dialect also evidences creolization, in ways similar to what we saw above for the Huálóu *zhènghuà* dialects. Examples of words in Nánpíng that are more typical of the surrounding Mǐn 閩 dialects and other southern dialects than of Mandarin, and thus must have become mixed into the dialect over the years, include:

Mandarin		Meaning	Nánpíng	
jīntiān	今天	'today'	[kiŋ¹tsiau¹]	今朝
mǔzhū	母豬	'sow'	[tsü¹p'o²]	豬婆
gōngjī	公雞	'rooster'	[ki¹koŋ¹]	雞公
xiǎojī	小雞	'chick'	[ki¹tsai³]	雞仔
zǎoshàng	早上	'morning'	[ts'au³k'i³]	早起
wénzi	蚊子	'mosquito'	[moŋ³tsi]	蠓子
yòuzi	柚子	'pomelo'	[p'au¹p'au¹]	棓棓
kāishuǐ	開水	'boiled water'	[kuəŋ³t'aŋ¹]	滾湯
máobǐ	毛筆	'writing brush'	[sui³pi²]	水筆
xiàmiàn	下面	'underside'	[xa⁴ti³]	下底
duōshǎo	多少	'how much'	[ki³to¹]	幾多

The Jīnxiāng 金鄉 dialect in Zhèjiāng

Farther north and originating half a century earlier we find the Jīnxiāng 金鄉 dialect in Zhèjiāng. Jīnxiāng was a Míng costal fort (*wèichéng* 衛城) that was established in the 1380s by Tāng Hé 湯和 (1326–1395) to guard the coast against Japanese pirates. Tāng Hé was a close associate and principal lieutenant of Zhū Yuánzhāng, with whom he shared his native village, Fèngyáng. In 1384 he was dispatched to tour Fújiàn and Zhèjiāng to inspect and improve military defenses (Goodrich 1976, II.1248–1251). Táng Hé ultimately established the *wèichéng* at Jīnxiāng. The dialect of Jīnxiāng is the vernacular spoken by the descendants of the imperial troops stationed there, who came primarily from northern Zhèjiāng and the Jiāng-Huái region of Jiāngsū and Ānhuī (Wēn Duānzhèng 1991, 28). On the basis of its origin, it can be classified as a type of *jūnhuà*.

The Jīnxiāng dialect is similar in many ways to the Old Hángzhōu dialect (formed more than 200 years prior) in its phonology and vocabulary, which contrasts

---
8. Personal communication.

with surrounding dialects in many ways. Representative Mandarin words in the dialect, and shared with Old Hángzhōu, include:

1. The third-person pronoun is *tā* 他 [tʻa⁵⁵] (not the pronoun *yī* 伊 seen in nearby Wú 吳 dialects); the suffix for the plural is -*men* 們 [mʌŋ].
2. The plain negative is *bù* 不 [poʔ⁵⁴] (not a word with a nasal labial or dentilabial initial as seen in the nearby dialects).
3. The attributive particle is *de* 的 [ti⁴²] (not a particle with a velar initial as seen in the surrounding dialects).
4. *liǎn* 臉 [li³] 'face' (not *miàn* 面 as seen in Wú dialects)
5. *wén* 聞 [vʌŋ²] 'smell' (not *xiù* 嗅 as seen in Wú dialects)
6. *wà* 襪 [vəʔ⁸] 'sock' (not [məʔ⁸] with a nasal initial as seen in Wú dialects)
7. *rè* 熱 [zyøʔ⁸] 'hot' (not [ɲieʔ⁸] with a nasal intial as seen in Wú dialects)
8. *yǎo* 咬 [iɔ³] 'bite' (not [ŋɔ³] with a nasal initial as seen in Wú dialects)
9. *érzi* 兒子 [l²tsɿ⁰] 'son' (not [ŋ²] or other words seen in Wú dialects)
10. *lěng* [lʌŋ⁴⁵] 'cold' (main vowel is not [a], as in [lã³] seen in the Wú dialects)

Jīnxiāng tones also match the Old Hángzhōu pattern:

	Píng 平	*Shǎng* 上	*Qù* 去	*Rù* 入
Yīn 陰	55	45 (includes *cìzhuó*)	42	<u>54</u>
Yáng 陽	33		212	<u>21</u>

The Old Hángzhōu tonal paradigm is descended from the Kāifēng dialect that migrated to the city in the Southern Sòng. Jīnxiāng closely matches Hángzhōu in that syllables with sonorant *cìzhuó* initials are in the upper *shǎng* tone, which is evidence of a Mandarin origin or Mandarin influence. The prestige of the Hángzhōu dialect, in combination with the influence of the surrounding Wú dialects, is the likely cause of Jīnxiāng's preservation of a seven-tone system.

In sum, we can identify the following characteristic Mandarin phonological features in Jīnxiāng:

1. Syllables reflecting the traditional *rì* and *wéi* initial categories do not have nasal initials. Other examples include *ròu* 'meat' 肉 [zyøʔ²¹], *ruǎn* 'soft' 軟 [ɕyø⁴⁵], and *rén* 'person' 人 [zyoŋ³³] with initial *rì*, and *wèn* 'ask' 問 [vʌŋ²¹²] with initial *wéi*.
2. Words in the *rù* tone (such as 'sock' and 'hot' cited above) end in a glottal stop. This is evidence that the dialect belonged to the southern Mandarin type.
3. The *jiàn-kāi-èr* set of syllables have medial -i-: *jiān* 'room' 間 [tɕi⁵⁵], *jiǎn* 'decrease' 減 [tɕi⁴⁵], *jiǎng* 'to talk' 講 [tɕiã⁴⁵], *gǎng* 'harbor' 港 [tɕiã⁴⁵].

4. Syllables with sonorant, *cìzhuó* initials in the *shǎng* tone include: *mǎ* 'horse' 馬 [ma⁴⁵], *nǚ* 'female' 女 [ny⁴⁵], *mǎi* 'buy' 買 [mɛ⁴⁵], *lǎo* 'old' 老 [lɔ⁴⁵], *mǎn* 'full' 滿 [mø⁴⁵].
5. The words for 'five' *wǔ* 五 [vu⁴⁵] and 'fish' *yú* 魚 [fiy³³] have non-nasal initials.
6. The attributive particle is *de* 的 [ti⁴²].
7. Mandarin words generally not seen in surrounding dialects include *fángzi* 房子 'house' [vã³³⁻²¹tsʅ⁵⁵], *fángjiān* 房間 'room' [vã³³⁻²¹tɕi⁵⁵], *érzi* 兒子 'son' [ʅ³³⁻²¹tsʅ⁵⁵], *liǎn* 臉 'face' [li⁴⁵], *kāishuǐ* 開水 'boiled water' [k'ɛ⁵⁵sai⁴⁵], *dàn* 蛋 'egg' [dɛ²¹²], *gōngjī* 公雞 'rooster' [koŋ⁵⁵tsʅ⁵⁵], *dōngxi* 東西 'thing' [toŋ⁵⁵sʅ⁵⁵].

The creole nature of the Jīnxiāng dialect, as a form of *jūnhuà*, is illustrated by various non-Mandarin words that it shares with surrounding dialects, including 'mother' [m̥⁵⁵mə⁵⁴] 姆媽, 'left hand' [tɔ³¹pa⁴⁵ɕiu⁰] 倒把手, 'right hand' [zioŋ²¹²⁻²¹pa⁴⁵ɕiu⁰] 順把手, 'clothing' [i⁵⁵ɲiã⁰] 衣[裳], 'chopsticks' [dʑy²¹²] 箸, 'mosquito' [mʌn³³⁻²¹dʑyoŋ³³] 蠓蟲, 'sleep' [k'uʌŋ⁴²] 睏, and 'corner, horn' [kəʔ⁵⁴] 角.

This concludes our look at frontier Mandarin dialect islands descended from Míng times. The following table summarizes the Southern Mandarin features that are shared by most or more than one of the dialects we looked at and the correspondence of each dialect to those features. Note that the first five features listed are phonological features, while the latter five are lexical features:

Feature	Huálóu *cūn zhènghua*	Pínghǎi *jūnhuà*	Nánpíng	Jīnxiāng
1. Has a *rù* tone	✓	✓	✓	✓
2. *Píng* tone has two registers (but not *shǎng* and *qù*)	✓	✓	✓	X
3. *Rì* and/or *wéi* initials are non-nasal	*wéi*	*wéi*	*rì, wéi*	*rì, wéi*
4. Words with sonorant initials remain in the *shǎng* tone	✓	✓	✓	✓
5. *Jiàn-kāi-èr* syllables have medial -i-	X	X	✓	✓
6. The 3rd-person pronoun is *tā* 他	✓	✓	✓	✓
7. Has the Mandarin negative *bù* 不	X	✓	✓	✓
8. The attributive particle is *de* 的	✓	(✓ partial)	✓	✓
9. The Mandarin word for 'five' 五 has no nasal element	✓	✓	✓	✓
10. Has other diagnostic Mandarin words: 'face' 臉, 'stand' 站	臉, 站	臉, 站	臉, (站?)	臉, (站?)

Next, we examine a record of Guānhuà by a Míng scholar that is descriptive of his contemporary dialect and that shares many distinctive features with the previously noted Mandarin dialect islands.

Míng Phonology and Innovation

Míng records of Guānhuà stand at the vanguard of innovations in linguistic description that brought traditional Chinese phonological tools to the portrayal of contemporary pronunciation. Stimulated by innovations seen in the Yuán (1271–1368) northern Mandarin rime book *Zhōngyuán yīnyùn* 中原音韻 (completed 1324) by Zhōu Déqīng 周德清 (1277–1365), the Míng was a time of burgeoning inventiveness in phonology. A great number of original ideas were brought to the rime book and rime table tradition, and many began to incorporate elements of the compilers' contemporary dialects.

Where they depart from the *Qièyùn* 切韻 tradition, Míng rime tables often incorporate elements from contemporary dialects. But where they parallel the tradition we need to consider whether (1) they are simply following tradition even though their underlying dialect is different, or (2) their contemporary colloquial naturally matches the traditional model. If their compilers are willing to depart from tradition in innovating, it seems that the second of these possibilities is the most likely. But the compilers may still follow tradition in areas where they do not necessarily perceive a change that has actually taken place. Though this state of affairs often leaves them as less than ideal witnesses to earlier forms of Chinese, there is still much that we can learn from the Míng rime tables.

Lán Mào's *Yùnlüè yìtōng*

The Míng scholar Lán Mào 蘭茂 (1397–1476, *zì* 字 Tíngxiù 廷秀) was born at the end of the Hóngwǔ reign in Sōngmíng 嵩明, Yúnnán 雲南, to a family that had migrated from Luòyáng 洛陽 in Hénán 河南, likely as members of a military garrison *wèisuǒ* group living in a *jūntún*. An authority on Chinese medicine and author of a compendium on the curative herbs of Yúnnán and Hénán, Lán Mào was a polymath who also compiled the first southern Guānhuà rime book, the *Yùnlüè yìtōng* 韻畧易通 'Intelligible sketch of rimes' (Gěng Zhènshēng 1992, 16, 197). His connection to both central and southwestern China at this formative period in the history of Mandarin means that the language reflected in his rime book was informed by the colloquial linguistic conventions that prevailed at the time. As such it contains many clues to the nature of the Guānhuà that became the *lingua franca* of the Míng empire.

Completed in 1442, *Yùnlüè yìtōng* was among the earliest of the innovative Míng rime books. The phonology of the volume is reflective of the actual speech of the author's time and community, containing both innovations and conservative features. Lán Mào has essentially the same set of rimes as the *Zhōngyuán yīnyùn*, but with the addition of the rime labeled *jū-yú* 居魚, making 20 rimes altogether.

The following chart lists the rimes of *Yùnlüè yìtōng*, numbered, named, and ordered following Lán Mào's own scheme. Beside the rimes, we list his finals as determined by medial and final consonant distinctions. Phonemic renderings of each final are determined by reference to modern dialects in order to reflect the salient phonemic and phonetic distinctions embodied in the *Yùnlüè yìtōng* phonology. The values for the initials and finals are thus derived through a kind of triangulation process, which we designate with a small triangle '▿'.[9]

Main vowel and/or medial: Corresponding modern *hū* 呼: Tone (if not *píng/shǎng/qù*):	▿a/ ▿e/ ▿o *kāikǒu* 開口 *rù*	▿i *qíchǐ* 齊齒 *rù*	▿u *hékǒu* 合口 *rù*	▿y *cuōkǒu* 撮口 *rù*
1. *dōng-hóng* 東洪	▿oŋ	▿ok	▿ioŋ ▿iok		
2. *jiāng-yáng* 江陽	▿aŋ	▿ak	▿iaŋ ▿iak	▿uaŋ ▿uak	
3. *zhēn-wén* 真文	▿en	▿et	▿in ▿it	▿uen ▿uet	▿yen ▿yet
4. *shān-hán* 山寒	▿an	▿at	▿ian ▿iat	▿uan ▿uat	
5. *duān-huán* 端桓				▿uon ▿uot	
6. *xiān-quán* 先全			▿iæn ▿iæt		▿yæn ▿yæt
7. *gēng-qíng* 庚晴	▿eŋ	▿ek	▿iŋ ▿ik	▿ueŋ ▿uek	▿yeŋ ▿yek
8. *qīn-xún* 侵尋	▿em	▿ep	▿im ▿ip		
9. *jiān-xián* 緘咸	▿am	▿ap	▿iam ▿iap		
10. *lián-xiān* 廉纖			▿iæm ▿iæp		
11. *zhī-cí* 支辭	▿ï				
12. *xī-wēi* 西微	▿ei		▿i	▿uei	
13. *jū-yú* 居魚					▿y
14. *hū-mó* 呼模				▿u	
15. *jiē-lái* 皆來	▿ai		▿iai	▿uai	
16. *xiāo-háo* 蕭豪	▿au		▿iau		
17. *gē-hé* 戈何	▿o			▿uo	
18. *jiā-má* 家麻	▿a			▿ua	
19. *zhē-shé* 遮蛇			▿iæ		
20. *yōu-lóu* 幽樓	▿eu		▿ieu		

Lán Mào's most striking innovation was his explicit identification and naming of each initial category in his phonology.[10] He composed a short four-line poem, of

---

9. They are not reconstructions of proto-forms, as they are not derived strictly by the comparative method. Also see Zhāng Yùlái (1999) for an in-depth treatement of the phonology of *Yùnlüè yìtōng*.
10. Zhào Yìntáng noted that Lán Mào went beyond the *Zhōngyuán yīnyùn* and was the first to clearly and unambiguously reassign the voiced set of initials ("*zhuóshēng* 濁聲") of the traditional *Qièyùn* based phonology to the voiceless initial categories that they corresponded to in Mandarin and thus "truly laid the foundation for a new phonology of Mandarin 實奠北音新等韻之基" (1957, 209–10).

five syllables per line, in which each syllable represents an initial. Using our rendering of Lán Mào's phonology, the poem is as follows:[11]

Dōng fōng pò zǎu méi.   東風破早梅。   The east wind falters by early-blooming plums.
Hiàng nuǒn yit zhī kāi.   向暖一支開。   Turned toward warmth, a single blossom.
Bīng syaet vú rén giàn,   冰雪無人見,   Icy snow out of sight to all,
Chuēn cóng tiāen shàng lái.   春從天上來。   Spring settles in from the heavens.

As can be seen, there are a total of 20 initials in his system:

Phonemic rendering	Following Pīnyīn
ᵛp, ᵛp', ᵛm, ᵛf, ᵛv	*b, p, m, f, v*
ᵛt, ᵛt', ᵛn, ᵛl	*d, t, n, l*
ᵛts, ᵛts', ᵛs	*z, c, s*
ᵛtẓ, ᵛtẓ', ᵛṣ, ᵛr	*zh, ch, sh, r*
ᵛk, ᵛk', ᵛh, ᵛØ	*g, k, h, Ø/y/w*

This set of initials exactly matches the *Zhōngyuán yīnyùn* and is the most common for Mandarin prior to the palatalization of the velars *g, k,* and *h* before high front vowels. That palatalization did not happen until the mid- to late Qīng and was eventually followed by palatalization of *z, c,* and *s* (ts, ts', s) in the same environment. In terms of initials, then, the phonology that Lán Mào outlines is definitely Mandarin.

Yùnlüè yìtōng phonology has the usual southern Mandarin set of 5 tones: *yīnpíng, yángpíng, shǎng, qù,* and *rù*. Lán Mào indicates tone by separating *xiǎoyùn* 小韻 'homophone groups' with small circles—*niǔ* 紐—in which he writes name of the tone for each group, *píng* 平, *shǎng* 上, *qù* 去, and *rù* 入. In rimes that have both *yīnpíng* and *yángpíng*, the *niǔ* for the lower *píng* tone is an empty circle. (This was a novel use of the *niǔ* mark that had conventionally separated initial categories.)

Exploring the innovations found in the *Yùnlüè yìtōng*, we find the following similarities with the *Zhōngyuán yīnyùn*, from which Lán Mào must have taken inspiration:

1. The *Yùnlüè yìtōng* has no voiced obstruent initials.
2. *Píng* tone syllables in the *Yùnlüè yìtōng* that reflect *Qièyùn* voiced obstruents are listed with the aspirates.
3. Lán Mào includes initial categories corresponding to the traditional *rì* and *wéi* initials: *rì* initial is reflected by ᵛr and *wéi* is reflected by ᵛØ (zero) and ᵛv.
4. Lán Mào treats medials ᵛi, ᵛu, ᵛy as a subcategories under the initials, starting a new set of *niǔ* 紐 for the tones when the medial changes. The

---

[11]. In this transcription ᵛŋ is written *ng*, and initials and tones follow the conventions of Hànyǔ *pīnyīn* 漢語拼音, but with the *rù* tone indicated by final consonants -*p*, -*t*, and -*k* and not a diacritic.

Zhōngyuán yīnyùn also keeps syllables with contrasting medials under different *xiǎoyùn*; but the *Yùnlüè yìtōng* is much clearer and more systematic about the grouping (see below).

There are also other, additional innovations in the *Yùnlüè yìtōng* that are not seen in the *Zhōngyuán yīnyùn*, including:

1. The *Yùnlüè yìtōng* explicitly lists all the initials and gives specific names to each.
2. The *Yùnlüè yìtōng* is organized by final first, as is *Zhōngyuán yīnyùn*, but then by initial within final categories—with headings for each initial, then by medial, and then by tone, whereas *Zhōngyuán yīnyùn* sorts by tone within final categories and then by initial, which includes medial distinctions. Hence in Lán Mào's system the initials are far more prominent.
3. In its names for the rimes, the *Yùnlüè yìtōng* consistently uses one *yīnpíng* syllable and one *yángpíng* syllable.
4. Within rimes, the *Yùnlüè yìtōng* clearly sorts *xiǎoyùn* homophone groups into four categories depending on the medial: Lán Mào has different groups for syllables with no medial, and those with medial ˅i, medial ˅u, and with medial ˅y. These four categories correspond to what is now called the *sì-hū* 四呼, though that phonological conceptualization had not yet been explicitly named.[12]

Lán Mào's *Yùnlüè yìtōng* also contains some apparently conservative features as compared to *Zhōngyuán yīnyùn:*

1. The *Yùnlüè yìtōng* treats the *rù* tone as regular tone and not as an optional or alternate tone or one that has merged into one of the other three tones.
2. The *rù* tone syllables in *Yùnlüè yìtōng* have ˅-p, ˅-t, ˅-k endings.

Aside from these differences in tone and consonant endings in the finals, the phonology of the *Yùnlüè yìtōng* parallels that of the *Zhōngyuán yīnyùn*, including the presence of the final nasal ˅-m.

In overall perspective, the phonology of the *Yùnlüè yìtōng* evidences all of the Mandarin phonological features we found to be shared by the four frontier Mandarin dialects discussed earlier:[13]

---

12. See Simmons (2016b) regarding the evolution of the *sìhū* and their reflection in *Yùnlüè yìtōng*.
13. The nature and content of the *Yùnlüè yìtōng* do not allow us to determine whether or not Lán Mào's dialect also evidenced the lexical features it might have shared with the four frontier Mandarins.

Feature	Lán Mào's *Yùnlüè yìtōng*	Huálóu *cūn zhènghuà*	Pínghǎi *jūnhuà*	Nánpíng	Jīnxiāng
1. Has a *rù* tone	✓	✓	✓	✓	✓
2. *Píng* tone has two registers, but *shǎng* & *qù* do not	✓	✓	✓	✓	X
3. *Rì* and/or *wéi* initials are non-nasal	rì, wéi	wéi	wéi	rì, wéi	rì, wéi
4. Words with sonorant initials remain in *shǎng* tone	✓	✓	✓	✓	✓
5. *Jiàn-kāi-èr* syllables have medial -i-	✓	X	X	✓	✓

Examples

3. *Rì* initial: *rén* 'person' 人 ▿ ʐen², *rè* 熱 'hot' ▿ ʐiæt; *wéi* initial: *wén* 'mosquito' 蚊 ▿ ven², *wǎn* 'late' 晚 ▿ van³.
4. Syllables with sonorant initials in the *shǎng* tone: *lěng* 'cold' 冷 ▿ leŋ³, *mǐ* 'raw rice' 米 ▿ mi³, *niǎo* 'bird' 鳥 ▿ niau³, *wǎn* 'late' 晚 ▿ van³.
5. *Jiàn-kāi-èr* syllables with medial -i-: *jiān* 'room' 間 ▿ kian¹, *jiàn* 'to see' 見 ▿ kian⁴, *jiāng* 'river' 江 ▿ kiaŋ¹, *jiǎng* 'to talk' 講 ▿ kiaŋ³, *gǎng* 'harbor' 港 ▿ kiaŋ³.

So from a purely phonological perspective, *Yùnlüè yìtōng* adheres to the same Míng southern Mandarin type preserved in the four dialect islands we discussed earlier. Below we take a closer look at the nature and details of the Míng Mandarin underlying the *Yùnlüè yìtōng*.

What *Yùnlüè yìtōng* reveals about early Míng southern Mandarin

The inclusion of ▿-p, ▿-t, ▿-k, and ▿-m endings in Lán Mào's *Yùnlüè yìtōng* is something of a conundrum. In the Yuán period, though the northern Mandarin reflected in the *Zhōngyuán yīnyùn* still maintained final -m, it had already lost the *rù* tone and final consonants -p, -t, and -k. By the late Míng, the final -m is seen to have been lost in the southern-type Mandarin recorded by Nicolas Trigault in his *Xīrú ěrmùzī*; and though the *rù* tone remained in the *Xīrú ěrmùzī* phonology, the three final consonants had merged into a single glottal-stop ending, -ʔ (Coblin 1997). It is thus unclear whether Lán Mào is simply following older *Qièyùn*-based tradition in preserving these features in his phonology, even though his own speech may have been different, or whether his contemporary southwestern colloquial actually did reflect a tripartite distinction in *rù* tone syllable endings parallel to -p, -t, -k and the nasal endings with the final -m. The general consensus of modern scholars is toward the former interpretation. For example, Nìng Jìfú 甯忌浮 insists that Lán Mào was just following tradition in his rendering of the *rù* tone finals (2009, 188).

Korean descriptions of Mandarin from the early Míng period reflect the final -m in the more conservative *zhèngyīn* 正音 'standard readings' recorded by Sin Sukchu in his *Sasông t'onggo* 四聲通考 'Thorough examination of the four tones' (completed ca. 1450). But it is merged with final -n in the more colloquial *súyīn* 俗音 'popular readings' Sin records. Sin Sukchu makes clear that the finals -p, -t, and -k had been lost in the *zhèngyīn* and had merged together as a glottal stop -ʔ, even though they were distinct in the imperially commissioned *Hóngwǔ zhèngyùn* 洪武正韻 'Standard rimes of the Hóngwǔ reign' completed in 1374 in Nánjīng. Yet this could be because Sin Sukchu is describing the pronunciation of *northern* varieties of Chinese (Kim Kwangjo 1991, 81; Coblin 2000a). Hence, it is not impossible that the early Míng *southern* Mandarin of Lán Mào's time did in fact preserve these final consonants and that they were only slowly lost later.

Reconstructions of proto-Mandarin phonologies by Baxter (2006) and Akitani (2017) both variously point to one or more of these final consonants in earlier forms of Mandarin. Baxter includes final *-t and *-k, with *-p seen to have merged with *-t, in his alternative Proto-Macro-Mandarin (PMM2). He explains that this makes for a simpler reconstruction, especially with regard to the vowels (2006, 16–18). Akitani postulates a final -m in the proto-Fénhé 汾河 that he reconstructs for a set of dialects at the boundary between Shǎanxī 陝西 and southwestern Shānxī 山西. In this respect, proto-Fénhé is similar to both the *Zhōngyuán yīnyùn* and *Yùnlüè yìtōng*. Akitani's proto-Fénhé also has a *rù* tone (with *yīn* and *yáng* registers), but ending in a glottal stop, and not in the consonants -p, -t, and -k.

We saw that the Huálóu *cūn zhènghuà* and Pínghǎi *jūnhuà* dialects also have a *rù* tone with syllables ending in -p, -t, and -k, as well as a final -m in addition to finals -n and -ŋ in non-*rù* syllables with consonant endings. *Yùnlüè yìtōng* matches the Huálóu *cūn* and Pínghǎi dialects quite exactly in this set of features. It has been assumed that the Huálóu *cūn* dialects were influenced by the surrounding Yuè, Hakka, and Mǐn dialects in having these final consonants and that they must have developed in the Huáluó *zhènghuà* due to outside influence (Chén Yúnlóng 2005, 63). But in such a case the strict regularity of the correspondence would have been undone by imperfect borrowing, or overdone by hyper-compensation, and a remnant glottal stop would have lingered in some syllables. Also, it is unlikely that the correct ending would have been preserved in forms that were not colloquial in non-Mandarin dialects. For example, we saw that the word for 'table' in Huálóu *cūn* is the Mandarin *zhuō* 桌 [tsok²¹³], but is another word in the other dialects, as the Cantonese *tái* 檯 [tʻai¹³]. It is unlikely that the colloquial of Huálóu *cūn* could have restored a final -k (the regular reflex, as in CDC *ciok⁷) on this syllable if it had originally been a glottal stop -ʔ.[14]

There is no glottal stop ending in Huálóu *cūn* or Pínghǎi *rù* tone syllables, which maintain -p, -t, -k endings as regularly as the *Yùnlüè yìtōng*. If we consider that Huálóu *cūn* and Pínghǎi Mandarin established themselves in southern Guǎngdōng in 1394 and 1385, respectively, while the *Yùnlüè yìtōng* was completed just 50 years later in 1442, it is probable that some sub-varieties of Southern Mandarin of the late fourteenth and early fifteenth centuries still preserved the -p, -t, -k endings. If so,

---

14. Here and following CDC (Common Dialectal Chinese) forms follow Norman (2006).

both Huálóu *cūn*, Pínghǎi, and Lán Mào's dialects all had the endings. They were then preserved over the years in Huálóu *cūn* and Pínghǎi *zhènghuà* through the influence of the surrounding dialects. But after Lán Mào's time they were lost in varieties of southwestern Mandarin.

Similarly, final -m was a feature of Huálóu *cūn* colloquial from the beginning. Such words as [nam²¹³] 南 'south', [ɬam³³] 三 'three', and [iɐm³³] 音 'sound' could not have recovered the final -m if it had been merged with -n. This is most certainly the case for colloquial words that are not found in neighboring dialects, such as Huálóu *cūn* [tsam⁵⁵] *zhàn* 站 'to stand', which is not seen in the surrounding non-Mandarin dialects. As the final -m was also maintained in the northern language of the *Zhōngyuán yīnyùn* language, it must have also existed in the language of Lán Mào and his *Yùnlüè yìtōng*. It was preserved in the Huálóu *cūn zhènghuà* dialects due to influence from the surrounding Yuè, Hakka, and Mǐn dialects, but lost in subsequent varieties of southwestern Mandarin.

Evidence of a lingering memory of the pronunciation of the final -m and the *rù* tone -p, -t, -k endings where they were fading is found connected to the Nánqǔ 南曲 'southern song' performance tradition in the late Míng. In "On the Closed-Lip Syllables" (*Lùn bì kǒu zì* 論閉口字) in his *Qǔlǜ* 曲律 'Conventions and principles for lyric drama', Wáng Jìdé 王驥德 (d. 1623) describes the articulation of the various endings and calls for their preservation in the performance tradition (1624, 2.16a–17a):[15]

> The open and closed endings of a syllable (*zì* 字), are as *yīn* is to *yáng* and as male is to female. Those of earlier times who composed rhyme, when they organized their rhymes in the categories of *qīn* 侵 CDC *tshim¹, *tán* 覃 CDC *dom², *yán* 鹽 CDC *yam², and *xián* 咸 CDC *ham², poets referred to this as "mute rhyming" *yǎyùn* 啞韻. They meant that it was necessary to pronounce them with closed lips, preventing the voice from expanding. In *cí* and *qǔ* the rhyming of open and closed syllables with it is strictly proscribed. The closed lip rhymes are not pronounced by opening the lips and then abruptly closing them, but rather by drawing the source syllable out of the open mouth, then gently extending the pronunciation though the nose. This way the singing is effortless, and the enunciation naturally draws to a close. It is what is referred to as a "nasal sound" *bíyīn* 鼻音.
>
> With regard to this, [Shěn] Cíyǐn [沈]詞隱 [Shěn Jǐng 沈璟 1553–1610] was especially adamant, and would circle every syllable [ending in -m in the scores]. This was most likely because the people of the Wú region do not have syllable ending in -m. They pronounce *qīn* 侵 CDC *tshim¹ like *qīn* 親 CDC *tshin¹, *jiān* 監 CDC *kam¹ like *jiān* 奸 CDC *kan¹, and *lián* 廉 CDC *liam² like *lián* 連 *lian². Thus 3 of the 19 rhymes are missing. This abuse has taken firm, unbreakable root and is passed on through the generations, doing great harm.
>
> Only in the termination of the *rù* tone, in syllables such as *hé* CDC 合 *hop⁸, *yè* 葉 CDC *yap⁸, and *qià* CDC 洽 *hap⁸, with the closing of the lips no voicing

---

15. I am indebted to Kevin Conrad Schoenberger for bringing this passage to my attention. I have added CDC forms to illustrate the relevant phonological features.

is emitted.[16] . . . If desiring to be simply approximately similar, and intermingle regional accents, with the result that within the five tones there is not a single syllable that ends in -m, would that not be a significant wrong?!

Wáng Jìdé was from Kuàijī 會稽 (in the area of modern Shàoxīng 紹興) in the northern Wú dialect region and is describing a pronunciation found in the prestige southern Mandarin of his time. He began writing *Qǔlǜ* around 1610 but did not complete it until just before his death in 1623; it was not published until 1624 (Fei 2002, 61; Shen 2005, 145). In this passage Wáng Jìdé tells us that Shěn Jǐng (who was from the Sūzhōu district of Wújiāng 吳江) circled syllables in his scores that had the final -m so as to preserve a fading distinction. An examination of Shěn Jǐng's *Zēngdìng nánjiǔgōng qǔpǔ* 增定南九宮曲譜 'Expanded collection of southern scores in the nine modes' reveals that indeed Shěn Jǐng consistently circled such syllables. For example, in his edit of the song "Zào luó páo" 皂羅袍 'Black silk robe' by Chén Duó 陳鐸 (*zì* 字 Dàshēng 大聲, who was from the Jīnlíng 金陵, modern Nánjīng, and active during the Míng Zhèngdé 正德 reign 1505–1521), Shěn Jǐng circles the syllables we have rendered in italics in the following transcription (modified to illustrate characteristic features of the period pronunciation):[17]

Tsuì bèi *gīm* siāo hán zhòng,	翠被㉠宵寒重,	The emerald quilt tonight is frigid and heavy,
Tīng siāosiāo loqyeq luàn tzǒu *liám*-lóng,	聽蕭蕭落葉亂悉㉠櫳,	Rustling leaves fall in a tumble by the curtained window,
Duī *zhěm* hiāng yún *nèm* péngsōng,	堆㉠香雲㉠鬆鬆,	Heaped pillows, a cloud of fragrance, ever so soft,
Būzhī liù kueq *gīm* chāi fòng,	不知溜却㉠釵鳳,	Unknowingly my phoenix hairpin has slipped away,
Nǎorén giē hià tsītsī hòu chóng,	惱人堦下淒淒候虫,	Annoyingly near the steps, a cold murmur of insects in the background,
Gīng *sīm* lóushàng dāngdāng hiǎo-zhōng,	驚㉠樓上噹噹曉鐘,	Startled by the ding-dong of the morning bell upstairs,
Wúduān huàgioq shēng *sām* nòng.	無端畫角聲㉠弄。	Then without cause three blasts from the bull-horn trumpet.

The late Míng playwright Féng Mènglóng 馮夢龍 (1574–1646) also followed the convention of circling the closed-lip syllables having final -m in his collection of songs titled *Tàixiá xīnzòu* 太霞新奏 'Magnificent clouds rendered anew' (preface 1627). The preservation of final -m in song performance advocated by Shěn Jǐng and Wáng Jìdé was clearly highly influential.

---

16. That is to say that in its enunciation, final "-m" can continue to carry the tune while the final "-p" halts voicing and cannot carry a tune.
17. Transcribed from *juàn* 1.14a/121 in the *Shànběn xìqǔ cóngkān* edition of Shěn Jǐng's *Zēngdìng nánjiǔgōng qǔpǔ*.

It is also significant that Wáng Jìdé describes the articulation of *rù* syllables that end in -p, where he says in the above-cited passage that "only in the termination of the *rù* tone, in syllables such as *hé* CDC 合 *hop⁸, *yè* 葉 CDC *yap⁸, and *qià* CDC 洽 *hap⁸, *with the closing of the lips no voicing is emitted*" (emphasis added). Perhaps like -m it was an enunciation that lingered in the memory of the Míng playwrights and their performance tradition. This bolsters our conjecture that Lán Mào's preservation of the three-way contrast of final ᵛ-p, ᵛ-t, and ᵛ-k in *rù* tone syllables reflects a real pronunciation still found in varieties of southern Mandarin in the early Míng.

Older, more conservative features are generally held to have high prestige in Chinese tradition. In Shěn Jǐng's scores and Wáng Jìdé's admonition we see an effort to preserve such features in an oral tradition, and to reflect it in the musical scores that recorded and represent that tradition. Wáng Jìdé's description is that of someone who knows how the pronunciation should work and how it sounds. His emphasis on the need to preserve the enunciation of final -m in the Nánqǔ performance tradition is parallel to the maintenance of the *jiān-tuán* distinction (noted above) in Běijīng opera tradition, though it probably faded from Běijīng pronunciation 150 to 200 years ago (Branner 2006, 220). Hence final -m may have still been heard rather widely in sixteenth- and even seventeenth-century Mandarin. It would have been lost earlier in Wú than in southern Mandarin, as the weakening of final nasals tends to be more advanced in Wú. Hence Shěng Jǐng and Wáng Jìdé were motivated to preserve this Mandarin prestige feature in the southern singing tradition as they saw it threatened by its loss in the colloquial Wú of their time and place.

Concluding Thoughts

We have looked at frontier Mandarin dialect islands (*jūnhuà* and *zhènghuà*) that formed in the Míng and explored a Míng period description of periphial Mandarin represented in the *Yùnlüè yìtōng*. We find that the languages reflected these various sources reveal a set of shared features characteristic of Mandarin, even within their regional variation. Their differences also reflect traces of changes that were taking place in Mandarin from the early Míng and into the Qīng. The changes we have observed in the living languages of the dialect islands and in the contemporary descriptions of textual sources show us that the changes were dynamic and varied across China's vast geography, with some happening earlier in some places and later in others.

The principal common elements in the various versions of Mandarin that had traveled across the map of the Míng empire generally included all or most of the following phonological features:

1. A five-tone system with a two-register *píng* tone and a *rù* tone.

2. A single (*yīn*)*shǎng* tone category which included syllables with sonorant initials that generally were in *yángshǎng* 陽上 or other tone categories in non-Mandarin dialects.
3. Preservation of the *rì* and/or *wéi* initials as separate categories and without any nasal elements.
4. A medial -i- following velar initials in the set of syllables belonging to the category that is labeled *jiàn-kāi-èr*.

And it included all or most of the following lexical features:

5. Third-person pronoun tā 他
6. The Mandarin negative bù 不
7. The attributive particle is de 的
8. The Mandarin word for 'five' 五 (non-nasal)
9. Other diagnostic Mandarin words such as 'face' 臉, 'stand' 站

The evidence reveals that the type of four-tone Mandarin represented in the *Zhōngyuán yīnyùn* had not spread widely in the south by the start of the Míng. Instead, a more conservative five-tone southern version of Mandarin that had garnered great prestige through its proximity to, and association with, the Míng founder Zhū Yuánzhāng and his troops traveled widely across southern China's east and west. In its early years, it may have had reminant elements of earlier Mandarin types, certainly including final nasal -m and maybe even final consonants -p, -t, and -k. Thus it is entirely possible that the southwestern Mandarin of Lán Mào's *Yùnlüè yìtōng* is much as he described it and that Lán Mào was not simply slavishly following tradition with the inclusion of ˅-p, ˅-t, ˅-k and ˅-m endings in his finals. By the same token, the -p, -t, and -k endings in the Huálóu *cūn* and Pínghǎi *rù* tone syllables are likely a preservation of an early Míng feature of the Mandarin that settled there, and not a restoration of categories due to the influence of surrounding dialects.

In overall perspective, the Míng Guānhuà that our various sources depict comprised a core set of features within a *lingua franca* that encompassed regional varieties with their own particular characteristics. This Guānhuà reached across a wide sweep of territory in southern China, from east to west, and coexisted with non-Mandarin southern dialects. It had an adaptable nature that could vary outside its set of core features, thus giving rise to regional forms. Those regional varieties in turn would change across time, subject to the influence of their neighbors. Hence the Guānhuà of the Míng had a flexible resilience that was no doubt the reason for its long life and deep, lasting influence—a life and influence that reached well into the Qīng dynasty that followed.

References

Primary sources

Féng Mènglóng 馮夢龍 (1574–1646). Preface dated 1627. *Tàixiá xīnzòu* 太霞新奏 [Magnificent clouds rendered anew]. Facsimile scan of the edition held by the Peking University Library at ctext.org and archive.org.

Lán Mào 蘭茂 (1397–1476). (1442) 1995. *Yùnlüè yìtōng* 韻畧易通 [Intelligible sketch of rimes]. *Xùxiū Sìkù quánshū* 續修四庫全書 edition. Vol. 259. Shànghǎi: Shànghǎi gǔjí.

Míng shílù 明實錄 [Veritable records of the Míng]. Dates vary: each section was composed following an emperor's reign. Reprint, Nán'gǎng 南港：Zhōngyāng yánjiūyuàn lìshǐ yǔyán yánjiūsuǒ 中央研究院歷史語言研究所, 1962–1968; also available at ctext.org.

Shěn Jǐng 沈璟 (1553–1610). n.d. *Zēngdìng nánjiǔgōng qǔpǔ* 增定南九宮曲譜 [Expanded collection of southern scores in the nine modes]. *Shànběn xìqǔ cóngkān* 善本戲曲叢刊 edition. Reprint, Taipei: Táiwān xuéshēng shūjú, 1984.

Trigault, Nicolas (Jīn Nígé 金尼閣, 1577–1628). 1626. *Xīrú ěrmù zī* 西儒耳目資 [An aid to the eye and ear of Western scholars]. 3 vols. Hángzhōu 杭州: Wáng Zhēng 王徵. Facsimile reprint by Guólì Běijīng dàxué 國立北京大學, 1933. Subsequent reprinting in *Pīnyīn wénzì shǐliào cóngshū* 拼音文字史料叢書. Běijīng: Wénzì gǎigé chūbǎnshè, 1957.

Wáng Jìdé 王驥德 (d. 1623). 1624. *Qǔlǜ* 曲律 [Conventions and principles of lyric drama]. Facsimile scan of the edition held by the Peking University Library at ctext.org and archive.org.

Yú Zhèngxiè 俞正燮 (1775–1840). 1833. *Guǐsì cúngǎo* 癸巳存稿 [Collected writings in the *guǐsì* year (1833)]. Peking University Library scan of *Lián Jūnyí cóngshū* 連筠簃叢書 edition held in Zhejiang University Library, accessible at ctext.org and archive.org.

Zhōu Déqīng 周德清 (1277–1365). 1341. *Zhōngyuán yīnyùn* 中原音韻 [Rimes of the central plains]. Scan of Qīndìng Sìkù quánshū 欽定四庫全書 edition digitized by China-America Digital Academic Library and online at ctext.org and archive.org.

Secondary sources

Akitani Hiroyuki 秋谷裕幸. 2017. *Zhōngyuán Guānhuà Fénhé piàn yīnyùnshǐ yánjiū* 中原官話汾河片音韵史研究 [Research in the history of the Central Plains Mandarin dialects of the Fénhé sector]. PhD diss., Kobe City University of Foreign Studies 神戸市外国語大学. http://id.nii.ac.jp/1085/00002119/.

Baxter, William H. 2006. "Mandarin dialect phylogeny." *Cahiers de linguistique – Asie Orientale* 35 (1): 71–114.

Branner, David Prager. 2006. "Some Composite Phonological Systems in Chinese." In *The Chinese Rime Tables: Linguistic Philosophy and Historical-Comparative Phonology*, edited by David Prager Branner, 209–54. Amsterdam: John Benjamins.

Brook, Timothy. 1998. *The Confusions of Pleasure: Commerce and Culture in Ming China*. Berkeley: University of California Press.

Cáo Shùjī 曹樹基. 1997. *Zhōngguó yímín shǐ—Míng shíqī* 中國移民史—明時期 [History of migration in China—the Míng period]. Vol. 5. Fúzhōu 福州: Fújiàn rénmín chūbǎnshè.

Chen, Chung-yu 陳重瑜. 1981. "Towards an Affiliation of the Nanping Mandarin Dialect of Fujian." *Journal of Chinese Linguistics* 9: 151–209.
Chén Yúnlóng 陳雲龍. 2003. "Guǎngdōng Diànbái jiùshí zhènghuà" 廣東電白舊時正話 [The old *zhènghuà* dialects of Diànbái in Guǎngdōng]. *Fāngyán* 方言 [Dialect] 3: 265–76.
Chén Yúnlóng 陳雲龍. 2005. "Cóng jiùshí zhènghuà kàn Míng dài Guānhuà 從舊時正話看明代官話 [*Jiùshí zhènghuà* from the perspective of Míng dynasty Mandarin]. *Yǔwén yánjiū* 語文研究 [Research in language] 2005 (1): 60–64.
Chén Yúnlóng 陳雲龍. 2006. *Jiùshí zhènghuà yánjiū* 舊時正話研究 [A study of the *jiùshí zhènghuà* dialects]. Běijīng: Zhōngguó shèhuì kēxué chūbǎnshè.
Chow, Chung-yu Chen 陳重瑜. 1974. *A Study of the Nanping Mandarin Dialect of Fukien.* PhD diss., Cornell University. Ann Arbor: UMI Dissertation Services.
Coblin, W. South. 1997. "Notes on the Sound System of Late Ming Guanhua." *Monumenta Serica* 45: 261–307.
Coblin, W. South. 2000a. "A Diachronic Study of Míng Guānhuà Phonology." *Monumenta Serica* 48: 267–335.
Coblin, W. South. 2000b. "A Brief History of Mandarin." *Journal of the American Oriental Society* 120 (4): 537–52.
Coblin, W. South. 2007. *Modern Chinese Phonology: From Guānhuà to Mandarin. Collection des Cahiers de linguistique – Asie Oriental* 11.
Faure, David. 2007. *Emperor and Ancestor: State and Lineage in South China.* Stanford: Stanford University Press.
Fei, Faye Chunfang, ed. and trans. 2002. *Chinese Theories of Theater and Performance from Confucius to the Present.* Ann Arbor: University of Michigan Press.
Gěng Zhènshēng 耿振生. 1992. *Míng Qīng děngyùnxué tōnglùn* 明清等韻學通論 [Survey of rime table studies in the Míng and Qīng]. Běijīng: Yǔwén chūbǎnshè.
Goodrich, L. Carrington, ed. 1976. *Dictionary of Ming Biography, 1368–1644.* 2 Vols. New York: Columbia University Press.
Huáng Xiǎodōng 黃曉東. 2007. "Hànyǔ jūn huà gàishù 漢語軍話概述" [Introduction to the Chinese *jùnhuà* dialects]. *Yǔyán jiāoxué yǔ yánjiū* 語言教學與研究 2007 (3): 21–27.
Kerswill, Paul. 2004. "Koineization and Accommodation." In *The Handbook of Language Variation and Change*, 669–702. Oxford: Blackwell Publishing.
Kim Kwangjo. 1991. "A Phonological Study of Middle Mandarin: Reflected in Korean Sources of the Mid-15th and Early 16th Centuries." PhD diss., University of Washington. Ann Arbor: UMI Dissertation Services.
Leonhard, Jürgen. 2013. *Latin: Story of a World Language.* Translated by Kenneth Kronenberg. Cambridge, MA: Belknap Press of Harvard University.
Lú Zēngfū 盧增夫. 2010. "Dèng Màoqī zhī luàn shǐliào chuánchéng kǎo biàn" 鄧茂七之亂史料傳承考辨 [Examination of the historical sources on the Dèng Màoqī Rebellion]. *Míng dài yánjiū* 明代研究 [Studies on the Míng Dynasty] 14: 45–66.
McWhorter, John H. 1998. "Identifying the Creole Prototype: Vindicating a Typological Class." *Language* 74: 788–818.
Nìng Jìfú 甯忌浮. 2009. *Hànyǔ yùnshū shǐ—Míng dài juàn* 漢語韻書史—明代卷 [History of Chinese rime books—volume on the Míng dynasty]. Shànghǎi: Shànghǎi rénmín chūbǎnshè.
Norman, Jerry (Luó Jiéruì 羅杰瑞). 2006. "Common Dialectal Chinese." In *The Chinese Rime-Tables: Linguistic Philosophy and Historical-Comparative Phonology*, edited by David

Prager Branner, 233–54. Amsterdam and Philadelphia: John Benjamins; Chinese translation: Hànyǔ fāngyán tōngyīn 漢語方言通音, translated by Richard VanNess Simmons 史皓元 and Zhāng Yànhóng 張艷紅. *Fāngyán* 方言 [Dialect] 2: 97–116.

Pān Jiāyì 潘家懿. 1998. "Jūnhuà yǔ Guǎngdōng Pínghǎi 'jūnshēng'" 軍話與廣東平海'軍聲' [*Jūnhuà* (garrison dialects) and the *jūnshēng* (garrison pronunciation) of Pínghǎi in Guǎngdōng]. *Fāngyán* 方言 [Dialect] 1: 41–47.

Qiū Xuéqiáng 丘學強. 2005. *Jūnhuà yánjiū* 軍話研究 [A study of Jūnhuà]. Běijīng: Zhōngguó shèhuì kēxué chūbǎnshè.

Shen, Grant Guangren. 2005. *Elite Theatre in Ming China, 1368–1644*. London and New York: Routledge.

Siegel, Jeff. 1985. "Koines and Koineization." *Language in Society* 14 (3): 357–78.

Simmons, Richard VanNess. 2016a. "The Dōngběi varieties of Mandarin: A Brief Look at Their History and Classification." *Journal of Asian Pacific Communication* 26 (1): 56–80.

Simmons, Richard VanNess. 2016a. 2016b. "The Evolution of the Chinese Sìhū 四呼 Concept of Syllable Classification." *Historiographia Linguistica* 43 (3): 251–84.

Thomason, Sarah Grey, and Terrence Kaufman. 1988. *Language Contact, Creolization, and Genetic Linguistics*. Berkeley: University of California Press.

Tong, James. 1991. *Disorder under Heaven: Collective Violence in the Ming Dynasty*. Stanford: Stanford University Press.

Trudgill, Peter. 1986. *Dialects in Contact*. Oxford: Blackwell Publishing.

Wēn Duānzhèng 溫端政. 1991. *Cāngnán fāngyán zhì* 蒼南方言志. Běijīng: Yǔwén chūbǎnshè.

Zhāng Yùlái 張玉來. 1999. Yùnlüè yìtōng *yánjiū* 韻略易通研究 [Research on *Yùnlüè yìtōng*]. Tiānjīn: Tiānjīn gǔjí.

Zhào Yìntáng 趙蔭棠. 1957. *Děngyùn yuánliú* 等韻源流 [A history of Děngyùn]. Shànghǎi: Shāngwù yìnshūguǎn.

14
On the Variation of the *Rù* Tone in the Shānyīn Dialect of Shānxī

Guō Lìxiá

Introduction

Among the dialects in northern China, the Jìn 晋 group stands apart from others in its preservation of a distinct *rù* 入 tone category with syllables ending in a glottal stop [ʔ]. But this situation appears to be changing in at least one Jìn dialect, that of Shānyīn 山陰 in northern Shānxī 山西. In a 1990 study of that dialect, Yáng Zēngwǔ 楊增武 observed that a set of syllables of the *rù* tone category had lost the glottal stop. This appears to have been the start of the kind of change that dramatically altered the phonology of the Guānhuà dialects, with which the Jìn are closely related. The question before us now, three decades after Yáng's Zēngwǔ's initial observation, is whether the *rù* 入 tone category in Shānyīn has lost the glottal stop on additional syllables, and, if so, what the extent of the loss may be as of the present and what forces have influenced this change. This chapter presents a sociolinguistically oriented survey of *rù* 入 tone syllables that was undertaken in the Shānyīn dialect in an effort to answer these questions.

Previous research on the history and nature of the *rù* in the Jìn dialects tone has focused on:

(1) the evolution of *rù* tone syllables in terms of local dialects;
(2) the phenomenon of the loss of the glottal stop in *rù* tone syllables, as well as a reverse of this process;
(3) experimental research on the *rù* tone;
(4) linguistic strata in the evolution of the *rù* tone; and
(5) sociolinguistic research on the *rù* tone.

Most studies to date have focused on the first four areas. Sociolinguistic research on the *rù* tone has been neglected. Yet sociolinguistic influences are of critical importance with regard to the historical evolution of the *rù* tone in the Guānhuà and Jìn dialects. Moreover, while the phonology of the Shānyīn dialect has been well-documented, the *rù* tone and its variation in the dialect is still poorly documented.

Hence the present study will focus on the phonology of the *rù* tone in Shānyīn from the perspective of its sociolinguistic variation.

Below, we first describe the phonology of the Shānyīn tones and the distinguishing features of the dialect's *rù* tone. Next we outline the methodology of our sociolinguistic-oriented survey, providing details of the sample composition and the elicitation technique. We then present and analyze the results. The details center on a description of the variation of the *rù* tone observed in the Shānyīn dialect and the internal linguistic rules for the variation. Our main finding is that the Shānyīn dialect has undergone a dramatic loss of *rù* 入 tone syllables. Almost half of all *rù* tone syllables in Shānyīn have shifted, or are shifting to non-*rù* tone, and show a loss of the glottal stop ending. We also find a reverse of this process, with some non-*rù* tone syllables shifting to *rù* tone. The most prominent reason for the variations observed is the influence of Modern Standard Chinese (Pǔtōnghuà). Variation due to factors internal to the dialect, such as word frequency and linguistic register (whether more literary or colloquial) are also seen, but appear to be less significant. We end the chapter with a brief consideration of the possible future development of the *rù* tone in the Shānyīn dialect.

Shānyīn Tones

Shānyīn County is in northern Shānxī 山西, which shares a border with Héběi 河北 and Nèiménggǔ 內蒙古. The Shānyīn dialect belongs to the Dàbāo 大包 subgroup of the Jìn dialects and has four contrastive tones (*Zhōngguó yǔyán dìtújí* 中國語言地圖集): *píng* 平, *shǎng* 上, *qù* 去, and a *rù* tone. The isolation contours of the four Shānyīn tones are as follows:

1. *Píng* tone is high level [55]
3. *Shǎng* tone is high to mid falling [52]
4. *Qù* tone is mid to mid-high rising [24]
5. *Rù* tone is short and ends in a glottal stop [ʔ4]

Shānyīn has a single *rù* tone category with a glottal stop [ʔ] ending and two contrasting vocalisms (main vowels). Including medials, they are [aʔ, iaʔ, uaʔ, yaʔ] and [əʔ, iəʔ, uəʔ, yəʔ].

In traditional Chinese linguistic practice, a *rù* tone is a tone that is realized within a syllable with a stop ending (coda), while a non-*rù* tone (or *shūshēng* 舒聲) is a tone that is realized within a syllable with an open or sonorant ending (Zhāng 1998). Shěn Míng 沈明 (2005) divides the *rù* tone syllables listed in the *Fāngyán diàochá zìbiǎo* 方言調查字表 [Character syllabary for dialect fieldwork] into four categories with regard to their occurrence in the Jìn dialects. The first category contains obsolete words, such as, *duó* 踱 'stroll' and *miè* 篾 (as in *zhúmiè* 竹篾 'bamboo strip'). The second category is comprised of syllables that are *rù* tone in the traditional conceptualization of Middle Chinese (MC) but that have been pronounced as non-*rù* tone for quite some time, such as *lā* in *lā-dùzi* 拉肚子 'have diarrhea', and *yè* in *yètǐ* 液體 'liquid'. The third category contains syllables derived from literary forms or neologisms, for example, *qià* in *qiàdàng* 恰當 'perfectly suitable', *nuò* in *xǔnuò* 許諾 'promise', *xù* in *chǔxù* 儲蓄 'savings deposit'. The fourth category contains syllables that are frequently used in colloquial speech. In the present study, we focus on the third and fourth categories, with a primary emphasis on the fourth.

Table 14.1 lists the *rù* tone syllables we investigated, together with their regular *rù* tone pronunciation in the Shānyīn dialect, that is, the pronunciation when variation is not observed. For reference, Table 14.1 also indicates Common Dialectal Chinese (CDC) forms and the traditional *shè* 攝 classification of the Middle Chinese *Qièyùn* 切韻 system (*Qy*):[1]

Table 14.1: The Shānyīn pronunciations of *rù* tone syllables

Shānyīn final	Qy Shè	CDC	Examples	Shānyīn final	Qy Shè	CDC	Examples
aʔ	咸	*vap⁸	*fá* 乏 'lack'	əʔ	深	*cip⁷ *ship⁷	*zhī* 汁 'juice' *shī* 濕 'wet'
		*kot⁷	*gē* 割 'to cut'		臻	*zhit⁸ *shit⁷ *it⁷	*shí* 實 'real' *shī* 失 'to lose' *yī* 一 'one'
	山	*cat⁷ *shat⁷	*zhā* 紥包紮 'to tie' *shā* 殺 'to kill'			*mut⁸	*méi* 沒 'not'
		*chiat⁷ *nhiat⁸	*zhè* 浙 (Zhèjiāng) *rè* 熱 'hot'		曾	*jik⁸ *zhik⁸	*zhí* 直 'straight' *shí* 食 'food'
		*pot⁷	*bō* 鉢 'bowl'		梗	*chiak⁷	*chǐ* 尺 'ruler'
		*fat⁷	*fà* 髮 'hair'			*phuk⁷	*bú* 醭 'fungus'
	宕	*pok⁷ *kok⁷	*bó* 博 'ample' *gè* 各 'each'		通	*fuk⁷	*fù* 覆 'recover'
	江	*pok⁷	*bō* 剝 'to peel'				
	曾	*shek⁷	*sè* 色 'color' cf. 太原 səʔ⁷文 saʔ⁷白				
	梗	*jiak⁸	*zé* 澤 'lake'				

(continued on p. 251)

---

1. CDC forms follow Norman (2006; 2011).

Table 14.1 (continued)

Shānyīn final	Qy Shè	CDC	Examples	Shānyīn final	Qy Shè	CDC	Examples
iaʔ	咸	*diat⁷	diē 跌 'to fall'	iəʔ	深	*zip⁸ *dzip⁸	xí 習 'to study' jí 集 'collect'
		*xat⁷	xiā 瞎 'blind'			*kip⁷ *khip⁷	jí 急 'anxious' qì 泣 'to cry'
	山	*biat⁸ *giat⁸ *xiat⁷ *piat⁷ *thiat⁷ *kiat⁷	bié 別 'do not', jié 傑 'great' xiē 蠍 'scorpion' biē 憋 'stifle (self)' tiě 鐵 'iron' jié 結 'knot'		臻	*pit⁷ *khit⁷	bǐ 筆 'pen' qī 七 'seven' qǐ 乞 'to beg'
					曾	*pek⁷	běi 北 'north'
	宕	*kiok⁷ *iok⁷	jiǎo 腳 'foot,' yuē 約 'approximate'			*lik⁸ *sik⁷	lì 力 'strength' xí 媳 'daughter-in-law'
	江	*k(i)ok⁷	jiǎo 角 'antler'		梗	*ngiak⁸ *piak⁷ *tshiak⁷	nì 逆 'opposite' bì 璧 'jade disk' qī 戚 'relative'
	梗	*pak⁷ *mak⁸	bǎi 百 'one hundred' mài 脈 'pulse'				
uaʔ	山	*thot⁷ *uat⁷ *shiot⁷	tuō 脫 'take off' wā 挖 'dig' shuō 説 'say, speak'	uəʔ	臻	*kut⁷ *chiut⁷	gǔ 骨 'bone' chū 出 'to go out'
	宕	*thok⁷ *dzok⁸ *lok⁸ *nhiok⁸ *kuok⁷	tuō 托 'entrust' zuó 昨 'yesterday' lè 樂 'enjoyment' ruò 弱 'weak' Guō 郭 [a surname]			*mvut⁸	wù 物 'thing'
					宕	*xuok⁷	huò 霍 [a surname]
	江	*ciok⁷	zhuō 桌 'table'		通	*duk⁸ *ciuk⁷	dú 獨 'alone' zhú 竹 'bamboo'
yaʔ	山	*siot⁷ *yot⁸ *yot⁸	xuě 雪 'snow' yuè 閲 'to read' yuè 越 'more'	yəʔ	臻	*khiut⁷	qū 屈 'suffer wrong'
					通	*tsiuk⁷ *ziuk⁸ *khiuk⁷	zú 足 'sufficient' sú 俗 'vulgar' qǔ 曲 'song'
		*xiot⁷	xuè 血 'blood'				
	臻	*giut⁸	jué 倔 'stubborn'				
	宕	*tsiok⁷	què 雀 'bird'				

Methodology and Data Collection

Most of the data used in this chapter were obtained during a field study carried out in Shānyīn in 2014. The interviewees included thirteen male speakers and five female speakers of the Shānyīn dialect. They were all born and raised in Dàiyuè 岱岳, a county town of Shānyīn, and were all between twelve and seventy-nine years of age. Table 14.2 provides a summary of the informants' backgrounds (with speakers' names surpressed).

Table 14.2: List of informants by background

Speaker No.	Gender	Birthday	Education	Occupation	Remarks
1.	Male	1935.12	初中 Junior High School	Civil servant	
2.	Male	1947.10	高中 Senior High School	Teacher	Lǎopài 老派 senior speakers (60–79 years old)
3.	Female	1937	小學 Primary School	Housewife	
4.	Female	1954.6	初中 Junior High School	Worker	
5.	Male	1951.9	小學 Primary School	Worker	
6.	Female	1974.5	大學 University	Teacher	
7.	Male	1970.3	技校 Technical School	Office clerk	
8.	Male	1978.9	高中 Senior High School	Office clerk	Zhōngpài 中派 middle-aged speakers (30–44 years old)
9.	Male	1970.7	高中 Senior High School	Office clerk	
10.	Male	1980.7	高中 Senior High School	Office clerk	
11.	Female	1984.11	中專 Technical Secondary	Office clerk	
12.	Male	1980.8	高中 Senior High School	Office clerk	
13.	Male	1973.5	高中 Senior High School	Office clerk	
14.	Male	2001.12	初中 Junior High School	Student	
15.	Male	1996.6	大學 University	Student	Qīngpài 青派 junior speaker (12–18 years old)
16.	Female	1997.6	高中 Senior High School	Student	
17.	Male	2000.5	初中 Junior High School	Student	
18.	Male	2002.11	初中 Junior High School	Student	

The survey elicited the pronunciations of the 84 most frequently used *rù* tone syllables. They are listed in Table 14.3 by traditional *shè* category and classified by Common Dialectal Chinese voicing type of the initial consonant; this was factored into our later analysis of the data.

Table 14.3: List of the *rù* tone syllables surveyed

Traditional grouping	With voiceless initials *Qīng rù* 清入 (47)	With voiced initials *Quánzhúo rù* 全濁入 (18)	With sonorant initials *Cìzhúo rù* 次濁入 (19)
Xián shè 咸攝	*jiē* 接 'to meet'; *hē* 喝 'to drink'		*niè* 聶 [a surname]; *yè* 葉 'leaf'
Shēn shè 深攝	*gěi* 給 'to give'; *shī* 濕 'wet'	*shí* 十 'ten'; *xí* 習 'to exercise'	
Shān shè 山攝	*bā* 八 'eight'; *guā* 刮 'to scratch'; *gē* 割 'to cut'; *jié* 節 'holiday; *shuō* 説 'to speak'; *xiā* 瞎 'blind'; *xuè* 血 'blood'; *Xuē* 薛 [a surname]; *xuě* 雪 'snow'; *yē* 噎 'to choke'; *tiě* 鐵 'iron'	*huó* 活 'to live'	*niē* 捏 'to pinch'; *rè* 熱 'hot'; *wà* 襪 'stocking'; *yuè* 月 'moon'
Zhēn shè 臻攝	*bǐ* 筆 'pen'; *bù* 不 'no'; *gǔ* 骨 'bone'; *shī* 蝨 'louse'; *hù* 忽 'suddenly'; *qī* 七 'seven'; *qī* 漆 'paint'; *yī* 一 'one'; *chū* 出 'to go out'	*zhí* 姪 'nephew'; *shù* 術 'art'; *bì* 弼 'to help'	*mì* 蜜 'honey'; *méi* 沒 'not'; *rì* 日 'sun'
Dàng shè 宕攝	*bó* 博 'rich', *jiǎo* 腳 'foot', *Guō* 郭 [a surname], *Hǎo* 郝 [a surname], *Huò* 霍 [a surname]	*báo* 薄 'thin'	*yào* 藥 'medicine'; *yào* 鑰 'key'
Jiāng shè 江攝	*jiǎo* 角 'horn or antler'; *shuò* 朔 'used in place names'; *zhuō* 桌 'table'	*xué* 學 'to study'	*yuè* 岳 'mountain, [a surname]'; *yuè* 樂 'music'
Zēng shè 曾攝	*běi* 北 'north'; *sè* 色 'color'; *hēi* 黑 'black'; *xí* 媳 'daughter-in-law'	*Zhí* 直 'straight-edge',; *zhí* 值 'to value',; *zéi* 賊 'thief'	*lì* 力 'strength'; *mò* 墨 'ink'
Gěng shè 梗攝	*bǎi* 百 'one-hundred'; *bó* 伯 'primary'; *gé* 隔 'divide'; *zhǎi* 窄 'narrow'; *chǐ* 尺 'ruler'; *chī* 吃 'to eat'; *tī* 踢 'to kick'; *kè* 客 'guest'	*bái* 白 'white', *shí* 石 'rock', *xí* 席 'a seat'	*mài* 麥 'wheat'; *mài* 脈 'pulse'
Tōng shè 通攝	*fú* 福 'good fortune'; *shū* 叔 'uncle'; *kū* 哭 'to cry'	*dú* 毒 'poison'; *fù* 複 'complex'; *jú* 局 'office'; *shǔ* 屬 'to belong to'	*lǜ* 綠 'green'; *mù* 木 'wood'

This study also includes data from an unpublished report written by a Peking University team that investigated the Shānyīn dialect in 1959. The linguistic informant at the time was a 24-year-old (born in 1935) male fluent in the Shānyīn dialect. These data are cited as "Wáng 王 1959." The data for the 1990s in the following sections are based on Yáng Zēngwǔ 楊增武 (1990) for which the interviewees were two male speakers of the Shānyīn dialect, one 74 years old and the other 36 years old at the time.

Results: Changes Observed in the Pronunciation of Shānyīn *Rù* Tone Syllables

Overall in our data, 47 of the 84 *rù* tone syllables maintain the *rù* tone glottal stop, which amounts to about 56 percent of all the *rù* tone syllables we investigated. Only four *rù* tone syllables have changed tone category completely and are pronounced as non-*rù* tone: *wà* 襪, *zhí* 侄, *zéi* 賊, and *mù* 木. Thirty-three syllables have variants. Also noteworthy is the influence of certain features from Pǔtōnghuà (Modern Standard Chinese) that have been adopted in the pronunciation of *rù* tone syllables. For example, *tiě* 鐵 and *yuè* 岳 still keep the glottal stop, while the initial and medial have changed from [tɕ'] to [t'] and from [i] to [y], respectively, in the speech of some junior speakers.

Back in 1959, all 84 syllables were pronounced as *rù* tone, even including *zéi* 賊 [tsaʔ], *mài* 麥 [miaʔ], *yào* 鑰 [iaʔ], *wà* 襪 [uaʔ], and *dú* 毒 [tuəʔ]. This is not the case in the data from Yáng Zēngwǔ 1990 and from our investigation. In Yáng Zēngwǔ (1990), 76 syllables keep the glottal stop while the remaining eight syllables lose the glottal stop. Those syllables are *wà* 襪, *zhí* 侄, *yào* 鑰, *zéi* 賊, *mài* 麥, *dú* 毒, *jú* 局, and *mù* 木. Table 14.4 illustrates the current conditions of syllables with regard to the preservation or loss of the glottal stop.

The data reveal that syllables having voiced initials in Middle Chinese (and CDC) are more likely to become non-*rù* tone in Shānyīn. In many of the modern dialects, the correspondence with MC/CDC tones is remarkably regular. Table 14.4 shows the correspondence of Shānyīn tones (by number: 1 for *píng*, 3 for *shǎng*, 4 for *qù*, and 5 for *rù*) with Middle Chinese/CDC initial types:

Table 14.4: The correspondence of Shānyīn tones with Middle Chinese initial types

MC/CDC initial type	MC/CDC tones:	*Píng*	*Shǎng*	*Qù*	*Rù*
		\multicolumn{4}{c}{Corresponding Shānyīn tones}
Voiceless – *Qīng* 清		1	3	4	1, 3, 4, 5
Voiced – *Quánzhuó* 全濁		1	5	4	1, (4 弼), 5
Sonorant – *Cìzhuó* 次濁		1	3	4	4, 5

The varied reflection of the Middle Chinese/CDC *rù* tone syllables with voiceless initials appears to be random, a situation partly due to dialect contact. It is very rare for MC/CDC *rù* tone syllables with *quánzhuó* initials to become *qù* tone 4. This developmental pattern is specific to the *bì* 弼 in the name Bìmǎwēn 弼馬溫 and is very likely influenced by Pǔtōnghuà.

As the sociolinguistic factors behind variations in the evolution of the Shānyīn *rù* tone were a primary motivating factor for this study, we focused on identifying the *rù* tone syllables that have become non-*rù* tone in present-day pronunciation. There are 33 of these syllables: *yè* 葉, *gěi* 給, *huó* 活, *rè* 熱, *yuè* 月, *shī* 蝨, *shù* 術, *bì* 弼, *mì* 蜜, *rì* 日, *bó* 博, *hǎo* 郝, *huò* 霍, *báo* 薄, *yào* 藥, *yào* 鑰, *jiǎo* 角, *xué* 學, *yuè* 岳, *yuè* 樂, *zhí* 直, *zhí* 值, *mò* 墨, *zhǎi* 窄, *kè* 客, *mài* 脈, *xí* 席, *bái* 白, *mài* 麥, *shū* 叔, *dú* 毒, *jú* 局, *lǜ* 綠. Table 14.5 provides the variant pronunciations observed in 21 of these 33 syllables, classified according to the age and gender of the speakers for each variant type.

Table 14.5: Variant pronunciations on *rù* tone syllables

Syllable	Pronunciations	Number of speakers	Year of birth	Gender
gěi 給 'to give'	[kə˧]	3	1937 (1), 1947 (1), 1951 (1)	Male (2), Female (1)
	[˩kei] or [kə˧]	10	1935 (1), 1954 (1), 1970 (2), 1973 (1), 1974 (1), 1978 (1), 1980 (2), 1984 (1)	Male (7), Female (3)
	[˩kei]	5	1996 (1), 1997 (1), 2000 (1), 2001 (1), 2002 (1)	Male (4), Female (1)
rè 熱 'hot'	[ẓa˧]	3	1937 (1), 1980 (1), 2000 (1)	Male (2), Female (1)
	[ẓə˧] or [ẓa˧]	10	1935 (1), 1947 (1), 1951 (1), 1954 (1), 1970 (2), 1978 (1), 1980 (1), 1984 (1), 1996 (1)	Male (8), Female (2)
	[ẓə˧]	5	1973 (1), 1974 (1), 2001 (1), 2002 (1), 1997 (1)	Male (3), Female (2)
yuè 月 'moon'	[yɛ˧] or [ya˧]	9	1935 (1), 1947 (1), 1951 (1), 1954 (1), 1970 (1), 1973 (1), 1978 (1), 1980 (1), 1996 (1)	Male (8), Female (1)
	[yɛ˧]	9	1937 (1), 1970 (1), 1974 (1), 1980 (1), 1984 (1), 1997 (1), 2000 (1), 2001 (1), 2002 (1)	Male (5), Female (4)
shù 術 'art'	[ʂuə˧]	14	1935 (1), 1937 (1), 1947 (1), 1951 (1), 1954 (1), 1970 (2), 1973 (1), 1974 (1), 1978 (1), 1996 (1), 1997 (1), 2000 (1), 2001 (1)	Male (10), Female (4)
	[ʂu˧]	4	1980 (2), 1984 (1), 2002 (1)	Male (3), Female (1)
bì 弼 'to help'	[piə˧]	4	1937 (1), 1951 (1), 1954 (1), 1970 (1)	Male (2), Female (2)
	[pia˧]	2	1935 (1), 1947 (1)	Male (2)
	[pi˧]	12	1970 (1), 1973 (1), 1974 (1), 1978 (1), 1980 (2), 1984 (1), 1996 (1), 1997 (1), 2000 (1), 2001 (1), 2002 (1)	Male (9), Female (3)

(continued on p. 256)

Table 14.5 (continued)

Syllable	Pronunciations	Number of speakers	Year of birth	Gender
mì 蜜 'honey'	[miəʔ]	1	1970 (1)	Male (1)
	[miəʔ] or [miˀ]	2	1970 (1), 1978 (1)	Male (2)
	[miˀ]	15	1935 (1), 1937 (1), 1947 (1), 1951 (1), 1954 (1), 1973 (1), 1974 (1), 1980 (2), 1984 (1), 1996 (1), 1997 (1), 2000 (1), 2001 (1), 2002 (1)	Male (10), Female (5)
bó 博 'rich'	[paʔ]	16	1935 (1), 1937 (1), 1947 (1), 1951 (1), 1954 (1), 1970 (2), 1973 (1), 1974 (1), 1980 (2), 1978 (1), 1996 (1), 2000 (1), 2001 (1), 2001 (1)	Male (13), Female (3)
	[paʔ] or [˔puə]	1	1984 (1)	Female
	[˔puə]	1	1997 (1)	Female
Hǎo 郝 [surname]	[xaʔ]	12	1935 (1), 1937 (1), 1947 (1), 1951 (1), 1954 (1), 1970 (2), 1973 (1), 1974 (1), 1978 (1), 1980 (1), 1984 (1)	Male (8), Female (4)
	[xaʔ] or [˥xɔɔ]	1	1980 (1)	Male
	[˥xɔɔ]	5	1996 (1), 1997 (1), 2000 (1), 2001 (1), 2002 (1)	Male (4), Female (1)
Huò 霍 [surname]	[xuəʔ]	13	1935 (1), 1937 (1), 1947 (1), 1951 (1), 1954 (1), 1970 (2), 1973 (1), 1974 (1), 1978 (1), 1980 (2), 1984 (1)	Male (9), Female (4)
	[xuəˀ]	5	1996 (1), 1997 (1), 2000 (1), 2001 (1), 2002 (1)	Male (4), Female (1)
báo 薄 'thin'	[paʔ] or [˔puə]	11	1935 (1), 1937 (1), 1947 (1), 1951 (1), 1954 (1), 1970 (2), 1974 (1), 1978 (1), 1980 (2)	Male (8), Female (3)
	[˔puə]	7	1973 (1), 1984 (1), 1996 (1), 1997 (1), 2000 (1), 2001 (1), 2002 (1)	Male (5), Female (2)
yào 藥 'medicine'	[iaʔ]	6	1937 (1), 1947 (1), 1951 (1), 1970 (1), 1980 (2)	Male (5), Female (1)
	[iaʔ] or [iɔɔˀ]	6	1935 (1), 1970 (1), 1973 (1), 1974 (1), 1978 (1), 1996 (1)	Male (5), Female (1)
	[iɔɔˀ]	6	1954 (1), 1984 (1), 1997 (1), 2000 (1), 2001 (1), 2002 (1)	Male (3), Female (3)

(continued on p. 257)

Table 14.5 (continued)

Syllable	Pronunciations	Number of speakers	Year of birth	Gender
jiǎo 角 'horn'	[tɕiaʔ]	16	1935 (1), 1937 (1), 1947 (1), 1951 (1), 1954 (1), 1970 (2), 1973 (1), 1974 (1), 1978 (1), 1980 (2), 1984 (1), 1996 (1), 2000 (1), 2002 (1)	Male (12), Female (4)
	[tɕiaʔ] or [˚tɕiɔo]	2	1997 (1), 2001 (1)	Male (1), Female (1)
Yuè 岳 [surname]	[iaʔ]	3	1937 (1), 1947 (1), 1951 (1)	Male (3)
	[yaʔ]	15	1935 (1), 1954 (1), 1970 (2), 1973 (1), 1974 (1), 1978 (1), 1980 (2), 1984 (1), 1996 (1), 1997 (1), 2000 (1), 2001 (1), 2002 (1)	Male (10), Female (5)
yuè 樂 'music'	[iaʔ]	6	1935 (1), 1947 (1), 1951 (1), 1970 (1), 1980 (2)	Male (6)
	[yaʔ]	12	1937 (1), 1954 (1), 1970 (1), 1973 (1), 1974 (1), 1978 (1), 1984 (1), 1996 (1), 1997 (1), 2000 (1), 2001 (1), 2002 (1)	Male (7), Female (5)
zhí 直 'straight'	[tʂəʔ]	15	1937 (1), 1947 (1), 1951 (1), 1954 (1), 1970 (2), 1973 (1), 1974 (1), 1978 (1), 1980 (1), 1996 (1), 1997 (1), 2000 (1), 2001 (1), 2002 (1)	Male (11), Female (4)
	[tʂəʔ] or [˳tʂʅ]	3	1935 (1), 1980 (1), 1984 (1)	Male (2), Female (1)
mò 墨 'ink'	[miəʔ]	8	1935 (1), 1937 (1), 1947 (1), 1951 (1), 1954 (1), 1970 (1), 1973 (1), 1974 (1)	Male (5), Female (3)
	[miəʔ] or [moˀ]	9	1970 (1), 1978 (1), 1980 (2), 1984 (1), 1996 (1), 1997 (1), 2000 (1), 2001 (1)	Male (7), Female (2)
	[moˀ]	1	2002 (1)	Male
kè 客 'guest'	[tɕiaʔ] or [kʻaʔ]	16	1935 (1), 1937 (1), 1947 (1), 1951 (1), 1954 (1), 1970 (2), 1973 (1), 1974 (1), 1978 (1), 1980 (2), 1984 (1), 1996 (1), 1997 (1), 2000 (1)	Male (11), Female (5)
	[tʻiaʔ] or [kʻaʔ]	1	2002 (1)	Male
	[kʻaʔ]	1	2001 (1)	Male

(continued on p. 258)

Table 14.5 (continued)

Syllable	Pronunciations	Number of speakers	Year of birth	Gender
mài 脈 'pulse'	[miaʔ]	14	1935 (1), 1937 (1), 1947 (1), 1951 (1), 1954 (1), 1970 (2), 1973 (1), 1978 (1), 1980 (2), 1984 (1), 1996 (1), 2000 (1)	Male (11), Female (3)
	[miaʔ] or [mɛeˀ]	1	1974 (1)	Female
	[mɛeˀ]	3	1997 (1), 2001 (1), 2002 (1)	Male (2), Female (1)
mài 麥 'wheat'	[miaʔ] or [mɛeˀ]	4	1935 (1), 1947 (1), 1951 (1), 1973 (1)	Male (4)
	[mɛeˀ]	14	1937 (1), 1954 (1), 1970 (2), 1974 (1), 1978 (1), 1980 (2), 1984 (1), 1996 (1), 1997 (1), 2000 (1), 2001 (1), 2002 (1)	Male (9), Female (5)
dú 毒 'poison'	[tuəʔ] or [˗tu]	3	1947 (1), 1970 (1), 2002 (1)	Male (3)
	[˗tu]	15	1935 (1), 1937 (1), 1951 (1), 1954 (1), 1970 (1), 1973 (1), 1974 (1), 1978 (1), 1980 (2), 1984 (1), 1996 (1), 1997 (1), 2000 (1), 2001 (1)	Male (10), Female (5)
lǜ 綠 'green'	[lyəʔ]	9	1947 (1), 1951 (1), 1954 (1), 1970 (2), 1973 (1), 1978 (1), 1980 (2)	Male (8), Female (1)
	[lyəʔ] or [lyˀ]	4	1935(1), 1937(1), 1974(1), 2001(1)	Male (2), Female (2)
	[lyˀ]	5	1984 (1), 1996 (1), 1997 (1), 2000 (1), 2002 (1)	Male (3), Female (2)

Discussion: Analysis of Results

Both our findings and preceding reports from Yáng Zēngwǔ (1990) indicate that the younger Shānyīn speakers are losing the glottal stop and that this process is happening slowly but steadily. As William S. Y. Wang (1969) stated in his well-known theory of lexical diffusion, there are three stages for this process: unchanged, ongoing change, and changed. In other words, this is a dynamic process; and we can divide the 84 syllables into three types, as indicated in Table 14.6. Below we consider the factors affecting the syllables in the "in-progress" category that are in the stage of ongoing-change.

Table 14.6: The state of change in the *rù* tone syllables surveyed

	Unchanged	Ongoing-change	Changed
Syllables	接,喝,聶,濕,十,習,八,刮,割,節,説,瞎,血,薛,雪,噎,鐵,捏,筆,不,骨,忽,七,漆,一,出,沒,腳,郭,朔,桌,北,色,黑,媳,力,百,伯,隔,尺,吃,踢,石,福,哭,複,屬 (47)	葉,給,活,熱,月,虱,術,粥,蜜,日,博,郝,霍,薄,藥,鑰,角,學,岳,樂,直,值,墨,窄,客,脈,席,白,麥,叔,毒,局,綠 (33)	襪,侄,賊,木 (4)

The direction and pace of *rù* tone syllable variation

Findings from the current study as well as those from Yáng Zēngwǔ (1990) clearly reveal that the variation of the *rù* tone is increasingly prominent. Yet we also find cases of the opposite process, in which some non-*rù* tone syllables tend to become *rù* tone. There are various reasons for this kind of change. We can safely conclude that although more and more *rù* tone syllables are changing to non-*rù* tone, it is almost impossible for the change to be completed within just a few decades. Aside from the influence of Modern Standard Chinese (Pǔtōnghuà), dialects have their own autonomous systems and motivations that are equally important in language development. This includes the phenomenon of non-*rù* tone syllables changing to *rù* tone in parallel with *rù* tone syllables dropping the glottal stop. The former process serves as the compensating mechanism for the mainstream process.

The *rù* tone syllables that are undergoing variation can be divided into two groups: one group is influenced by Pǔtōnghuà and the other developed on its own following normal Shānyīn dialect evolution. The number of syllables in the first group is the largest, with 30 out of the 33 syllables. The non-*rù* version of 28 of these 30 corresponds exactly to Pǔtōnghuà: *yè* 葉 [iɛ²⁴], *gěi* 給 [kei⁵²], *huó* 活 [xuə⁵⁵], *rè* 熱 [zə²⁴], *yuè* 月 [yɛ²⁴], *shī* 虱 [ʂʅ⁵⁵], *shù* 術 [ʂu²⁴], *bì* 粥 [pi²⁴], *mì* 蜜 [mi²⁴], *rì* 日 [ʐʅ²⁴], *bó* 博 [puə⁵⁵], *hǎo* 郝 [xɔɔ⁵²], *huò* 霍 [xuə²⁴], *báo* 薄 [puə⁵⁵], *yào* 藥 [iɔɔ²⁴], *yào* 鑰 [iɔɔ²⁴], *jiǎo* 角 [tɕiɔɔ⁵²], *zhí* 直 [tʂʅ⁵⁵], zhí值 [tʂʅ⁵⁵], *mò* 墨 [muə²⁴], *zhǎi* 窄 [tʂɛɛ⁵²], *mài* 脈 [mɛɛ²⁴], *xí* 席 [ɕi⁵⁵], *bái* 白 [pɛɛ⁵⁵], *mài* 麥 [mɛɛ²⁴], *dú* 毒 [tu⁵⁵], *jú* 局 [tɕy⁵⁵], and *lǜ* 綠 [ly²⁴]. Of the remaining syllables, *kè* 客 [k'aʔ] 'guest' shares its initial with Pǔtōnghuà and *yuè* 樂 [yaʔ] 'music' shares its medial with Pǔtōnghuà, The only two syllables that have not been influenced by Pǔtōnghuà are *xué* 學 [ɕyaʔ] and shū 叔 [ʂu⁵⁵]. Variation in the syllable *yuè* 岳 is in between these two types: the *rù* tone version [yaʔ] shares its medial with Pǔtōnghuà, while a non-*rù* tone variant [iɔɔ⁵²], found in the local place name Dàiyuè 岱岳 [tɛɛ²⁴iɔɔ⁵²], originated long ago and was not influenced by Pǔtōnghuà.[2]

---

2. All speakers in Shānyīn use the non-*rù* variant in 'Dàiyuè 岱岳 [tɛɛ²⁴iɔɔ⁵²]', not just the eighteen speakers of our survey.

We find that the change from *rù* tone to non-*rù* tone was gradual. Some words changed to non-*rù* tones and then the *rù* tone and non-*rù* tone versions coexisted for a period of time. As time passed, non-*rù* tone forms gradually developed. For example, *rù* 褥 has two variants, [zuə?] and [zu˒] in Wang (1959), while in Yáng Zēngwǔ (1990) only the [zu˒] is left.[3]

While more and more *rù* tone syllables are losing the glottal stop, more than 50 percent of the *rù* tone syllables retain it. At the same time, some non-*rù* tone syllables are evolving into *rù* tone. None of these variations and changes in the Shānyīn dialect are isolated phenomena. Corresponding developments are seen in some neighboring *Jìn* dialects as well. The relationship between *rù* tone and non-*rù* variants within the *Jìn* dialect speech community is an important sociolinguistic phenomenon that we examine more closely below.

The influence of Pǔtōnghuà in variants

The most important factor behind *rù* tone syllables evolving to non-*rù* tone is the influence of Pǔtōnghuà. Upon closer examination of the *rù* tone data, we find that the main vowel goes through a significant change in these cases. In concurrence with the definite drop of the glottal stop, the vowels become diphthongs. The *rù* tone version of both *yào* 藥 and *yào* 鑰 is [ia?], while the non-*rù* tone version is [iɔo˒]. Other examples are *hǎo* 郝 and *zéi* 賊, with the former pronounced [xa?] by senior and middle-aged speakers, and as [ᶜxɔo] by younger students. The latter has the pronunciation [tsa?] in Wang (1959), while in our survey we found it has changed to [ᴄtsei] or [ᴄtsɛe]. Both situations are clear results of the influence of Pǔtōnghuà.

Some *rù* tone syllables keep the glottal stop but take on specific features of Pǔtōnghuà in their initial. For example, the initial of both *tiě* 鐵 and *tī* 踢 follow the Pǔtōnghuà, becoming [t'] from [tɕ']. Some changes also involve the medial. For instance, *bái* 白, *mài* 麥, and *mài* 脈 have a medial 'i' in the *rù* tone version but lose the medial in the non-*rù* tone version. Examples include 白 [pia?] > [ᴄpɛe], 麥 [mia?] > [mɛe˒], and 脈 [mia?] > [mɛe˒].

There is also a degree of instability in the variation of *rù* tone syllables. With some speakers, certain *rù* tone syllables are pronounced in the *rù* tone in some cases but pronounced using the non-*rù* tone in other cases. Sometimes there is free variation in a single word. For instance, *Yuè* 月 is pronounced either [ya?] or [ye˒] in *yuèliàng* 月亮 'moon' by a male speaker born in 1935 and a female speaker born in 1954. Other times, the variation is lexicalized. For example, *Mò* "墨" is pronounced [muə˒] in *mòhér* 墨盒兒 'ink-box' and [miə?] in *mòzhī* 墨汁 '(liquid) ink' in the speech of a male speaker born in 1970. That speaker also has variation in his pronunciation of *rè* 熱, [za?] in *rèlì gōngsī* 熱力公司 and [zə˒] in *rèshuǐ* 熱水. Eight out of

---

3. For an explanation of the meaning of the semi-circular tone marks at the left and right of some transcribed syllables here and following, see Simmons (2017).

thirteen middle-aged speakers have a similar variation. Three speakers only have the non-*rù* tone version and two have the *rù* tone version. As for the five young speakers, only one of them renders it as the *rù* tone, three pronounce it as the non-*rù* tone, and the other one uses both pronunciations. Some young speakers also hesitate whether to use the *rù* tone version or non-*rù* tone version. In other words, *rù* tone variation follows a fuzzy regularity rather than a categorical rule.

Internal factors affecting *rù* tone syllable variation

That the same *rù* tone syllable can be pronounced differently is not unexpected. Variation is the result of competition between the dialect and Pǔtōnghuà as well as the result of phonetic developments within the dialect. The former is an external factor and the latter is an internal factor. Examination of the evolution of the tone system in Shānyīn dialect reveals that the internal factor is of equal weight to, if not more important than, the external factors. In Wáng 王 (1959), the dialect has five tones: *yīnpíng, yángpíng, shǎngshēng, qùshēng*, and *rùshēng*. In Yáng Zēngwǔ (1990), the five-tone system has become a four-tone system in which the two *píng* tones have merged. So the *píng* tone in the present-day Shānyīn dialect consists of both *yīnpíng* and *yángpíng* tone categories. This change has nothing to do with the influence of other dialects, for the surrounding dialects, as well as Pǔtōnghuà, all have the two *píng* tones. Thus, the merger of the *yīnpíng* and *yángpíng* tones into a single *píng* tone is a relatively recent change in the Shānyīn dialect. This should be a reminder to us that the influence of surrounding dialects does matter in dialect change and evolution; but it should not be overemphasized, as internal factors for change in dialects is critical as well.

Returning to the variation of *rù* tone syllables in the Shānyīn dialect, there are other reasons besides for variation. One is *érhuà* 兒化 'rhoticizaton', the effect of *ér* suffixization on a syllable. *Bó* 伯 and *shū* 叔 are both pronounced as a *rù* tone in *shūbó* 叔伯 [ʂuə?piaʔ] 'paternal cousins', while in the words *dàbór* 大伯兒 [ta²⁴piər⁵⁵] 'older brother-in-law' and *xiǎoshūr* 小叔兒 [ɕiɔ⁵²ʂuər²⁴] 'younger brother-in-law' they are [˳piər] and [ʂuərˀ], respectively. Some may argue that *shū* 叔 also has a non-*rù* tone version. But in fact [ʂuərˀ] is derived from [ʂuəʔ] and does not originate from [˳ʂəu]. Another example is *jiǎo* 角 [[tɕiaʔ]], which is pronounced [˳tɕyər] in *gējiǎor* 圪角兒 [kəʔtɕyər⁵²] 'corner'.

The relative weight of the influencing factors

The variations we observed are reflections of the fact that since the 1980s, more and more Jìn dialect speakers have adopted new pronunciations as many loan-words have entered the local dialects and more and more people have adapted their accent to Pǔtōnghuà. In light of this situation, next we address the following questions:

1. What is more important in the development of *rù* tone variation, the influence of Pǔtōnghuà or developments internal to the dialect?
2. Does word frequency matter in the process of sound change?
3. Are words in the literary strata more liable to drop the glottal stop than words in the colloquial strata?

The answer to the first question is that the influence of Pǔtōnghuà is more important. Yet while the dialect is primarily influenced by Pǔtōnghuà, age and education are also important catalysts. In probing into the development and evolution of the *rù* tone in Shānyīn from a sociolinguistic perspective, we found that age is the most important reason behind change, while education is an important secondary reason. The younger the speaker is, the more prominent are the effects of Pǔtōnghuà on their pronunciation, and the older the speaker the less prominent are those effects. Gender also makes a difference. Although there were only five female speakers in our survey, the number of syllables pronounced with the *rù* tone or spoken with two variants was relatively more frequent in their speech compared to that of the males.

The answer to the second question is that word frequency does not seem to have any consistent effect on the variation of *rù* tone. Some high-frequency words do have variants, for example, *xué* 學, *huó* 活, *báo* 薄, *rè* 熱, *yuè* 月, *lǜ* 綠, and *bó* 伯. Yet other high-frequency syllables all remain with a *rù* tone without variation. This includes the verbs *chī* 吃 [tʂəʔ], *hé* 喝 [xaʔ], *chū* 出 [tʂʰuəʔ], *jiē* 接 [tɕiaʔ], *kū* 哭 [kʰuəʔ], *niē* 捏 [ɲiaʔ], *yē* 噎 [iaʔ], and *gé* 隔 [kaʔ]; the nouns *jiǎo* 腳 [tɕiaʔ], *zhuō* 桌 [tʂuaʔ], *xí* 媳 [ɕiəʔ], *xuě* 雪 [ɕyaʔ], *xuè* 血 [ɕyaʔ], *sè* 色 [saʔ], *shí* 石 [ʂəʔ], *fú* 福 [fəʔ]; the numbers *yī* 一 [iəʔ], *qī* 七 [tɕʰiəʔ], *bā* 八 [paʔ], *shí* 十 [ʂəʔ], *bǎi* 百 [piaʔ]; negatives *bù* 不 [pəʔ], and *méi* 沒 [məʔ]; and the adjectives *shī* 濕 [ʂəʔ] and *hēi* 黑 [xəʔ]. This leads us to conclude that frequency is not a critical factor in the evolution of the *rù* tone in Shānyīn dialect.

The rise of new vocabulary and the loss of older words are influenced by social change. Some words that are less frequently used are often replaced by Pǔtōnghuà forms. For example, *shīzi* 蝨子 'louse' is a rare word in recent decades. Therefore, it is not surprising at all for two young speakers (one 12-year-old and one 13-year-old) to adopt the Pǔtōnghuà form [ʂʅ] as a loan word as they had no exposure to the older form in *shīzi* 蝨子 [saʔzə]. Yet all 16 of the other speakers pronounce it in the *rù* form as [saʔ], which reflects the more common status of the word in society. The variation within a category, however, is never as neat as might be expected.

In some cases, the *rù* tone form of a syllable has not disappeared but the speaker is not aware of the connection with a dialect form. In these cases, the syllables are usually prounounced as in Pǔtōnghuà. Examples include the *rù* tone syllables *bái* 白, *mài* 麥, and *mài* 脈, respectively in *báizhú* 白朮 [piaʔtʂuəʔ] 'macrocephala rhizome', *màidōng* 麥冬 [miaʔtuə̃⁵⁵] 'dwarf lilyturf', and *zhuōmài/hàomài* 捉脈 [tʂuaʔmiaʔ]/ 號脈 [xɔ²⁴miaʔ] 'feel the pulse'. Because most Chinese parents now seek doctors who practice Western medicine for help when their children are sick, children are unfamiliar with Chinese traditional medicine. Fifteen speakers did not know the word *màidōng* 麥冬 so they just pronounced the first syllable as [mɛe²⁴]. Only three speakers pronounce it [miaʔ]; and a male speaker born in 1935 pronounced the *mài* 麥 in *xiǎomài* 小麥 as [miaʔ], but did not know the word *màidōng* 麥冬. A similar situation was observed with *báizhú* 白朮, with one speaker pronouncing it [piaʔtʂuəʔ]. *Zhuōmài* 捉脈 saw a stronger preservation of the *rù* tone: fifteen speakers pronounced it as [tʂuaʔmiaʔ] (or [xɔɔ²⁴miaʔ] *hàomài* 捉脈) without prompting. One male speaker born in 1970 used the *rù* tone version of the syllable *mài* in the curse word *méimàihuò* 沒脈貨 [məʔ miaʔ xuə²⁴] 'pulse-less corpse'. This reveals that Shānyīn speakers are more familiar with traditional Chinese medicinal therapy than they are with the traditional herbal remedies. The process of *mài* 麥 [mɛe²⁴] and *bái* 白 [pɛe⁵⁵] replacing [miaʔ] and [piaʔ] in the names of herbal medicine will be complete within the next few decades, while *mài* 脈 [miaʔ] in its therapeutic sense will likely continue to be pronounced in the *rù* tone for quite a long time, although it definitely is not a high-frequency word.

Some syllables are much more susceptible to variance than others, even when they share the same word frequency. *Yàoshi* 鑰匙 [iɔɔ²⁴sŋ⁵⁵] 'keys', *wàzi* 襪子 [ua²⁴zə] 'socks', *shí* 石 [ʂəʔ] 'stone', *jiǎo* 腳 [tɕiaʔ] 'foot', *rè* 熱 [zə²⁴]/[zaʔ] 'hot', and *yuè* 月 [yɛ²⁴]/[yaʔ] 'moon' are all high-frequency words. We found that *yào* 鑰 and *wà* 襪 have lost the glottal stop of the *rù* tone; *shí* 石 and *jiǎo* 腳 have retained it; and *rè* 熱 and *yuè* 月 are in the process of variation.

Guō 郭, Xí 習, Niè 聶, Yè 葉, Hǎo 郝, Huò 霍, and Bó 薄 are all family names which are not frequently used. All eighteen speakers pronounce Guō 郭 and Xí 習 as [kuaʔ] and [ɕiəʔ], respectively. In Niè 聶 [niaʔ], the glottal stop is preserved by all speakers except one male speaker born in 1996. All the speakers from twelve to eighteen years of age pronounce Hǎo 郝 and Huò 霍 with a non-*rù* tone, [xɔɔ⁵²] and [xuə²⁴] respectively. The two names Yè 葉 [iaʔ]/[iɛ²⁴] and Bó 薄 [puə⁵⁵]/[paʔ] are in the middle stage of variation between *rù* and non-*rù* forms.

The above analysis of some of the phenomena from the perspective of sociolinguistics reveals that the Shānyīn dialect is rapidly taking on many characteristics of Pǔtōnghuà. Some *rù* tone syllables in Shānyīn dialect have changed remarkably in terms of pronunciation under the influence of Pǔtōnghuà.

Some *rù* tone syllables have a Pǔtōnghuà-influenced counterpart, which might still be *rù* tone, such as *kè* 客, *tī* 踢, *tiě* 鐵, and *yuè* 樂. In the speech of three young speakers, the initial of *tī* 踢 [tɕʻiəʔ] and *tiě* 鐵 [tɕʻiaʔ] has changed to [tʻ] which is a feature of Pǔtōnghuà, as noted earlier, while the glottal stop is still preserved. One speaker pronounces both variants for each word, [tɕʻiəʔ] or [tʻiəʔ] for *tī* 踢 and [tɕʻiaʔ] or [tʻiaʔ] for *tiě* 鐵. Seventeen speakers pronounce the syllable *kè* 客 in *kèrén* 客人 'guest' as [tɕʻiaʔ]. Only one male speaker born in 2001 pronounces it as [kʻaʔ], apparently influenced by Pǔtōnghuà. But in the words *kèyùn zhān* 客運站 [kʻaʔyɤ̃²⁴tsɛ²⁴] 'passenger station' and *kèdū* 客都 [kʻaʔtu⁵⁵] '*Kèdū* [supermarket]' all the speakers say [kʻaʔ]. Twelve speakers pronounce *yuè* 樂 in *yīnyuè* 音樂 [iə̃⁵⁵iaʔ] 'music' as [yaʔ]. The medial [y] is the result of partial assimilation by Pǔtōnghuà. Six speakers pronunce it as the original dialect [iaʔ], with a medial [i]. As for the meaning 'happy' written with the same graph, the pronunciation is *lè* 樂 [luaʔ]. *Lǜ* 綠 'green' has *rù* and non-*rù* variants [lyəʔ] and [ly²⁴]. In overall perspective, quantitatively speaking, there emerges a rather dominant trend in which the *rù* tone is changing to the non-*rù* tone. Far more *rù* tone syllables change to non-*rù* tone syllables than follow the opposite process.

Finally, the answer to the third question is in the negative: the tendency for loss of the *rù* tone pronunciation is not affected by literary or colloquial usage. In the early stages, all the literary words were pronounced in their *rù* tone version, including, for example, the *rù* syllables in *bóshì* 博士 [paʔsʅ²⁴] 'doctor', *suànshù* 算術 [suɛ²⁴ʂuəʔ] 'arithmetic', *bóruò* 薄弱 [paʔʐua] 'weak', Yuè Fēi 岳飛 [yaʔ fei⁵⁵], and Bì Mǎwēn 弼馬溫 [piəʔ ma⁵² uə̃⁵⁵]. But as time passes, more and more literary words are also coming to be pronounced in the non-*rù* tone version, such as *màidōng* 麥冬 [mɛɛ²⁴tuə̃⁵⁵] and *shīzi* 虱子 [ʂʅ⁵⁵zə] discussed earlier.

Conclusion

This study is based on a relatively small-scale investigation. While we still can safely conclude that the Shānyīn *rù* tone category will persist for quite a long time, there are several obvious indications that dramatic change is in progress. The mainstream cause behind the trend is the influence of Pǔtōnghuà. First, some *rù* tones syllables have changed to non-*rù* tone. Second, medials have become similar to Pǔtōnghuà. For most *rù* tone syllables that have both literary and colloquial versions, the only difference is in the medial, such as we saw with *yuè* 岳 and *yuè* 樂 [iaʔ]/[yaʔ]. Third, the initial is influenced by Pǔtōnghuà, as seen with *kè* 客 [tɕ'iaʔ]/[k'aʔ], *tī* 踢 [tɕ'iəʔ]/[t'iə ʔ], and *tiě* 鐵 [tɕ'ia]/[t'iaʔ].

In the data of Wáng (1959), the five *rù* tone syllables *zéi* 賊 [tsaʔ], *mài* 麥 [miaʔ], *yào* 鑰 [iaʔ], *wà* 襪 [uaʔ], and *dú* 毒 [tuəʔ] have changed to non-*rù* tone. Our survey found that now only *mài* 麥 is pronounced [miaʔ] in *màidōng* 麥冬 in the speech of a few senior citizens. It can be conjectured that this version will disappear soon. To illustrate, in Wáng (1959), *rù* 褥 has both *rù* tone and non-*rù* tone versions. But both our survey and Yáng Zēngwǔ (1990) found no *rù* tone variant of this syllable. The loss was completed within forty years.

In broader perspective, the disappearance of the glottal stop within Shānyīn phonology has been a slow but steady process over quite a long period. The loss of the glottal stop in *rù* tone syllables is more gradual across the complete lexicon, generally following a pattern of lexical diffusion.

Having examined the patterns of variation in the Shānyīn dialect *rù* tone syllables, both between speakers and within a single speaker's usage, we found that the variation is not affected by word frequency, as we initially expected. Alongside the inevitable influence of the standard language (Pǔtōnghuà), age and education markedly affect the realization of the variant pronunciations. We observed gradual change happening along a variety of tracks: from younger to older speakers, from less-educated speakers to more well-educated speakers, from loan words to local words, and also from syllabic segment to the whole syllable. The variation then, is the result of ongoing diachronic change, observed across data collected both at different times and in apparent time in the synchronic variants observed between speakers of different generations.

References

Norman, Jerry. 2006. "Common Dialectal Chinese." In *The Chinese Rime Tables*, edited by David Branner, 233–54. Amsterdam: Benjamins. Chinese translation: Shǐ Hàoyuán 史皓元 [Richard VanNess Simmons] and Zhāng Yànhóng 張艷紅. 2011. "Hànyǔ fāngyán tōngyīn" 漢語方言通音 *Fangyan* 方言 2: 97–116.

Shěn Míng 沈明. 2005. "Jìn dōngnán Jìnyǔ rùshēngdiào de yǎnbiàn" 晉東南晉語入聲調的演變 [The evolution of the *rù* tone in the Jìn dialects of southeastern Shānxī]. *Yǔwén yánjiū* 語文研究 2005 (4): 52–62.

Simmons, Richard VanNess. 2017. "Pre-modern tonal notation for Chinese." *Encyclopedia of Chinese Language and Linguistics*, vol. 4, 321–26. Leiden: Brill.

Wáng 王. 1959. Unpublished report written by a Peking University team held in the Peking University archives.

Wang, William S-Y. 1969. "Competing Changes as a Cause of Residue." *Language* 45: 9–25.

Yáng Zēngwǔ 楊增武. 1990. *Shānyīn fāngyánzhì* 山陰方言志 [A record of the Shānyīn dialect]. Běijīng: Yǔwén chūbǎnshè.

Zhang, Jie. 1998. "A Typology of Ru Tones in Chinese Dialects: Evidence for Phonetically-Driven Phonology." *Papers from the Regional Meetings, Chicago Linguistics Society* 34 (1): 439–53.

15
Tonal Features Based on Acoustic Analysis and Historical Development in Mùlěi Mandarin in Xīnjiāng

Liú Xīnzhōng

Introduction

Lányín 蘭銀 Mandarin in Xīnjiāng 新疆 is mainly distributed from Shāwān 沙灣 county to the east of Hāmì 哈密 city, along the north Tiānshān 天山 area, including twenty-two major cities, among which are Shāwān 沙灣, Mǎnàsī 瑪納斯, Hūtúbì 呼圖壁, Chāngjí 昌吉, Urumqi 烏魯木齊, Mǐquán 米泉, Jimsar 吉木薩爾, Qītái 奇台, Mùlěi 木壘, Barkol 巴里坤, and Hāmì 哈密. A characteristic feature of Lányín Mandarin is a reduced number of tones, with a three-tone system being quite common. This chapter examines the tone system of present-day Mùlěi Lányín Mandarin as represented in the speech of one middle-aged male speaker who provided recordings of 3,595 monosyllabic words. In light of our analysis of the tone system represented by this speaker, we argue for categorizing the Mùlěi tones into the three categories of *píng*, *shǎng*, and *qù*.

Data and Methods

After the recordings were made, all the data were extracted and analyzed using software and program scripts developed by Mr. Xióng Zǐyú 熊子瑜, technical researcher at the Chinese Academy of Social Sciences. The main process is as follows:

(1) The basis for the design of the survey of dialect word lists was the *Fāngyán diàochá zìbiǎo* 方言調查字表 [Syllabary for dialect fieldwork], edited by the Linguistic Institute of the Chinese Academy of Social Sciences.
(2) The sounds were recorded with xRecorder audio recording software, and a script automatically generated a text grid with annotation for each voice file; then another script, "tabular data manipulation," checked the recording.
(3) A PitchTier data object was generated and calibrated with a script.
(4) Smoothed processing of PitchTier objects was conducted; for each syllable we measured the start and end point of the pitch.
(5) We defined ten pitch points for means analysis and graphing.

(6) Extracted tonal duration, F0, and annotation data were extracted; discriminant analysis was then conducted.

The Tonal System of Mùlěi Mandarin

Through analysis of the tone data of the 3,595 Chinese syllables, we obtained tone data for all the syllables recorded. In the results, *píng* tone has 251 syllables, *shǎng* tone has 1,467 syllables, and *qù* tone has 1,407 syllables, as shown in Table 15.1.

Table 15.1: The average value of Mùlán Mandarin tones (pitch_Hz, duration_ms, and number of syllables)

Tones	T1	T2	T3	T4	T5	T6	T7	T8	T9	T10	Duration ms	No. of syllables
Píng	132	131	131	131	130	129	128	128	127	125	377	721
Shǎng	148	146	142	137	129	119	109	100	93	88	326	1467
Qù	108	102	98	96	94	94	96	101	107	111	386	1407

To mimic perception, we converted the pitch values to a logarithmic scale. For Table 15.2, we converted the values in Table 15.1 according to the following formula, developed by Shí Fēng 石锋 (1987):

T=5*(logX − logMin) / (logMax−LogMin)

Where X is the pitch points in Hz and Max and Min are extremes of the pitch.

Table 15.2: The value of Mùlán Mandarin tones (logarithm value)

Tones	T1	T2	T3	T4	T5	T6	T7	T8	T9	T10	Value of tone
Píng	3.90	3.83	3.83	3.83	3.75	3.68	3.60	3.60	3.53	3.38	44
Shǎng	5.00	4.87	3.90	4.26	3.68	2.90	2.06	1.23	0.53	0.00	51
Qù	1.97	1.42	1.04	0.84	0.63	0.63	0.84	1.33	1.88	2.23	213

Using this formula, all pitches are distributed in the interval from 0 to 5. In Mùlěi Lányín Mandarin, the *píng* tone's value is 44, the *shǎng* tone is 51, and the *qù* tone is 213. Figure 15.1 shows the graphical representation of the data in Table 15.2.

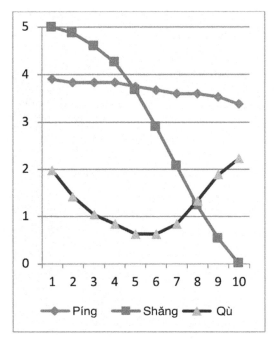

Figure 15.1: Contour of Mùlán Mandarin tones

To Denominate the Tone System and Its Correspondence with the Common Dialectal Chinese Tone System

The three Lányín Mandarin tones have been conventionally identified as *yīnpíng*, *yángpíng*, and *qù*. In this formulation, the *píng* tone was divided into *yīn* and *yáng* registers and was seen to have absorbed the other tones, such as the *shǎng* tone. But does this reflect the actual situation? Below we show the correspondence between the ancient common dialectal tones and today's tones in Mùlěi Lányín Mandarin.

Common Dialectal Chinese (CDC) follows the traditional analysis of four tones—*píng*, *shǎng*, *qù*, and *rù*, with each divided into two registers—*yīn* and *yáng*, making a total of eight CDC tone categories.[1] We subdivided the eight tones into 16 types according to the manner of articulation of the CDC initials with which they occur: voiceless unaspirated (voiceless 1), voiceless aspirated (voiceless 2), voiced obstruent (voiced 1), and sonorant (voiced 2). We then extracted the corresponding modern tone data, the pitch value of the tones in articulation, in order to observe the distribution of the tone types in Mùlěi Lányín Mandarin. The results are shown in Table 15.3.

---

1. See Liú Fù (1925) and Yuen Ren Chao (1922, 1933), who laid the foundation for the study of the tone of modern Chinese, for the foundational studies that led to the established paradigm of four tones in two registers. The CDC adoption of this analysis is based on Norman (2006; 2011).

Table 15.3: The correspondence of tone categories with the tone pitch of modern Mùlěi

Mùlěi tone	CDC Tone & initial	T1	T2	T3	T4	T5	T6	T7	T8	T9	T10	Duration ms	No. of syllables
Píng	Píng Voiceless 1	131	130	130	131	130	130	129	129	128	127	378	548
Píng	Píng Voiceless 2	133	132	131	131	130	129	127	127	126	124	376	173
Píng	Píng Voiced 1	154	151	147	141	133	122	110	100	92	87	312	379
Píng	Píng Voiced 1	148	148	145	140	132	122	111	101	93	88	323	321
Shǎng	Shǎng Voiceless 1	147	145	141	135	127	117	107	99	92	87	326	304
Shǎng	Shǎng Voiceless 2	154	150	146	141	133	122	110	100	93	87	323	97
Shǎng	Shǎng Voiced 2	142	142	140	134	127	117	107	99	93	88	343	166
Shǎng	Rù Voiced 1	141	139	134	129	122	114	106	100	96	94	327	140
Shǎng	Shǎng Voiced 1	107	100	96	93	92	92	94	99	107	111	380	133
Qù	Qù Voiceless 1	105	97	93	91	90	91	94	99	107	113	384	368
Qù	Qù Voiceless 2	106	99	95	93	92	93	96	101	109	114	372	129
Qù	Qù Voiced 1	106	99	94	92	91	92	94	99	107	111	381	196
Qù	Qù Voiced 2	103	99	96	93	91	91	94	99	107	113	410	185
Qù	Rù Voiceless 1	120	116	113	110	107	104	102	103	105	106	371	234
Qù	Rù Voiceless 2	115	109	105	102	101	100	101	103	108	109	369	90
Qù	Rù Voiced 2	101	97	94	92	91	91	94	100	108	113	420	132
													3595

With the data in Table 15.3, we have mapped the correspondence of the CDC tones against the modern tones of Mùlěi Lányín Mandarin. Figure 15.2 displays how the four CDC tones (without register distinction) correspond to the modern tone contours in Mùlěi when sorted according to CDC initial types: voiceless unaspirated (VL1), voiceless aspirated (VL2), voiced obstruent (V1), and sonorant (V2).

The syllables of the CDC *píng* tone can be seen to fall into two contrasting contours that respectively parallel the CDC voiceless and voiced categories of the initials and thus also correspond to the *yīnpíng* and *yángpíng* tonal registers. The syllables of the *yīnpíng* category have a distinct pitch contour in Mùlěi, whereas the syllables in the *yángpíng* category have the same tone contour as the *shǎng* tone syllables that correspond to both CDC voiceless categories and the sonorant voiced category.

In Mùlěi, CDC *shǎng* tone syllables for the most part fall into a single discrete category, with the exception of the syllables whose initials correspond to the CDC voiced obstruent category, which have a contour corresponding to the *qù* tone syllables.

The CDC *qù* tone syllables (of both registers) all fall together in Mùlěi Mandarin.

The evolution of the CDC *rù* tone appears to be more complex on the surface. But the syllables whose initials correspond to the CDC voiced obstruent category have the same contour as the *shǎng* tone. Among syllables reflecting the other three kinds of CDC initials (voiceless, voiceless aspirated, sonorant) the *rù* tones have somewhat variant pitch curves. But in fact, these pitch values are allophonic with the Mùlěi *qù* tone and can be incorporated into it.

The evolution of CDC tones within Mùlěi Mandarin can be summarized as follows:

1. CDC *píng* tone syllables with voiceless initials (both unaspirated and aspirated) remain in the *píng* tone, maintaining a correspondence with the CDC *yīnpíng* category.
2. CDC *píng* tone syllables with voiced initials (both obstruent and sonorant), that is, those that correspond to the CDC *yángpíng* category, have merged with the *shǎng* tone.
3. CDC *shǎng* tone syllables all remain in the *shǎng* tone, except for those with voiced obstruent initials (i.e., excluding those with sonorant initials), which have merged with the *qù* tone.
4. CDC *qù* tone syllables all remain in the *qù* tone.
5. CDC *rù* tone syllables with voiced obstruent initials merged first with the CDC *yángpíng* category tones and then moved together with the *yángpíng* syllables into the *shǎng* tone. The remainder of the *rú* tone syllables have effectively merged with the *qù* tone.

The result of this exercise is our determination that the tones of Mùlěi's three-tone system should be named *píng*, *shǎng*, and *qù*. This conclusion is based, first,

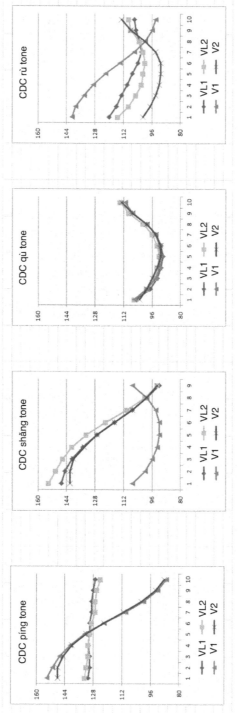

Figure 15.2: CDC tone correspondence to the three tone contours of Mùlán Mandarin

on the actual distribution of the contrastive tone pitch types against the CDC tone categories. Second, the names of tones in the modern Chinese dialects are all usually based on their correspondence to the ancient tones, which also correspond to the CDC tone categories. The derivation of Mùlěi Mandarin tones from the CDC system can be outlined as below.

1. *Píng* tone syllables are all derived from the CDC *yīnpíng* category.
2. *Shǎng* tone syllables include syllables from the following CDC categories:
   a. *Yīnshǎng*, including syllables with sonorant initials.
   b. *Yángpíng* plus *yángrù*, but the latter excluding syllables with sonorant initials.
3. *Qù* tone syllables include syllables from the following CDC categories:
   a. *Yīnqù* and *yángqù*.
   b. *Yángshǎng*, but excluding syllables with sonorant initials.
   c. *Yīnrù*, including syllables with sonorant initials.

Zhōu Lěi 周磊 (2005) argued that "based on their sandhi behavior, the *rù* tone syllables with voiced Middle Chinese initials correspond with *yángpíng*." So he maintained the *yángpíng* category and included in it the Mùlěi syllables from the CDC *shǎng* tone. But our data show that statistically the distribution of the tones of the syllables recorded correspond in overall aggregate to the categories from which they evolved: *píng*, *shǎng*, and *qù*. There is no need to identify the categories according to tone sandhi effects when a more direct correspondence to actual evolutionary origin can be discerned. Moreover, it is likely that the *rù* syllables in the CDC voiced obstruent category merged first with *yángpíng* at some earlier stage and then subsequently moved to the *shǎng* tone concurrently with *yángpíng* in Mùlěi Mandarin.[2] Since the great majority of *shǎng* tone syllables fall together in a tone with a discrete pitch contour in Mùlěi, there is no need to think of them as having merged with *yángpíng*. Hence it is more natural and balanced to conceive of the overall system as the three tones, *píng*, *shǎng*, and *qù*, with *yángpíng* merged into *shǎng*.

Of course, the particular nomenclature does not affect the actual nature of the tones and their system. However, the names assigned to the tones should consider the phonetic, phonological, and evolutionary factors behind them. This way, (1) the names can show the overall distribution of the reality of the phonetic features and pronunciation, and (2) the names can clarify the regularity of their evolution, especially the development of the ancient tones into their modern counterparts. The conditional factors affecting the evolution of the tones and the characteristics of subsequent splits and mergers can be discussed in the light of historical evolution and the distribution of phonological types or categories. Moreover, the names *píng*, *shǎng*, and *qù* also can successfully capture most of the evolutionary conditions, such as those described

---

2. Thanks to the editor of the present volume for this observation.

by Zhōu Lěi wherein "syllables reflecting Middle Chinese voiceless initials in the *rù* tone are now pronounced as the *qù* tone in Lányín Mandarin" (Zhōu Lěi, 2005).

The quantity of the affected syllables in each category is also an impact factor. In our data, there are 700 syllables that correspond to CDC syllables with voiced initials in the *píng* tone. This number is greater than the 567 syllables corresponding to the CDC *shǎng* tone. There are 721 syllables that correspond to the CDC *píng* tone syllables with voiceless initials. These have not merged with other tones, instead retaining the identity of the *píng* tone category, even when the *yángpíng* syllables are identified as having merged with the *shǎng* tone. This conceptualization reflects the actual evolution of the tonal system from CDC to the present. Additionally, tones in Urumqi Mandarin cannot be analyzed as *yīnpíng, yángpíng, qù*. And a set of names combining categories, such as that used for the Yínchuān dialect, "*yīnpíng* (44), *yángpíng-shǎng* (53), and *qù* (13)," provides a rather erratic solution in using the "*yángpíng-shǎng*" name for the merged category.

Conclusion

The present chapter has presented an experimental study based on relatively big data to research both the phonetic reality of the articulation of tones in Mùlěi and the historical evolution of the categories the tones fall into. The main results are:

(1) A descriptive snapshot of the synchronic tone system of the dialect and all the actual phonetic values of the tones found in the large dataset.
(2) A classification of the tones within the system as revealed by a comparative analysis of their historical evolution and outcome in the modern tones.

Where acoustic values were not completely consistent with the evolutionary tone categories and showed a merging of traditional categories, we matched the evolution of the CDC tones against the actual pronunciation of the modern tones, and concluded that Mùlěi Mandarin reveals that Lányín Mandarin in northern Xīnjiāng has three tones: *yīnpíng* is a level tone, *shǎng* is a falling tone, and *qù* is a low falling-rising tone.

We argued against eliminating *shǎng* as a tone category and maintained that the CDC *yángpíng* category should be seen as having merged into *shǎng* in the three-tone system of Lányín Mandarin.

Research on tone in Chinese has made great progress, from methods to content, over the past hundred years. As in many of the tone languages of the world (Goldsmith, Hume, and Wetzels 2010; Hyman 1973; Pike 1961), the tones in Chinese dialects create phonemic contrasts between morphemes; they can also vary in their effects on phonological structure and grammatical category. The study of tone in the Chinese dialects must account for the historical evolution of tones from the ancient phonologies to the modern system. Moreover, the syllables surveyed must be carefully chosen, and the realities of the actual speech must be taken into account. In this way the results of the research will be both reliable and reasonable.

Note: This study was supported in part by: (1) The study of acoustic features on Cantonese, National Social Science Fund, Grant No 2014-14BYY038; (2) a phonetic study on Guangdong Cantonese, Fund of Guangdong key research center of Humanity and Social Science 2012, Grant No 2012JDXM_0007; (3) Dictionaries of Chinese Dialects and their Digitization, Major projects of the National Social Science 2013, Grant No.13ZD135; (4) The protection project for endangered Chinese dialects of Chinese language resources, 2016, Fuma Dialect of Hainan, Grant No.YB1618A009. A previous version of this chapter appeared in Chinese as "Xīnjiāng Mùlěi fāngyán de dānzì diào: yī xiàng jīyú shēngxué shùjù de yánjiū 新疆木垒方言的單字調: 一項基於聲學數據的研究," *Fāngyán* 方言 2017 (3): 336–40. Thanks to Liáng Jiāyíng 梁嘉瑩 for assistance with some of the preliminary research for this chapter.

References

Chao, Yuen Ren 趙元任. 1922. "Zhōngguó yǔyán zìdiào di shíyàn yánjiūfǎ" 中國言語字調底實驗研究法 [The Methodology of experimental study of Chinese tone]. *Kēxué* 科學 7 (9): 871–82.

Chao, Yuen Ren 趙元任. 1933. "Hànyǔ de zìdiào gēn yǔdiào 漢語的字調跟語調" [Tone and intonation in Chinese]. *Bulletin of the Institute of History and Philology* 4 (2): 121–34.

Goldsmith, John A., Elizabeth Hume, and W. Leo Wetzels, eds. 2010. *Tones and Features: Phonetic and Phonological Perspectives*. Berlin: De Gruyter.

Pike, Kenneth L. 1961. *Tone Languages*. Ann Arbor: University of Michigan Press.

Hyman, Larry M., ed. 1973. *Consonant Types & Tone*. Southern California Occasional Papers in Linguistics, no. 1, July 1973. Los Angeles: The Linguistics Program, University of Southern California.

Liú Fù 劉復. 1925. *Étude Expérimentale Sur les Tons du Chinois*, Paris: Société d'Édition les Belles Lettres.

Norman, Jerry. 2006. "Common Dialectal Chinese." In *The Chinese Rime Tables*, edited by David Branner, 233–54. Amsterdam: Benjamins. Chinese translation: Shǐ Hàoyuán 史皓元 [Richard VanNess Simmons] and Zhāng Yànhóng 張艷紅. 2011. "Hànyǔ fāngyán tōngyīn" 漢語方言通音. *Fangyan* 方言 2: 97–116.

Shí Fēng 石鋒. 1987. "Tiānjīn fāngyán dānzìyīn shēngdiào fēnxī" 天津方言單字音聲調分析 [Tianjin dialect single syllable tone acoustical analysis]. *Yǔyán yánjiū lùncóng* 語言研究論叢 4: 69–82.

Zhōu Lěi 周磊. 2005. "Lányín Guānhuà de fēnqū (gǎo) 蘭銀官話的分區(稿)" [The classification of Lányín Mandarin (draft)]. *Fāngyán* 方言 3: 271–78.

Contributors

David Prager Branner (林德威，號茶米) is a sinologist who studies Chinese language and lexicography. His interests are diverse, and his recent study has covered traditional reading practice of literary texts, historical linguistics in the service of literature, and literary translation. Branner trained initially with Robert Austerlitz in dialect field methods and with Jerry Norman in Chinese historical-comparative linguistics. He was granted a doctorate at the University of Washington (1997) and academic tenure at the University of Maryland (2004).

Marjorie K. M. Chan (陳潔雯) is an associate professor of Chinese linguistics in the Department of East Asian Languages and Literatures at The Ohio State University, on the main campus in Columbus, Ohio. Her research publications and teaching in linguistics (at graduate and undergraduate levels) encompass phonetics, phonology (synchronic and diachronic), dialectology, the writing system (including dialect-writing and other East Asian scripts), and sociolinguistic topics such as humor and gender-linked issues. Her teaching assignments have also included traditional Chinese culture and Chinese opera, both national and regional.

Kengo CHIBA (千葉謙悟) obtained his PhD in 2007 from Waseda University, Japan, before taking up the post of professor at Chuo University in Tokyo. His research interests range across lexicography, especially the formation of modern Chinese neologisms, sociolinguistics, and Chinese pedagogy as well as historical phonology in Mandarin. His publications include *Linguistic and Cultural Exchange in Modern Chinese* (2010, in Japanese) and *The Basic Crown Dictionary of Chinese* (2019, with Xiong Jin).

Weldon South Coblin (柯蔚南) was born in Lexington, Kentucky, in 1944. He took his BA in 1967 and PhD in 1972 in Chinese at the University of Washington. In 1973 he joined the faculty of the Department of Asian Languages and Literature at the University of Iowa, where he taught for thirty-seven years, retiring as professor emeritus of Chinese language and linguistics. During the course of his career, his scholarly interests have included Chinese historical linguistics, Chinese historical and comparative dialectology, Chinese koines, Old Tibetan language and linguistics, and Sino-Tibetan comparative and historical linguistics.

GUŌ Lìxiá (郭利霞) is professor in the College of Chinese Language and Culture at Nánkāi University, China. She holds a PhD in Chinese dialectology from Peking University and has been visiting scholar at Rutgers University and visiting assistant professor at MingDao University in Taiwan. Her primary areas of research include Chinese dialectology and teaching Chinese as second language (TCSL). She has published extensively on the grammar of the Jìn dialects and the history of Mandarin. Most recently, she has been researching the evolution of technical terminology in the late Qīng dynasty and early Republic of China.

Henning Klöter (韓可龍) PhD, Leiden University 2003, is professor of modern Chinese languages and literatures at the Institute of Asian and African Studies (IAAW), Humboldt-Universität zu Berlin. He has previously held positions at the universities of Göttingen, Mainz, Bochum, and National Taiwan Normal University. His major publications are *Written Taiwanese* (2005) and *The Language of the Sangleys: A Chinese Vernacular in Missionary Sources of the Seventeenth Century* (2011).

HUÁNG Lín (黃霖) is professor emeritus at Fùdàn University in Shànghǎi, where he has served as director of the Institute of Chinese Language and Literature and director of the Center for Chinese Ancient Literature Research. He has also served as president of the Ming Dynasty Literature Association of China, of the Modern Chinese Literature Association, and of the Shanghai Society for Classical Chinese Literature. His graduate degree was received in 1967 at Fùdàn University. His primary areas of research include the history of Chinese literary criticism and the literature of the Ming and Qing dynasties.

HUÁNG Xiǎodōng (黃曉東) is professor in the Faculty of Linguistic Sciences at Beijing Language and Culture University. He holds a MA degree in Chinese Philology and a PhD degree in linguistics and applied linguistics from Beijing Language and Culture University. He has been a visiting scholar at the Kanazawa University in Japan, and Rutgers University and the University of Pennsylvania in the United States. His research areas include Chinese dialectology, sociolinguistics, and geographical linguistics.

LIÚ Xīnzhōng (劉新中) is professor in the College of Liberal Arts at Jinan University, where he is director of the phonetics laboratory and dean of the Research Institute of Chinese Dialects. His academic expertise includes Chinese dialectology, phonetics, linguistics, and applied linguistics. His primary research focus in recent years is on the study of the combination of acoustics, articulatory phonetics, and cognition of distinctive features in Chinese dialects. He has published more than sixty papers and six monographs and has directed over eleven projects in recent years.

NÍ Zhìjiā (倪志佳) is a PhD student in the Department of Chinese Language and Literature at Peking University. He received his bachelor's degree in Chinese language and literature from Shāndōng University and has a master's degree in Chinese linguistics from Peking University. He has also been an exchange student in the Department of Chinese Language and Literature at East China Normal University and was a visiting student in the Department of Asian Language and Cultures at Rutgers University. His main research direction is Chinese dialectology, especially in the areas of Guānhuà (Mandarin) dialects, Wú dialects, dialect phonology and lexicology, dialect geography, and dialect contact.

SHÍ Rǔjié (石汝杰) is professor at Kumamoto Gaku'en University. He has also served as professor in the Chinese Department at Sūzhōu University and associate professor at Kyushu University. He received his graduate degree Chinese at Fùdàn University. His primary fields of research include Chinese dialects, with a focus on Wú dialects and their history, Chinese dialect geography, and Chinese phonology. His major publications include *The Míng and Qīng Wú Dictionary* (co-edited with Ichiro Miyata, 2005) and *Research in Wú Dialect Lexicon and Its Written Form* (2018).

Richard VanNess Simmons (史皓元) is professor and director of the Chinese Language Center in the School of Chinese at the University of Hong Kong and professor emeritus of Chinese in the Department of Asian Languages and Cultures at Rutgers University. He holds a PhD in sinology and Chinese dialectology from the University of Washington, Seattle. Simmons's research areas include dialectology, dialect geography, historical linguistics, history of Chinese, history of Mandarin, and Chinese sociolinguistics. He has done extensive fieldwork investigating and mapping China's Mandarin and Wu dialects.

ZĒNG Xiǎoyú (曾曉渝) is professor in the School of Arts at Nánkāi University. She holds a master's degree in Chinese history from the Chinese Department of Southwest Normal University and a PhD in minority languages and literature from the Chinese Department at Nánkāi University. She has been visiting scholar at Centre National de la Recherche Scientifique, Centre de recherches linguistiques sur l'Asie orientale (CNRS-CRLAO) in Paris and in the Department of Linguistics of the University of Kansas. Her areas of research include historical Chinese phonology, Chinese dialects, Kam-Tai languages, language contact, and historical linguistics.

ZHĀNG Huìyīng (張惠英) is a native of Chongming, in Shànghǎi municipality, China. She is research professor in the Institute of Linguistics at the Chinese Academy of Social Sciences and professor at Hǎinán Normal University. She has also been a visiting scholar at the Harvard-Yenching Institute, Leiden University, Hong Kong City University, and the University of Hong Kong and has served as visiting professor in the Department of Asian Languages and Literature at the University of Washington. Her areas of research expertise include Chinese dialects, the comparison of Chinese dialects and minority languages, and the history of Chinese.

ZHĀNG Měilán (張美蘭) is professor in the Department of Chinese Language and Literature at Hong Kong Baptist University and previously served for nineteen years in the Chinese Department of Tsinghua University. She holds a PhD in the history of Chinese from Nanjing University and has undertaken post-doctoral research at Peking University and Harvard University. Her research areas include Chán language studies, the history of the Chinese lexicon and grammar, particularly the evolution of common Chinese vocabulary as reflected in early modern texts, the history of Chinese language education, and Běijīng colloquial vocabulary.

Index

Terms

Ānhuī (安徽), 7, 179–82, 186–87, 189–90, 201–2, 220, 224–25, 232

báihuà (白話) 2, 89, 222, 225; *báihuàwén* (白話文), 1, 10; Mandarin and, 1, 90, 114

běifānghuà (北方話). *See under* Mandarin

Běijīng (北京), 6, 8–9, 224, 230; dialect, 109, 118, 129, 155–56, 157 table 8.1, 158, 168–69, 195–97, 198 table 11.1, 199, 200, 200 table 11.2, 202; opera, 44, 47, 243

cantillation: contemporary performance of, 15, 18; in Taiwan, 16; phonology of, 22; prolonged syllables in, 23; styles of, 17; tradition of, 16

Cantonese, 15, 36, 225, 227; colloquial, 40, 46, 47, 49, 51; historical background of, 38, 40; Hong Kong, 36–38, 47, 49, 50–51, 53–54, 155; vernacular, 36; wordplay, 52–54; written forms of, 41; Yuè (粵) dialects, 143, 153, 225–26, 240, 241

Cantonese opera, 45–47; Canto-pop and, 50, 51; history of, 48; libretti, 49; post-WWII, 48; sanitation of, 48–49; vernacular and, 40, 48; writing and, 43, 47, 50

Central Plains. *See Zhōngyuán* (中原)

Chángshā (長沙), 137, 153

chanting. *See* cantillation

Chéngdū (成都), 6, 112, 153–54, 157 table 8.1, 158–59, 12–63, 164n23, 165–69

Chóngqìng (重慶), 154, 165–66, 168

classical Chinese, 25, 84, 88–89, 90, 107, 216

code mixing, 36

colloquial Chinese: in dialects, 1; influence on written language, 1, 140, 144; phonetic loaning in, 41; phonology of, 10, 21; post-Táng, 1; reflections of Cantonese in, 39; stories, 106

Common Dialectal Chinese (CDC), 61–64, 88, 118n5, 119, 183–91, 240, 240n, 241, 241n, 243, 250–51, 252, 254 table 14.4, 268, 269 table 15.3, 270–74

dialect performance: cantillation as a form of, 3; Cantonese opera as a form of, 38; Cantonese written vernacular and, 3; female literacy and, 41–42, 43; origins of Cantonese opera, 44–45; vernacular and, 44

dialects, 137; in texts, 3, 5–6, 36; islands, 7–8, 179–90, 220–23, 224, 229, 234, 239, 243; mixing, 4, 37, 61; modern, 142; phonology of, 182–91, 195–203, 221, 225–27, 228–29; prestige, 5–6, 8–9, 10, 121, 221, 222, 224, 225, 244; Shànghǎi, 98, 121; southern, 142; textbooks, 5; written tradition and, 2. *See under* Cantonese: Yuè (粵) dialects; Gàn (贛) dialects; Hakka dialects; Jìn (晉) dialects; Mandarin; Mǐn (閩)

dialects; Wú (吳) dialects; *Shānyīn* (山陰) dialect
diglossia, 36, 216; in the Philippines, 206, 210–11, 215–17; occasional, 211, 215
Dōngběi (東北) Mandarin. *See under* Mandarin
Dream of Red Mansions. See *Hónglóu mèng* (紅樓夢)

èrhuà (兒化). *See* rhotacization

Fāngyán diàochá zìbiǎo (方言調查字表), 249, 266
fǎnqiè (反切). See under *Qièyùn* (切韻)
finals, 6, 16, 61–62, 63, 119, 156, 156n8, 157, 158, 173–77, 183n7, 186, 187–89, 191, 195–202, 226, 227, 229, 235–36, 237n, 238–42, 242n, 243, 244, 250–51
folk literature, 39
Fújiàn (福建), 142, 145, 206, 209, 222, 223, 229–32

Gàn (贛) dialects, 41n9, 143
Guǎngdōng (廣東), 37, 41, 42, 43, 143, 145, 176, 179, 222, 223, 224, 228–29, 240
Guǎngxī (廣西), 143, 145, 222
Guǎngzhōu (廣州), 44, 49, 153, 181, 225
Guānhuà (官話). *See under* Mandarin
Guānhuà zhǐnán (官話指南), 4, 121–22; Běijīng dialect in, 129–30; Mandarin in, 123–24
Guide to Guānhuà. See *Guānhuà zhǐnán* (官話指南)
Guide to Kuan Hua. See *Guānhuà zhǐnán* (官話指南)
Guide to the Local Dialect (of Shànghǎi). See *Tǔhuà zhǐnán* (土話指南)
Guide to the Shànghǎi Dialect. See *Hùyǔ zhǐnán* (滬語指南)
Guìzhōu (貴州), 112, 159, 201

Hǎinán (海南), 179, 201, 222
Hakka dialects, 143, 225–26, 227, 240, 241; Kèjiā (客家) dialects, 41n9
Hángzhōu (杭州), 5, 99, 114, 144, 145n, 146, 222–23, 232–33

Hànyǔ fāngyán dà cídiǎn (漢語方言大詞典), 112
Hànyǔ fāngyán dìtújí (漢語方言地圖集), 142
Hànyǔ fāngyán tōngyīn (漢語方言通音). *See* Common Dialectal Chinese
Héběi (河北), 89, 249
Hénán (河南), 7, 8, 112, 143, 144, 179–92, 195, 230, 235
Hokkien dialect. *See under* Mǐn (閩) dialects
Hong Kong. *See under* Cantonese dialects
Hónglóu mèng (紅樓夢), 105–6, 107
Hóngwǔ (洪武), 220, 235, 240
Huājiān jì (花箋記), 39–40, 52
Húběi (湖北), 112, 143, 180, 181
Hú'nán (湖南), 143
Hùyǔ zhǐnán (滬語指南), 4, 121–22; Mandarin in, 127, 135; Shànghǎi dialect in, 133; southern dialects in, 128; Wú (吳) dialects in, 131

initials, 9, 18, 19, 22, 101, 110, 113, 119, 155, 156, 157, 157n12, 158, 174–75, 183–86, 188, 189, 190–91, 195–202, 225, 227, 228, 230–31, 233–34, 236–39, 244, 252–54, 259, 260, 263, 264, 268, 269 table 15.3, 270, 272–73
Inner Monglia. *See* Nèiménggǔ (內蒙古)

Jiānghuái (江淮) Mandarin. *See under* Mandarin
Jiāngsū (江蘇), 7, 112, 116, 118, 146, 153, 179–82, 186–87, 189–90, 194, 201–2, 220, 224, 230, 232
Jiāngxī (江西), 142, 143, 145, 181
Jìn (晉) dialects, 9, 143, 260
Jīn Píng Méi (金瓶梅): *cíhuà* (詞話), 88; dialects in, 4–5, 94–95, 97, 99–101, 105; dialect mixing in, 104; homophony in, 4, 99, 105, 109–10, 113–14, 116; *Shuǐhǔ zhuàn* (水滸傳) and, 90–94, 97–98, 99; translation of, 1; typographical discrepancies in, 100–102; vernacular in, 4, 88–90, 96–97; wordplay in, 104–5, 107–8, 110–12, 118

Index

Jìndài Hànyǔ (近代漢語), 1
Jīnxiāng (金鄉), 232–34, 239
Jíyùn (集韻), 140, 145n
Journey to the West. See Xīyóu jì (西遊記)
jùběn (劇本). *See* libretti
jūnhuà (軍話), 179, 201, 221, 222, 223, 240
jūntún (軍屯), 201, 220, 221, 235
Jurchens, 145, 220
Jyutping. *See under* transliteration

Kūnmíng (昆明), 154, 165, 168

libretti, 42, 44, 47, 49
Linguistic atlas of Chinese dialects. See Hànyǔ fāngyán dìtú jí (漢語方言地圖集)
loanwords, 46, 50, 261; in Cantonese, 46

Mandarin, 153n1, 154, 215–16, 220, 225; *běifānghuà* (北方話), 106; Dōngběi (東北) 222, 223; frontier, 221–23, 243, 238, 243; Guānhuà (官話), 2, 5, 7–10, 44, 153, 173, 175–77, 179, 194, 196, 200, 202, 206, 207–8, 220–22, 224, 227–28, 234–35, 244, 248; Jiānghuái (江淮), 7, 8, 62n, 143, 194, 195, 197, 199–202, 220, 230; koine, 5–8, 10, 145, 173, 179, 194, 199, 202, 207, 220, 221, 223–24, 223n3, 227–28; influence on dialects, 60, 61, 145, 226, 232, 244, 254, 259, 260–64; Modern Standard Chinese, 3, 8–9, 10, 61n1, 123n, 174, 249, 254, 259; Nánpíng (南平), 229–32, 239; officials, 209, 210–12, 215; Old/Early, 1–2; phonology of, 6, 8, 155–58, 164, 195, 200 table 11.2, 220, 230–31, 236–40, 243–44, 268; prestige varieties of, 5–6, 202, 225, 243; Pǔtōnghuà (普通話), 9, 48, 69–70, 153, 162–63, 166n29, 201–2, 259, 260–61; in *Shāngē* (山歌), 59; Southern, 146, 194, 200, 224, 234, 240–41; Southwestern, 143, 220, 241; Western, 153–69, 157n12, 266–74

medials, 6, 7, 17, 20, 21, 63, 186, 187, 188, 191, 231, 233, 234, 235, 236, 237–39, 244, 249, 254, 259, 260, 263–64
melisma, 24–25
Middle Chinese (MC), 1, 9, 156, 187, 195–98, 199, 200 table 11.2, 201–2, 221, 225, 228, 230, 249–51, 254, 254 table 14.4, 272–73
Mǐn (閩) dialects, 2, 7, 41n9, 73, 143, 179, 210, 214, 225–26, 227, 232, 240, 241; Hokkien dialect, 15, 206, 208, 210, 212, 213–16, 225
Míng (明) dynasty, 6–8, 38–39, 42, 62n, 65, 82, 84, 89, 104, 107–8, 114–15, 125, 141, 153–54, 162, 165, 173–77, 179, 194–95, 196, 199, 201, 202–3, 207–8, 212, 223–24, 227, 228, 229, 234–35, 239–40, 243, 244
missionaries: Mandarin and, 6, 154, 156, 157, 159, 160, 160n, 161, 165–68, 214; impact on dialects, 5, 10, 121, 221
Modern Standard Chinese. *See under* Mandarin
mùyúgē (木魚歌), 39, 42

Nánjīng (南京), 6, 7, 9, 115, 154, 155–56, 157 table 8.1, 157n12, 158, 160, 168–69, 181, 194–203, 224, 240, 242
Nánpíng (南平). *See under* Mandarin
Nèiménggǔ (內蒙古), 249
Notitia Linguae Sinicae, 156n8, 176
Nǚzhēn (女真). *See* Jurchens

overseas Chinese, 7–8, 206–17

phonology, 15–16; impact on Cantonese opera, 45; of cantillated literature, 22, 25–26
Pínghǎi (平海), 228–29, 239
píngshēng (平聲). *See under* tones
píngzè (平仄), 16, 18, 23, 25, 225, 228, 230; prolonged syllables and, 23, 25
pīnyīn (拼音). *See under* transliteration
The Plum in the Golden Vase. See Jīn Píng Méi (金瓶梅)

prestige dialects. *See under* dialects
prosody, tonal: prolonged syllables in, 23; syllable length, 22
Pǔtōnghuà (普通話). *See under* Mandarin

Qièyùn (切韻), 21, 174, 195, 221, 235, 237, 250–51; *fǎnqiè* (反切), 46, 174
Qīng (清) dynasty, 7, 10, 38–39, 42, 43, 44, 121, 125, 135, 141–44, 153, 153n1, 154, 156, 177, 180, 181, 199, 207, 222–23, 243
qùshēng (去聲). *See under* tones

Republican period, 44, 142, 143, 144, 222
rhotacization, 261
rhyming, accommodated (協韻), 19–20, 25
Romance of the Three Kingdoms. See *Sānguó yǎnyì* (三國演義)
Romanization. *See under* transliteration
Rúlín wàishǐ (儒林外史), 106
rùshēng (入聲). *See under* tones

sandhi, tone, 24n
Sānguó yǎnyì (三國演義), 88
Shǎanxī (陝西), 94, 112, 142, 144, 146, 240
Shāndōng (山東), 1, 4, 97, 113, 230; dialects of, 89, 105
Shāngē (山歌), 4, 59, 106; conjunctions in, 73–75; dialects in, 106–7; disposal construction in, 75–76; Guānhuà (官話) in, 81, 84; negative imperative in, 81; passive markers in, 70–73; position and existence markers in, 76–81; pronouns in, 64–68; rhyme in, 61–64; substantives in, 68–70; Wú (吳) dialects in, 8, 83, 84
Shànghǎi (上海), 153–54, 155; dialects of, 5, 89, 90n, 95, 98, 101, 113, 118n4, 121–35
shǎngshēng (上聲). *See under* tones
Shānxī (山西), 9, 94, 112, 140,142, 144, 146, 240, 248–65
Shānyīn (山陰) dialect, 9, 248–65
Shítou jì (石頭記). See *Hónglóu mèng* (紅樓夢)

Shuǐhǔ zhuàn (水滸傳), 4, 88, 95–96, 97, 107; dialects in 98–99; vernacular in, 96–97
shūshēng (舒聲). *See under* tones
Sìchuān (四川), 6, 112, 154, 158n13, 159, 160, 165–66, 168
Sòng (宋) dynasty, 137, 143–44, 220, 222, 224, 233
súyǔ (俗語), 4, 89–90
Sūzhōu (蘇州), 4, 59, 62–63, 65–66, 70, 81, 106–7, 131, 153

taboo words, 109
Tàipíng (太平) Rebellion, 44, 180, 181
Taiwan, 3, 15–26
Táng (唐) dynasty: dialect transcription, 17; literature, 15; phonology, 20; poetry, 15, 18; rhyming practice, 21
tones, 16, 189, 191, 197, 198 table 11.1, 227, 266; categories of, 9, 17, 21, 23 table 1.6, 24 table 1.8; contours of, 24, 190–91; non-*rù*, 187, 189, 191, 195, 227, 240, 249, 254–55, 259–61, 263–64; *píngshēng* (平聲), 189, 191, 197, 198, 199, 200, 201, 227, 229, 230, 233, 234, 237, 239, 243, 249, 254 table 14.4, 261, 266, 267, 269 table 15.3, 270–74; pitch value of, 268; *qùshēng* (去聲) 21, 22, 189, 191, 195, 198, 227, 229, 230, 233, 234, 237, 239, 249, 254 table 14.4, 261, 266, 267, 269 table 15.3, 270–74; *rùshēng* (入聲), 15, 117, 157 table 8.1, 187, 189, 191, 195, 197, 199, 200, 201, 227, 229, 230, 233, 234, 237, 239, 243, 244, 248–65, 268, 269, 270–74; *shǎngshēng* (上聲), 21, 22, 189, 191, 195, 197, 198, 227, 229, 230, 233, 234, 237, 239, 244, 249, 254 table 14.4, 261, 266, 267, 269 table 15.3, 270–74; *shūshēng* (舒聲), 249
transliteration, 196, 199, 200, 213–14; Jyutping, 37, 40, 53; *pīnyīn* (拼音), 17, 61n1, 84, 123n; Romanization, 6, 17, 155, 156, 156n8, 164, 195
Tǔhuà zhǐnán (土話指南), 4, 121–22; Shànghǎi dialect in, 126–27, 131–32,

Index

133, 135; Wù (吳) dialects in, 129–30, 131

vernacular: dialects, 3, 36, 225, 232; in literature, 5, 42, 82, 84, 88–90; in opera, 49, 50, 115; written forms of, 36, 38, 45, 51, 54; 104, 105, 106, 118, 177

Wáng (王), 253, 260, 261, 264
Water Margin. See *Shuǐhǔ zhuàn* (水滸傳)
wèichéng (衛城), 232
wèisuǒ (衛所), 220, 223, 224, 225, 235; *zhílì wèisuǒ* (直隸衛所), 230
wéndú (文讀), 15, 18; phonology of, 18, 19, 20, 22, 25; in Taiwanese, 25; written Chinese and, 18
wényán (文言). See classical Chinese
Wēnzhōu (溫州), 114, 117
Wú (吳) dialects, 98, 121, 140, 143, 145n, 153, 233, 243; colloquial, 88; dialect mixing, 59, folk songs, 81; homophony in, 60, 81, 109–10, 117; literature, 4–5; wordplay, 59–60, 109–10
Wǔhàn (武漢), 137, 154, 165, 168

Xī'ān (西安), 112
Xiāng (湘) dialects, 143, 153
Xīnjiāng (新疆), 112, 266–74
Xīrú ěrmùzī (西儒耳目資), 175, 195, 200, 221, 239
Xīyóu jì (西遊記), 107

yínsòng (吟誦). See cantillation
Yuán (元) dynasty, 220, 224, 228, 235, 239; *Yuán qǔ* (元曲), 106
Yuè (粵) dialects. See under Cantonese
Yùnlüè yìtōng (韻畧易通), 221, 227, 235–41, 243–44
Yúnnán (雲南), 8, 201, 220, 235

zhànhuà (站話), 220, 222–23
Zhèjiāng (浙江), 5, 7, 118, 142, 144, 145–46, 145n, 153, 179–84, 186–87, 189–90, 224, 232–34
zhènghuà (正話), 221, 222, 223, 224, 225–27, 229, 232, 234, 240

Zhōngguó yǔyán dìtújí (中國語言地圖集), 249
Zhōngyuán (中原): dialects of, 7, 144, 145–46, 145n, 194–95, 197, 199, 200, 201–2
Zhōngyuán yīnyùn (中原音韻), 235, 237–41, 244

Authors

Akitani Hiroyuki (秋谷裕幸), 240
Amundsen, Edward, 166, 166n27
Ang Ui-jin (洪惟仁), 210

Bái Jūyì (白居易), 17, 21–22, 27
Bái Wǎnrú (白宛如), 142n
Bào Shìjié (鮑士杰), 145n, 180n, 181n2, 192
Bauer, Robert, 36
Baxter, William H., 240
Bernal, Rafael, 211
Blair, Emma Helen, 211
Bond, Geo J., 165
Branner, David Prager, 243
Brockey, Liam, 208
Brook, Timothy, 230n6

Cài Fùwǔ (蔡復午), 141
Cano, Glòria, 211
Cáo Shùjī (曹樹基), 180, 222n1
Cáo Zhìyún (曹志耘), 142, 145n
Chao, Yuen Ren (趙元任), 160, 268n
Chén Liánxiāng (陳蓮香), 139n
Chén Shìyuán (陳士元), 140
Chén Xiǎo (陳曉), 196
Chén Yúnlóng (陳雲龍), 224, 225, 226, 240
Chén Zhāngtài (陳章太), 179
Chén Zhìchāo (陳智超), 144n
Chen, Chung-yu (陳重瑜), 229
Chia, Lucille, 209
Chow, Chung-yu Chen (陳重瑜). *See* Chen Chung-yu (陳重瑜)
Chu, Richard T., 216
Coblin, W. South, 173n3, 176, 206, 207, 213, 214, 221, 228, 239, 240
Conde-Silvestre, J. Camilo, 206

Couvreur, Séraphim, 159

Dài Bùfán (戴不凡), 99
Dèng Yīngshù (鄧英樹), 163
Diaz, Francisco, 175, 176
Dīng Bāngxīn (丁邦新), 179
Dīng Fēng (丁鋒), 196, 197n, 198

Edkins, Joseph, 156n8, 157, 158, 159, 159n, 160, 168
Endicott, James, 161, 162, 165, 166
Endo Mitsuaki (遠藤光曉), 196, 197n, 198, 200
Èrchūn Jūshì (二春居士), 83, 84

Fasold, Ralph, 215
Faure, David, 225
Fei, Faye Chunfang, 242
Felix, Alfonso, 214
Féng Mènglóng (馮夢龍), 4, 59, 60, 61, 63, 70, 81, 82, 83, 84, 105, 106, 108, 109, 242
Ferguson, Charles A., 216
Fishman, Joshua A., 215
Fù Chóngjǔ (傅崇矩), 164n23
Furuya, Akihiro (古屋昭弘), 162

Gao Yongan (高永安), 208
Gě Qìnghuá (葛慶華), 180, 181n4
Gěng Zhènshēng (耿振生), 195, 235
Goldsmith, John A., 273
Gonzalez, Andrew, 214, 215
Goodrich, L. Carrington, 232
Grainger, Adam, 158, 161, 162n18, 163, 165
Guō Lì (郭力), 195
Guō Xī (郭熙), 180, 181, 187, 191

Hán Shìqí (韓世琦), 142
Hanan, Patrick, 104, 106
Hernández-Campoy, Juan M., 206, 207
Hirata, Shōji (平田昌司), 153
Hóng Mài (洪邁), 139
Hóng Zénán (洪澤南), 17, 18, 27
Horsley, Margaret Wyant, 209
Hú Wényīng (胡文英), 141
Huáng Hóng (黃宏), 144n

Huáng Jiànbǎo (黃健保), 139n
Huáng Tíngjiān (黃庭堅), 138, 139, 139n, 143
Huáng Xiǎodōng (黃曉東), 181, 223
Huáng Xuězhēn (黃雪貞), 154
Huáng Zàn (黃瓚), 173
Huáng Zhàohàn (黃兆漢), 45, 46, 46n, 47
Hume, Elizabeth, 273
Hyman, Larry M., 273

Ingle, James Addison, 165, 166n27, 167n

Jīn Nígé (金尼閣). See Trigault, Nicolas

Kamiya, Toshio (神谷俊郎), 169n33
Kaske, Elisabeth, 153
Kaufman, Terrence, 223n3
Kerswill, Paul, 223n3
Kilborn, Omar Leslie, 158, 161, 162, 164, 164n23, 166, 167
Kim, Kwangjo, 174, 221, 240
Kim, Youngman, 174
Klöter, Henning, 208, 209, 212, 214
Kwan, Uganda Sze Pui (關詩珮 [Guān Shīpèi]), 155n5
Kwok, Bit-chee, 210

Labov, William, 202, 207
Lamarre, Christine, 153, 165n25
Lán Mào (蘭茂), 221, 235, 236, 236n10, 237, 238, 238n13, 239, 240, 241, 243, 244
Lánlíng Xiàoxiào Shēng (蘭陵笑笑生), 90, 99, 105, 107
Ledyard, Gari, 173n2
Lee, Fabio Yuchung, 212
Leonhard, Jürgen, 223n3
Levi, Joseph A., 214
Lǐ Kāixiān (李開先), 115
Lǐ Rúlóng (李如龍), 140n, 142n, 179
Lǐ Shí (李實), 165
Lǐ Wúwèi (李無), 196
Lǐ Xīnkuí (李新魁), 195
Lǐ Zhǔn (李準), 112
Li, Fang-Kuei (李方桂), 159, 174
Lín Fèngshān (林鳳珊), 46n16

Index

Líng Méngchū (凌濛初), 82, 84
Liú Fǎng (劉昉), 139
Liú Fù (劉復), 268n
Loon, Piet van der, 210, 216
Lǚ Guóyáo (魯國堯), 194
Lǚ Shūxiāng (呂叔湘), 145, 146
Lù Shìè (陸士諤), 83
Lú Zēngsfū (盧增夫), 230n6
Luó Chángpéi (羅常培), 160

Mǎ, Zhēn (馬真), 163n22
Mài Yún (麥耘), 194, 195
Mair, Victor, 38
Máo Kūn (毛坤), 159
Mateer, Calvin Wilson, 156, 156n9, 157, 157n11
McWhorter, John H., 223n3
Meadows, Thomas Taylor, 155, 155n5, 155n6
Medhurst, Walter Henry, 207, 208
Méi Jié (梅節), 100, 101
Menegon, Eugenio, 209
Mèng Jìyuán (孟濟元), 142n
Mèng Yuánlǎo (孟元老), 138, 143, 144n
Möllendorff, Paul Georg von, 159
Morrison, Robert, 40
Murata, Yūjirō (村田雄二郎), 153

Nakamura, Masakyuki (中村雅之), 155n4
Nevius, John Livingstone, 169n34
Ní Zhìjiā (倪志佳), 137, 139
Nìng Jìfú (寧忌浮), 195, 200, 239
Norman, Jerry, 106, 145, 146, 183n, 232, 240n, 250n, 268n

Pān Jiāyì (潘家懿), 223, 224, 228
Parker, Edward Harper, 166n28
Peng, Chia Oai, 210
Platt, John, 215
Pettus, W. B., 166
Pike, Kenneth L., 273
Pínghuā Zhǔrén (評花主人), 83
Prémare, Joseph Henri Marie de, 156n8, 176

Qián Nǎiróng (錢乃榮), 122, 125, 126, 127, 128, 130, 132, 133

Qián Nányáng (錢南揚), 114, 115
Qīu Xuéqiáng (丘學強), 179, 223, 228, 228n
Qú Yuán (蘧園), 84

Ricci, Matteo, 176, 202, 207–8
Robertson, James Alexander, 211
Rokkaku Tsunehiro (六角恒廣), 196, 202
Ruǎn Yǒngméi (阮咏梅), 118n5
Ruggieri, Michele, 176

Sarashina Shinichi (更科慎一), 196
Schilling, Natalie, 207
Setoguchi Litsuko (瀨戶口律子), 196, 200
Shào Jìngmǐn (邵敬敏), 121n
Shěn Jǐng (沈璟), 116, 241, 242, 242n17, 243
Shěn Míng (沈明), 249
Shen, Grant Guangren, 242
Shí Fēng (石鋒), 267
Shī Nàiān (施耐庵), 99
Siegel, Jeff, 223n3
Simmons, Richard VanNess, 2, 6n, 8, 145n, 156n7, 203, 222n2, 223, 238n12, 260n
Sin Sukchu (申叔舟, 1417–1475), 6, 173, 174, 175, 177, 221, 239–40
Skinner, G. William, 216
Snow, Don, 36n1, 38, 42, 47n, 49
Stephenson, Frederic Clarke, 160
Stewart, James Livingstone, 167
Sūn Yízhì (孫宜), 195

Takata, Tokio (高田時雄), 155, 169
Táo Huán (陶寰), 129, 130, 133
Thomason, Sarah Grey, 223n3
Thoms, Peter Perring, 39n4
Ting, Pang-hsin. See Dīng Bāngxīn (丁邦新)
Toqto'a [脫脫 Tuōtuō], 144
Trigault, Nicolas [Jīn Nígé 金尼閣], 195, 198, 200, 202, 221, 239
Trudgill, Peter, 223n3

Wade, Thomas Francis, 123, 155, 155n5, 156
Walmsley, Lewis C., 166
Wáng Gōngxiān (王恭先), 140
Wáng Jìdé (王驥德), 241, 242–43

Wáng Yǔchēng (王禹偁), 98
Wang, William S-Y, 258
Weightman, George Henry, 209
Wēn Duānzhèng (溫端政), 232
Wetzels, W. Leo, 273
Wickberg, Edgar, 209
Williams, Samuel Wells, 154, 155, 156
Wills, John E., 209, 214
Witek John W., 208
Wú Chéng'ēn (吳承恩), 141
Wú Qǐtài (吳啟太), 121
Wú Xìntiān (吳信天), 84
Wúzhōng Pèihéngzǐ (吳中佩蘅子), 82

Xiāo Xù (蕭旭), 137
Xiè Liúwén (謝留文), 140n, 142n
Xiè Yùxīn (謝育新), 196, 200
Xíng Xiàngdōng (邢向東), 142n
Xióng, Jìn (熊進), 163n21
Xǔ Bǎohuá (許寶華), 129, 130, 133

Yán Déliàng (閆德亮), 179, 182n5
Yáng Shífēng (楊時逢), 158n13
Yáng Zēngwǔ (楊增武), 248, 253, 254, 258, 259, 260, 261, 264
Yang, Paul F. M., 176n7
Yoshikawa, Masayuki (吉川雅之), 153n1, 155
Yóuxì Zhǔrén (遊戲主人), 82, 107
Yú Zhèngxiè (俞正燮), 223, 223n4
Yuán Jiāhuá (袁家驊), 153n2, 154n
Yùchí, Zhìpíng (尉遲治平), 173n2

Zēng Xiǎoyú (曾曉渝), 195, 196, 200, 201
Zhāng Bǐnglín (章炳麟), 137
Zhāng Dài (張岱), 140
Zhāng Huìyīng (張惠英), 2, 4, 5, 101
Zhāng Měilán (張美蘭), 2, 5
Zhāng Míngfēi (張冥飛), 89, 9
Zhāng Qǐhuàn (張啟煥), 191
Zhāng Qīngyuán (張清源), 163
Zhāng Shìfāng (張世方), 184
Zhāng Sìwéi (張四維), 13
Zhāng Wèidōng (張衛東), 194, 195
Zhāng Yīzhōu (張一舟), 16
Zhāng Yùlái (張玉來), 236n9
Zhāng Zìliè (張自烈), 141
Zhang, Jie, 249
Zhào Yìntáng (趙蔭棠), 236n10
Zhèng Gāngzhōng (鄭剛中), 138, 143, 144n
Zhèng Yǒngbāng (鄭永邦), 121
Zhèng Yǒngxiǎo (鄭永曉), 139n
Zhèng-Zhāng Shàngfāng (鄭張尚芳), 137, 181
Zhōu Déqīng (周德清), 235
Zhōu Lěi (周磊), 272–73
Zhōu Yún (周芸), 142n
Zhū Xiǎonóng (朱曉農), 194
Zhuāng Chūshēng (莊初升), 179
Zōng Jìchén (宗繼辰), 140

CPSIA information can be obtained
at www.ICGtesting.com
Printed in the USA
JSHW051336080622
26433JS00002B/10